HOUSTON
& THE TEXAS GULF COAST

ANDY RHODES

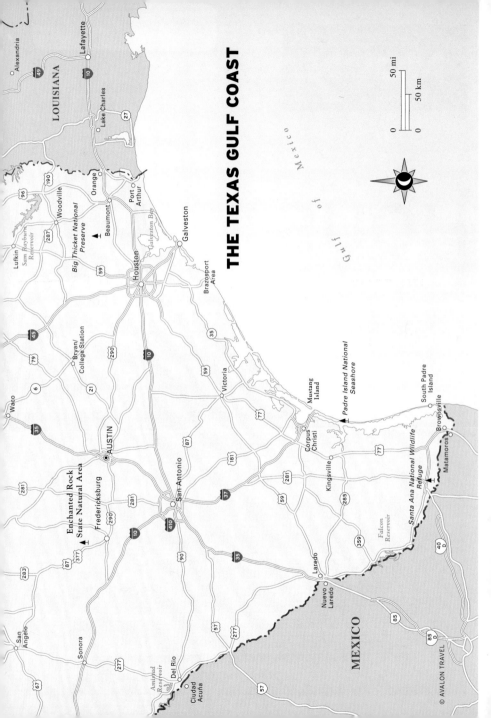

THE TEXAS GULF COAST

LOUISIANA

MEXICO

Gulf of Mexico

Big Thicket National Preserve

Brazosport Area

Galveston Bay

Padre Island National Seashore

Mustang Island

South Padre Island

Santa Ana National Wildlife Refuge

Enchanted Rock State Natural Area

Falcon Reservoir

Amistad Reservoir

Sam Rayburn Reservoir

Alexandria
Lafayette
Lake Charles
Lufkin
Woodville
Orange
Beaumont
Port Arthur
Houston
Galveston
Victoria
Corpus Christi
Kingsville
Brownsville
Matamoros
Laredo
Nuevo Laredo
San Antonio
AUSTIN
Fredericksburg
Bryan/College Station
Waco
San Angelo
Sonora
Del Rio
Ciudad Acuña

0   50 mi
0   50 km

© AVALON TRAVEL

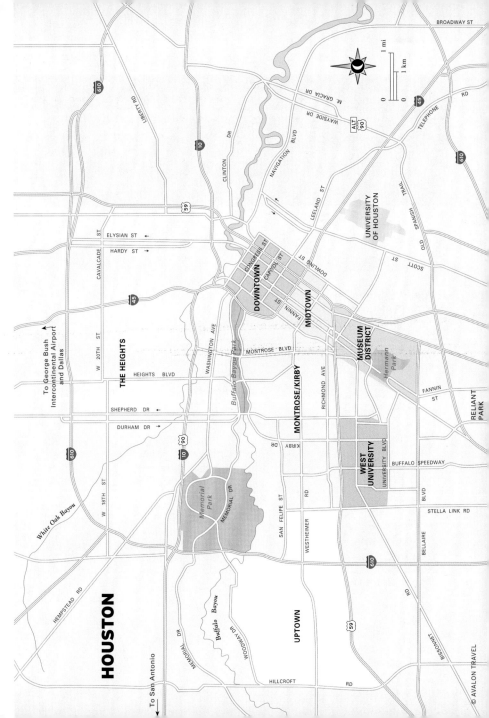

Contents

▶ **Discover Houston
& the Texas Gulf Coast** **6**
Planning Your Trip 8
Explore Houston
& the Texas Gulf Coast 11
• The Best of Houston 11
• Cowboy Culture 13
• Coasting Along the Gulf 14
• Foodie Favorites............... 16
• Family Road Trip............... 17
• High Points in History 18

▶ **Houston** **21**
Sights...................... 28
Sports and Recreation 39
Entertainment and Events 42
Shopping 50
Accommodations 54
Food 58
Information and Services........ 69
Getting There and Around 72

▶ **The Gulf Coast** **73**
Galveston..................... 76
Brazosport Area 92
Corpus Christi 98
Mustang Island 112
Kingsville 118
South Padre Island 122

▶ **East Texas Getaways** **135**
Beaumont and Vicinity.......... 138
Big Thicket National Preserve 145

Piney Woods National Forests..... 148
Lufkin....................... 154
Nacogdoches and Vicinity 159
Tyler 163
Marshall 167
Jefferson.................... 171

▶ **Background**................. **175**
The Land 175
Flora and Fauna............... 178
History 182
Economy and Government....... 185
People 186
Arts and Culture 189

▶ **Essentials** **192**
Getting There 192
Getting Around 194
Sports and Recreation 195
Food 200
Tips for Travelers 202
Health and Safety 203
Information and Services........ 204

▶ **Resources** **205**
Suggested Reading............. 205
Internet Resources 207

▶ **Index**........................ **208**

▶ **List of Maps** **215**

Discover Houston & the Texas Gulf Coast

Everything about Houston and the Texas Gulf Coast is larger than life. From towering skyscrapers to endless stretches of sandy coastline to high-powered humidity, this region of the Lone Star State exemplifies grandiosity, all with a hearty sense of Texas pride.

Naturally, this results in excessive opportunities for exploration. As the country's fourth-largest city, Houston offers travelers a cosmopolitan playground to discover, but with a Texas flair that sets it apart from other urban landscapes. And when you've had your fill of bustling restaurants and active nightlife, the calming waves of the Gulf Coast beckon just hours away.

Mention the word "Houston" and iconic images immediately start gushing, from oil booms to NASA, from *Urban Cowboy* to Enron. The Texas mystique lives large in Houston, just like the diverse characters that have called the city home, including Beyonce, Roger Clemens, and George H. W. Bush.

Travelers in Texas and across the country often associate a visit to Houston with the words "business trip." Fortunately, there are countless attractions and destinations beyond the city's convention center and hotel

room walls. Its 8,000-plus restaurants (that's not a misprint) specialize in the regional cuisine of lesser-known countries far beyond most cities' standard fare. The multifaceted nightlife ranges from down-home honky-tonks to stylish, sophisticated dance clubs. And the city's surprisingly efficient and navigable public transportation system makes it easy to get out and explore.

Just down the road, the Gulf Coast boasts more than 350 miles of shoreline, appealing to all types of recreational travelers. Salty fishermen escape to Galveston or Mustang Island near Corpus Christi for no-frills fishing while South Padre Island draws visitors from the opposite extreme: road-tripping families and spring breakers who frolic on the pristine white beaches.

Houston may never top the list of trendy destinations, but its distinctive characteristics as a cosmopolitan Southern city with an independent spirit befitting of Texas's colossal charm make it a worthy destination for anyone seeking a memorable escape.

Planning Your Trip

▶ WHERE TO GO

Houston

The fourth-largest metropolis in the country offers all the amenities of big-city living—plus a distinctive Texas twist. Spanning several miles, the Museum District hosts nearly a dozen attractions, including parks and cultural facilities ranging from the small Buffalo Soldiers Museum to the enormous Museum of Natural Science. Sample tasty local cuisine here from authentic barbecue to Cajun and real Tex-Mex. Nightlife options are refreshingly laid-back, from trendy beer joints in the Heights to live blues clubs in the West University neighborhood. Some of the can't-miss sights are outside the city limits. NASA Space Center is an absolute must, the Kemah Boardwalk is a fun place for families to frolic, and the San Jacinto Battleground is where Texas won its legendary independence.

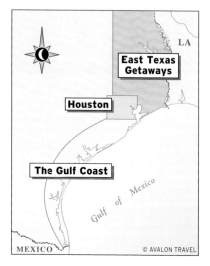

Houston Museum of Fine Arts

San Jacinto Battleground Historic Site

South Padre Island

The Gulf Coast

Stretching more than 350 miles along the Gulf of Mexico, this region of sun, sea, and sand offers the ultimate escape from cities, suburbs, and small towns. Occasionally referred to as the country's "Third Coast," its moderate beaches and waves don't attract crowds the way Florida's mighty surf does, but the call of the ocean draws casual beachcombers, lifelong fishermen, and frolicking families. For those with limited time who need a quick saltwater fix, there's nearby Galveston Island, just 50 miles southeast of Houston. Though the beaches aren't exactly pristine, they're close and easily accessible. Less crowded and more inviting is Mustang Island near Corpus Christi (about 3.5 hours from Houston), offering steady waves and wide-open stretches of sand. Texas's preeminent beach—think soft white sand and surfable waves—is on South Padre Island, a nearly five-hour drive from Houston but well worth the effort for those wanting to truly kick back, relax, and soak up the warm Texas sun.

East Texas Getaways

Houstonians escape to East Texas to play in the Piney Woods. From national forests to Main Street communities to historical attractions, this abundant area offers plenty of recreational and leisure activities to chase away the intensity of urban life. Spend a day in Angelina National Forest for a woodsy hike to the abandoned Aldridge Sawmill. Up the road, you can enjoy the clickety-clack of the Texas State Railroad as it rambles along historic tracks through the pines. Nearby Lufkin and Diboll boast fantastic facilities—the Texas Forestry Museum and the History Center, respectively—dedicated to the region's logging heritage. If you have a few extra days, take time to smell the 35,000 roses at Tyler's famous Rose Garden and Museum. Or bust a move to the northeast, where Marshall bills itself as the "Birthplace of Boogie Woogie."

sunset in Angelina National Forest

▶ WHEN TO GO

The region is downright pleasant in spring and fall, quite tolerable during the mild winter months, and absolutely hellish in the summertime.

Spring is the ideal time to visit, so plan for March or April. Vegetation is blooming in parks and gardens, festivals capitalize on sunny 73-degree days, and people enjoy the final few months they'll be able to spend outside. Fall is the next-best season. By late October, things begin to "cool" down to the 80s, drawing cabin-fever sufferers out of their homes to restaurant patios and neighborhood parks.

Winter is a distinct season, but snowflakes and icy roads are rare. Temperatures can be erratic, jumping from the 30s to the 70s in just a few hours. This is a good time to plan a trip to South Padre Island.

Houston has gone to great lengths to accommodate its sweltering humid weather during summer (May through mid-October), mainly via overpowered air-conditioning systems and subterranean downtown tunnels. The constant flow of air-conditioning and water recreation allows residents and visitors to (barely) tolerate the heat. The coastal communities don't have these fancy amenities, but the constant 15-mph wind coming off the water is a welcome change from oppressive urban humidity.

Explore Houston & the Texas Gulf Coast

▶ THE BEST OF HOUSTON

With dozens of worthy attractions and hundreds of notable restaurants in greater Houston, choosing an itinerary may be challenging. But who can complain about having too many good options?

Day 1

Begin your odyssey in Houston's Museum District, starting with the enormous Museum of Natural Science, which introduces visitors to the area's cultural heritage—from prehistoric creatures to modern oil-drilling techniques. Grab lunch at El Real Tex-Mex Cafe in the nearby Montrose-Kirby area, and then head back to the Museum District for an afternoon of amazing art at the Houston Museum of Fine Arts, the Contemporary Arts Museum

of Houston, or both. For dinner, head back to Montrose-Kirby for some lip smackin' Goode Co. Barbeque, followed by a nightcap at Anvil Bar & Refuge—its Nitro Cuba Libre is the fanciest rum and Coke ever made.

Day 2

Return to the Museum District to wrap up your cultural tour of Houston by sampling from attractions dedicated to animals (the zoo), children, health, history, and photography. For your lunch break, try some regional Cajun cuisine at Treebeard's in the nearby downtown business district. After a couple days of museum hopping, treat yourself to a nice downtown dinner at III Forks and a few cocktails at Dean's Credit Clothing.

Houston's Museum of Natural Science

Rienzi's house and gardens are home to its fine art collection.

Day 3

Explore additional cultural attractions inside The Loop, beginning with a morning in the Montrose-Kirby area. The Menil Collection and Rienzi house fantastic fine art collections. Nearby West University is a hotbed for shopping (Rice Village and Kuhl-Linscomb, in particular), and a dinner at Uchi or Underbelly can be a Houston highlight, but be sure to make reservations well in advance. Afterward, stay in the neighborhood for some live Bayou City blues music at the legendary Big Easy Social and Pleasure Club.

Day 4

For those who still want to soak up the city scene, there are plenty of urban attractions to be found. The Heights is the hip place to find trendy shops, including boutiques like Hello Lucky and Latin American folk art at Casa Ramirez. Enjoy a hearty lunch at Gatlin's Barbecue, and then walk it off in the Uptown district at the Arboretum nature sanctuary. If you have time, squeeze in a visit to the intriguing Orange Show art collective, and then enjoy a traditional Mexican dinner at Molina's. Nearby, the Firehouse Saloon offers genuine country-and-western culture with live music on weekends.

Day 5

It's finally time to escape The Loop, so head southeast of Houston to NASA Space Center for an otherworldly experience. If you have kids in tow, visit the nearby Kemah Boardwalk for some traditional touristy fun on amusement park rides. Those interested in the Lone Star State's legendary heritage should go to the San Jacinto Battleground Historic Site, where Texas famously won its independence in 1836. Top the day off with a seafood dinner at the bayside TopWater Grill.

COWBOY CULTURE

Goode Co. Barbeque

The *Urban Cowboy* legend was born in Houston in the early 1980s, and in some parts of the city, it's never left. Visitors can get a good feel for the cowboy culture by sampling a few of Houston's western-themed nightlife options and restaurants. Although you won't see too many Houstonians wearing oversized belt buckles or cowboy hats, Texas's influence on this cosmopolitan city is still apparent in pockets all around town. Take a gander (and a listen) at these Houston watering holes and vittle halls:

NIGHTLIFE

- **PBR** tips its hat to cowboy culture with mechanical bull riding, two-stepping, and multiple country-and-western dance floors downtown (page 43).

- **Alice's Tall Texan** is a true no-frills experience in the Heights, with friendly folks chatting above the din of classic jukebox country music and clinking bottles of Lone Star beer (page 46).

- **Armadillo Palace** in the Montrose-Kirby area features pure honky-tonk sounds coming from live bands that prompt people to two-step near the small stage (page 47).

- **Firehouse Saloon** west of Uptown is a genuine local spot, with some big ol' shiny belt buckles, fancy light machines, Vegas-style video games, and country cover bands (page 47).

- **Big Texas Dance Hall and Saloon** southeast of town is even more local, with western decor and boot-scootin' worthy live music on Thursdays (page 47).

RESTAURANTS

- **Goode Co. Barbeque** in Montrose-Kirby specializes in classic Texas-style 'cue—sausage, ribs, chicken, and the signature tender and juicy brisket—all topped with a succulent and smoky sauce (page 61).

- **Sammy's Wild Game Grill** is a modern-day urban cowboy's dream in the Heights, with exotic seasonings on wild critters—we're talkin' elk tacos, pheasant hot dogs, and python chili fries (page 64).

- **Gatlin's Barbecue** is another Heights-based meat-lover's paradise, offering perfectly smoked beef brisket and hearty sausage and pork ribs (page 64).

► COASTING ALONG THE GULF

Combining a Houston trip with excursions along the Gulf Coast is not only possible, it's encouraged. For those with limited time who need a quick saltwater fix, there's nearby Galveston Island, just 50 miles southeast of Houston on the Gulf Freeway (I-45). Though the beaches aren't exactly pristine, they're close and easily accessible. Less crowded and more inviting is Mustang Island near Corpus Christi, offering steady waves and wide-open stretches of sand. Texas's preeminent beach—think soft white sand and surfable waves—is on South Padre Island, a nearly five-hour drive from Houston but well worth the effort to truly kick back, relax, and soak up the warm Texas sun.

The following itinerary offers a solid introduction, but most visitors may prefer to enjoy these coastal towns at their leisure. To truly experience more than one of these destinations, plan for at least five or six days. Factor in driving time: from Houston, it will take about three-and-a-half hours to reach Corpus Christi via U.S. Hwy. 59 through Victoria (State Hwy. 35 along the coast is more picturesque but takes about 45 minutes longer). The five-and-a-half-hour drive to South Padre Island on U.S. Hwy. 77 is pretty lengthy, but absolutely rewarding once your feet hit the soft sand.

Galveston Island
DAYS 1-2

Just an hour southeast of Houston, welcoming waves beckon at Galveston Island. Visit The Strand district, a 36-block National Historic Landmark District that features New Orleans-style hotels, restaurants, art galleries, boutiques, and a seaport museum with the 1877 tall ship *Elissa*. Enjoy a local lunch at Mosquito Café. In the afternoon, you can choose your adventure based on the weather—if it's nice outside, visit Pleasure Pier for the amusement park rides; if it's too hot, windy, or rainy, head to the indoor pyramids at Moody Gardens for aquariums and

the Moody Gardens Festival of Lights on Galveston Island

Galveston's historic Strand district

Port Isabel Lighthouse, South Padre Island

exhibits. Dinner and drinks await at the tremendous Saltwater Grill.

If you want to extend your stay, consider spending the night at Tremont House, a stunning 1879 Victorian hotel in The Strand district. Spend the morning at Broadway Street's stately historical mansions—Bishop's Palace and Moody Mansion—then enjoy lunch at Fisherman's Wharf, with a deck overlooking the bay, before heading to your next coastal stop.

Corpus Christi
DAYS 2-3
A few hours down the coastline, Corpus Christi offers wide-open beaches on Mustang Island. Named for the wild horses that once roamed free on the island, the park offers five miles of outstretched beach, perfect for swimming, fishing, sunbathing, and beachcombing. Those seeking recreational fun can rent a kayak or windsurfing equipment and tackle the gulf waters. Be sure to schedule time for a meal at Water Street Seafood Co. Stay at the Radisson, located right on the sand of Corpus Christi Beach.

On your next day, hit one of the top-notch cultural attractions like the USS Lexington or Texas State Aquarium.

South Padre Island
DAYS 4-5
Serious beachcombers should alter their schedules to spend a few days on South Padre Island. Soft white sand and bright blue water are major attractions, and so is the marine life at Sea Turtle, Inc. and on dolphin tours. It's also well worth the 74-step climb up the tight spiral staircase to experience the breathtaking views from the Port Isabel Lighthouse.

The seafood here is the best in Texas, so be sure to catch a lunch or dinner at Pier 19 or Sea Ranch. If it's too hot outside, play indoors at Schlitterbahn Beach Waterpark.

East Texas Excursions
If you happen to be heading back from the coast along U.S. Hwy. 77, be sure to visit the legendary King Ranch to experience Texas's cattle culture where it was born. Then hightail it to one of East Texas's national forests for some camping or cabin time.

El Real Tex-Mex Cafe

Houston has more than 8,000 restaurants—the array of options is overwhelming, from lowly fast food to lofty haute cuisine. The city's enormous international population offers authentic fare from all corners of the globe. This being Texas, the options also include a fair number of home-grown varieties, including some of the state's finest barbecue, Tex-Mex, and good ol' fashioned down-home Southern cookin'. Here's the best of the bunch, by neighborhood:

DOWNTOWN

· **Ill Forks** is known throughout Texas for its sumptuous steaks, with featured cuts including the double-cut strip, filet mignon, and porterhouse (page 58).

· **Brennan's** is one of the best places to experience authentic Cajun cuisine, offering classic Gulf Coast flavors such as étouffée, lump crab cakes, and pecan-crusted amberjack (page 59).

· **Oxheart** is known for its bold flavor combinations, like the smoked tuna accompanied by chickpeas, seaweed, and caramelized tomatoes (page 58).

· **The Breakfast Klub** is famous in Houston for its magnificent chicken and waffles. Locals gladly wait up to an hour to experience it (page 59).

THE HEIGHTS

· **Gatlin's Barbecue** has been receiving rave reviews from Houston's culinary professionals and fans of succulent brisket and savory smoked sausage (page 64).

· **Sammy's Wild Game Grill** may look tame from the outside, but the selection of exotic meats inside is downright crazy. For example, the menu includes a kangaroo burger with a side of python chili fries (page 64).

· **The Blue Fish** is known for its generous portions of seafood with top-notch ingredients in popular items like yellowtail and eel rolls (page 64).

· **Mam's House of Snoballs** offers a refreshing frozen dessert (strawberry lemonade or gummy bear flavor for the kids), which is often a necessity in hot and humid Houston (page 65).

MONTROSE/KIRBY

· **El Real Tex-Mex Cafe** serves a stunning collection of traditionally inspired Tex-Mex dishes, derived from extensive research and attention to authentic recipes and ingredients (page 61).

· **Churrascos** draws from the rich well of Central American cuisine; instead of tortilla chips and enchiladas, think plantain chips and empanadas (page 61).

· **Underbelly** is helmed by a visionary chef who passionately champions regional produce like braised goat, tilefish with okra, snapper with bok choy, and lamb meatballs (page 60).

· **Uchi** features *Top Chef*-winning Paul Qui's exquisite flavor combinations that have somehow never been attempted before, such as salmon and Asian pear or yellowfin tuna and oranges (page 63).

Another option—via U.S. Hwy. 59 and State Hwy. 103—is to explore the Piney Woods by bike or canoe, or hike to the abandoned Old Aldridge Sawmill in Angelina National Forest. Learn about the region's logging heritage at Lufkin's forestry museum, or take a leisurely ride on the Texas State Railroad. At mealtime, be sure to sample a regional specialty like chopped beef barbecue or fried catfish. An East Texas day trip or overnight regional jaunt directly from Houston is also feasible.

► FAMILY ROAD TRIP

Houston and the Gulf Coast are ideal stomping grounds for frolicking families. The cities are brimming with museums and recreational pursuits, and the entire coastline is a natural playground. From toddlers to great-grandparents, there are activities for all ages and interests.

Houston
DAY 1
Houston's Museum District is a natural place to get things rolling on a family road trip. Start things off at the Museum of Natural Science, where kids and parents can learn about dinosaurs, mummies, gems, butterflies, and oil production through interactive exhibits. Another option is to actively participate in the fun exhibits at the Children's Museum. The Museum District is surprisingly lacking in walking-distance restaurants, so plan to get in the car for lunch or eat at the only restaurant available in the science museum, McDonald's. As that can sometimes be a necessary option (for silencing hungry children), it may be fitting to visit the nearby Health Museum next, where proper body maintenance is a main theme.

DAY 2
Head southeast of town for a day of family

the NASA Space Center in Houston

HIGH POINTS IN HISTORY

Bishop's Palace

Despite all the new-fangled sprawl and a notorious penchant for teardowns, Houston and its Gulf Coast neighbors retain impressive historical charm.

HOUSTON

- **San Jacinto Battleground** boasts a remarkable 570-foot-tall monument on a 1,200-acre site commemorating the legendary battle that secured Texas's independence (page 37).

- **Battleship *Texas*** is the only remaining battleship to serve in both World Wars I and II (page 38).

- **Buffalo Soldiers Museum** is dedicated to the African American Army troops who protected the Texas frontier in the late 1800s (page 32).

- **George Ranch Historical Park** is a working cattle ranch on an 1890s pioneer farmstead (page 38).

GALVESTON

- **The Strand District** was once Texas's second-busiest port, the "Wall Street of the South" (page 79).

- **Bishop's Palace,** an 1866 Victorian castle, exudes elegance, from its ornate fireplaces to its spectacular stained-glass windows (page 81).

- **Moody Mansion** is worth a visit, given its manicured grounds and exquisite furnishings, as well as the dining room's gold-leaf ceiling (page 82).

- **The 1887 ship *Elissa*** is the second-oldest operational sailing vessel in the world (page 81).

CORPUS CHRISTI

- **The USS *Lexington*** is a decommissioned World War II naval aircraft carrier now serving as a 33,000-ton floating museum (page 100).

- **Corpus Christi Museum of Science and History** celebrates maritime heritage with authentic recreations of Christopher Columbus's three ships, nautical exhibits, and a Children's Wharf (page 100).

- **King Ranch** tells the story of the Lone Star State's first cattle drives and legendary brands that forever changed Texas (page 118).

PINEY WOODS

- **The Aldridge Sawmill**'s enormous concrete walls are all that remain of the century-old lumber operation (page 151).

- **The Texas State Railroad** allows you to ride the rails on an enchanting steam locomotive, which chugs and charms its way through the Piney Woods (page 160).

- **The Texas Forestry Museum and the History Center** in the Lufkin area offer a fascinating look the growth of the region's lumber industry (page 154).

rhinos in the African forest exhibit at the Houston Zoo

fun at NASA and Kemah Boardwalk. Young children may not grasp the historical significance of viewing Mission Control, but they'll certainly appreciate Kids Space, a massive collection of exhibits, games, and hands-on activities. Grab some lunch on the bay at TopWater Grill, and then head to Kemah Boardwalk, featuring restaurants, shops, fountains, and an impressive collection of amusement park-style rides at the water's edge.

DAY 3

Stick around Houston for an animal-themed day, starting with the Houston Zoo. Five thousand animals keep adults and children entertained on those 55 acres, including a world of primates, Asian elephant habitat, lion and tiger exhibit, and children's zoo. Afterward, head to the Downtown Aquarium for lunch—the seafood restaurant on the second floor is extremely kid friendly and surprisingly tasty. Plan to spend a few hours at the aquarium mingling with marine life. Families will marvel at the enormous tanks, Shark Voyage train ride, and outdoor midway rides. If time permits, visit the Buffalo Soldiers Museum dedicated to the African American troops who protected the Texas frontier (Native Americans gave them this notable name because of their immense bravery and valor).

Galveston Island
DAY 4

Galveston Island, just an hour southeast of Houston, is one of the most popular getaways for local families, and for good reason. In addition to beach and recreational activities at Galveston Island State Park, visitors can spend a day or two riding roller coasters and rides at Pleasure Pier or strolling among rainforest and marine creatures within the indoor pyramids at Moody Gardens. For a completely different kind of adventure, spend the day on the water rides at Schlitterbahn Waterpark. At mealtime, be sure to order a family-sized batch of fried or boiled shrimp at Gaido's Seafood restaurant.

Corpus Christi
DAYS 5-6

It's worth making the three-and-a-half-hour drive from Houston to Corpus Christi just

the Aviator Ride at the Kemah Boardwalk

Fountains dance at Houston's Downtown Aquarium.

to play on Mustang Island. The wide open welcoming sand and surf are inviting natural playgrounds, and the steady breeze off the water keeps the temperatures tolerable. If it's too hot, head inside to the Texas State Aquarium, featuring a dolphin habitat, otter slides, and an exhibit showcasing menacing sharks. Find time to have a flavorful meal at Water Street Seafood Co., which serves everything tasty in the region—fresh seafood, Mexican influences, Cajun flavors, and good ol' Southern cooking. While in Corpus, consider taking a half-day jaunt to nearby Kingsville to experience the legendary King Ranch, where Texas's cowboy culture was born. Spend the night on the shoreline of Corpus Christi Beach at the comfy Radisson.

Piney Woods
DAY 7

Take a day trip to East Texas to play in the Piney Woods. The Angelina National Forest is a fun place to hike with kids and explore the abandoned Aldridge Sawmill. Up the road, you can enjoy the gentle charm of the Texas State Railroad as it rambles along historical tracks. Nearby Lufkin offers a surprisingly large and diverse zoo and the compelling Texas Forestry Museum.

HOUSTON

A city as big as Houston (metro population 2,099,451) deserves to be named after a larger-than-life figure: Sam Houston, president of the Republic of Texas who, as general of the Texas army, led the fight for independence from Mexico. Everything about Houston is huge—with more than five million people in the area, it's the largest city in Texas and fourth largest in the country. The Bayou City is notorious for its lack of zoning ordinances and its high humidity, resulting in unmitigated sprawl and unbearably hot summers. But it's not without its charm—Houston has world-class cultural and medical facilities, and its immense international population contributes to a truly cosmopolitan setting with world-renowned corporations, services, and restaurants.

The city even started out with grand ambitions. In the late 1830s, New York City brothers and entrepreneurs Augustus and John Allen claimed that the town would become the "great interior commercial emporium of Texas," with ships from New York and New Orleans sailing up Buffalo Bayou to its door. For most of the late 1800s, Houston was a typical Texas town, fueled by cotton farming and railroad expansion. Unlike other cities, however, Houston received a major financial and identity boom when oil was discovered at nearby Spindletop in 1901. The oil industry changed Houston forever, with major corporations relocating to the city and using its deep ship channel for distribution.

Houston received another identity change and financial surge in the mid-1900s, when it became a headquarters for the aerospace

© BRANDON SEIDEL/123RF

HIGHLIGHTS

LOOK FOR **C** TO FIND RECOMMENDED SIGHTS, ACTIVITIES, DINING, AND LODGING.

C Museum of Natural Science: Featuring an almost overwhelming array of exhibits and artifacts, this museum covers everything from dinosaurs to gems to ancient Egypt to Native American and Latin American cultures. Bonus: a beautiful butterfly atrium (page 29).

C Houston Museum of Fine Arts: Spanning several city blocks and boasting more than 64,000 pieces of art, the Fine Arts museum is a treasure trove of culture representing all major continents and eras, from antiquity to the present (page 30).

C Contemporary Arts Museum of Houston: One of the country's most respected modern art facilities, the Contemporary Arts Museum offers a compelling collection of paintings, sculpture, and objets d'art in a stunning stainless-steel building (page 30).

C NASA Space Center: For an otherworldly experience, shoot over to NASA, Houston's preeminent tourist attraction. Don't miss the awe-inspiring Mission Control building (page 36).

C The Orange Show: Postman-turned-artist Jeff McKissack glorified "the perfect food" by devoting thousands of square feet to orange-related folk art, including sculptures, masonry, and bizarre buildings (page 36).

C The Kemah Boardwalk: Located southeast of Houston on Galveston Bay, the boardwalk is pretty touristy but offers nostalgic fun with amusement park rides, a massive aquarium, and a train, along with restaurants, shops, and fountains (page 37).

C San Jacinto Battleground Historic Site: With its remarkable 570-foot-tall monument (15 feet taller than the Washington Monument) honoring Texas's victory for independence, this 1,200-acre site commemorates the legendary battleground where Texian troops defeated the Mexican Army under General Sam Houston in 1836 (page 37).

industry. NASA established the Manned Spacecraft Center in 1961, which eventually became the epicenter of the country's space program with its earth-shattering Gemini and Apollo missions.

With the proliferation of air-conditioning around the same time, Houston's brutal humidity was no longer a year-round deterrent, resulting in corporations and their workers relocating from colder climes. The population boomed even more in the 1970s when the Arab Oil Embargo caused Houston's

petroleum industry to become one of the most vital assets in the country. The world oil economy in the 1980s caused a recession in Houston, and although the city eventually recovered, it received another black eye in the late 1990s as a result of the Enron accounting fraud scandal.

Texans typically don't consider Houston a viable travel destination, but they should. Most people within the state prefer to visit natural wonders such as Big Bend or South Padre Island, but a dose of cosmopolitan life is good for the soul. Houston's sense of style is a step ahead of the Lone Star State's masses, its restaurants often specialize in the regional cuisine of lesser-known countries (offering tantalizing taste-bud sensations beyond standard eatery fare), and the city's public transportation system is surprisingly comprehensive in its coverage. Incidentally, you'll be able to identify a native by the way they say their city's name—locals don't always pronounce the *H* (resulting in YOO-ston) for some reason.

A drive through Houston's inner-core neighborhoods reveals what happens when a city doesn't prioritize zoning regulations. Depending on who you ask, it's good (Texans in particular don't like to be told what they can or cannot do with their property) or bad (significant historic neighborhoods and homes are routinely leveled to make room for McMansions). Regardless, it's part of Houston's character, even if that means a 150-year-old home sits in the shadow of a monstrous contemporary house across the street from a gargantuan pseudo-historical retail and residential complex.

Houston may never equal San Antonio in visitation numbers, but its distinctive characteristics—a Southern cosmopolitan city with an independent spirit befitting of Texas—make it a worthy destination for more than just business travelers.

PLANNING YOUR TIME

Houston is often considered more of a business obligation than a tourist destination, which is unfortunate, since many of the city's museums and cultural attractions are first-rate. Those who make the effort to visit, be it for personal or professional reasons, will discover several days' worth of intriguing activities.

To maximize your experiences in a during a brief visit, first head to the Museum District, where nearly a dozen attractions—ranging from the enormous Museum of Natural Science to the small Buffalo Soldiers Museum—appeal to the entire cultural spectrum. Visitors can realistically make it to about three destinations in a day before losing steam, so pick a few topics

of interest (from art to health to history) and make the most of it.

If you're the kind of traveler who prioritizes unique-to-location experiences, make sure NASA is near the top of your list since nowhere else in the world can claim Houston's distinctive connection to the space program. It's about a half hour outside of downtown, so you'll need at least a half a day to fully appreciate the experience. Other uniquely Houston sites like the impressive San Jacinto Monument and Battleship *Texas* also involve a 30-minute drive, so be sure to plan accordingly.

ORIENTATION

Known for its seemingly endless suburban sprawl, Houston is defined by its highways and loops—in fact, there are three loops: *The* Loop (Loop 610, the original and inner loop), the Belt (aka Beltway 8, Sam Houston Parkway, and Sam Houston Tollway), and the Grand Parkway (aka State Highway 99, an unfinished outer loop that will be the longest in the United States when finally completed). While many of Houston's suburbs and outlying communities are worthy of exploration, the primary focus of this book is in or around the inner Loop.

With downtown as Houston's historical epicenter, the city's noteworthy historical attractions begin to expand mainly to the west, including museums, Rice University, and now-kitschy mid-century modern architecture. To the north of these neighborhoods is Houston Heights (The Heights), a formerly low-key residential area that has transformed over the past decade into a trendy place to live and do business. Well-heeled Houstonians have traditionally lived in ritzy suburbs to the west, most notably the Uptown area anchored by the high-end Galleria shopping district. Because the Houston Ship Channel was dredged eastward to provide lucrative access to the Gulf of Mexico, this side of the city is almost entirely industrial, with the exception of two large college campuses—University of Houston and Texas Southern University—southeast of downtown.

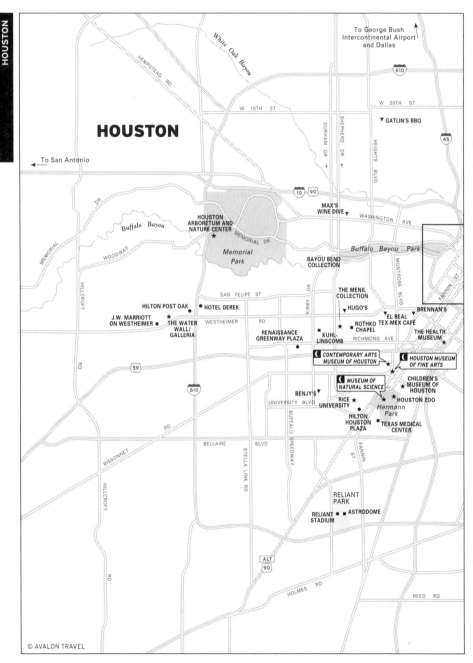

HOUSTON

To San Antonio ←

To George Bush
Intercontinental Airport
and Dallas

White Oak Bayou

HEMPSTEAD RD

W 18TH ST

W 20TH ST

DURHAM DR

SHEPHERD DR

HEIGHTS BLVD

▼ GATLIN'S BBQ

610

45

10 90

MAX'S
WINE DIVE ▼

WASHINGTON AVE

Buffalo Bayou

MEMORIAL DR

MEMORIAL DR

HOUSTON
ARBORETUM AND
NATURE CENTER ★

Memorial
Park

Buffalo Bayou Park

WOODWAY

BAYOU BEND
COLLECTION

MONTROSE BLVD

MAIN ST

HILLCROFT

SAN FELIPE ST

KIRBY DR

THE MENIL
COLLECTION

▼ HUGO'S

BRENNAN'S

HILTON POST OAK ● ● HOTEL DEREK

J.W. MARRIOTT
ON WESTHEIMER ● ★ THE WATER
WALL/
GALLERIA

WESTHEIMER RD

RENAISSANCE
GREENWAY PLAZA

★ ROTHKO
CHAPEL

EL REAL
TEX-MEX CAFÉ

THE HEALTH
MUSEUM ★

● KUHL-
LINSCOMB

RICHMOND AVE

59

610

BENJY'S ▼

UNIVERSITY BLVD

BUFFALO SPEEDWAY

RICE ★
UNIVERSITY

(CONTEMPORARY ARTS
MUSEUM OF HOUSTON ★

(HOUSTON MUSEUM
OF FINE ARTS ★

(MUSEUM OF
NATURAL SCIENCE ★

CHILDREN'S
★ MUSEUM OF
HOUSTON

★ HOUSTON ZOO

Hermann
Park

HILTON
HOUSTON
PLAZA

■ TEXAS MEDICAL
CENTER

FANNIN ST

RD

BELLAIRE BLVD

STELLA LINK RD

BISSONNET

HILLCROFT

RD

RELIANT
PARK

RELIANT
STADIUM ■ ■ ASTRODOME

ALT
90

HOLMES RD

REED RD

© AVALON TRAVEL

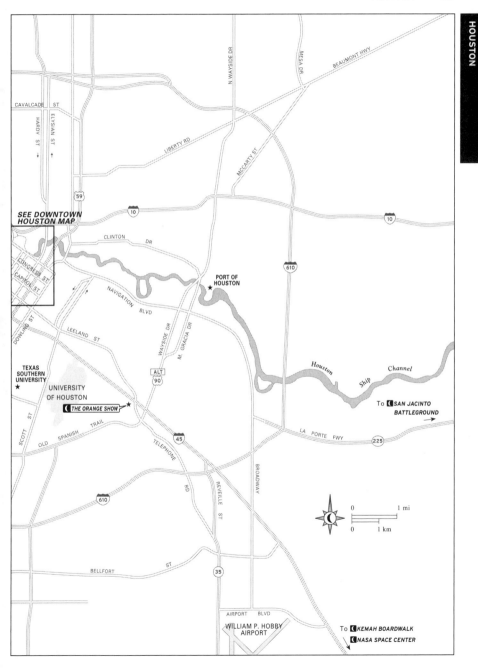

SEE DOWNTOWN
HOUSTON MAP

PORT OF
HOUSTON
★

Houston Ship Channel

To (C SAN JACINTO
BATTLEGROUND →

TEXAS
SOUTHERN
UNIVERSITY
★
UNIVERSITY
OF HOUSTON
(C THE ORANGE SHOW ★

0   1 mi
0   1 km

WILLIAM P. HOBBY
AIRPORT

To (C KEMAH BOARDWALK
(C NASA SPACE CENTER

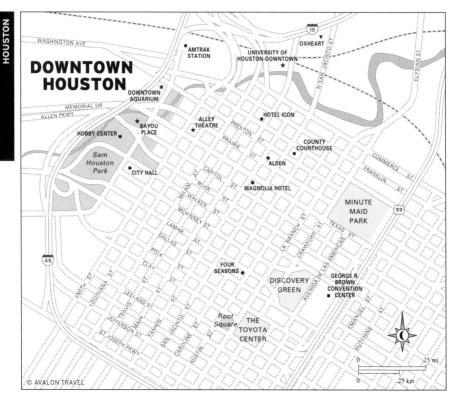

DOWNTOWN HOUSTON

WASHINGTON AVE
AMTRAK STATION
UNIVERSITY OF HOUSTON-DOWNTOWN
OXHEART
10
DOWNTOWN AQUARIUM
MEMORIAL DR
ALLEN PKWY
HOTEL ICON
ALLEY THEATRE
PRESTON ST
PRAIRIE ST
COUNTY COURTHOUSE
COMMERCE ST
BAYOU PLACE
HOBBY CENTER
Sam Houston Park
CITY HALL
ALDEN
FRANKLIN ST
CAPITOL ST
RUSK ST
MILAM ST
WALKER ST
MAGNOLIA HOTEL
MINUTE MAID PARK
59
MCKINNEY ST
LAMAR ST
DALLAS ST
LA BRANCH ST
CRAWFORD ST
TEXAS ST
AVENIDA DE LAS AMERICAS
POLK ST
CLAY ST
45
FOUR SEASONS
DISCOVERY GREEN
GEORGE R. BROWN CONVENTION CENTER
SMITH ST
LOUISIANA ST
LEELAND ST
TRAVIS ST
Root Square
THE TOYOTA CENTER
EMANUEL ST
HUTCHINS ST
JEFFERSON ST
MAIN ST
FANNIN ST
SAN JACINTO ST
CAROLINE ST
AUSTIN ST
ST. JOSEPH PKWY
N. SAN JACINTO ST
ELYSIAN ST

0 .25 mi
0 .25 km

© AVALON TRAVEL

Downtown

Once practically deserted after dusk, key investments since the 1990s have remade downtown Houston into a destination for more than just work. Just a few of the major draws are sporting-entertainment facilities that host Houston's professional baseball, basketball, and soccer franchises; the Downtown Aquarium; the **George R. Brown Convention Center;** and the **Theater District.** The addition of light rail and its continued expansion have made it easier than ever to get downtown. Downtown is vast, with pockets of nightlife, dining, and entertainment zones throughout—and even a subterranean network of air-conditioned tunnels that basically function as a shopping mall.

Midtown

Bordering downtown to the northeast and Montrose-Kirby to the west, Midtown embodies the ethos of Houston: change. The revitalization of downtown since the 1990s has transformed Midtown along with it. What was once a commercial and low-income residential district has become a commercial and high-income residential district. Expensive modern condos and townhomes abound, as well as pockets of dining and nightlife options. One unique district is **Little Saigon,** which has some of the city's best Vietnamese restaurants, as well as street signs in both English and Vietnamese.

Museum District

The name gives it away: Museums are the main attraction in this area southwest of Midtown. There are many major medical facilities here too, but what sounds more inviting: Museum

District or Hospital District? With more than a dozen museums to explore within a manageable area, this is Houston's most-visited part of town. With the added bonus of welcoming greenery in manicured parks and lush tree canopies, it's an ideal neighborhood to showcase to visitors.

Montrose-Kirby

Long the antithesis of Houston's sterile suburbs, the Montrose-Kirby area has been the bastion of the **LGBT community,** artists, hippies, punks, and various bohemian types for decades. But the freak scene has lost some of its edge of late. The forces of gentrification have been at work, leaving the Montrose-Kirby of today much different than the neighborhood of even a decade ago—meaning higher rents, ever more fancy restaurants, and less seediness. That said, it remains an artsy, avant-garde hub, with world-class museums, plentiful galleries, eclectic nightlife, and renowned restaurants.

West University

Officially known as West University Place (aka West U) for its proximity to **Rice University,** this enclave is actually a neighborhood municipality within the Houston Metropolitan Area. It is predominantly a residential district, generally with a mix of cottages and bungalows attracting professorial types and wealthy families. The adjacent **Rice Village** is a 16-block zone that is packed with shops, restaurants, and bars.

The Heights

If the Heights' Victorians and tree-lined roads could speak, they might report on the massive social changes taking place in the district over more than a century. The journey from streetcar suburb to city center has taken a predictable path: from desirable residential neighborhoods to post-war decline to revitalization/gentrification. The constant throughout has been its residential vibe. While it has a laid-back and somewhat bohemian feel like Montrose-Kirby, it has long been known more for its antique shops and thrift stores than its of-the-moment clubs and boutiques—though it is not lacking in the latter.

Uptown

Anchoring Uptown is the **Galleria,** one of the largest shopping centers in the United States and a major Houston attraction. Located just west of Loop 610, the Galleria's lavish sensibility is carried over into the district surrounding it, which features more upscale shops, luxury hotels, and office buildings. Uptown is, in fact, the second major business district in Houston, behind downtown. Beyond the business district, the vast and hard-to-define Uptown has many exclusive residential neighborhoods.

Greater Houston

Not surprisingly, this category represents the outlying parts of town, typically beyond the Loop 610. Atttractions in Greater Houston include cultural sites like **NASA, Kemah Boardwalk,** and **San Jacinto Battlefield** to the southeast and east. To the west are shopping and dining destinations such as **Chinatown** and the **Kirby Outlet Malls.** Otherwise, this part of the city is filled mainly with Houston's legendary sprawling suburbs.

Sights

A city of Houston's size offers countless attractions, most of them cultural in nature. The Museum District is a loose collection (not logically planned, but what in Houston is?) of facilities dedicated to art, science, and children's sites located just southwest of downtown. The urban core features occasional historic buildings and theaters among the modern skyscrapers, and the city boasts several offbeat spots outside of town worth checking out for fun, including the folk-art wonder of the Orange Show, and the historically significant state park featuring the San Jacinto Battleground site and the Battleship *Texas*.

DOWNTOWN

The terms "downtown Houston" and "tourist attractions" aren't typically used together. There are plenty of shiny skyscrapers, hotel and convention facilities, and sports arenas, but not many cultural sites for travelers. Regardless, it's worth checking out the downtown area just to experience Texas's version of cosmopolitan life. And to explore the bizarre subterranean tunnel system.

Downtown Aquarium

Mingle with marine life at the modestly sized **Downtown Aquarium** (410 Bagby St., 713/223-3474, www.aquariumrestaurants.com, 10am-9pm Sun.-Thurs., 10am-11pm Fri.-Sat., $9.25 adults, $8.25 seniors, $6.25 children ages 2-12, additional fees for rides and parking). Not as extensive or awe-inspiring as some other big-city aquariums, Houston's version is focused on fun, and there's plenty to be had here. Families will marvel at the enormous tanks, touch pools, and (slightly unexpected) midway rides outside.

Regardless of your age, it's always awe inspiring to stand face-to-face with a grouper, piranha, or shark. And speaking of sharks, one of the aquarium's highlights is the Shark Voyage, in which a train takes visitors into a clear tunnel surrounded by blacktips, whitetips, and zebra sharks. Other notable exhibits are the Gulf of Mexico tank with barracuda and snappers, and the Discovery Rig, where kids can get a handle on horseshoe crabs and stingrays. The aquarium also includes a seemingly unrelated yet interesting exhibit area with several majestic white tigers.

The on-site restaurant is better than expected, so consider planning your visit around a mealtime to enjoy a decent seafood plate while gazing at happily living sea creatures in the surrounding 150,000-gallon aquarium. Stick with the basics here (the flaky and flavorful whitefish or succulently seasoned shrimp), and you'll be pleasantly satisfied with your day of sensory sea-related experiences.

Incidentally, be sure to step outside and pony up for a few of the midway rides, just to add a different element to the fun factor. A medium-sized Ferris wheel offers spectacular views of downtown Houston, and the merry-go-round (with sea creatures in place of horses) will bring genuine smiles of delight to your family's faces.

Downtown Tunnels

Houston's bizarre yet fascinating **Downtown Tunnels** (713/650-3022, tour info at 713/222-9255, www.downtownhouston.com) are more of a local shopping and errand-running destination than tourist attraction, but their uniqueness is worth noting. The seven-mile subterranean system connects 77 downtown buildings, offering an air-conditioned respite from triple-digit surface temperatures. Interestingly, the tunnels started as a small system to connect three downtown theaters in the 1930s; now, tunnelers can find scores of services, ranging from banks to restaurants to clinics to clothing boutiques, 20 feet below the surface.

The tunnel system is accessible primarily from elevators, stairways, and escalators inside commercial buildings and parking garages situated above the passageways. The only building offering direct access to the tunnels from the street is the Wells Fargo Plaza (1000 Louisiana

Downtown Aquarium

their experiences in a minimal amount of time. Spanning a several-mile area with parks (and medical facilities), the district offers nearly a dozen attractions—ranging from the enormous Museum of Natural Science to the medium-sized Children's Museum to the small Buffalo Soldiers Museum—appealing to the entire cultural spectrum. Visitors can realistically make it to about three destinations each day before losing steam, so pick a few topics of interest (from art to health to history) and make the most of it.

◖ Museum of Natural Science

One of the best places in Houston for a family adventure is the **Museum of Natural Science** (1 Hermann Circle Dr., 713/639-4629, www.hmns.org, 9am-5pm daily, $15-36 adults, $10-29 seniors and students, based on exhibits, free 2pm-5pm Thurs.). The museum features an almost overwhelming array of exhibits and artifacts covering everything from dinosaurs to gems and minerals to ancient Egypt. Its permanent collection is especially impressive, most notably the Hall of the Americas, with its compelling exhibits depicting the stories of how people arrived on the continent (including Native American, Mayan, and Aztec cultures) and their ways of life once they became permanent residents.

As if the museum didn't already have enough amazing exhibits, in 2012 it added an entire wing devoted to paleontology. Featuring dramatically lit dinosaur fossils and exhibits dedicated to evolution and early humans, the hall is a sight to behold, especially with its action-packed scenes of predators and prey.

Children will never want to leave the museum's Discovery Place on the lower level, featuring interactive exhibits dedicated to light and sound waves; machines with levers, pulleys, and gears; and a simulated weather studio. Kids (and parents) will also be drawn to Energy Hall, an extensive area showcasing the importance of the oil and gas industry to Houston and the region. Interactive hands-on and touch-screen displays about oil density, drilling, and delivery allow children to learn through

St.). If you're interested in spending some time exploring the system (an appealing getaway on a sweltering summer day in Houston), consider starting at the Macy's parking garage (located at Lamar and Travis Streets) and accessing the tunnels from the garage or department store.

Once below ground, there are plenty of maps and signs to help you get oriented. You'll need them, too, since it can get pretty confusing to keep track of your location when you don't have traditional visual landmarks (street signs, buildings, etc.). Things move pretty quickly in the tunnels, and after a while, you'll realize that most people are there to do things citizens and workers do in cities all around the world: run errands and grab a bite to eat. They just don't normally do these things 20 feet below the earth's surface. To plan ahead, consult the helpful color-coded maps at www.downtown-houston.com.

MUSEUM DISTRICT

More inspiring than its name implies, the city's Museum District allows visitors to maximize

the Museum of Natural Science's butterfly exhibit

play, which is always a winning combo. Also, kids will be (perhaps unexpectedly) interested in the museum's large gemstone exhibit, featuring colorful and sharply cut gems in fascinating backlit displays.

The museum's butterfly exhibit is a bit pricey ($7-8) but worthwhile, especially to see the thousands of colorful, lithe winged creatures peacefully meander throughout the towering domed Mayan rainforest habitat. A lengthy waterfall flows gently in the background, and the butterflies occasionally drop by for a personal visit. The museum also contains a McDonald's, but be forewarned: At lunch and dinner the scene can be as crazy as Times Square on New Year's Eve.

◖ Houston Museum of Fine Arts

Another Museum District hot spot is the **Museum of Fine Arts** (1001 Bissonnet St., 713/639-7300, www.mfah.org, 10am-5pm Tues.-Wed., 10am-9pm Thurs., 10am-7pm Fri.-Sat., 12:15pm-7pm Sun., $13 adults, $8 seniors

and students 6-18, free on Thurs.). Billing itself as "the largest art museum in America south of Chicago, west of Washington, D.C., and east of Los Angeles," the Houston Museum of Fine Arts contains several major buildings offering 300,000 square feet of display space and 18 acres of public gardens and draws more than two million people annually. Be sure to look for the main entrance on Bissonnet Street because the museum complex stretches over several blocks. Free parking is available at several nearby street lots, or for $6 in an adjacent parking garage on Binz Street.

The museum's collection contains nearly 64,000 pieces of art representing all major continents and dating from antiquity to the present. Soaking up the significance of each collection in a half-day visit is challenging, so consider planning ahead by visiting the museum's website to see what inspires you.

European masters are always a compelling option, including impressively bold Italian Renaissance paintings and the mesmerizing French impressionist works. Also make a point to visit the Arts of North America wing, offering quality examples of nascent American landscape paintings, stunning black-and-white photographs, vintage jewelry, and well-known sculptures.

The museum is acclaimed throughout the national arts scene for its impressive collection of rare and diverse work. Its ancient Asian holdings are especially notable, including sculpture from Japan's pre-Buddhist days and a Chinese boat dating to circa 2400 BC. Other significant collections include masterworks by famed Western artist Frederic Remington, and the Glasswell Collection of African Gold, considered the best of its kind in the world.

◖ Contemporary Arts Museum of Houston

As big-city museums go, this is one of the best, with intriguing and captivating (and sometimes head-scratching) objets d'art down every hall. Located in the heart of the Houston Museum District, **CAM** (5216 Montrose Blvd., 713/284-8250, www.camh.org, 10am-7pm Tues., Wed., and Fri., 10am-9pm Thurs., 10am-6pm Sat., noon-6pm Sun., free admission) is unmistakable, housed in a distinctive stainless-steel building designed by prominent architect Gunnar Birkerts.

As a non-collecting museum, the facility focuses on current and new directions in art, with regularly changing exhibits and acclaimed education programs. The museum grew steadily in the 1970s and '80s to reach significant status in the nation's art world with celebrated exhibits featuring contemporary still-life painting, thematic installations, performance pieces, and other mediums.

If you're visiting on the last Friday of the month, be sure to drop by the museum's Steel Lounge for an *art*ini while you browse the exhibits and visit the amazing shop, featuring whimsical toys and objects, large posters, decorative items, and exceptional gifts.

The Health Museum

Since Houston is one of the country's leading medical centers, it makes sense to have the **Health Museum** (1515 Hermann Dr., 713/521-1515, www.mhms.org, 9am-5pm Tues.-Sat., noon-5pm Sun., $8 adults, $6 seniors and children ages 3-12, occasional fees for traveling exhibits). Located in the Museum District, this modest-sized facility is dedicated to educating visitors (kids, mostly) about the importance of good health. The museum includes one of the best exhibits in town, the *Amazing Body Pavilion*, where you can experience a human body by walking through it. Start by entering through the mouth and exploring the various systems and organs via innovative, interactive displays. Vocal chords, lung capacity, stomach acids, and blood content are portrayed through games, hands-on activities, and informative models. The museum also features traveling exhibits related to children's health issues and a fancy gift shop with fun toys, games, and knickknacks.

Houston Zoo

Consistently rated one of the city's top attractions is the lush, welcoming, and occasionally stinky **Houston Zoo** (6100 Hermann Park Dr., 713/533-6500, www.houstonzoo.org, 9am-6pm daily, $14 ages 12-64, $10 children ages 2-11, $7.50 seniors). Five thousand animals keep adults and children entertained on 55 acres of various ecosystems of the world. Be sure to drop by the world of primates, the Asian elephant habitat, the lion and tiger exhibit, and the grizzly bear habitat. Kids will also love the children's zoo, featuring a petting area with various farm animals and a "Meet the Keeper" program, offering behind-the-cage insight. Families with children will want to set aside time for a little excursion on the train, which takes a short journey through the park along the zoo's border. Also, if you have children in tow, consider bringing some extra clothes since most kids love the water play area and will undoubtedly get soaked.

Children's Museum of Houston

A must-see if you're in the Museum District with kids is the **Children's Museum of Houston** (1500 Binz St., 713/522-1138, www.cmhouston.org, 10am-6pm Tues.-Sat., until 8pm Thurs., noon-6pm Sun., $9 adults and children ages 1 and up, $8 seniors). The building itself is a sight to behold—an appropriately playful take on classical architecture with giant colorful details. The fun continues inside, where nine galleries engage children's minds through various subjects including science, geography, performing arts, and history. One of the most popular and informative attractions is the multilevel exhibit *How Does It Work?* Parents may even pick up a few pointers on how mobile phones function and how turning a key gets an engine running. Younger kids will relish the opportunity to sit in a model car with the freedom to push and pull every button and lever in sight. Other fun activities include an interactive Mexican village, art stations, live shows, and a café with healthy snacks. An added bonus: The Teacher and Family Resource Center has loads of books and items related to child development and parenting for the grown-ups who may need a break from all the incessant noise and questions.

HOUSTON'S HUGE HEALTH CENTER

Houston has become a worldwide destination for people in search of a cure. The **Texas Medical Center,** southwest of downtown, bills itself as the largest medical center in the world.

The sheer size of the complex–1,000-plus acres (billed as "approximately the size of Chicago's inside loop")–is impressive, as are the number of patients: 160,000 daily visitors with more than six million annual patient visits.

The medical center's origins date to the 1930s when businessman Monroe Dunaway Anderson proposed a medical center consisting of hospitals, academic institutions, and support organizations. Land was provided free of charge to institutions as an incentive to build within the complex.

Over the decades, the medical center has flourished, with dozens of facilities and specialists flocking to the enormous complex. It now contains one of the world's highest densities of clinical facilities for patient care and medical research. The center contains 49 medicine-related institutions, including 13 hospitals, 2 medical schools, 4 nursing schools, and several schools for other health-related practices (pharmacy, dentistry, public health, etc.).

In true Texas braggadocio style, the Texas Medical Center proudly touts many of its accomplishments:

- It performs more heart surgeries than anywhere else in the world.
- It has delivered 19,500 babies.
- It has 21,000 physicians, scientists, researchers, and other advanced-degree professionals.
- It has 71,500 students, including those in high school, college, and health-profession programs.
- It has 93,500 employees.
- It boasts $7.1 billion in approved building and infrastructure for future growth.

The Buffalo Soldiers Museum

The specialized **Buffalo Soldiers Museum** (3816 Caroline St., 713/942-8920, www.buffalosoldiersmuseum.com, 10am-5pm Mon.-Fri., 10am-4pm Sat., $10 adults, $5 students) moved from a modestly sized facility to a larger building in 2012. Appropriately, the subject matter is deserving of this greater space. The museum's name is derived from the term associated with the African American troops who served in the U.S. Army and protected the Texas frontier in the late 1800s. The Native Americans reportedly referred to them as Buffalo Soldiers because of to their immense bravery and valor. Fittingly, the museum honors the legacy of African Americans' contributions to military service for the past 150 years. This is a unique collection of materials dedicated to a compelling aspect of both Texas's and America's heritage. Two stories of exhibits feature artifacts, photos, and maps detailing the importance of legacies being passed on to future generations. It's a true learning experience, and it's inspiring to see the groups of area students making connections with their past as interpretive guides offer insight about the uniforms, flags, and equipment.

Holocaust Museum Houston

A somber subject is handled admirably at the **Holocaust Museum Houston** (5401 Caroline St., 713/942-8000, www.hmh.org, 9am-5pm Mon.-Fri., noon-5pm Sat.-Sun., free admission, not recommended for children under 10). The museum's mission is to educate people about the dangers of prejudice and hatred in society, and it certainly makes an impact on everyone who walks through its doors. Visitors learn about the historical and personal stories associated with the Holocaust in the museum's permanent exhibit called *Bearing Witness: A Community Remembers*, which focuses on the stories of Holocaust survivors living in the Houston area. Displays chronicle the Nazi rise to power and the imprisonment in

© ANDY RHODES

Holocaust Museum Houston

concentration camps. Artifacts, photos, films, informative panels, and a research library serve as testament to the suffering, with the hope that this educational experience will help prevent future atrocities from occurring.

Houston Center for Photography

One of the best little museums in the region is the **Houston Center for Photography** (1441 W. Alabama St., 713/529-4755, www.hcponline.org, 11am-5pm Wed.-Sun., free admission). Located in a funky building at the edge of the Museum District, the HCP's mission is to encourage and educate people about art and photography. Exhibits showcase local and national photographers, and programs and services strive to stimulate dialogue about the art form through digital workstations, presentations about methods and critique, and community collaboration.

Asia Society Texas Center

Even if you're not an architectural aficionado, you'll be impressed by the contemporary building that houses **Asia Society Texas** (1370 Southmore Blvd., 713/496-9901, www.asiasociety.org/texas, 11am-6pm Tues.-Sun., building admission is free, exhibits are $5), which opened in 2012. Located in a residential neighborhood just a block away from the Museum District, the graceful structure blends in perfectly with its surroundings and offers panoramic views of downtown Houston from its enormous second-story windows. Designed by Harvard-educated Yoshio Taniguchi, the 40,000-square-foot building is impeccable, with clean sight lines and exquisite materials.

Research and community outreach are the center's primary focus at this point, but there are several public displays and an outdoor sculpture garden reflecting its mission. For example, an exhibit titled *What Are You?*, about how individuals identify themselves racially, invites visitors to write their answer to the question and post it with a Polaroid photo to the display, prompting a wide range of emotional responses.

© ANDY RHODES

the Menil Collection's Rothko Chapel

MONTROSE-KIRBY
The Menil Collection

What do you do when you have too much fine art to handle? If you're art collectors John and Dominique de Menil, you open your own museum: **The Menil Collection** (1515 Sul Ross St., 713/525-9400, www.menil.org, 11am-7pm Wed.-Sun., free admission, parking at 1515 W. Alabama St.). Located among comfortable homes at the edge of the trendy Heights neighborhood, the Menil is an ideal place to spend a few hours soaking up some magnificent art spanning many ages. The grounds are expansive and inviting, with an abundance of trees, installation artwork, and even a wooden swing.

The Menils have passed on, but they left a legacy of approximately 16,000 paintings, sculptures, prints, drawings, photographs, and rare books. Most of the works are modern with an emphasis on the surrealist movement, but there are also African pieces and works from the Byzantine period on display. Be sure to check around each nook and cranny since some

of the Menil's most rewarding experiences are in solitary areas where artwork and gardens are bathed in natural light.

The Menil compound also includes several noteworthy structures near the main museum building that are worth an extra hour of time. Two blocks south of the main building is a fascinating Dan Flavin light installation, housed inside a former grocery store. The vertical-oriented fluorescent tubes on the side walls are a sensory delight, drawing your eye to the spacious open room and toying with color in your peripheral vision. Also be sure to set aside at least 15 minutes to experience the **Rothko Chapel,** a block east of the main museum building. From the outside, the chapel is disarmingly stark (it's no Sistine), with bland rectangular brick walls. Inside, it's similarly subdued, but the silence screams reverence. Even if you're not religious, the experience of being completely quiet (either alone or among others) in a public space surrounded by muted colors is absolutely sacred.

Bayou Bend Collection

The affluent home of unfortunately named Ima Hogg, a respected Texas philanthropist, now houses the **Bayou Bend Collection** (1 Westcott St., 713/639-7750, www.mfah.org, self-guided tours 10am-5pm Tues.-Sat., 1-5pm Sun.; guided tours 10-11:30am Tues.-Thurs., 1-2:45pm, 10-11:15am Fri.-Sat., $10 adults, $8.50 seniors, $5 students ages 10-17). This spectacular 1928 home is one of Houston's cultural treasures, and it's filled with an impressive collection of nearly 5,000 antique objects showcasing American decorative arts from 1620 to 1870. "Miss Hogg," as she was known, also had a hand in the design of the opulent home and grounds, featuring lush gardens and distinctive decorations spanning from the colonial to antebellum eras. Visitors are encouraged to call in advance to make tour reservations, and it should be noted that children under age 10 are not permitted in the home (apparently some old-fashioned customs are still retained along with the objects).

Rienzi

Another art museum located in an impressive homestead is **Rienzi** (1406 Kirby Dr., 713/639-7800, www.mfah.org, 10am-5pm Wed.-Sat., 1pm-5pm Sun., $13 adults, $8 seniors, $6 students, free on Thursday). Dedicated to European decorative arts, Rienzi features paintings, furnishings, and miniatures in the former home of local philanthropists Carroll Sterling Masterson and Harris Masterson III. The home was designed by noted Houston architect John Staub in 1952, and the name references Harris Masterson's grandfather Rienzi Johnston, a prominent Houston newspaperman and politician.

The collection is best known for its fine English ceramics and furniture, European jewelry, and sculpture, including the picture hall's main attraction, an early-1800s white marble sculpture of the goddess Venus. The surrounding four-acre grounds are also impressive, with welcoming shade trees and lush gardens. Drop-in visits are welcome, but reservations are recommended (except Sundays).

Rice University

Considered one of the finest universities in the South, Rice University is an oasis of intellectualism (and plant life) in this sprawling metropolis. With an exclusive undergraduate enrollment of approximately 3,700 students, the university has a reputation for its high-quality educational instruction, especially research in the medical, science, and engineering fields. Interestingly, the institution did not charge tuition until 1965.

To soak up the collegiate scene, consider dropping by the **Rice Student Center** (6100 Main St., 713/348-4096). Here, you can pick up a T-shirt or ball cap, grab a coffee, visit the gardens, and even have a beer at Willy's Pub. Another noteworthy place for visitors to explore is the nearby **Rice University Art Gallery** (ground floor of Sewall Hall, 713/348-6069, 11am-5pm Tues.-Sat., noon-5pm Sun.), offering a modest collection of site-specific installation works by international painters, sculptors, and photographers. Visitors can take self-guided tours, allowing them to interact with the large-scale artwork.

Garnering the most attention lately is the spectacular **Skyspace building,** adjacent to the university's Shepherd School of Music. Opened in early 2013, the pyramid-esque structure was designed for music, but the visual effect is profound. The two-story structure appears as a large grass-covered mound topped by a futuristic light show that projects LED-based colors onto the enormous 72-foot square roof, which opens to the sky.

Visitor parking is available at six campus locations. For a detailed map with parking locations and fees, visit www.rice.edu/maps.

UPTOWN
Houston Arboretum and Nature Center

Experience Houston's oft-forgotten natural side at the **Houston Arboretum and Nature Center** (4501 Woodway Dr., 713/681-8433, www.houstonarboretum.org, trails and grounds open 7am-7pm daily, Discovery Room open 10am-4pm Tues.-Sun., free admission). Located on the west side of near-downtown Memorial Park, the 155-acre nature sanctuary is a green oasis in a city known for its sprawling concrete. Native plants and animals are the focal point, with interactive exhibits and activities educating residents and visitors about the importance of not paving over everything. The park area is beautifully landscaped, and kids will love the Discovery Room's pondering pond and learning tree. Stroll the five miles of trails, hear the sweet sounds of birds, and get a glimpse of Houston's version of the natural world.

The Water Wall

Houstonians take immense pride in their beloved **Water Wall** (2800 Post Oak Blvd., 713/621-8000, 8am-6pm weekdays). Located in a strangely unoccupied area among office buildings and Galleria parking garages, this six-story structure is exactly what it sounds like—a giant wall of cascading water. But it needs to be experienced to be truly appreciated. The structure is semicircular shaped, and the hypnotic sound of falling water is especially mesmerizing. The gentle mist provides a soothing respite from a hot summer day, and the experience is even cooler at night thanks to the dramatic lighting (and "cooler" temperatures in the 80s). Considered by many to be the most romantic spot in town, the water wall is typically bustling with couples on dates, getting their photograph taken, or even getting married. The nearby colossal 64-story-tall Williams/Transco Tower offers a nice urban complement to the scene. Parking can be a hassle—instead of driving around in search of a nonexistent street spot, head directly to the nearby West Drive parking garage, which doesn't charge a fee after 9pm on weekdays or weekends.

GREATER HOUSTON
◖ NASA Space Center

Light years away from ordinary cultural attractions is **NASA Space Center** (1601 NASA Pkwy., 281/244-2100, www.spacecenter.org, 10am-5pm weekdays, 10am-6pm weekends, extended summer hours, $22.95 adults, $21.95 seniors, $18.95 children ages 4-11, check for online discounts). NASA is about as big as it gets for Houston tourist attractions, and it's one of the only cities in the United States to host such a distinct icon of contemporary American history. However, this might not be apparent when you step through the front gates. There are no time lines or text panels dedicated to the history of America's proud space program; instead, there's a 40-foot-tall playground and exhibits about nature's slimiest animals. At this point it becomes apparent that NASA is about two very distinct experiences: kids and adults. Fortunately, it works well.

Those who want to experience the significance and history of the facility should go directly to the tram tour at the far end of the main building. The open-air tram transports visitors to the space center's significant buildings, including the remarkable Mission Control Center. Here, visitors can learn (or relive) the fascinating saga of the Apollo manned spacecraft missions. A knowledgeable and entertaining guide takes you on a descriptive tour of the

extraordinary manned spacecraft experience as you peer through a glass partition at the dated yet iconic original gray-paneled equipment and flat monitor screens. Goosebumps involuntarily rise on your neck as you realize you're in the exact same room where the words "The Eagle has landed" and "Houston, we have a problem" were first heard. Next door, you'll get to see real astronauts in action at the Space Vehicle Mockup Facility, containing space shuttle orbital trainers, an International Space Station trainer, a precision air-bearing floor, and a partial gravity simulator.

Children may not understand the historical significance of Mission Control, but they'll certainly appreciate Kids Space, a massive collection of exhibits, games, and hands-on activities. Most of NASA's main facility features educational and entertainment-related elements, including an enormous playground for kids, interactive flight simulators for young adults, and the compelling Starship Gallery for all ages, offering life-sized models and an educational effects-filled film.

◖ The Orange Show

You know that burst of inspiration that enters your brain and encourages you to take an idea, no matter how ambitious, and follow through with it? Jeff McKissack, a Houston postman-turned-artist, actually did it. He built an enormous folk-art monument dedicated to oranges. McKissack glorified his favorite fruit with 3,000 square feet of space filled with orange-related folk art now known as **The Orange Show** (2402 Munger St., 713/926-6368, www.orangeshow. org, noon-5pm most weekends, $1). Standing among modest suburban homes just east of downtown, this bizarrely compelling artwork is comprised primarily of brick and concrete, accompanied by metal sculptures, mosaic tilework, and various random objects (birdhouses, windmills, statues). McKissack once delivered oranges throughout the South, and he apparently became obsessed enough with them to fashion this whimsical collection of objects found along his mail route. The absurdity-bordering-on-lunacy factor is rather fascinating,

HOUSTON, WE HAVE A LEGACY

Space exploration used to be major international news; now, we hardly know when a mission is taking place. Throughout the past four tumultuous decades, NASA's Johnson Space Center in Houston has been the hub of America's celestial activity.

The facility was established in 1961 as the Manned Spacecraft Center and renamed in honor of former president and Texas native Lyndon B. Johnson in 1973. The Johnson Space Center will forever be associated with its earth-shattering early missions with resoundingly extraterrestrial names, such as Gemini and Apollo.

The famous Mission Control Center was known as the nerve center of America's human space program, and the facility's remarkable guided tours shed light on the fascinating activities that took place here. Grainy TV footage from the manned Apollo missions comes to life as visitors absorb the significance of being in the same room where the words "the Eagle has landed" and "Houston, we have a problem" were first heard.

Mission Control handled all the activity related to the space shuttle and International Space Station programs. Training for these missions took place in an adjacent building, where astronauts and engineers prepared for their time in orbit by using the Space Vehicle Mockup Facility. This enormous edifice houses an International Space Station trainer, a precision air-bearing floor, and a partial gravity simulator. Although the future of the space program remains unclear, NASA expects to play a role in exploring the outer reaches of our known universe, however that may occur. For the past 40 years, this uniquely American entity has helped humans transcend the physical boundaries of Earth to enhance our knowledge about the universe.

To learn more about Johnson Space Center, visit www.nasa.gov/centers/johnson/home.

and the devotion to his subject is admirable in a disturbing kind of way. McKissack apparently believed his life work (it took him nearly 25 years to assemble his collection into a publicly accessible venue) would become a major tourist destination, but somehow it never quite caught on with the masses. Regardless, it remains an intriguing folk art environment unlike any other you'll ever encounter. Incidentally, you'll know you're in the right spot as soon as you see the local folk art organization's colossal 70-foot-tall blue saxophone, an enormous sculpture that's comprised of oil field pipes, an entire VW Beetle, and even a surfboard.

The Kemah Boardwalk

Located about 25 miles southeast of downtown on Galveston Bay, the popular **Kemah Boardwalk** (215 Kipp Ave., 281/535-8100, www.kemahboardwalk.com, open daily, all-day ride passes are available: $22 for adults, $18 for children) features restaurants, shops, fountains, and an impressive collection of amusement-park-style rides at the water's edge. Though it's touristy by nature (and draws suburbanites by the thousands for an escape from their 'hoods), the boardwalk offers a much-needed summertime diversion for families along with a nostalgic sense of fun. The restaurants are more notable for their bayside views than adventurous fare, but there's plenty of excitement nearby in the form of rides—including a bona fide roller coaster, Ferris wheel, and double-decker carousel along with bouncy, swingy, and spinny diversions. Other attractions include a 50,000-gallon aquarium with more than 100 different species of tropical fish, a marvelous meandering train, and an interactive stingray reef.

San Jacinto Battleground Historic Site

Two distinctly different, yet remarkably significant, historic attractions lie adjacent to each other near the Houston Ship Channel 20 miles east of the city. The **San Jacinto**

Battleground Historic Site (3523 Hwy. 134, 281/479-2431, www.tpwd.state.tx.us) tells the stories of valiant warriors in disparate settings fighting for freedom.

Perhaps most significant to Texas history is the San Jacinto Battleground site, with its remarkable 570-foot-tall monument (15 feet taller than the Washington Monument) commemorating Texas's victory for independence. The 1,200-acre site and its adjoining San Jacinto Museum of History preserve and interpret the legendary battleground where Texian troops under General Sam Houston defeated the Mexican Army in an 18-minute battle on April 21, 1836. The magnificent monument—topped by a 34-foot star symbolizing the Lone Star Republic—is dedicated to the "Heroes of the Battle of San Jacinto and all others who contributed to the independence of Texas."

The ground level houses the San Jacinto Museum of History, containing nearly 400,000 objects, documents, and books spanning 400 years of Texas history. Be sure to watch the fascinating 30-minute movie *Texas Forever! The Battle of San Jacinto.* The site's highlight is the observation deck, a 490-foot-tall vantage point offering stunning, sweeping views of the battlefield, ship channel, reflecting pool, and surrounding scenery.

Battleship *Texas* Historic Site

Just across the street from San Jacinto Battleground lies an important piece of the state's history: the **Battleship *Texas***. This impressive 1911 vessel is unique—the only remaining battleship to serve in both World Wars I and II and the first U.S. battleship to mount antiaircraft guns and launch an aircraft.

The mighty ship's multiple decks reveal what life was like for the crew, who bravely defended the stars and stripes during crucial combat situations while enduring overcrowded conditions. The elaborate system of massive guns remains impressive, and visitors can occupy one of the artillery seats to get a feel for the challenging precision required to operate the heavy machinery. Head below deck to see the cramped cots, officers' quarters, galley, engine room, medical facilities, and other slices of life to get a true appreciation for the distinguished service provided by the men of the *Texas.*

Since the ship has been moored at the site (in the brackish water of the Houston Ship Channel) since 1948, it has experienced significant weakening in its hull. The approval of a 2007 bond package included funds for dry-berthing the ship, which hasn't always gone as smoothly as expected. It's currently slated for a 2017 dry-berth completion.

George Ranch Historical Park

For a step back in time and away from the urban pace, consider a jaunt to **George Ranch Historical Park** (10215 FM 762 in Richmond, 281/343-0218, www.georgeranch.org, 9am-5pm Tues.-Sat., $10 adults, $9 seniors, $5 students ages 5-15). Located about 30 miles southwest of downtown near the community of Richmond, the site showcases four generations of family members on a 484-acre living-history site. The namesake George family were the last descendants of the site's original settlers, who began ranching operations here in the 1820s.

Visitors discover what life was like for Texans on a working cattle ranch through exhibits and displays at the pioneer farmstead, an 1890s Victorian mansion, and a 1930s ranch house. The enormous ranch house and its nearby barns and working pens help sharpen the site's focus on 1930s and '40s ranching operations. Visitors should plan to devote a few hours to exploring this truly Texan locale, where they can attend daily demonstrations about tending to livestock (horses, pigs, chickens), participate in hands-on activities such as corn gringing and weaving, and help harvest seasonal crops. You can even watch honest-to-goodness cowboys roping cattle. If (and when) it gets too hot outside, escape to the air-conditioned ranch house to see exhibits, photographs, and artifacts about pioneer and farming life on the George Ranch.

Sports and Recreation

Houston is home to several professional sports franchises as well as myriad opportunities for year-round outdoor activities, including golf, hiking, and biking. Pro sports teams are the big draw, especially because so many Houston residents are transplants from other parts of the country in search of opportunities to see their hometown heroes on the field. Natives have had reason to jump on the bandwagon for several sports, most notably the Texans football team's recent postseason appearances.

PARKS

Most big cities have a showcase central park offering an inviting natural oasis amid the harsh urban environs. Houston's version is Hermann Park just outside of downtown in the Museum District. Running a close second is Memorial Park, a haven for local hikers and bikers, as opposed to Hermann's visiting strollers. The city operates dozens of neighborhood-oriented

parks for families (visit www.houstontx.gov/parks to find one close to the part of town you're visiting). For an outdoor experience near NASA, be sure to drop by the Armand Bayou Nature Center.

Hermann Park

The huge green swath (for Houston) in the middle of most city maps is **Hermann Park** (6001 Fannin St., 713/524-5876, www.houstontx.gov). Located in the heart of the Museum District just southwest of downtown, Hermann Park is a 400-acre magnet for joggers, dog walkers, bikers, and families in search of some rare green space in a city known for its rampant development. Trails and trees are abundant here, as are the amenities and services, including a theater, golf course, and garden center. The park is filled with statues, too; look for monuments to Sam Houston, Mahatma Gandhi, and namesake George Hermann.

Memorial Park

Hugging the northwest corner of the city's inner loop is **Memorial Park** (6501 Memorial Dr., 713/845-1000, www.houstontx.gov, 6am-11pm daily). What sets Memorial Park apart from other parks in the city are its recreational facilities, primarily the hike and bike trails. Located on 1,400 acres formerly dedicated to World War I-era Camp Logan, Memorial Park is now a magnet for all varieties of athletes and exercisers (see Hiking and Biking entries for trail information). The park's other recreational opportunities include a full-service tennis center, swimming pool, golf course, fitness center, baseball diamonds, a croquet field, and sand volleyball courts.

Armand Bayou Nature Center

Farther outside of town but worth the 30-minute drive is **Armand Bayou Nature Center** (8500 Bay Area Blvd. in Pasadena, 281/474-2551, www.abnc.org, 9am-5pm Tues.-Sat., noon-5pm Sun., $4 adults, $2 seniors and

© ANDY RHODES

Hermann Park

students ages 4-12). Located near NASA on the west side of Galveston Bay, the nature center offers residents and visitors a chance to learn about native plant and animal species, hike on the discovery trails, or see the live animal displays featuring the likes of bison, hawks, and spiders. The main area of the park contains a boardwalk traversing the marshes and forests and providing a glimpse of the beautiful bayou region of East Texas. The best way to experience this natural wonder is by boat—consider taking a tour on the Bayou Ranger pontoon boat or signing up for a guided canoe tour.

HIKING

Despite a few national reports claiming Houston (and the South, in general) is one of the least fit places in the nation, a large number of residents are active and interested in exercise and health. Many opt for a gym membership since the city does not offer an abundance of hiking trails and coordinated recreational facilities.

The city's most popular outdoor destination for exercisers is **Buffalo Bayou** (1800 Allen Pkwy., 713/845-1000, www.buffalobayou.org). Those interested in a slightly less-crowded area should head to the nearby **Seymour Lieberman Exercise Trail** in **Memorial Park.** The three-mile trail is popular with residents who have a daily workout routine and utilize the exercise stations and restrooms along the route. More dedicated runners use the nearby asphalt timing track to work on speed and develop skills while the **Memorial Park Picnic Loop** offers a smooth surface for in-line skaters, traditional roller skate enthusiasts, and hikers. Dogs are welcome and even encouraged at the park— canine drinking fountains are conveniently located at ground level along the jogging trails. Just remember to keep your pooch on a leash and to bring a doggie bag.

Those willing to go a few miles outside of town will be rewarded by the scenic, tree-filled **Houston Arboretum & Nature Center** (4501 Woodway Dr., 713/681-8433, www. houstonarboretum.org, open 7am-dusk daily). The arboretum's outer loop is a two-mile trail for longer-distance hikers who enjoy combining exercise with bird and wildlife viewing. The trail's natural setting distinguishes it from other available urban options for hikers. For a topographically diverse alternative, consider a trek on the **R.A. Vines Trail,** offering up-close views of shallow wetlands, fish, and a boardwalk.

BIKING

Mountain bikers enjoy the challenging terrain along the city's **Buffalo Bayou** (1800 Allen Pkwy., 713/845-1000, www.buffalobayou. org), an urban greenbelt with the namesake waterway as its centerpiece. With the towering Houston skyline as a backdrop, the park draws bikers, joggers, art lovers, and walkers from across the city who relish its riverside trails and bustling activity. In addition to the smooth wide trail system, the 124-acre park contains exercise stations, a recreation center, a disc golf course, a children's playground, and a popular dog recreation area. Public art abounds along the jogging trail, from stainless-steel objects representing tree roots on an overpass to the large stone blocks, now turned sculpture, that remain from the city's demolished civic auditorium. Visit the park's website to download PDFs of trail maps. The southwest section of adjacent Memorial Park contains color-coded trails with maps at the trailheads, and Infantry Woods provides an advanced trail for those with superior skills.

GOLF

Houston's **Parks and Recreation Department** (www.houstontx.gov) operates seven respectable municipal golf courses, a worthy city service in an urban environment that features year-round moderate temperatures and developers ready to capitalize on any available open space. Three of the most popular courses are located within the loop, drawing golfers and hackers to the links' well-maintained grounds and affordable greens fees.

The gem of the downtown-area muni courses is **Memorial Park Golf Course** (1001 E. Memorial Loop Dr., 713/862-4033), a

MID-CENTURY MOD

Now that "modern" architecture is officially becoming historic, the term "mid-century" is emerging as a distinctive style and era (1950s-60s). Since Houston experienced one of its population booms during this time, the city is becoming well known in architectural circles for its fascinating collection of mid-century buildings that have survived the wrecking ball (so far).

Houston Mod (www.houstonmod.org), an organization dedicated to 1960s architecture in the Houston area, is making an impressive effort to document and preserve dozens of the city's significant mid-century structures. Perhaps most iconic is the **Astrodome,** which opened in 1965 and served as home field for the Astros and Oilers during the teams' glory years. However, finding a new use for the building, once hailed as the Eighth Wonder of the

World, has been a challenge, leaving it in danger of demolition.

Another historically significant structure is the 1963 **Humble Oil Building** (now Exxon Mobil). The 600-foot tall, 44-story edifice is one of downtown Houston's most recognizable mid-century buildings. For a short time, it even boasted the title of "tallest building west of the Mississippi." To Exxon Mobil's credit, it has been faithfully restoring the structure's exterior.

Also instilling pride in Houston's mid-century fans is the **Alley Theatre building,** which opened in 1968 to national critical acclaim. Known for its flowing and curvilinear use of raw concrete, the Alley is also associated with an architectural style known as brutalism, coined in 1953 and derived from the French term *béton brut* (raw concrete).

600-acre oasis of rolling fairways and challenging greens. Originally constructed as a nine-hole sand green course for soldiers at Camp Logan (now Memorial Park), the links feature lush landscapes, putting and chipping greens, a golf museum, a contemporary clubhouse, and an always-packed driving range offering shade and lighting.

Located adjacent to the city's Museum District, **Hermann Park Golf Course** (2155 Cambridge St., 713/526-0077) is another natural escape from the surrounding urban scenery. Lengthy fairways, snug out-of-bounds areas, and occasional water hazards make Hermann a favorite among serious golfers, who appreciate the shade of the ancient oaks and steady surface of the Bermuda-grass greens. While at the turn, be sure to order a hot dog or two from the clubhouse kitchen.

Farther south of town is **Wortham Park Golf Course** (7000 Capitol St., 713/928-4260), a former private course now operated by the city. The sportiest of the three downtown-area courses, Wortham Park features hilly terrain, tight turns, and several short par fours. The

course also offers a practice green and bunker, a chipping green, and a full driving range.

SPECTATOR SPORTS

Houston is a football town. Once home to the storied Houston Oilers football franchise (before they bolted for Tennessee and became the Titans), the city is now the home to the NFL's **Houston Texans.** As an expansion team, the Texans were slow to gain their footing in the NFL but are building a formidable franchise that, regardless of their spot in the standings, continues to draw substantial crowds to Reliant Stadium (1 Reliant Park). For Texans ticket and schedule information, contact the team at www.houstontexans.com or 832/667-2000.

Sports fans are also drawn to the venerable (at least from the local perspective) **Houston Astros.** In 1965, the Astros became the primary occupants of the then-futuristic Astrodome, referred to as the Eighth Wonder of the World. Indeed, it was a sight to behold and an especially welcome respite from Houston's horrendous humidity. The Astros assembled some worthy teams in the 1980s, most notably with hometown hero Nolan Ryan, and two decades later they attained similar success with another local legend Roger Clemens at the helm and a powerhouse offense featuring the "Killer Bs"—Craig Biggio, Jeff Bagwell, and Lance Berkman. By this time, the Astros had fled the Eighth Wonder for the comfy confines of the downtown Minute Maid Park (501 Crawford St.), a classic urban ball field with a modern retractable roof. For Astros ticket and schedule information, contact the team at www.houston. astros.mlb.com or 713/259-8000.

Basketball isn't as big a draw in Texas as other sports, but the **Houston Rockets** have always had a considerable following. Their successful 1990s teams, featuring top-notch talent such as Clyde "The Glide" Drexler and Hakeem "The Dream" Olajuwon, were the talk of the NBA during their glory years, when they won the NBA title in 1993 and '94. The Rockets hold court at the downtown Toyota Center (1510 Polk St.). For ticket and schedule information, contact www.nba.com/rockets or 713/627-3865.

Entertainment and Events

The *Urban Cowboy* legend was born in Houston in the early 1980s, and in some parts of town, it's never left. Visitors can get a good feel for the scene by sampling a few of the city's many nightlife options. Houston has a healthy blues scene, and the bars and dance clubs are reminders of the city's cosmopolitan culture. The performing arts in Houston are truly befitting of the nation's fourth-largest city, particularly its internationally renowned opera and ballet companies and spectacular symphony.

NIGHTLIFE

Covering the nightlife scene in the country's fourth-largest city is a daunting task, especially given the fluid nature of clubs. Instead of attempting to capture the trend-of-the-moment venue (which will likely change in style or name within a year), the following listings tend to be established sites that have proven their venerability by keeping the drinks and good times flowin' while the trends come and go.

Downtown

Downtown Houston can be unexpectedly quiet at night, and it doesn't tend to spawn scenes. Still, there are many notable clubs that boast a distinctive vibe and treat visitors to a uniquely Houston experience.

One of the more interesting spots in town to grab a cocktail is **Dean's Credit Clothing** (314 Main St., 713/227-3326, www.deanshouston.

com, 8pm-2am daily, no cover). Nope, that's not a misprint. Housed inside a historic downtown 1930s clothing store, Dean's strives to maintain as much of its early charm as possible. Original features include the elevator (one of the first in Texas), the ornate flooring, and the checkout area that's been transformed into a bar. Even the clothing racks remain stocked with vintage items, available for purchase at the bar. Local fashion shows are held here on occasion, and best of all, the drink prices are almost as dated as the surroundings—$2 for cans of Pabst Blue Ribbon and $5 well drinks.

Nearby is the low-key and comfy **Warren's Inn** (307 Travis St., 713/247-9207, 11am-2am Mon.-Fri., noon-2am Sat., 2pm-2am Sun., no cover). A longtime downtown lounge, Warren's is a dark and mellow place where the regulars look like they've occupied their spots at the bar for decades. Be sure to check out the jukebox with appropriate soundtrack music from the 1940s to 1960s.

In search of an urban dance-club experience? Head to **Club Venue** (719 Main St., 713/236-8150, www.venuehouston.com, 9pm-2am weekends, cover charge). Locals have been lining up here for years to dance the night away to über-trendy house and techno beats. Call in advance for bottle service or to reserve a VIP table.

Those not as interested in keeping up with the latest trends or worrying about specifically appropriate footwear should head to **La Carafe** (813 Congress St., 713/229-9399, noon-2am Mon.-Fri., 1pm-2am Sat.-Sun.). Known for its laid-back vibe and legendary jukebox, La Carafe is in a historic brick building that exudes character. Order some wine, punch in a little Otis Redding on the jukebox, and settle in for a long and cozy evening.

Somewhat defying categorization is **Dirt Bar** (1209 Caroline St., 713/426-4222, www.dirtbar.com, 6pm-2am daily, no cover). Located across from the city's House of Blues and just a few blocks away from the Toyota Center, Dirt Bar is an ideal after-show venue, where concert attendees can keep the party going with loud rock (and sometimes metal) blasting from the jukebox.

Not quite as rock n' roll (yet usually rockin') is **PBR** (534 Texas St., 281/300-7568, 10pm-2am Thurs.-Fri., 9pm-2am Sat., no cover). A multiplex for the senses, PBR has mechanical bull riding, two-stepping, stripper poles, and multiple dance floors. Show up early for drink specials, but stick around after midnight for the crowds to arrive. An outdoor patio offers a different vibe (and a chance to see loitering hobos' funky dance moves).

Midtown

The often overlooked Midtown area is worth exploring for its interesting mix of nightlife options. One of the most popular is **13 Celsius** (3000 Caroline St., 713/529-8466, www.13celsius.com, 4pm-2am daily, no cover), a wine bar in a distinctive building: a refurbished 1920s dry cleaner. Though the vibe is laid-back, the patrons take their wine pretty seriously, and waitstaff will speak in knowing terms without much interest in teaching basics. Not surprisingly, the wine selection is extensive and impressive, and the prices mirror this richness.

On the complete opposite end of the scale is **The Alley Cat** (3718 Main St., 713/522-9985, 5pm-2am Tues.-Fri., 7pm-2am Sat., no cover). A two-story club and live-music venue, the Alley Cat features a small bar in front (with a surprisingly diverse drink selection) and

raucous rock 'n' roll bands upstairs in the back. Though mainly a local scene, it's sometimes interesting for visitors to sneak a peek at the city's burgeoning bands.

Skewing more toward the dance crowd is **Escobar** (2905 Travis St., 832/443-5781, www.escobarhouston.com, 10pm-2am Thurs.-Sun., no cover). Look for the "Suite A" sign and prepare for a packed party scene, with hip-hop beats and moving bodies boosting the energy levels in the small space.

Montrose-Kirby

One of the most colorful and crazy places to spend a late night is **Poison Girl** (1641 Westheimer Rd., 713/527-9929, 4pm-2am Mon.-Sun.). The first thing you'll notice are the bright pink walls; the next will be the incredible selection of bourbons and pinball machines. Even if you're not a bourbon fan, it's worth chatting with the bartender to help pick your, um, poison. Be sure to spend some time on the back patio, where you'll be in the presence of a fun-lovin' crowd and the largest statue of the Kool-Aid Man you'll ever see (or attempt to climb).

Far more refined is the cocktail-minded **Anvil Bar & Refuge** (1424 Westheimer Rd., 713/523-1622, 4pm-2am Mon.-Sun., www.anvilhouston.com). This is a place for people who take their booze seriously, and judging by the steady crowds Anvil has drawn for the past few years, many Houstonians do. Though the bartenders shun the term "mixologists," they're absolutely deft at concocting a perfect cocktail. One of the bar's most popular drinks is the Nitro Cuba Libre, the fanciest rum and Coke you'll ever experience (dispensed via a nitrogen tap). Or consider ordering a First Growth, made with gin, pineapple juice, elderflower, and sage.

Houston has perhaps the largest **gay scene** in the South, drawing all walks of life, from the understated to the overblown, and most of it is centered on the city's Montrose District. So this is also where most of the gay bars are. One of the newer clubs on the scene is **JR's** (808 Pacific St., 713/521-2519, www.

LITTLE SAIGON: THE SEQUEL

In the 1960s, hundreds of Vietnamese residents fled their country and settled in and around Houston, where they found jobs in fishing and shrimping (and working in manufacturing and retail) in a humid coastal environment reminiscent of their homeland. Today, Houston's Vietnamese community of approximately 70,000 is the third largest in the nation, according to U.S. Census figures.

During the past few decades–particularly 2000-2010–tens of thousands of Vietnamese residents relocated from California and their native country to purchase homes and open businesses, mostly along a four-mile stretch of Bellaire Boulevard in southwestern Houston (after being priced out of an initial enclave in Midtown). Comparatively cheap housing drew the Californians, many who lived in Los Angeles's famed Little Saigon district.

Word soon got out that Vietnamese families were selling their pricey L.A. abodes and purchasing homes in Houston for a third of the cost. Their remaining funds were often invested in new Vietnamese-centered enterprise businesses, including restaurants, real estate firms, medical facilities, and supermarkets.

The result is a vibrant community, and its neighboring enclaves–shops and residences representing cultures from Chinese to Latino to Pakistani–add to Houston's cosmopolitan and diverse atmosphere. What was once the Vietnamese "best-kept secret" is quickly becoming a high-profile area.

jrsbarandgrill.com, noon-2am daily, cover charge), drawing a semiprofessional crowd for drink specials, karaoke, and male dancers. Parking is hard to come by, so consider using the valet service across the street at the old-school (and somewhat outdated) **Montrose Mining Company** (805 Pacific St., 713/529-7488, 4pm-2am Wed.-Sun.). Next door to

JR's is the popular **South Beach** (810 Pacific St., 713/529-7623, www.southbeachthenightclub.com, 9pm-2am Thurs., 9pm-4am Fri.-Sun., no cover), a hot spot for dancing. South Beach attracts a primarily gay clientele, but everyone is welcome on the dance floor, where suspended jets spray liquid ice on the crowd to keep things cool. A bit farther away, yet still in the Montrose area, is **EJ's** (2517 Ralph St., 713/527-9071, www.ejsbar.com, 10am-2am daily, no cover). Pool is a popular draw here, as are the cheap drinks and a second-floor martini bar.

West University

Many Houston residents associate pub crawls with West University's **Rice Village** area, where a collection of English-style brewpubs has kept nearby university students out of libraries for decades. The following locales are ideal spots for grabbing a freshly poured pint, finding the jukebox of your dreams, and soaking up the freewheeling college scene: **The Ginger Man** (5607 Morningside Dr., 713/526-2770, www.gingermanpub.com, 2pm-2am Mon.-Fri., 1pm-2am Sat.-Sun., no cover) and **Hans' Bier Haus** (2523 Quenby St., 713/520-7474, www.hansbierhaus.com, 2pm-2am Mon.-Fri., noon-2am Sat.-Sun., no cover, be sure to play some bocce ball out back).

Similar in approach with an added dose of live music is **Big Easy Social and Pleasure Club** (5731 Kirby Dr., 713/523-9999, www.thebigeasyblues.com, 8pm-2am daily). Beer and blues are the key ingredients here, and the mix of students and former hipsters make this joint a fun place to kick back and soak up the scene. Don't be surprised if you have to pay a $5 cover at the door; fortunately, you'll make up for it quickly with the cheap beer.

Less of a dive, yet naturally cozy, is **Simone on Sunset** (2418 Sunset Blvd., 713/636-3033, www.simoneonsunset.com, 4pm-midnight Mon., 4pm-2am Tues.-Thurs., 2pm-2am Fri.-Sat., 2pm-midnight Sun., no cover). Intimate but comfortable, Simone's is a great place to order a specialty cocktail with a light bite (pear salad, slice of pizza, etc.). Incidentally, the

Moscow Mule cocktails (vodka, ginger, simple syrup) are scarily addictive.

The Heights

Transcending its former trendy reputation is **Max's Wine Dive** (4720 Washington Ave., 713/880-8737, www.maxswinedive.com, 4pm-midnight Mon.-Thurs., 10am-2am Fri.-Sat., 9am-midnight Sun., no cover). "Dive" is a misnomer since the dimly-lit, comfortable locale caters to an upscale clientele, but the pairings of drink and food are down 'n' dirty. You never realized a glass of red wine would complement a burger so well. Or a flute of champagne pairs perfectly with fried chicken. More than 150 wines are available by the glass or bottle, and many are available to go. An added bonus: Most of the beverages and food are Texas organic products.

Another worthy wine bar is **The Corkscrew** (1308 W. 20th St., 713/230-8352, 4pm-midnight Mon.-Thurs., 4pm-2am Fri.-Sat., 2pm-midnight Sun., no cover). Things are more laid-back at the Corkscrew, allowing customers to explore wine options without feeling the pressure of being knowledgeable about specific varieties or taste descriptions. The wine-inspired quotes on the wall skew a bit pun-like, but the open and inviting atmosphere, friendly and helpful waitstaff, and quality wine selection are far more endearing.

It's only appropriate that a trendy area like The Heights has **The Drake** (1902 Washington Ave., 713/869-8333, www.drakehouston.com, 8:30pm-2am Thurs.-Sat., VIP cover), an upscale club for dancing and socializing. It doesn't have the same vibe as the city's Downtown or Uptown venues; instead, you'll find the Drake's unique spin on the dance-floor experience, with a lofty two-story 10,000-square-foot space punctuated by chandeliers, red-velvet wallpaper, and chrome barstools. Bonus: Some nights, a live drummer takes center stage and pounds the skins along with the DJ's propulsive rhythms. A VIP lounge and bottle service are available.

For those who'd rather dress down than up, The Heights is especially accommodating. The best place to soak up a true Lone Star State experience is **Alice's Tall Texan** (4904 N. Main St., 713/862-0141, 10am-midnight Mon.-Fri., 10am-1am Sat., noon-10pm Sun., no cover). Alice's is a true no-frills experience (cafeteria-style seating in a modest brick building) with friendly folks chatting above the din of classic jukebox country music and clinking bottles of cheap beer. And speaking of cheap, for just $2 you can order a giant goblet of Texas draft beer (Lone Star or Shiner) accompanied by a $1 bag of popcorn. How-dee!

Another dive-ish option is **Big Star Bar** (1005 W. 19th St., 281/501-9560, www.bigstarbar.com, 4pm-2am daily, no cover). Dimly lit with a classic checkerboard floor, Big Star is a comfy place to kick back with a cheap bottle of beer and shoot a few rounds of pool while listening to Johnny Cash. An outdoor patio (with chain-link fence) offers a friendly place to chat and smoke, and the vintage furniture and picnic tables were designed with chillin' in mind.

Uptown

Outlasting the trendy aspects of "craft cocktailing" is **Prohibition** (5175 Westheimer Rd., 281/940-4636, www.prohibitionhouston.com, 4pm-midnight Mon.-Wed., 4pm-2am Thurs.-Sat., no cover). Exuding a speakeasy vibe, Prohibition is known for its attention to detail and its serious approach to crafting mixed drinks (some would say too serious). Still, there's an undeniable charm in witnessing a drink being "created," especially when they involve items such as eggs, cinnamon, and Bénédictine. Popular options include the Penicillin (Scotch, ginger, lemon, and honey) and, for the adventurous souls, a French 750 (gin, champagne, strawberries, and pop rocks). Be sure to make reservations on weekends to witness the bawdy burlesque show.

For a classic British-style pub, head to **Richmond Arms** (5920 Richmond Ave., 713/784-7722, www.richmondarmsonline.com, 11am-2am daily, no cover). It's an ideal place to watch a soccer game on TV, and you can easily identify fellow fans at outdoor picnic tables because they're painted with team and country flags. Not surprisingly, there are plenty of fine British ales on tap, and the food is surprisingly good for a British-themed establishment.

Wine aficionados should sample the **Tasting Room** (1101 Uptown Park Blvd., 713/993-9800, www.tastingroomwines.com, 11am-midnight Mon.-Fri., 11am-1am Sat., 11am-11pm Sun., no cover). The crowd here tends to be slightly older than the usual club scene, and the clothing and haircuts tend to be of the well-heeled variety. Regardless, it doesn't feel pretentious, and the staff is happy to offer suggestions to wine rookies and veterans.

Another popular option for oenophiles is **Phil's Wine Lounge** (1800 Post Oak Blvd., 713/439-1000, www.philippehouston.com, 4pm-10:30pm Mon.-Wed., 4pm-midnight Thurs.-Sat., no cover). Part of Philippe Restaurant, the lounge has become a popular destination unto itself, with 88 wines by the glass and in-house cocktail recipes. Most patrons eventually order a bite to eat because the restaurant's cuisine is top-notch. Cheese plates and meat samplers are among the favorites.

LIVE MUSIC
Blues

Mention blues towns and most people think of Memphis or Chicago, but Houston definitely belongs in the mix. It has a long-standing tradition of serving up swampy bayou blues, and some of the state's grittiest and most soulful players have emerged from the city's downtown African American neighborhoods. One of the best places to see them play is the legendary, lowdown **Etta's Lounge** (5120 Scott St., 713/528-2611, hours vary). You'll have to seek Etta's out because it has no sign in front, a testament to its unassuming vibe. Inside, you'll find the real deal—a no-frills, cavernous room allowing the focus to be on the stage. The refreshingly diverse clientele isn't there to be seen (just to hear). Etta's shines on Sunday nights, when Grady Gaines wows the crowd with his soulful sax. Bring your appetite for a tasty meal too since Etta's serves some fine soul food in the restaurant up front.

The **Continental Club** (3700 Main St., 713/529-9899, www.continentalclub.com, 7pm-2am Mon., Thurs.-Fri., 8pm-2am Wed., Sat.) doesn't stage blues exclusively—roots and alternative rock acts are often on the bill—but the local and touring blues bands that play here are typically the best around. An offshoot of the legendary Austin venue, Houston's version of the Continental is appropriately more sprawling but still dedicated to offering some of the most soulful music in the Bayou City.

Consistently topping Houston's annual "best blues club" lists is West University's **The Big Easy Social and Pleasure Club** (5731 Kirby Dr., 713/523-9999, www.thebigeasyblues. com, 8pm-2am daily). Locals have called it the "Big Sleazy" for so long, it may as well be the official moniker, but the quality musicianship waiting inside is the epitome of integrity. Weekends are set aside for top-notch touring acts and Houston's premiere local blues bands while weeknights offer themes like open jams and dance parties.

Another local favorite is **The Shakespeare Pub** (14129 Memorial Dr., 281/497-4625, www.shakespearepub.net, 4pm-2am Mon.-Sun.). Locals rule the stage here, including luminaries such as John McVey, Eugene Moody, and Texas Johnny Brown. If you get a chance, drop by at dinnertime on Sunday for Sparetime Murray's weekly "early blues jam."

Country and Western

Houston is the true home of the *Urban Cowboy,* so grab those boots if you're fixin' to head out for some two-steppin' at one of these fine dance halls. For a real-deal honky-tonk experience, go straight to **Blanco's** (3406 W. Alabama St., 713/439-0072, 11am-2am Mon.-Fri., closed Sat.-Sun. for private events). Located near downtown just north of the Rice University area, Blanco's is small in size but huge on character. Some of the best live acts in the state play here, and there's always a fascinating array of couples gliding across the dance floor, from octogenarians to college students. The music is

classic country, transporting all ages to a bygone era of bolo ties and beehive hairdos.

Less charming, yet more appealing to the masses, are the city's big-box country music venues. Located near the Galleria among the trendy upscale dance clubs is the refreshingly unhip **Firehouse Saloon** (5930 Southwest Fwy., 713/977-1962, www.firehousesaloon. com, check website for hours). You'll see some flashiness here—big ol' shiny belt buckles, fancy light machines, Vegas-style video games—but the crowd is genuinely friendly. Although cover bands take the stage most nights, you'll find the occasional worthy local band looking to catch their big break.

For an overwhelming dose of Lone Star State culture, drop by the **Big Texas Dance Hall and Saloon** (803 E. NASA Blvd., 281/461-4400, www.bigtexassaloon.com, 6pm-2am daily). It's a bit hokey—the decor is pseudo-rustic with cacti and Western "artifacts"—but the scene is vibrant, especially for singles. Live music is the big draw on Thursday, when regional acts get boots scootin', but DJs fill the dance floor most weekends.

More interested in drinking and listening to country music than dancing? Work up an appetite and drop by **Armadillo Palace** (5015 Kirby Ave., 713/526-9700, www.thearmadillopalace. com, noon-midnight Mon.-Sun. and until 2am on weekends), located among a cluster of barbecue restaurants. The Armadillo has a huge bar in the middle and tiny stage in the corner. Fortunately, the pure honky-tonk sounds coming from the bands are huge enough to fill the venue and even get a few people two-stepping in the limited space near the stage.

Jazz

One of the many benefits of being a music fan in a big city is access to quality jazz clubs. Houston is a major player on the jazz circuit, and it's a hotbed for some of the genre's rising stars. The stalwart on the scene is **Sambuca** (909 Texas Ave., 713/224-5299, www.sambucarestaurant.com, 11am-11pm Mon.-Wed., 11am-midnight Thurs., 11am-1:30am Fri., 6pm-1:30am Sat., 6pm-10:30pm Sun.).

Located in the stunning historic Rice Hotel, Sambuca is a jazz fan's dream—a classy downtown venue offering nightly performances from local and national performers like Norma Zenteno, Tianna Hall, and The McClanahans. Accompany your ideal evening with a juicy steak from the acclaimed restaurant and a postmeal or set-break visit to the cigar room.

For a truly intimate experience, visit **Cezanne** (4100 Montrose Blvd., 713/522-9621, www.cezannejazz.com, hours vary), a 40-seat venue in the trendy Montrose district. Cezanne is considered Houston's premier jazz club, which is nice for the aficionados who get a chance to sit merely feet away from national acts but unfortunate for the hundreds or even thousands of other music lovers who'd like to see the show. Regardless, every seat in this cozy spot is a good one, and you'll hear, see, and feel every note being played. Check the website for favorites such as Joshua Redman, Randy Brecker, and Pamela York.

Concert Venues

Since Houston is such a business- and convention-oriented city, visitors often find themselves in town for a few days in search of familiar rock acts or with an expense account to afford some pricey tickets. Virtually every touring act makes a stop in Houston, so out-of-towners also have an opportunity to catch shows that may not make it to their home turf until the second or third leg of the tour. These folks will likely want to browse the online calendar for the downtown entertainment complex **Bayou Place** (500 Texas St., 713/227-0957, www.bayouplace.com). The Bayou's **Verizon Wireless Theater** (713/230-1600, www.verizonwirelesstheater.com) covers the gamut from rock and country to comedy and musicals while the adjacent **Hard Rock Cafe** (713/227-1392, www.hardrock.com) offers its venerable blend of music and memorabilia. Nearby is the more club-oriented **Rocbar** (713/236-1100, www.rocbartx.com), where DJs and live acts keep the party going until 2am.

If you still want to rock but prefer to roll away from the hassle of downtown, head to the classic Houston venue **Fitzgerald's** (2706 White Oak Dr., 713/862-3838, www.fitzlivemusic.com). Housed in an enormous historic Polish dance hall, Fitz's features indie rock acts, classic Americana groups, and comfy local bands. The all-ages policy can rub some old-timers the wrong way, but they can always escape to the spacious back patio for a fresh breath of smoky air.

Also housed in a historic venue is the folkie **Anderson Fair** (2007 Grant St., 832/767-2785, www.andersonfair.com, Sat.-Sun., cash only). This tucked-away weekend club in the Montrose area has been hosting up-and-coming folk and roots rock acts for decades and continues to stage some of Texas's most popular Americana acts. Note: Anderson Fair is only open on weekends and only accepts cash.

PERFORMING ARTS
The Houston Grand Opera

A big-time city deserves a big-time opera company, and Houston has one in **The Houston Grand Opera** (713/228-6737, www.houstongrandopera.org). Performances are held at the downtown **Wortham Theater Center** (501 Texas Ave.), and the opera is considered one of the city's cultural crown jewels. This is the only opera company on the planet to win a Tony, two Emmys, and two Grammy awards, and it has a reputation for commissioning and performing new works, with dozens of world premieres in more than 50 years. The company tours extensively, bringing productions to Europe, Japan, and Egypt. On the home front, it's been lauded for its accessibility (tickets for some shows start at $15, and the casual dress series is popular among the younger crowd).

The Houston Ballet

Another world-class performing arts company is **The Houston Ballet** (713/523-6300, www.houstonballet.org). Also utilizing the beautiful **Wortham Theater Center** (501 Texas Ave.), the ballet has developed a national reputation for making stars of principal dancers and staging contemporary, edgy ballets. In recent years, the company has been an important diplomat for the city by taking its impressive show on the road to China, London, Canada, and Washington, D.C.'s Kennedy Center.

The Houston Symphony

Also highly respected in the city's performing arts scene is **The Houston Symphony** (713/224-4240, www.houstonsymphony.org). The symphony has been impressing audiences at the magnificent downtown **Jones Hall** (615 Louisiana St.) for more than four decades, and it currently performs more than 170 concerts attended by nearly 350,000 people annually. Shows include a classical season, pops series, *Messiah* performances at Christmas, and family concerts. In the summer, the symphony performs outdoor shows and stages children's performances throughout the region.

Theater

Houston boasts several high-quality theater companies, but two consistently emerge at the top of the playbill. The **Alley Theatre** (615 Texas Ave., 713/220-5700, www.alleytheatre.org) stages its productions in a facility that's a sight to behold—a brutalist fortress in the heart of downtown separated into two stages. The Alley is known and respected throughout Houston for its ability to embrace the old and the new. The company's classic and contemporary performances consistently draw wide audiences.

Also drawing rave reviews is the **Ensemble Theatre** (3535 Main St., 713/520-0055, www.ensemblehouston.com). Billed as the largest African American professional theater company in the country with its own productions and facility, the Ensemble regularly stages acclaimed dramas, comedies, and musicals for enthusiastic crowds. The company also runs an educational touring program and a popular summer training program for youth.

EVENTS
Winter

Each year in mid-January, the Antioch Missionary Baptist Church of Christ is a gathering site for the **Gardere Martin Luther King Jr. Oratory Competition** (500 Clay St., 713/867-3286, www.gardere.com). Sponsored by the Gardere law firm for nearly two decades, the event is a highly anticipated contest for elementary school students, who research, write, and deliver inspiring speeches dedicated to Dr. King's legacy. The competition also includes a spirited performance by the Salvation Army Choir. In mid-February, the **Texas Home and Garden Show** (8400 Kirby Dr., 800/654-1480, www.texashomeandgarden.com) offers interactive displays and more than 1,500 exhibitors at the Reliant Center to help Houstonians and visitors get their spring gardening plans growing.

Spring

Every March, the University of Texas Health Science Center presents the popular **Brain Night at the Museum** (7000 Fannin St., 713/521-1515, www.uthouston.edu), featuring presentations about how the brain works, a nauseating yet fascinating dissection of a sheep's brain, an informative video, and other brainy activities. In April, don't miss the **Bayou City Cajun Fest** (7979 N. Eldridge Pkwy., 281/890-5500, www.tradersvillage.com) at Traders Village. Patrons enjoy crawfish, po'boys, zydeco bands, and all kinds of Cajun culture. Another popular annual springtime event is the **Asian Pacific Heritage Festival** (11903 Bellaire Blvd., 713/784-1112, www.apaha.org), featuring an impressive parade, food booths, and cultural activities at the Alief Community Park in southwest Houston each May.

Summer

It gets downright sweltering in Houston during the summer months, but that doesn't deter locals from celebrating. One of the city's best-known annual events is **Juneteenth** (7800 Airport Blvd., 713/558-2600, www.houstonculture.org), commemorating the day in June that enslaved Texans learned about their freedom via the Emancipation Proclamation. Juneteenth activities include national gospel, blues, and jazz acts taking the stage at Hermann Park, along with plenty of good eats and revelry. Paper-folding aficionados won't want to miss the annual **Origami Festival at Tansu** (321 W. 19th St., 713/880-5100, www.tansustyle.com), held each July in the Heights. Participate in the interactive workshops, exhibits, and demonstrations. September is still the height of the summer in Houston, and residents celebrate by enjoying hot jazz at the **Houston International Jazz Festival** (520 Texas Ave., 713/839-7000, www.jazzeducation.org). Let the smooth sounds of local and nationally known jazz artists provide a cool breeze to beat the September heat. The event is held annually at the Bayou Music Center.

Fall and Holiday

Get your ghoul' on with the city's annual **Ghost Walks** (713/222-9255) throughout October. Previous events have used the Spaghetti Warehouse restaurant (901 Commerce St.) as a ghoulish gathering point. Participants ride on the Metro to different downtown locales where they can get freaked out by various urban legends and authentic historical death scenes. Speaking of deceased, locals and visitors descend en masse on downtown neighborhoods on November 2 as part of the **Day of the Dead Festival** (4912 Main St., 713/343-0218, www.lawndaleartcenter.org). Held in conjunction with the Lawndale Art Center, this important Latin American cultural event includes parades and festivals to honor the former lives of family and friends. In early December, City Hall becomes the gathering place for **Chanukah Fest** (901 Bagby St., 713/774-0300, www.chabadoutreach.org). The Chabad Lubavitch Outreach of Houston sponsors this annual event featuring traditional food, live music, craft demonstrations, and holiday activities.

Shopping

Mention the words "shopping" and "Houston," and most people will immediately mention the Galleria, an (appropriately) sprawling community unto itself on the western edge of the city's outer loop. It's a glassy bustling commercial destination that inspires some but intimidates others. Fortunately, Houston has plenty of shopping options for all types, from the exclusive high end (Galleria) to the funky bargain basement (The Heights). Despite being associated with the *Urban Cowboy* mystique, Houston does not have an overabundance of specialty shops with Western gear, though you'll likely find more flashy rhinestone-embellished clothing items here than anywhere else in Texas (except Dallas).

DOWNTOWN

Macy's (1110 Main St., 713/405-7035, www.macys.com, 9am-9pm Mon.-Sat., 9am-6pm Sun.) is the five-story department store in the heart of the historic business district. The venerable building housed the original Foley Bros. store, an establishment that went on to become a mall mainstay across the country. Now that it's been in place for a few years, Macy's ably continues the tradition of offering quality clothing, perfume, and accessories in a cosmopolitan environment. For a real urban experience, take the Metro to the Main Street rail stop and step out near Macy's grand front doors.

Another popular downtown shopping destination is the pleasantly modest **Shops at Houston Center** (1200 McKinney St., 713/759-1442, www.shopsathc.com, hours vary by location), comprised of nearly 50 specialty stores and boutiques beneath a canopy-style atrium. Look for jewelry, home decor items, and a quick bite to eat as you stroll the two-block complex among meandering visitors and beelining professionals. The shops are connected to Houston's bizarre yet fascinating **Downtown Tunnels** (713/650-3022, tour info at 713/222-9255, www.downtownhouston.com, 9am-5pm Mon.-Fri.), a seven-mile system of air-conditioned subterranean walkways that link more than 82 downtown buildings.

Locals are warming up to the corporate **Houston Pavilions** (1201 Fannin St., 832/320-1200, www.houstonpavilions.com, 10am-9pm Mon.-Sat., noon-6pm Sun.). More than just the "stores around the House of Blues," the Pavilions offer several chain clothing boutiques, health and beauty shops, and shoe stores. However, the charm lies in the entertainment venues, like Pete's Dueling Piano Bar and even a bowling alley (Lucky Strikes Lanes).

Many Houstonians have deemed the Pavilions' location of **BCBG Max Azaria** (1201 Fannin St., 713/654-7752, www.bcbg.com, 10am-9pm Mon.-Sat., noon-5pm Sun.) a hidden gem, especially as an alternative to the overcrowded and stuffy Galleria option. Specializing in a wide range of women's clothing, BCBG carries everything from business wear and cocktail dresses to casual outfits and comfy shoes. Bonus: The sales racks offer high-quality items at 30 to 80 percent off.

Another specialty option is **The Tipping Point** (1212 Main St., 713/655-0443, www.thetippingpointstore.com, 11am-6pm Mon.-Sat.), known for its sneakers and casual wear. Although it's smaller than other retail shops, the size lends an intimacy that helps patrons interact with staff on a more personal level. The shoe and clothing options (think T-shirts and hats) are clean and simple, reflecting the Tipping Point's easy vibe.

WEST UNIVERSITY

Aside from the Galleria, one of Houston's most popular and venerable shopping destinations is **Rice Village** (Rice Blvd. and Kirby Dr. just west of Rice University, www.ricevillageonline.com, hours vary). This 16-block complex has been a favorite place for bargain hunting, browsing, and people watching since the 1930s. The Village features scores of independent shops and eclectic boutiques along with local restaurants and services, some located in historic homes, others in modest 1950s strip centers.

The nearby **Highland Village** (4055 Westheimer Rd., 713/850-3100, www.shophighlandvillage.com, hours vary) is considered a more subdued version of the Galleria. It's an upscale collection of shops, but the stucco buildings and breezy palm trees give it a more relaxed feel than other high-end plazas. Home furnishings are big here, including retail giants Williams-Sonoma, Crate & Barrel, Restoration Hardware and the like, along with dozens of fancy clothing stores and restaurants.

Less charming in nature but still appealing for its sheer size and selection is **Kuhl-Linscomb** (2424 W. Alabama St., 713/526-6000, www.kuhl-linscomb.com, 10am-6:30pm Mon.-Fri., 10am-6pm Sat., 1pm-6pm Sun.). Focusing on design and lifestyle products, this enormous 70,000-square-foot destination is comprised of five buildings packed with everything from Texas-themed accessories to home decor items. It's like a housewares boutique on steroids.

Almost as alluring is its name is **Naked Body+Bath** (2516 Times Blvd., 713/942-8800, www.nakedbodyandbath.com, 10am-6pm Mon.-Sat., noon-5pm Sun.). Specializing in all-natural bath products, this store features an impressive collection of handmade and organic items such as soaps, lotions, essential oils, and salt scrubs. One of the most popular products is a "bath bomb," providing a naturally fizzy accompaniment to the traditional tub soak. Also appealing to organic-minded shoppers is **One Green Street** (3423 White Oak Dr., 281/888-9518, www.onegreenstreet.com, 11am-6pm Tues.-Thurs., 11am-7pm Fri.-Sat., 1pm-6pm Sun.). Located in a refurbished bungalow, One Green Street features separate rooms offering various natural products, ranging from recycled and repurposed merchandise to organic cosmetics and products from local businesses. True to its nature, One Green Street offers a discount to patrons who arrive by bike.

Drink in the city's cultural scene while drinking a latte at **Brazos Bookstore** (2421 Bissonnet St., 713/523-0701, www.brazosbookstore.com, 11am-8pm Mon.-Sat., noon-6pm Sun.). Fiercely loved by local book people (it was rescued from closure by a group of concerned citizens in 2006), Brazos Bookstore is an ideal place to spend an afternoon out of the heat by browsing, reading, and chatting with the knowledgeable and friendly staff.

Those who enjoy getting lost in a good mystery book will find all the answers at **Murder by the Book** (2342 Bissonnet St., 713/524-8597, www.murderbooks.com, 10am-6pm Mon.-Sat., noon-5pm Sun.). The definition of an independent bookstore, this specialty shop is a fun place to discover, even if you're not an exclusive fan of mystery novels. Mystery by the Book also offers an impressive collection of foreign fiction and hosts a busy event calendar with readings and book signings.

THE HEIGHTS

Shopping destinations in The Heights reflect the neighborhood's funky and trendy vibe. A good example is **Casa Ramirez** (241 W. 19th St., 713/880-2420, 10am-5pm Tues.-Fri., 10am-6pm Sat., 11am-5am Sun.). Featuring Latin American folk art and clothing items, Casa Ramirez offers customers a colorful view of traditional Latin American wares, from furniture to handbags to paintings. Be sure to look for Mr. or Mrs. Ramirez, who will gladly provide suggestions and explain stories behind the shop's many interesting items.

Just a block away is the equally fascinating **Chippendale Eastlake Antiques** (250 W. 19th St., 713/869-8633, www.chippendaleon19th. com, 10am-6pm Mon.-Sat., 11am-6pm Sun.). This welcoming shop is clean, bright, and filled with an eclectic collection of vendor "booths" offering everything from vintage toys to classic furniture to amusing artwork.

If you're interested in the culture (and animals) of rural America, head straight to **Wabash Antiques and Feedstore** (5701 Washington Ave., 713/863-8322, www.wabashfeed.com, 9am-6pm Mon.-Fri., 8:30am-6pm Sat., 10am-5pm Sun.). Although many Houstonians come here for their high-end pet food, others visit just to soak up the sounds and sights associated with farms, including antique equipment, lawn art, and plenty of hens, turkeys, kittens, and rabbits.

For another distinctive "shopping" experience, stop by **Adicks SculpturWorx** (2500 Summer St., www.adickes.net, hours vary), where the visual entertainment is sometimes more valuable than a purchase. Known around the city as "that place with the huge president sculptures," Adicks is actually a workspace and storage area for sculptors' works, including traditional works and contemporary pieces (like the Beatles and presidents).

If you're in search of a lil' ol' Texas-style fashion boutique, then come on down to **Hello Lucky** (1025 Studewood St., 713/864-3556, www.hello-lucky.com, 11am-5pm Wed.-Thurs., 11am-6pm Fri.-Sat., noon-5pm Sun.). Located in a small historic home, Hello Lucky is filled with Texas-themed clothing and knickknacks. Featured items include jewelry, T-shirts, tote bags, and accessories (like gold armadillo cufflinks).

UPTOWN

One of the city's most popular tourist and shopping destinations is the colossal **Galleria** (5085 Westheimer Rd., 713/622-0663, www. galleriahouston.com, 10am-9pm Mon.-Sat., 11am-7pm Sun.). This city within a city—the fourth-largest mall in the country—draws more than 24 million visitors annually. Noted for its remarkable glass atria and suspended balconies, the Galleria contains a popular ice-skating rink, two Westin hotels, and more than 375 shops, including top-notch retailers such as Nordstrom (the only location in Houston), Saks Fifth Avenue, Neiman Marcus, Cartier, Gucci, and Tiffany & Co. The best time to experience the Galleria is Saturday afternoon. It's an absolute madhouse, and you probably won't get much shopping done, but the people watching is the best the city has to offer. Grab a latte and keep an eye out for the girls in flashy gowns celebrating their *quinceañeras* (a Latin American rite of passage that occurs on a girl's 15th birthday).

Across the street is the slightly more eclectic **Centre at Post Oak** (5000 Westheimer Rd., 10am-9pm Mon.-Sat., 11am-7pm Sun.), offering a good mix of corporate giants and smaller independent stores. Barnes & Noble and Marshalls peacefully coexist alongside specialty

© ANDY RHODES

the Water Wall at the Galleria

shops such as J. Tiras Classic Handbags & Jewelry and Jeffrey Stone Ltd. Upscale dining options are also a part of this pedestrian-friendly environment.

Nearby is the charming **Uptown Park** (1400 Post Oak Blvd., 713/850-1400, www.uptownparkhouston.com, hours vary by location). Billed as "Houston's Italian-style piazza," Uptown Park features pleasant European-inspired buildings, lush landscaped walkways, and soothing fountains. Coffee shops, upscale clothing retailers, fancy jewelry stores, and luxury spas add to the ambience.

GREATER HOUSTON

An eclectic mix of Asian shops and restaurants awaits on **Harwin Drive,** roughly between Gessner and Fondren Streets. The area offers an epic mash-up of cultural diversity (Thai, Pakistani, Indian, and Chinese vendors and authentic eateries) in the unassuming form of typical American suburban sprawl (strip malls,

gaudy signs). Plan to spend an afternoon browsing for unexpected gems and bargain clothes, accessories, furniture, and knickknacks. Just a couple miles west on Harwin is **Chinatown,** a concentrated collection of Chinese establishments, including a mall with bookstores, music, gifts, and cooking items.

Located about 25 miles west of Houston is the immensely popular **Katy Mills** (5000 Katy Mills Cir., 281/644-5015, www.katymills.com, 10am-9pm Mon.-Sat., 11am-6pm Sun.), a destination for bargain hunters who thrive on finding discounted clothing and products from big-time retailers. Katy Mills goes a step beyond other outlet malls, however, by including a 20-screen movie theater, merry-go-round, and rock wall. It's the brand-name stores that offer the true thrills, however, including Tommy Hilfiger, Off 5th Saks Fifth Avenue, Books-A-Million, Bass Pro Shops, Last Call Neiman Marcus, Cole Haan, and Polo Ralph Lauren.

Accommodations

For all its Texas-worthy cosmopolitan charm, Houston remains primarily a business destination. And the city's hotels reflect that. Sure, there are a few upscale independent options (Hotels ZaZa and Derek, in particular), but most lodging is located on a busy interstate highway with easy access to other major traffic arteries connecting business centers. As a result, rooms are easy to book throughout the year and mostly generic with their amenities.

That being said, visitors can take full advantage of this phenomenon (almost exclusively downtown) by booking upscale establishments at especially affordable rates on weekends (around $115 nightly). The downtown action slows considerably during this time, allowing travelers to park and walk freely. With the absence of work-related traffic, driving back and forth from a high-end historic downtown hotel like the Magnolia to Museum District

© ANDY RHODES
the Magnolia Hotel

sites for a quick change of clothes or laptop break is easy.

DOWNTOWN
$50-150

One of the best ways to experience Houston—at an affordable rate, no less—is at the fabulous **◖Magnolia Hotel** (1100 Texas Ave., 713/221-0011, www.magnoliahotelhouston.com, $136 d). This historic downtown gem hosts many business guests and events, and the bustling activity adds to the cosmopolitan aura of the grand 1926 building. There's an undeniable charm to strolling in and out of a fancy hotel on a bustling urban streetscape, and it's always a bonus to be within walking distance of attractions and quality restaurants. The Magnolia offers an impressive number of complimentary services, including wireless Internet access, downtown car transportation, a full hot breakfast, and even better: free happy hour drinks and milk and cookies at bedtime. The rooms are on the small side, but that's to be expected in a downtown hotel in the nation's fourth-largest city. Also expected (yet dangerous) is the minibar stocked with beverages and snacks. The Magnolia's accessible library is stocked with an eclectic collection of classic (and not-so-classic) books to borrow, and its rooftop fitness center, lap pool, and hot tub make this impressive hotel one of Houston's top-notch lodging options.

At the complete opposite end of the chronological scale is the eco- and tech-minded **Element Houston Vintage Park** (14555 Vintage Preserve Pkwy., 281/379-7300, www.starwoodhotels.com, $99 d). Part of a "lifestyle center" in the bustling northwestern part of town, Element touts its environmentally friendly design and construction, as well as its thorough provision of widespread wireless access for computers, phones, and portable online devices. Other amenities include a hot breakfast, open-flow guest rooms with fully equipped kitchens, and an evening reception

(6pm-7:30pm Mon.-Thurs.) with hand-selected regional wines and beer, soft drinks, and appetizers.

$150-200

For a deluxe downtown lodging experience in a major city of Houston's size, it doesn't get much better than the **Alden** (the former Sam Houston Hotel at 1117 Prairie St., 832/200-8800, www. aldenhotels.com, $150 d). The Alden offers near-luxury accommodations without charging outrageous prices. Pamper yourself in this contemporary setting with fancy bathrooms (granite walls and glass-walled showers with plush robes and towels), quality bedding (400-thread-count sheets, down comforters and pillows, pillow-top mattresses), as well as DVD libraries, gourmet snacks, a minibar, and free Wi-Fi service.

For a slight price increase, consider **Hilton Americas** (1600 Lamar St., 713/739-8000, www.hilton.com, $159 d), a massive, visually striking hotel with more than 1,200 rooms towering over downtown. This is a big-time business destination because the Hilton is attached to the convention center, but weekends are a nice (and cheaper) time to stay as the hotel's many amenities are even more accessible. Highlights include three restaurants, several bars and lounges, and an impressive spa and health club with downtown views. Rooms feature free wireless Internet access, fancy linens (300 thread count), and an in-room refreshment center.

Another worthwhile option is the clean and spacious **Best Western Downtown Inn and Suites** (915 W. Dallas St., 713/571-7733, www. bestwestern.com, $150 d). Rooms and suites include microwaves, fridges, and free Wi-Fi service, and the hotel offers a free full breakfast every morning, happy hour cocktails (Monday-Thursday), a fitness center, a spa, and an outdoor pool.

Those seeking the comforts of home in a historic urban setting will enjoy the **Residence Inn Houston Downtown** (904 Dallas St., 832/366-1000, www.marriott.com, $159 d). The building itself is spectacular—the 1921 Humble Oil Building features well-restored Classical Revival details such as brass elevator doors, tall ceilings, and stately rose marble. Hotel amenities include free Internet access, free drinks at the evening social hour, a large pool, fitness center, and spacious suites with fully equipped kitchens and separate sleeping and living areas. Check out this over-the-top service: You can leave a grocery list at the front desk and return in the evening to a stocked kitchen.

Sometimes a visit to a cosmopolitan city requires a cosmopolitan lodging experience. In Houston, look no further than the **✪ Hotel Icon** (220 Main St., 713/224-4266, www.hotelicon.com, $179 d), offering dynamic contemporary lodging in the heart of downtown. This 12-story hotel is filled with bold colors and lavish details, including marble countertops, antique claw-foot tubs, luxury robes, and plush linens. In the mood for a bubble bath? Simply summon the Bath Butler for a perfectly drawn sudsy experience. Other amenities include free Wi-Fi service, Web TV, a stocked minibar, and fresh-cut flowers.

If a historic setting is more your style, consider the elegant **Lancaster** (701 Texas St., 713/228-9500, www.thelancaster.com, $189 d), considered Houston's original small luxury hotel. The Lancaster's posh aura is immediately apparent upon entering the lobby, decorated with large oil paintings, beveled glass, and dramatic lighting. The hotel's decor evokes a sense of European opulence, and the guest rooms capture this charm with dark wood two-poster beds, feather pillows and duvets, and brass furnishings. The Lancaster also offers free wireless Internet service, plush bathrobes, and free car service to nearby attractions.

Over $200

Those in search of five-star accommodations have several downtown options, including the reliably luxurious **Four Seasons** (1300 Lamar St., 713/650-1300, www.fourseasons.com, $200 d). The skyline views are outstanding here, as are the services, including the exquisite spa and salon, a spacious pool and fitness center, complimentary downtown car service, a tasty antipasti bar, and rooms featuring plush bathrobes, minibars, and Wi-Fi access.

Some of the most expensive lodging in town is at the **Inn at the Ballpark** (1520 Texas St., 713/228-1520, www.innattheballpark.com, $209 d), located within earshot of the cracks of the Houston Astros' bats. The location is one of the prime amenities here because the other services (aside from being five-star in quality) are not overly inspiring. The Inn at the Ballpark offers free transportation services around town as well as complimentary Internet access and a light breakfast.

WEST UNIVERSITY
$50-150

Downtown is pretty quiet most nights, but the West University area is usually hoppin'. Visitors often opt to stay here for the abundant nearby nightlife and cultural attractions. One of the best deals in the area is the **Courtyard Houston West University** (2929 Westpark Dr., 713/661-5669, www.marriott.com, $139 d), offering an outdoor pool/whirlpool, exercise room, book-filled library, and free Internet access.

Similarly priced yet slightly more up-scale is the **Renaissance Greenway Plaza** (6 Greenway Plaza E., 713/629-1200, www.marriott.com, $129 d), featuring spacious rooms with walk-in closets, luxury bedding, Internet access, a fitness center, and outdoor pool.

Another worthy option is the enormous **Hilton Houston Plaza** (6633 Travis St., 713/313-4000, www.hilton.com, $129 d). The Hilton includes large suites, minibars, Internet access, a fitness facility, heated swimming pool, and free transportation within a three-mile radius of the hotel.

Over $200

The lodging jewel of the city's crown is **C Hotel ZaZa** (5701 Main St., 713/526-1991, www.hotelzaza.com, rooms start at $259), located just east of the University neighborhood on the edge of the Museum District. Billed as an "urban resort with a mix of glamour and warmth, high style, and creature comforts," the

ZaZa is in a league of its own. Amenities include a poolside retreat and outdoor bar with private cabanas, the luxurious ZaSpa and fitness center, nightly turndown service, cordless phones, free Wi-Fi service, ZaZa guest robes, fancy linens, refrigerators, and an in-room "grab and go gourmet refreshment bar."

UPTOWN
$50-150

Some of the best bargains in the city are in the busy Uptown area west of downtown near the Galleria. Among them are **Drury Inn and Suites** (1615 W. Loop S., 713/963-0700, www.druryhotels.com, $99 d), offering a free hot breakfast, evening social hour, a fitness center, indoor/outdoor pool, and whirlpool. Guest rooms feature free Internet access, microwaves, and refrigerators.

Similarly priced and amenity packed is the adjacent **La Quinta Inn and Suites** (1625 W. Loop S., 713/355-3440, www.lq.com, $89 d), with a heated pool and spa, a fitness center, free deluxe continental breakfast buffet, and rooms with free Internet access.

For a modest increase in price, consider the impressive **Hilton Post Oak** (2001 Post Oak Blvd., 713/961-9300, www.hilton.com, $129 d). Each room includes a balcony offering impressive skyline views, as well as Wi-Fi access, minibars, and refrigerators. The hotel also offers complimentary shuttle service to destinations within a three-mile radius.

Another option favored by many Galleria shoppers is the **JW Marriott on Westheimer** (5150 Westheimer Rd., 713/961-1500, www.marriott.com, $139 d), a stately 23-floor hotel featuring wireless Internet access, a fitness center, indoor and outdoor pools, and a whirlpool.

$150-200

Enjoy a unique and memorable experience at **C Hotel Derek** (2525 W. Loop S., 866/292-4100, www.hotelderek.com, $189 d). This independent option is contemporary and sophisticated, with consistently reliable service. Hotel Derek's highlights include an outstanding pool with gushing waterfall, day-spa treatments, and the Derek Mobile, a black stretch SUV providing free transportation to the Galleria's nearby shopping locales (or business meetings). Rooms feature free Wi-Fi access, minibars, CD players with extensive libraries, bathrobes, and beds with goose-down duvets. The hotel's restaurant, Bistro Moderne, is a destination itself, with remarkable French cuisine.

Galleria visitors also enjoy setting up shop at **Embassy Suites** (2911 Sage Rd., 713/626-5444, www.embassysuites.com, $169 d). Guests are immediately greeted by an almost overwhelming lobby featuring a lofty atrium with a jungle-themed waterway that's home to swans. Hotel amenities include an indoor pool and whirlpool, a large fitness center, a free cooked-to-order breakfast, and an evening social reception. Rooms offer a private bedroom and separate living area with a sofa bed, minibar, refrigerator, microwave, and Internet access.

The Galleria draws some big spenders, and the surrounding area accommodates them with several pricey lodging options. Among them are **Doubletree Guest Suites** (5353 Westheimer Rd., 713/961-9000, www.doubletree.com, $159 d). In addition to its ideal location, the hotel offers spacious one- and two-bedroom suites with wireless Internet access, a fancy fitness center, and a large outdoor pool area with sundeck and whirlpool.

Over $200

If shopping is a priority, consider staying in a hotel connected to the country's fourth-largest mall. The **Westin Galleria Houston** (5060 W. Alabama St., 713/960-8100, www.starwoodhotels.com, $200 d) is in a prime location, allowing guests to walk straight from the hotel to the massive attached shopping center. After a full day of browsing stores (or even leaving the hotel to explore nearby restaurants, taverns, and cultural attractions), you can unwind in a spacious room with Internet access (for a fee) and high-quality furnishings.

Another worthy option is **Staybridge Suites Houston Galleria Area** (5160 Hidalgo St., 800/465-4329, www.ichotelsgroup.com, $209 d), featuring full kitchens, separate sitting and work areas, free Internet access and printing, a fitness center, and an outdoor pool.

CAMPING

Houston's best camping is about 30 miles southwest of the city at **Brazos Bend State Park** (21901 FM 762, 979/553-5102, www.tpwd.state.tx.us, $7 daily per person 13 and older). Covering roughly 5,000 acres, this popular state park offers hiking, biking, equestrian trails, and fishing on six easily accessible lakes. However, visitors are cautioned about alligators (seriously), which are numerous in some areas of the park. Facilities include restrooms with showers, campsites with water and electricity, screened shelters, primitive equestrian campsites, and a dining hall. Many visitors make Brazos Bend a weekend destination because of its abundant activities, including free interpretive programs and hikes. A nature center with informative displays contains a "hands-on" alligator discovery area, a model of the park, a freshwater aquarium, live native snake species, and the **George Observatory** (3pm-10pm Sat.).

Closer to town is the unremarkable yet convenient **Alexander Deussen County Park** (12303 Sonnier St., 713/440-1587, call for reservation information). Named after a respected Houston geologist, Deussen Park offers basic camping services, including site pads, fire pits, picnic areas, and restrooms. Pets are allowed, but they must be kept on a leash.

Food

Houston has more than 8,000 restaurants (that's not a misprint). People here love eating out, and the array of options is overwhelming, from lowly fast food to lofty haute cuisine. Visitors and residents benefit from the city's enormous international population, offering authentic fare from all corners of the globe, including specific regional styles not found in most midsize cities. This being Texas, the options also include a fair number of home-grown varieties, including some of the state's finest barbecue, Tex-Mex, and good ol' fashioned down-home Southern cookin'.

DOWNTOWN
Contemporary and Fusion
Houston's culinary crowd is completely in love with **C Oxheart** (1302 Nance St., 832/830-8592, www.oxhearthouston.com, 5:30pm-10pm Sun.-Mon., Thurs., 5:30pm-10:30pm Fri.-Sat., $14-42, reservations recommended). More than just a trendy destination for "lo-covores" (those who eat food grown locally), Oxheart is known for its bold flavor combinations, which work surprisingly well or are at least impressive in their attempts. For example, one of the restaurant's most popular dishes is a smoked tuna accompanied by chickpeas, seaweed, and caramelized tomatoes. Others are subtler, like a leafy salad containing bonus flavors of turnip, pecans, and beef fat. Consider sharing the dessert treat of tomato tart on a shortbread crust.

Another favorite restaurant for those interested in locally sourced food is **Sparrow Bar and Cookshop** (3701 Travis St., 713/524-6922, www.sparrowhouston. com, 10am-midnight Tues.-Sat., $12-39). Considered a forerunner of the now popular farm-to-table trend, the Sparrow is an appropriately contemporary spot with immensely flavorful menu items. Can't-miss options include the mushroom dumplings topped with a honey-based blue cheese sauce, the beet salad accompanied by pickled feta and pine nuts, and

a postmodern macaroni and cheese, containing pork belly, peas, and topped with an egg yolk.

More traditional in nature, yet still somewhat adventurous with its flavor combinations, is **17** (1117 Prairie St., 832/200-8888, www.17food.com, 6:30am-2pm Mon.-Sat., 5:30pm-10pm Mon.-Sun., 7am-11am Sun., $11-33). Don't let the colorful "light wall" in the back room distract you from the tasty food on the table, including a delectably creamy beet soup (served cold), a refreshing option on a characteristically humid evening. For meat lovers, the deconstructed beef Wellington is surprisingly good (more meaty goodness than fluffy pastry).

Even more traditional in atmosphere and menu options is **Bistro Lancaster** (701 Texas St., 713/228-9502, www.thelancaster.com, 6:30am-10pm Mon.-Fri., 7am-11pm Sat.-Sun., $14-38). Located inside the historic Hotel Lancaster, the Bistro transports diners to a more simple and elegant time with knowledgeable waitstaff, exquisitely presented food, and quality ingredients. The crab cakes are wonderful, as are the tamale-style shrimp and ribeye steak. Be sure to split a slice of the dense and flavorful cheesecake.

Steak Houses
A steak house doesn't have to be stodgy. The scene is downright comfortable at **C III Forks** (1201 San Jacinto St., 713/658-9457, www.iiiforks.com, 11am-10pm Mon.-Thurs., 11am-11pm Fri., 4pm-11pm Sat., $13-42). Sumptuous steaks take center stage here, with featured cuts including the double-cut strip, filet mignon, and porterhouse. The meat is perfectly prepared and the sides (they cost extra but are well worth it) are ideal accompaniments, including the popular spinach and six-cheese potatoes. If possible, try to save some room for the Texas pecan cake.

For a well-heeled, but not traditionally bedecked, downtown steak house, head to **Vic & Anthony's** (1510 Texas St., 713/228-1111,

© ANDY RHODES

Oxheart

www.vicandanthonys.com, 4pm-10pm Sun.-Thurs., 11am-11pm Fri., 4pm-11pm Sat., $15-40). Chic, minimalist, and tightly packed, Vic & Anthony's wisely sticks with the basics—a simple menu offers high-quality cuts of meat and a few seafood and chicken options. The salads and appetizers here are outstanding (the pear salad and oysters, in particular), and the wine selection is impressive, if a bit pricey. The steaks are enormous, and the bone-in ribeye is considered among the best in town.

Cajun

Houston is one of the few places in the country that serves authentic Cajun cuisine. The Bayou City has direct access to the seafood, sauces, spices, and swamps—the style's integral ingredients. It doesn't get much better than the legendary New Orleans family establishment **◖Brennan's** (3300 Smith St., 713/522-9711, www.brennanshouston.com, 11am-2pm, 5:45pm-10pm Mon.-Sat., 10am-2pm, 5:45pm-10pm Sun., $10-36). Located in a historic brick mansion, Brennan's offers classic Louisiana

flavors such as étouffée, lump crab cakes, and pecan-crusted amberjack. The breakfasts at Brennan's are legendary, and the eggs and delectable sauces taste even better paired with live jazz music during the weekend New Orleans Jazz Brunch.

Less formal is the popular downtown lunch chain **Treebeard's** (several locations, including 315 Travis St., 713/228-2622, www.treebeards.com, 11am-2pm weekdays, $6-13). All the Creole classics are here—shrimp étouffée, jambalaya, gumbo, and a hearty dose of red beans and rice. Be sure to order a side of jalapeño corn bread, and save room for the bread pudding with whiskey sauce. The only drawback: Treebeard's isn't open on weekends or for dinner.

Breakfast

The first thing you'll hear about when anyone mentions **◖The Breakfast Klub** (3711 Travis St., 713/528-8561, www.thebreakfastklub.com, 7am-2pm Mon.-Fri., 8am-3pm Sat., 9am-2pm Sun., $9-20) is the long line. The next thing you'll hear about is their famous chicken and waffles. And then you'll hear that it's absolutely worth waiting up to an hour to experience this dish (and most others) on the menu. As for the line, it moves fairly quickly and is far shorter the earlier you arrive (plan for sometime before 9 a.m.). If you're stuck waiting, however, you'll be struck by the tremendous diversity of your fellow line mates, offering a refreshing perspective of this international city with a love for good food. Speaking of which, the chicken and waffles are absolutely worth ordering, with both items perfectly prepared (tender and flavorful centers surrounded by lightly-crisped goodness). The "biskuits" and gravy are also flaky and flavorful and serve as a delicious reward for a long wait in line.

Not nearly as famous but still known for its quality breakfast fare is **Corner Bakery Cafe** (1000 Main St., 713/651-0854, 6:30am-4pm Mon.-Fri., $4-10). Considered a superior alternative to Panera Bread Co., the Corner Bakery, a Southern U.S. chain, is a perfect place to grab a pastry and coffee. Popular items include the lemon pound cake, and cinnamon pecan rolls. There's heartier fare, too, like the steel-cut oatmeal and breakfast panini.

MONTROSE-KIRBY
Contemporary and Fusion

A small stretch of Westheimer Road near the intersection of Montrose Boulevard has become the epicenter of Houston's foodie scene, and for good reason. In addition to Japanese restaurant Uchi, several Texas-minded restaurants are drawing national attention for their bold flavors and chefs. Chief among them is **C Underbelly** (1100 Westheimer Rd., 713/528-9800, www.underbellyhouston.com, 11am-3pm, 5pm-10pm Mon.-Fri., 5pm-11pm Sat., $13-43, reservations strongly recommended). Helmed by a visionary chef who passionately champions regional produce and seafood, Underbelly is earning its accolades by offering consistently quality dishes, like the extremely popular Korean braised goat with dumplings, a wonderfully savory meal brimming with rich flavors that you'd never associate with goat meat. Other beguiling options include tilefish with okra and the bizarre-sounding yet fabulous-tasting vinegar pie with salt brittle. Located in the same building and operated by the same culinary team is the bar-oriented **Hay Merchant** (713/528-9805, www.haymerchant.com, 3pm-2am Mon.-Fri., 11am-2am Sat.-Sun., $6-19). Specializing in craft brews, Hay Merchant also offers an impressive (yet limited) menu that elevates pub grub to an art form. Locals are abuzz with the pig ears, a crispy pork treat that tastes wonderful if you don't think too much about the source. More traditional offerings include a fantastic soft pretzel and seasoned chicken wings.

Just down the road is another of Houston's favorite dining destinations, **Mark's American Cuisine** (1658 Westheimer Rd., 713/523-3800, www.marks1658.com, 11am-2pm, 5:30pm-11pm Mon.-Fri., 5pm-midnight Sat., 5pm-10pm Sun., $15-48, reservations strongly recommended). As its name implies, the restaurant focuses on American food. In this case, it's bold, flavorful, and prepared with top-notch

ingredients. The setting is equally inspiring, inside a remodeled church with a lofty ceiling and soft lighting. Popular menu items include the bourbon short ribs, pork tenderloin (topped with an amazing ginger-maple sugar rub), and prime rib.

Closer to the Rice University campus is **Local Foods** (2424 Dunstan Rd., 713/521-7800, www.houstonlocalfoods.com, 10am-8pm daily, $11-30). Contemporary, classy, and casual, Local Foods is an ideal spot to enjoy a long lunch in a welcoming environment. The restaurant is perhaps best known for its scrumptious Crunchy Chicken sandwich, a fresh and flavorful dish with a variety of complimentary tastes and textures (the pretzel bun is worth ordering on its own). Pair it with the clean-tasting lemongrass soup and the flavorful kale.

Houstonians go berserk over **Backstreet Café** (1103 S. Shepherd Dr., 713/521-2239, www.backstreetcafe.net, 11am-10pm Mon.-Thurs., 11am-11pm Fri.-Sat., 10am-9pm Sun., $10-26). This wildly popular two-story New American venue is revered for its crafty chef (Hugo Ortega of Hugo's), who specializes in quality comfort food. Backstreet is particularly known for its "crusted" dishes, including mustard-crusted salmon and sesame-crusted shrimp. The most popular entrée is the meat loaf tower, an aptly named stack of seasoned meat, garlic mashed potatoes, sautéed spinach, and mushroom gravy. Backstreet breakfasts are also legendary, as is the Sunday jazz brunch (11am-3pm).

Also popular with the locals is **C Benjy's** (2424 Dunstan Rd., 713/522-7602, www.benjys.com, 11am-9pm Mon.-Sun., 11am-10pm Tues.-Thurs., 11am-11pm Fri.-Sat., $11-28), a contemporary venue with outstanding food and service. Things change often here, from the artwork to the menu, keeping things fresh for the regulars and kitchen staff. Seafood is the specialty (smoked salmon, seasoned shrimp), but Benjy's also serves comfort food with modern flair, including distinctive sandwiches and entrées such as the pecan- and pistachio-crusted chicken with mixed potato gratin. Locals flock

© ANDY RHODES

El Real Tex-Mex Cafe

and the signature tender and juicy brisket—all topped with a succulent and smoky sauce. The side items are better than average, including a sweet coleslaw and jalapeño corn bread with a kick.

Mexican and Tex-Mex

This part of town covers a lot of Mex-inspired ground, from Mexico City street food to retro Tex-Mex chic to traditional Latin American specialties. Garnering the most attention for its bold flavors (and building) is **El Real Tex-Mex Cafe** (1201 Westheimer Rd., 713/524-1201, 11am-10pm Mon.-Wed., 11am-midnight Thurs.-Sat., 10am-10pm Sun., www.elrealtex-mex.com, $10-27). Housed in a former movie theater (you can't miss the enormous sign and marquee), El Real is a flavorful culinary venture organized by one of Houston's most-respected chefs and a food writer. The result is a stunning collection of traditionally inspired Tex-Mex dishes, derived from extensive research and attention to authentic recipes and ingredients. Start your meal with a tasty prickly pear margarita while enjoying the free chips and salsa. Save enough room for the main event, including popular options like the Tin Can Tacos (perfectly seasoned meats encased in freshly made tortillas) and the Jefferson Plate (gooey cheese enchiladas with a crispy beef taco and bean chalupa). Enhance the wonderful flavors by adding a fried egg on top or an extra dose of hearty chili. An added bonus: throughout your meal, you'll be treated to an old-school Western movie on the big screen above.

Another twist is on the menu at the Latin-American flavored **Churrascos** (2055 Westheimer Rd., 713/527-8300, www.cordua.com, 11am-9:30pm Mon.-Thurs., 11am-10:30pm Fri., 11:30am-10:30pm Sat., 10:30pm-9pm Sun., $9-22). Instead of tortilla chips and enchiladas, think plantain chips and empanadas. Drawing from the rich well of Central American cuisine, Churrascos offers a tantalizing blend of flavors that differ mightily from traditional Texas versions of Mexican food. Empanadas contain unexpected taste bursts from raisins and pecans,

to Benjy's for brunch, and their Bloody Marys are some of the best in the city (they use wasabi instead of regular horseradish).

Another trendy and tasty option is **Mockingbird Bistro** (1985 Welch St., 713/533-0200, www.mockingbirdbistro.com, 11:30am-2pm, 5:30pm-10pm Mon.-Fri., 11am-3pm, 5:30pm-10pm Sun., $11-32), nestled in a dark but comfy historic building in a well-heeled neighborhood. Diners can elect to go small (the "bar bites" offer mini portions of ribs, risotto, and mussels) or large (the entrées are generously sized). Popular menu items include the onion soup, seared tuna steak, pork chop, and steak au poivre. Save room for the chocolate-themed desserts.

Barbecue

Goode Co. Barbeque (5109 Kirby Dr., 713/522-2530, www.goodecompany.com, 11am-10pm daily, $9-19) is a funky spot that's always packed with students, young professionals, and working-class carnivores. Goode's specializes in classic 'cue—sausage, ribs, chicken, and seafood dishes are topped with mushrooms and cotija cheese.

Those interested in authentic Mexican food of a different type should head to **100% Taquito** (3245 Southwest Fwy., 713/665-2900, www.100taquito.com, 11am-10pm Mon.-Thurs., Sun., 11am-11pm Fri.-Sat., $9-20). Don't be afraid to load up on several different varieties of tacos here: The street-food style means they're smaller than most traditional restaurants, and double wrapped in tasty corn tortillas. A great place to start is the *al pastor* seasoned pork topped with onion and cilantro. Another super-savory option is the tinga torta, featuring a juicy shredded brisket on homemade bread. Mix things up by making your order quesadilla style, and be sure to accompany your meal with a sweet *agua fresca* (nonalcoholic fresh-fruit drink).

Not nearly as exciting but representing a significant role in the Mexican-inspired food scene is the West University-area **Fajita Pete's** (4050 Bellaire Blvd., 713/723-8100, www.fajitapetes.com, 11am-2:30pm, 4:30pm-8:30pm Mon.-Fri., noon-8:30pm Sat., noon-8pm Sun., $7-13). This is about as no-frills as it gets: a small, noisy, counter-service spot in a strip mall. But it's not about the ambience at Fajita Pete's. It's about the savory flavor of perfectly seasoned fajita meat (beef and chicken are equally tasty)—and a warm handmade tortilla to place it in. Toss in some grilled peppers and onions with a dollop of guacamole (and a Dos XX beer), and you'll have everything you need for a low-key, flavor-filled, affordable feast.

Many locals believe a visit to this part of town is incomplete without a meal at the tremendous ◖ **Hugo's** (1600 Westheimer Rd, 713/524-7744, www.hugosrestaurant. net, 11am-10pm Mon.-Thurs., 11am-11pm Fri.-Sat., 10:30am-9:30pm Sun., $12-33). This open-air, chic hacienda serves trendy Mexican dishes sizzling with *sabor* (flavor). Start with Hugo's signature velvety margarita, paired with a tantalizing appetizer, such as the squash-blossom quesadillas or one of four varieties of ceviche. Entrées range from savory pork carnitas to tender snapper Veracruzana. Desserts are legendary at Hugo's, especially the options containing freshly roasted and ground cocoa beans (flan, Mexican hot chocolate).

Another trendy spot with fantastic food is **Armando's** (2630 Westheimer Rd., 713/520-1738, www.armandosrestaurant.com, 4pm-10pm Tues.-Wed., 4pm-11pm Thurs.-Sat., 4pm-9pm Sun.-Mon., $10-22). Hipsters and regulars arrive early for the potent happy-hour margaritas and stick around for the classic Tex-Mex dishes with a twist. Enchiladas are filled with crab and vegetables, and beef dishes are prepared with savory sauces. Unfortunately, the beans are bland, but Armando's is known around town for its tasty *sopapillas* (pillowy pastries topped with honey and powdered sugar).

Italian

Montrose-area residents can't seem to get enough risotto; fortunately, they (and visitors to their trendy neighborhood) have several worthy Italian restaurant options to satisfy their craving. Chief among them is **Divino** (1830 W. Alabama St., 713/807-1123, www.divinohouston.com, 5:30pm-10pm Mon.-Thurs., 5:30pm-10:30pm Fri.-Sat., $13-44). The words most often used to describe Divino are "fresh," "authentic," and "homemade." Not a bad trio. Locals love the Parma style risotto, though the Boar Sausage style is also highly commendable. In-house pasta specialties include the Merlin's Papardelle (especially for mushroom lovers). Any of the seasonal seafood dishes are consistently excellent.

Another notable destination is **DaMarco** (1520 Westheimer Rd., 713/807-8857, www.damarcohouston.com, 11:30am-2pm, 5:30pm-10pm Tues.-Fri., 5:30pm-10pm Sat., $14-46). Quaint and fancy at the same time, DaMarco is known for its top-notch ingredients and the inventive flavor combos of renowned chef Marco Wiles. Diners are faced with the daunting task of choosing from Tuscan- to Texas-inspired dishes, including savory Chianti-braised pork ribs, sea bass with grilled grapefruit, flavorful lamb chops, and roasted Texas quail. Other suggested menu items include the lamb chops (with an unbelievably tasty cumin-based yogurt sauce), a truffle risotto/pasta (opt for the pasta since it's served tableside), and the sweet corn lobster ravioli.

Those in search of a romantic evening should head directly to **Sorrento** (415 Westheimer Rd., 713/527-0609, www.sorrentohouston. com, 11am-10pm Mon.-Fri., 4pm-10pm Sat., 11am-3pm, 4pm-9pm Sun., $13-44). Feel free to take your time and savor the experience at Sorrento, starting with a flavorful appetizer of roasted garlic on homemade bread accompanied by a fine wine. For main course options, consider the succulent veal chop or the wild mushroom risotto (the accompanying cheese wheel is magnificent).

Indian

This part of town is brimming with Asian-inspired restaurants, but the Indian cuisine consistently draws diners from across the city for authentic high-quality flavor combinations. At the top of most destination lists is **Indika** (516 Westheimer Rd., 713/524-2170, www.indikausa.com, 11am-2pm, 6:30pm-10pm Tues.-Thurs., 11am-2pm, 6:30pm-10:30pm Fri., 6pm-10:30pm Sat., 10:30am-2:30pm Sun., $11-29). Prepared with the perfect amount of spicy goodness, dishes at Indika are bold and inventive with an extra touch of class not always found at other establishments. For example, Indika's tandoori quail is a step up from the traditional chicken variety, and the curry-based seafood dishes are extraordinary. Top your meal off with an order of the pumpkin flan.

Far more old school (and bordering on downright old) is the neighborhood stalwart **Madras Pavilion** (3910 Kirby Dr., 713/521-2617, 11:30am-3pm, 5:30pm-9:30pm Mon.-Fri., 11:30am-10pm Sat.-Sun., $8-20). Though most people order the buffet (a worthy option for those inclined to sample multiple flavors), it's also worth taking a look at the menu. Stick with traditional favorites here (saag paneer, curried cauliflower, mushroom masala), and you

won't be disappointed. Watch out for the heat since the spicy afterburn can catch up to you.

Japanese

It's not often that Houston imports a trend from its little sibling Austin. It happened in 2012 as a result of the Capital City's culinary scene exploding onto the national level. Much to Austin's chagrin, Houston's version of the unparalleled Japanese restaurant **◖ Uchi** (904 Westheimer Rd., 713/522-4808, www.uchirestaurants.com, 5pm-10pm Mon.-Thurs., Sun., 5pm-11pm Fri.-Sat., $14-43, reservations recommended) is just as good as the original. *Top Chef*-winning Paul Qui creates exquisite flavor combinations that had somehow never been attempted. Before getting too far into your unprecedented culinary journey, order a bottle of wine and the fried Brussels sprouts—the slightly smoky and caramelized flavors are perfect complements to the leafy green vegetables. And speaking of flavor combinations, the sushi rolls are a delight to behold with their seemingly disparate yet instantly perfect intertwined tastes. A few examples include the salmon and Asian pear or yellowfin tuna and oranges. The *hamachi nabe* is another wonderful dish, with tuna topped by a soy-based broth and an egg. Each of the uniquely and unexpectedly crafted dishes are expertly explained by the waitstaff, who politely suggest menu items and recommend dishes based on the level of adventure (and budget) of each individual diner. You'll savor each individual bite and discuss the distinctive flavor combinations for hours (and weeks).

Known for its stylish social scene as much as its hip sushi rolls, sleek **Ra Sushi** (3908 Westheimer Rd., 713/621-5800, www.rasushi.com, 11am-midnight daily, $5-17) draws a young crowd of busy singles. Popular items include the spicy lobster roll, scallop dynamite, and Viva Las Vegas roll with light tempura, crab, tuna, and lotus root. Consider ordering one of the seaweed salads or a more substantial item from the Pacific Rim-themed full menu. It's a great option for lunch; stick around for the happy hour scene at Ra's Flying Fish Lounge.

THE HEIGHTS
Barbecue

For possibly Houston's best barbecue—go directly to **⊂ Gatlin's Barbecue** (1221 W. 19th St., 713/869-4227, www.gatlinsbbq.com, 11am-7pm Tues.-Sat., $11-29). Located in an extremely small building on a strangely desolate street, Gatlin's has been receiving rave reviews from Houston's culinary professionals and fans of perfectly smoked meat. Even if you're not a barbecue sandwich orderer, it's worth sampling a Gatlin sandwich just to taste the amazing bun, a buttery toasted delight. The meat is the main draw, though, so be sure to experience the tender and succulent brisket or savory smoked sausage.

Carnivores also line up at **Pizzitola's Bar-B-Cue** (1703 Shepherd Dr., 713/227-2283, 11am-8pm Mon.-Sat., $9-20), a legendary barbecue joint just south of the Heights. This old-fashioned locale has been around since the 1930s, when it was known as Shepherd Drive Barbecue, and the decades of hickory-smoked goodness have lingered ever since. Tender ribs and brisket are the big draw here, and the spicy sauce subtly enhances both. Another bonus: Warm towels are available for sauce removal, post-feast. Be sure to save room (or place a takeout order) for the amazing desserts, particularly the coconut pineapple cake and banana pudding.

Burgers

Looking for meat? This is Texas, after all. So a creative menu devoted to crafty carnivores in one of the Lone Star State's trendiest neighborhoods is certainly appropriate. **⊂ Sammy's Wild Game Grill** (3715 Washington Ave., 713/868-1345, www.sammyswildgamegrill. com, 11am-10pm Mon.-Thurs., Sun., 11am-11pm Fri.-Sat., $13-39) may look like a tame burger restaurant from the outside, but the selection of exotic meats inside is downright crazy. Consider this wild pairing: a kangaroo burger with a side of python chili fries. Feeling less adventurous? There are elk tacos and pheasant hot dogs. Still too exotic? There's always an angus burger with sweet potato fries.

Incidentally, all the wild game here is expertly prepared, with complimentary seasonings that enhance the unique flavors found in these distinctive menu items.

Some of the best burgers in Houston are being served out of a school bus. Check online to see where you can find **Bernie's Burger Bus** (281/386-2447, www.berniesburgerbus. com, $8-14); then make a beeline to wherever they are to sample the hearty, beefy creations. These hand-formed patties of three natural beef cuts take time, so expect a 15-minute wait. As soon as you sink your teeth into the flavorful burger, you'll find it's worth every minute. For an extra kick, order a Cheerleader Burger with jalapeño ranch.

Japanese

One of the city's most consistent high-quality sushi spots is **⊂ The Blue Fish** (5820 Washington Ave., 713/862-3474, www.thebluefishsushi.com, 11am-2pm, 5pm-10:30pm Mon.-Fri., 1pm-10:30pm Sat.-Sun., $8-14), just south of the Heights. Known for its generous portions of seafood, the Blue Fish offers top-notch ingredients with knowledgeable staff. Popular sushi items include the yellowtail rolls (the samurai has a sweet and spicy kick, and the piñata includes crab and shrimp) as well as the eel and avocado roll and spicy salmon tartare.

A block away is the equally commendable **Soma** (4820 Washington Ave., 713/861-2726, www.somasushi.com, 10:30am-11pm Mon.-Wed., Fri., 11:30am-midnight Thurs., noon-11pm Sat.-Sun., $7-12). Though it's known for its tasty traditional sushi rolls and near-perfect tempura, Soma is famous in Houston's food circles for the Crazy Irishman. One of the most bizarre and spicy sushi rolls you'll ever experience, the Irishman includes tuna, salmon, and avocado wrapped in a soy bean paper and flash fried. Then it's topped with a crazy-hot mayo sauce and some onion and roe for good measure. Go Irish!

Looking for a hearty dose of rock with your rolls? Head to **Sushi Tora** (920 Studemont St., 713/864-8672, 6pm-10pm Mon.-Sun., 11:30am-10pm Tues.-Thurs.,

11:30am-10:30pm Fri.-Sat., $7-13). The blaring music can be almost too distracting, but it sets the tone for the brash and fun restaurant. Popular menu items include the Dylan roll (tuna topped with roasted garlic and avocado) and the Gary roll (crab on a spicy tuna).

Desserts

In hot and humid Houston, a refreshingly frozen dessert is sometimes a necessity. For a simple pleasure any time of day, drop by 🄲**Mam's House of Snoballs** (20th St. at Rutland St., 713/868-4545, www.mamshouseofice.com, 2pm-6:30pm Tues.-Fri., 1pm-6:30pm Sat.-Sun., $2-5). Though it may be challenging to find at first (the trailer is usually parked across from a bank in an empty dirt lot), Mam's is always rewarding with its perfectly shaved soft ice and extensive flavor options. Favorites include the tiger's blood (with a fruity condensed milk flavoring), strawberry lemonade, and gummy bear for the kiddos.

If you're looking for a snack to accompany your sweet tooth, head to **Happy Fatz** (3510 White Oak Dr., 713/426-3554, www.happy-fatz.com, 7am-10pm Wed.-Sat., $4-8). Located in a quaint residential neighborhood, Happy Fatz is best known for its hot dogs but also offers a tantalizing selection of baked goodies. Most folks order the sumptuous cake bites, but consider taking a chance on the carrot cake or Oreo cheesecake.

UPTOWN
Contemporary and Fusion

Locals can't get enough of the classy **RDG Bar Annie** (1728 Post Oak Blvd., 713/840-1111, www.rdgbarannie.com, 11:30am-4pm Mon.-Fri., 6pm-10pm Mon.-Thurs., 6pm-10:30pm Fri.-Sat., 11am-2:30pm, 5pm-9pm Sun., $13-41). Elegance exudes from the decor and the dishes, starting with tantalizing appetizers such as goat cheese crepes and continuing with entrées like the cinnamon-roasted pheasant and cocoa-roasted chicken. Haute Texas cuisine is well represented in the cilantro-enhanced mussel soup and barbecued sweet potatoes. Take note: Many locals still refer to this locale as Café Annie, its previous name. Reservations are highly recommended.

Another high-quality option with intriguing taste twists is **Masraffs** (1753 Post Oak Blvd., 713/355-1975, www.masraffs.com, 10:30am-10pm Mon.-Thurs., 10:30am-11pm Fri., 5:30pm-11pm Sat., $13-32). This is the kind of place where an appetizer is almost a necessity, mainly because they're so good you'll consider returning just to make a meal of them. A perfect example is the crab cakes, expertly prepared with just the right subtleties: crust, seasoning, and sauce. Masraffs is known for its seafood, so err on surf options if you're having trouble deciding on a menu item. The fillet of sole is exquisite, as are the halibut and sea bass. For meat lovers, the options are just as notable, including the bison steak and lamb chops.

Steak Houses

Although Uptown is lacking the historic charm of Downtown, it can claim a few of the city's most popular and esteemed steakhouses. The favorite among locals is **Pappas Brothers Steakhouse** (5839 Westheimer Rd., 713/780-7352, www.pappasbros.com, 4pm-10pm Mon.-Thurs., 4pm-11pm Fri.-Sat., $13-45). This is where steak lovers gather to get their carnivorous fix: perfectly marbled cuts of top-notch beef. The filets are Pappas Brothers' specialty, and their somewhat-lofty prices (upper $40s) become a wise investment once you're savoring each tender bite. The sides are also top notch; suggested options include potatoes au gratin and asparagus.

Just down the street is another tremendous steakhouse, albeit with an international flair. **Chama Gaucha** (5865 Westheimer Rd., 713/244-9500, www.chamagaucha.com, 11:30am-2:30pm, 5pm-10pm Mon.-Thurs., 11:30am-2:30pm, 5pm-10:30pm Fri., 4:30pm-10:30pm Sat., 4pm-9pm Sun., $12-42) is a Brazilian-style establishment, meaning the staff serves a plethora of meat options with sharp and shiny knives. The filet mignon and sirloin are excellent, but there are other styles to consider, such as the bacon-wrapped variety and a cut of lamb. A word of caution: Although the introductory salad bar may tempt you with its leafy goodness, colorful vegetables, and bread medallions, try not to overdo it at the expense of the magnificent meat.

Mexican and Tex-Mex

Those looking for a traditional Mexican restaurant should head directly to **Molina's** (7901 Westheimer Rd., 713/782-0861, www.molinasrestaurants.com, 11am-9pm Mon., 11am-10pm Tues.-Wed., Sun., 11am-11pm Thurs., Sat., 11am-midnight Fri., $8-15) on the western edge of Uptown. A Houston institution for nearly seven decades, Molina's is the ultimate destination for old-school Tex-Mex. The signature Mexico City Dinner captures it all: chili con queso, tamale, tostada, taco, and enchilada with requisite rice and beans.

Similar in approach and quality is **El Patio Mexican Restaurant** (6444 Westheimer Rd., 713/780-0410, www.elpatio.com, 11am-10pm Sun.-Weds., 11am-11pm Thurs., 11am-midnight Fri.-Sat., $8-18). El Patio is also known for its rollicking bar Club No Minors, named for the legal notice posted on the door. The other main draw here is the fajita plate, a steaming dish of savory beef and chicken accompanied by cheddar cheese and piquant pico de gallo. The chicken enchiladas and chiles rellenos are also popular menu items.

Middle Eastern

One of the benefits of being in a cosmopolitan environment is the abundance of international cuisine in various formats. Houston's Uptown area contains several noteworthy informal lunch venues, and the best among them serve savory Lebanese food. One of the favorites is **Mary'z Lebanese Cuisine** (5825 Richmond Ave., 832/251-1955, www.maryzcuisine.com, 11am-10:30pm Mon.-Thurs., Sun., 11am-11pm Fri.-Sat., $6-15). It's a tiny place, but the tastes are huge, especially in fresh-made favorites like kabobs, falafel, shawarma, and baba ghanoush. Complement your meal with a Lebanese beer like Almazo. At night, Mary'z becomes a hot spot for young adults who toke on hookahs and exchange phone numbers.

A larger and more traditional option is **Café Lili Lebanese Grill** (5757 Westheimer Rd., 713/952-6969, www.cafelili.com, 11am-9pm Mon.-Thurs., 11am-10pm Fri.-Sat., 11am-4:30pm Sun., $7-16). This mom-and-pop establishment is a no-frills operation that focuses on the most important things: exemplary food and service. Start off with spinach pie, hummus, or tabouleh, and proceed to the kafta kabobs or lamb dishes. Top it all off with the signature strong coffee.

Deli

Enormous sandwich spot **Kenny & Ziggy's** (2327 Post Oak Blvd., 713/871-8883, www.kennyandziggys.com, 7am-9pm Mon.-Fri., 8am-9pm Sat.-Sun., $13-32) is a true deli, unfortunately a rarity in Texas. This is the place Northerners go to get a slice of homestyle goodness. Not surprisingly, the corned beef and pastrami are favorites, especially piled high on Reubens and rye sandwiches. The portions are enormous, so consider splitting a plate or plan to arrive extremely hungry. It's worth saving some precious space for the potato salad and pickles.

GREATER HOUSTON
Cajun

With its regional claim to Cajun culture, it's somewhat surprising that Houston doesn't have more top-notch restaurant options. Regardless, a favorite among locals is **Beaucoup Bar & Grill** (3102 Old Spanish Trl., 713/747-5100, www.beaucoupbarandgrill.com, 11am-10pm Mon.-Thurs., 11am-midnight Fri.-Sat., noon-7pm Sun., $9-27). Located in an odd zone south of Midtown between the medical facilities and South Freeway, Beaucoup is worth finding for the crawfish bread alone. Locals have made an entire meal out of this item, with its sumptuous crawfish flavor accompanied by a buttery, crunchy French bread. Crawfish also figures prominently in the hearty gumbo, and the curry shrimp po'boy is an absolute highlight. Many Houstonians will tell you Beaucoup serves the best seasoned chicken wings in town—or anywhere else.

Burgers

Burger fans take note: **Becks Prime** (www. becksprime.com, 11am-10pm Mon.-Fri., 11am-11pm Sat.-Sun., $7-18) is just about as good as it gets. Upscale burgers with top-quality meat and sensational seasonings are typically found only in fancier restaurants with tablecloths and wine menus. Not here. The fast-food vibe tricks your senses with lowered expectations, but the massive burger you hold in your hands has all the makings of a classic: thick, juicy high-quality ground beef and fresh toppings on a soft, sweet bun. You'll never want to bite into a chain-store burger again. Becks also serves equally tantalizing steaks (and milkshakes). Becks operates several locations throughout greater Houston, but the Galleria-area location (2615 Augusta Dr., 713/266-9901) has especially pleasant scenery, thanks to several colossal outstretched oak trees on the grounds.

Mexican and Tex-Mex

Just outside the Loop in the Bellaire neighborhood is the fantastic **Pico's** (5941 Bellaire Blvd., 713/662-8383, www.picos.net, 9am-10pm Mon.-Thurs., Sun., 9am-11pm Fri.-Sat., $9-23). Billing itself as "Mex-Mex," Pico's offers interior Mexican food with some flair. Specialties include the bacon-wrapped shrimp with poblano pepper stuffing, *pollo pibil* (marinated chicken wrapped in banana leaves), and smooth yet spicy mole sauce. Things get a bit festive here, especially on weekends, when diners enjoy margaritas and mariachis on the *palapa*-covered patio.

For a more traditional Tex-Mex experience, head to the Gulfgate area southeast of the city for **Doneraki Restaurant** (300 Gulfgate Mall, 713/645-6400, www.doneraki.com, hours vary, $9-20). This is a classic joint, complete with a massive Diego Rivera mural. The taste is huge here, too, especially in the perfectly seasoned meat dishes. Try the beef fajitas and chicken enchiladas, and appreciate the fact that the chips, salsa, and bowl-scraping chili con queso are free at lunch.

For some of the best Mexican home-style cooking in Houston, visit **Otilia's Mexican Restaurant** (7710 Long Point Rd., 713/681-7203, www.otiliasmexican.com, 11am-9pm Mon.-Thurs., noon-10pm Fri.-Sat., 11am-10pm Sun., $8-19) located in Spring Branch, northwest of the Loop. What Otilia's lacks in atmosphere (it's housed in a former fast-food drive-in) it makes up for in spectacular-tasting food. Like most interior-leaning locales, the velvety mole sauce is outstanding here, but the á la carte items make a visit to Otilia's imminently worthwhile. Load up on gorditas, chiles rellenos, *cochinita pibil*, and the *tres leches* cake for an unforgettable experience in a forgettable building.

If you're interested in sampling Houston's burgeoning food truck scene, head directly to the University of Houston area (specifically in a Kroger parking lot) to feast at **Taco Keto** (1401 Cullen Blvd., 713/224-1898, hours vary, $4-10). Not surprisingly, tacos are the top draw here, and you can't go wrong with most of the options. Try the trio sampler, and be sure to include fajita beef as one of your choices. The slightly spicy sauce provides a nice kick, and the grilled veggies (onions, potatoes, jalapeños) are a perfect accompaniment. Be sure to grab an extra handful of napkins because the greasy goodness will be running down your chin and arms.

Seafood

Those craving fresh seafood won't regret the 30-mile drive to **TopWater Grill** (815 Ave. O in the small town of San Leon, 281/339-1232, www.topwatergrill.com, 11am-11pm daily, $8-24). Nestled in an unassuming building on the bay, Top Water is high on the list of angler favorites, thanks to the quality fresh catches and understated but effective seasoning and preparation. Start with the plump and flavorful peel-and-eat shrimp (or fried, or grilled), and complete your feast with the swordfish or redfish. Fill up on the fresh seafood; don't waste valuable stomach space with the iceberg-lettuce salad or fried side items (hush puppies and fries).

Chinese

Houston has a sizable Chinese population, and the plethora of restaurants provide an impressive representation of the various styles of that national cuisine. Topping most foodies' lists is **Fung's Kitchen** (7320 Southwest Fwy., 713/779-2288, www.fungskitchen.com, 11am-10pm Mon.-Thurs., Sun., 11am-11pm Fri.-Sat., $10-36), located near Sharpstown, southwest of the city. This is fancy stuff, so don't be surprised by the somewhat lofty yet completely worthwhile prices. Many of the seafood items are still swimming in tanks when you order them, including the soon-to-be lightly seasoned and heavily flavorful lobster, crab, and cod. With more than 400 items to choose from, the menu is somewhat overwhelming but ultimately tantalizing in its impressive array of items. Dim sum fans will be pleasantly surprised and rewarded with the vast number of quality options.

Less distinguished but more appealing to the masses is **Yao Restaurant & Bar** (9755 Westheimer Rd., 832/251-2588, www.yaorestaurant.com, 11am-10pm Mon.-Thurs., 11am-11pm Fri., noon-11pm Sat., noon-10pm Sun., $10-29), located in the Westchase neighborhood, west of town. Run by the parents of former Houston Rockets basketball star Yao Ming, this upscale establishment focuses on the classics—Peking duck, Szechuan prawn, and mu shu pork—in a modern Asian setting with several large-screen televisions broadcasting sporting events. The food isn't very adventurous, but it's high-quality stuff. In fact, it may be one of the best meals you'll experience while watching a game on TV.

Located east of downtown in an area some locals refer to as EaDo, **Kim Son** (2001 Jefferson St., 281/222-2461, www.kimson.com, 10am-8pm daily, $10-30) is an interesting place to go for dim sum (the traditional Chinese custom of ordering individual items from roving carts). Though it's technically a Vietnamese restaurant, the dim sum custom, like many families in Houston, crosses cultures. If you've never experienced this unique approach to enjoying a meal, this is the place to do it: Pan-fried and steamed seafood dumplings, sticky rice, seaweed-wrapped shrimp, and mushroom-capped meatballs are just a few of the dozens of enticing items awaiting your selection at Kim Son.

Indian

For a cheap and flavorful veggie meal, drop by the magnificent **Shri Balaji Bhavan** (5655 Hillcroft Dr., 713/783-1126, 11am-9:30pm Mon., Wed.-Sun., $4-12), located near Gulfton, west of the city. This is hot stuff, but for the price—most entrées average around $5—you can't go wrong. The cuisine is primarily South Indian, including spicy well-balanced dishes such as *rasam* soup, *chole,* and dal.

Vegetarian

Houston is generally more about beef than veggies, but vegetarians have a few safe havens. The most acclaimed spot, **Baba Yega** (2607 Grant St., 713/522-0042, www.babayega.com, 11am-9pm Mon.-Thurs., 11am-10pm Fri., 10am-10pm Sat., 9:30am-9pm Sun., $8-21) is between Midtown and Montrose. While it's not exclusively vegetarian, the meat-free dishes are some of the city's finest. The salads, pasta, and sandwiches here are legendary, including the tasty veggie club (turkey, fake bacon, and provolone) and the Tuesday Italian Special (pasta and wine combo). The owner's adjacent herb shop is the source for many of Baba Yega's fresh and flavorful seasonings.

Also not technically a full vegetarian restaurant, the popular **Hobbit Cafe** (2243 Richmond Ave., 713/526-5460, www.myhobbitcafe.com, 11am-9:30pm Mon.-Thurs., 11am-10:30pm Fri., 10:30am-10:30pm Sat., 10:30am-9pm Sun., $7-17), located near the Greenway and Upper Kirby neighborhoods, serves earthy fare in a forest-like setting surrounded by a white picket fence. Soups and salads are the specialty here, including the ambrosial fruit salad and tropical chicken salad, and the veggie burgers are as charming as the mystical decor. The Hobbit Cafe also has a well-deserved reputation for serving delicious desserts, and the moist carrot cake and tangy Key lime pie live up to that.

Information and Services

VISITOR INFORMATION AND TOURS

Because Houston isn't a big-time vacation destination, it doesn't have an abundance of visitors centers offering maps and brochures. In fact, it only has one. Fortunately, the **Greater Houston Convention and Visitors Bureau** (901 Bagby St., Ste. 100, 713/437-5200, www.visithoustontexas.com, 9am-4pm daily) can handle just about everything. The CVB's impressive offices at City Hall (Bagby Street location) are chock full of literature and knowledgeable staff members. Similar services are available southwest of town at the Bay Area Houston Visitors Center (913 North Meyer Ave. in Seabrook, 281/474-9700) and a Houston CVB kiosk at Katy Mills Mall (on I-10 about 15 miles west of town).

Tours of Houston and the surrounding area are also available. Contact **HoustonTours.net** (888/838-5894, www.houstontours.net) to choose from activity types or location. This operator also offers a selection of "most popular tours," including motorcycle rentals and helicopter rides in the area. Another company, **Houston Tours, Inc.** (8915 Bellaire Blvd., 713/988-5900, www.houstontours.com, 8am-8pm daily) features traditional bus tours of downtown, outlying neighborhoods, and treks to Galveston.

For something more educational (and quirky), consider taking part in one of the Orange Show Foundation's **Eyeopener Tours** (713/926-6368, www.orangeshow.org/eyeopener-tours, typically the second weekend of the month). Inspired by "places that made you stop, look and look again," Eyeopener Tours are dedicated to itineraries involving compelling food, stories, and sightings in the Houston area and beyond. Tours typically involve a fancy bus with snacks and drinks (averaging around $65 for the entire package) en route to the interesting objet d'folk art, architectural wonders (or disasters), and enigmatic ethnic enclaves of the city.

For those venturing beyond Bayou City, the **Texas Forest Trail Region** (headquarters 202 E. Pilar St. #214, Nacogdoches, 936/560-3699, www.texasforesttrail.com) is an ideal place to prepare for a Piney Woods adventure. Check out the website or drop by the main office to get help with determining an East Texas itinerary.

If you're entering East Texas by vehicle from Louisiana, look for the Texas Department of Transportation's **Travel Information Center** at two spots on the state border. The largest facility is in Orange (1708 E. I-10, 409/883-9416) on I-10 en route from New Orleans. The other is in Waskom (1255 N. I-20 E., 903/687-2547) on I-20 from Shreveport. Visit www.dot.state.tx.us for road-related travel information, or check out www.tx.roadconnect.net to find out about the nearest rest area or travel center with free Wi-Fi access.

The best source for news and information in Houston and southeast Texas is the **Houston Chronicle** (www.chron.com), containing thorough coverage of city and state happenings as well as detailed listings of restaurants and entertainment venues. For specific information about local politics, touring shows, and movie listings, pick up a free copy of the **Houston Press** (www.houstonpress.com) at bars, coffee shops, and bus stations across town.

EMERGENCIES
Hospitals
Houston isn't any more dangerous (or safer) than other major U.S. cities, but in case you find yourself with a medical emergency and happen to be reading this book, there are several services you should contact immediately. A good place to start is the **Texas Medical Center** (2450 Holcombe Blvd., 713/791-6161, www.texasmedicalcenter.org), which operates a 24-hour emergency room in Central Houston. Another nearby option is **Ben Taub General Hospital** (1504 Taub Loop, 713/873-2000, www.harrishealth.org).

If you've suffered a minor emergency or need to see a doctor without an appointment, contact **NextCare Urgent Care** at 281/477-7490 or www.nextcare.com. For a dental emergency, receive a dentist referral by calling 1-800-DENTIST (800/922-6588). Finally, travelers with medical issues are encouraged to bring extra supplies of medications and copies of prescriptions. Local visitors centers can recommend the best pharmacy or medical center, if needed.

Police

Like the rest of the country, Houston's law enforcement responds to emergency telephone calls at 911 and nonemergencies at 311. Also, to request nonemergency police service for locations inside Houston's city limits, call 713/884-3131. The **Houston Police Department** can be reached at its main office downtown (1200 Travis St.). To find a substation in other parts of the city, contact 713/308-1200 or www.houstonpolice.org.

MEDIA AND COMMUNICATIONS
Newspapers

To find out what's going on in the city and beyond, pick up a copy of the respected *Houston Chronicle* (www.chron.com), the city's only metro daily. The *Chronicle* provides detailed coverage of city and state news, as well as detailed listings of restaurants and entertainment venues. For information about local politics and arts happenings, pick up a free copy of the *Houston Press* (www.houstonpress.com) at businesses and bus stations across town.

Radio and TV

Houston has dozens of radio and TV stations, and their formats, frequencies, and call letters change on a fairly regular basis. To keep up with the latest information about the city's 26 AM radio stations, 27 FM radio stations, or 13 local TV stations, visit www.entertainmenthouston.com.

Internet Access

Satellite and Wi-Fi connections are easily accessible throughout the city, but if you should find yourself without access to a computer or phone, consider the old-school approach of using a **public library** (find a location near you via 832/393-1300 or www.houstonlibrary.org). If you're in the West University or Montrose area, drop by **Copy.com** (1201 Westheimer St., 713/528-1201) to rent time on a computer.

Post Office

Houston's downtown **post office** (401 Franklin St., 713/226-3066) is open 9am-7pm Monday-Friday and 9am-noon Saturday. For information about other branch locations, visit www.houston.com/post-offices.

MONEY

It's always a good idea to have cash on hand for tips, bottles of water, and parking or tollway fees, but you can get by in most parts of Houston with a credit or debit card. Some smaller businesses still don't accept them (old-fashioned restaurants and "convenience" stores, in particular), but they're typically modern enough to have ATM machines nearby. Also available, yet not quite as accessible, are wire transfers and travelers checks. Call ahead for the bank's hours of operation because some institutions close at odd hours.

LUGGAGE STORAGE

Luggage storage is no longer provided at locations where it once was available (both of Houston's airports, the Galleria shopping area, various other public areas) because of security concerns. Check with your hotel or campground about individual policies or options.

QUICK GETAWAYS

To escape the hustle and bustle of the country's fourth-largest city, Houstonians and visitors often take a quick jaunt to **Brenham** (population 15,716), a quaint nearby Main Street community. Located about 75 miles northwest of Houston, this historical town is famous for producing the "best ice cream in the country" at **Blue Bell Creameries** (1101 S. Blue Bell Rd., 979/830-2197, www.bluebell.com, tours held at 10am, 11am, 1pm, 1:30pm, 2pm, 2:30pm Mon.-Fri., $5 adults, $3 children and seniors). A highlight is seeing the enormous processing machines with tubes and conveyer belts methodically churning out a carton's worth of ice cream. You'll feel like you're viewing a real-life episode of the Food Network's *Unwrapped.* Even more appealing are the free samples waiting at the end of the tour.

To get a feel for Brenham's small-town past, drop by the **Brenham Heritage Museum** (105 S. Market St., 979/830-8445, www.brenhamheritagemuseum.org, 1pm-4pm Wed., 10am-4pm Thurs.-Sat.). Experience the community's memorable tales through historical artifacts and photos in a 1915 Classical Revival post office. Next door, visitors are drawn to a rare 1879 Silsby steam-powered horse-drawn fire engine. Just down the street, melodic sounds beckon from Fireman's Park, featuring an early 20th-century antique merry-go-round that still works.

Another popular destination in Brenham is **Ellison's Greenhouses** (2107 E. Stone St., 979/836-0084, 8am-6pm Mon.-Fri., 10am-5pm Sat.-Sun.). Advertised as the only commercial wholesale greenhouse in Texas allowing public tours, Ellison's offers five acres of greenhouses producing annual crops of flowers and vegetables for the picking. Smaller greenhouses are filled seasonally with poinsettias, tulips, and lilies.

Heading in the opposite direction, **Lake Charles, Louisiana,** (population 71,933) offers locals and travelers an opportunity to visit another state and, perhaps more importantly, gamble. Although advertisements and websites will attempt to paint Lake Charles as a family-friendly destination (similar to Las Vegas's approach in the 1990s), the main reason most visitors make the trek is to play "games of chance" and see live performances. Because Texas lawmakers are apparently concerned gambling will sully its residents, fans of this "illicit" activity are forced to spend their money across the state line.

Even if they aren't rewarded with winnings, visitors to Lake Charles have the good fortune of experiencing fine casinos and decent food. The most popular casino (deservedly so) is **L'Auberge du Lac Hotel & Casino** (337/395-7777, www.llakecharles.com, rooms start at $119). Boasting nearly 1,000 rooms on 26 floors (reportedly the tallest building between Houston and Baton Rouge), the L'Auberge is surprisingly elegant for rural southwestern Louisiana. Featuring stylish design and comfortable rooms, the casino and hotel is the closest thing to Las Vegas available in these parts, offering a luxury spa, golf club, and entertainment (past performers include Jay Leno, Willie Nelson, and Lionel Richie). The casino itself is located on a riverboat, with blackjack, craps, and 1,600 slot machines drawing the biggest crowds.

For those who may not actually want to spend their entire visit on a riverboat, several cultural attractions are available in the Lake Charles area. The centerpiece is the Arts & Humanities Council of Southwest Louisiana's **Central School Arts and Humanities Center** (809 Kirby St., 337/439-2787, www.artsandhumanitiesswla.org, 9am-5pm Mon.-Fri.). Located in the pleasant Charpentier District, the stately historic building offers studios, galleries, and performance spaces.

The city's largest museum is **Imperial Calcasieu Museum** (204 West Sallier St., 337/439-3797, www.imperialcalcasieumuseum.org, 10am-5pm Tues.-Sat.). The facility features a permanent historical exhibit and an impressive art gallery. Another highlight is the Sallier oak tree, which is more than 400 years old.

Getting There and Around

GETTING THERE
Air

The major air hub in this part of the country is **George Bush Intercontinental Airport** (2800 N. Terminal Rd., 281/230-3100, www. fly2houston.com), located just north of the city. This is one of United Airlines's major hubs, and since this airport offers nonstop service to and from more than 170 cities around the world, it's typically hustling and bustling at all hours of the day and night. The city's old airfield, **William P. Hobby Airport** (7800 Airport Blvd., 713/640-3000, www. fly2houston.com) is now the center of activity for Southwest Airlines and hosts flights from several other major carriers. Located 10 miles southeast of downtown, Hobby is more accessible than Bush, but it's showing its age. That's often deemed forgivable by travelers who prefer the accessibility and cheaper cab fares (nearly $20 less than the trek from Bush to downtown Houston).

SuperShuttle (281/230-7275, www.supershuttle.com) offers shuttle service to and from area hotels and Bush Intercontinental and Hobby Airports. Look for the company's ticket counters in the lower-level baggage claim areas of Bush and Hobby. Many downtown-area hotels offer free shuttle service to and from Bush Intercontinental Airport, but check first to make sure they're running.

Train

Passenger trains arrive in town via **Amtrak's Sunset Limited line,** which runs cross-country between Orlando and Los Angeles. Look for arrivals and departures at the Houston **Amtrak station** (902 Washington Ave., 713/224-1577 or 800/872-7245, www.amtrak.com).

Bus

Those interested in traveling by bus can contact **Houston Greyhound** (2121 Main St., 713/759-6565 or 800/231-2222, www.greyhound.com).

GETTING AROUND
Car

Upon arriving at the airport, some travelers prefer to rent a car, and the powers that be at Bush Intercontinental have attempted to make things easier by establishing the **Consolidated Rental Car Facility** (281/230-3000, www.iahrac. com). All the major rental car companies are accessible from this shared location about five minutes away from the terminals. The rental companies share a shuttle system, designated by the white and maroon buses marked "Rental Car Shuttle" located outside the terminal.

Public Transportation

Houston has a decent public transportation system, but it can be confusing for out-of-towners who haven't yet developed a strong sense of direction. Regardless, a little homework can be helpful in strategizing plans via the Metro, aka the **Metropolitan Transit Authority of Harris County** (713/635-4000, www.ridemetro.org), which offers local and commuter light rail and bus service. Tickets are available in vending machines located at each station. Metro's red line services 16 stations near downtown's busiest commercial and recreational sites.

Taxi

Ground transportation employees outside each terminal of Bush Intercontinental Airport and near the lower-level baggage claim area (Curbzone 1) of Hobby Airport will half-heartedly hail travelers a taxi. All destinations within Houston's city limits to or from Bush Intercontinental are charged a flat zone rate or the meter rate, whichever is less. For more information on zone rates, check out the Ground Transportation section at www. fly2houston.com. To arrange for cab pick-up service from within the city, contact one of the following local companies: **Liberty Cab Company** (281/540-8294), **Square Deal Cab Co.** (713/444-4444), **Lonestar Cab** (713/794-0000), and **United Cab Co.** (713/699-0000).

THE GULF COAST

Stretching more than 350 miles along the Gulf of Mexico, this region of sun, sea, and sand offers the ultimate escape from cities, suburbs, and small towns. Its moderate beaches and waves don't attract crowds the way Florida's mighty surf does, but the call of the ocean draws casual beachcombers, fishing enthusiasts, and frolicking families.

Occasionally referred to as the country's "Third Coast," the gulf region offers something for everyone: quiet natural seashores, crazy spring-break parties, and world-class museum facilities. The constant breeze off the ocean keeps sailors and windsurfers blissfully cruising along the shore and keeps the temperatures down a few degrees (though the humidity is always hair-curling). The warm ocean water is inviting, but it sometimes approaches an uncomfortable soup-like temperature in the summer, and it's technically responsible for stirring up horrific hurricanes far out at sea. Unfortunately, the gulf region has been making headlines in the past decade for less-than-appealing reasons. Hurricane Ike (2008) wreaked havoc on Galveston, and the Deepwater Horizon oil spill (2010) caused visitors to avoid the beaches, albeit temporarily.

All along the Gulf Coast you'll find anglers of different stripes, from solo artists casting lines off a pier or from the surf's edge to groups of tourists on charter deep-sea boats with professional guides. Regardless, the promise of a fresh catch—flounder, trout, bull reds, and even shark and tuna—is a rewarding prospect and one of the region's main draws.

Naturalists flock to the area for the abundant

THE GULF COAST

HIGHLIGHTS

© AVALON TRAVEL

LOOK FOR ◖ TO FIND RECOMMENDED SIGHTS, ACTIVITIES, DINING, AND LODGING.

◖ **The Strand:** Experience Galveston's thriving historical district in all its New Orleans-style splendor, including hotels, restaurants, art galleries, and boutiques (page 79).

◖ **The *Elissa*:** Get a feel for seafaring life by walking across the sturdy wooden decks of this remarkable 1877 ship, the second-oldest operational sailing vessel in the world (page 81).

◖ **Texas State Aquarium:** Visitors experience Texas's Gulf Coast from the ground down at Corpus Christi's Texas State Aquarium, starting with birds and gators at sea level and descending to oil-rig depths with menacing sharks, a colossal grouper, and hundreds of other slippery species (page 98).

◖ **USS *Lexington* Museum:** Hop aboard the massive USS *Lexington* in the Corpus Christi Bay, where this decommissioned World War II naval aircraft carrier transports visitors back in time with vintage aircraft, tours of its 11 decks, and an impressive collection of historical memorabilia (page 100).

◖ **Padre Island National Seashore:** Not to be confused with its rambunctious little sibling to the south, Padre Island National Seashore is the longest remaining undeveloped stretch of barrier island in the world (page 112).

◖ **King Ranch:** This 825,000-acre "birthplace of American ranching" evokes the majesty and mystique of Texas culture, from Longhorn cattle to wide-open spaces to genuine cowboys on a vast expanse of coastal plains larger than Rhode Island (page 118).

◖ **Port Isabel Lighthouse:** It's well worth the 74-step climb up the lighthouse's tight spiral staircase to experience the breathtaking views—from the bug-size cars passing over the gorgeous Laguna Madre Bay to the remarkable view of classic downtown Port Isabel, the vantage point from this historic lighthouse is truly a sight to behold (page 123).

birding opportunities. The Great Texas Coastal Birding Trail ties together all 300-plus miles of shoreline, from hummingbirds near Galveston to whooping cranes and tropical species on Padre Island. Two major migratory flyways intersect along the Gulf Coast, allowing birders to potentially capture (on a camera viewfinder) an elusive species on their "must-see" list.

Although it's hard to imagine why anyone would want to abandon the recreational opportunities along the shoreline (perhaps your skin is already too parched), the cool air-conditioning at numerous Gulf Coast museums offers a welcome cultural respite. Galveston's Moody Gardens and several Corpus Christi attractions are world-class facilities for learning about regional history, wildlife, and art. Top your day off with a fresh catch from one of the seaside restaurants for a perfect ending to a Gulf Coast day.

Aside from the festive annual springtime activity in Galveston (Mardi Gras) and South Padre (spring break), most of the Gulf Coast is a year-round, slow-moving vacationland, where the biggest challenge is determining the day's activities—swimming, fishing, shell collecting, sunbathing, surfing, boating, or sand-castle building. Visitors responding to the call of the sea find the region to be as low-key as the gulf's lightly lapping waves.

PLANNING YOUR TIME

Coast-bound travelers tend to stay for a weekend in one area—Galveston, Brazosport, Corpus Christi, or South Padre—to lay claim to a beach condo or hole up in a fishing village as opposed to roaming the entire region. In fact, parking yourself on one beach is the best way to do it, unless you have time and money to spare and can enjoy your experience cruising along the coast in a boat (rentals are available).

In general, there are two types of Gulf Coast travelers: busy families looking for a getaway from the 'burbs and grizzled anglers looking for a getaway from the family. The South Padre Island beaches are considered the nicest, so if quality sand and surf are your top priorities, that's the best place to start. Plan to spend at least two to three days soaking up the sun, the soft white sand, and the gently rolling surf.

As you make your way up the coast, the beaches tend to be less scenic—the sand is a bit darker and the infiltration of civilization is more apparent (oil rigs, trash, tankers, commercial buildings, etc.). Regardless, the scent of salt water and the intrinsic lure of the sea are just as strong, but you have to deal with more traffic and city folk. It's worth spending a long weekend in Corpus Christi to soak up the pleasant scene on Mustang Island or nearby Padre Island National Seashore. The city's USS *Lexington,* Texas State Aquarium, and Museum of Science and History are well worth visiting for a family-friendly, air-conditioned change of pace.

The Brazosport Area offers fewer cultural amenities than its coastal cousins, which is precisely the reason why anglers prefer spending quiet weekends here sans water parks and booming car stereos. Things are more low key and less commercial in this unassuming corner of the coast, where retirees, fisherfolk, and professional beachcombers peacefully coexist.

Galveston is where the big-city Houstonians go to spend their money and get their beach and seafood fix. It's the least stunning of all the Gulf Coast beaches, but the waves are still welcoming, and the shopping and restaurant scene in the historical Strand district are certainly deserving of two travel days.

Most communities along the Gulf Coast have visitors centers where tourists can inquire about directions, equipment rental, and other travel-related assistance (information on each is included throughout this chapter). A couple of helpful websites provide more detailed information about the coast, including maps, resources, and notices about current conditions and events. The **Texas General Land Office** offers a Beach and Bay Access Guide with links to environmental reports and downloads (www. glo.state.tx.us/coastal/access), and the Texas Gulf Coast Real Estate organization has compiled a handy website with general information about coastal geology, beaches, parks, and map links (www.texasgulfcoastonline.com).

GETTING THERE AND AROUND

Most travelers arrive to the Gulf Coast by car from other locales within the state; however, airline service is available via Corpus Christi International Airport and Brownsville South Padre Island International Airport.

Because the majority of the coastline is undeveloped, there aren't any major freeways linking cities. State Highway 35 is the closest option—a primarily rural road stretching between Houston and Corpus Christi that passes through dozens of small towns along the way. The lengthy Padre Island National Seashore is only accessible by a park road near Corpus Christi; otherwise, the trek to South Padre

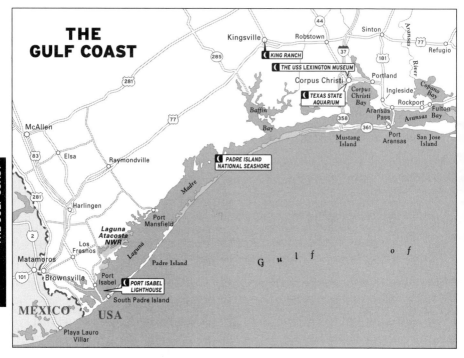

beaches is more than 20 miles inland via U.S. Highway 77 through Kingsville, Harlingen, and Brownsville.

To reach the beach in a hurry, get on the next flight to **Corpus Christi International Airport** (1000 International Blvd., 361/289-0171, www.cctexas.com/airport), offering service from American Eagle, United, and Southwest Airlines. South Padre is accessible via the **Brownsville South Padre Island International Airport** (700 S. Minnesota Ave., 956/542-4373, www.flybrownsville.com), served by United and American Eagle. Galveston is about an hour-long drive from Houston.

Galveston

Located on an island about 50 miles southeast of Houston, Galveston (population 47,743) is a hotbed for Texas history. Most people remember the Alamo, but they don't realize Galveston was once Texas's largest city and busiest port, with thousands of immigrants arriving each year. Unfortunately, recent hurricanes (2008's Ike, in particular) have been historic for all the wrong reasons, with devastating winds and waves destroying property and driving thousands of residents permanently out of town.

Galveston was founded in 1839, and the island town was emerging as a burgeoning commercial center until the Civil War put the brakes on its progress. An interesting historical side note: On January 1, 1863, Confederate troops recaptured the city while on the same day Abraham Lincoln signed the final draft of the Emancipation Proclamation.

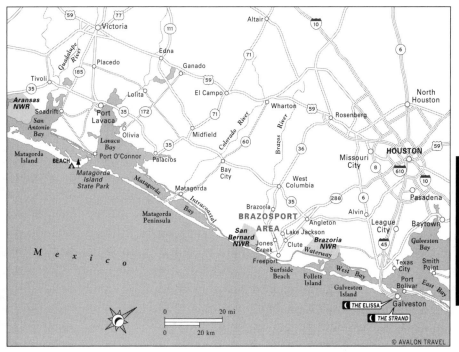

Word didn't make it to Galveston until June 19, 1865, when enslaved Texans officially (finally) received their freedom. Afterward, Galveston became the birthplace of the now-national Juneteenth celebration, which commemorates the June 19 announcement.

After the war, Galveston resumed its steady growth due to the hundreds of immigrants, primarily German, disembarking from ocean liners each day. Trade was prosperous, especially cotton exports, and for a while, Galveston was known as the "Wall Street of the South" because of its robust economy and cosmopolitan amenities, such as electric lights, telephones, and modern streetcars.

The stately mansions and downtown business buildings constructed during this era still stand as the heart of Galveston's historical district. Tourists from across the globe flock to the island to experience these intricate homes (most are now history museums) and ornate commercial architecture.

Galveston's fate was forever altered in 1900 when a massive hurricane decimated nearly a third of the island's buildings. The torrential 120-mile-per-hour windstorm caused an estimated 6,000 deaths, a number of casualties now inconceivable with today's 24-hour live-weather radar forecasts. As a result of the devastation, Galveston's industrial and residential populations shifted to Houston.

Galveston eventually recovered from its economically challenging times (thanks in part to the construction of a massive seawall to protect the northern part of the island) to become one of the state's top tourist destinations. Although Hurricane Ike caused widespread damage in 2008 (mainly from flooding), most of the island's cultural and historical attractions survived the storm and reopened for business. The beach remains the

THE GULF COAST

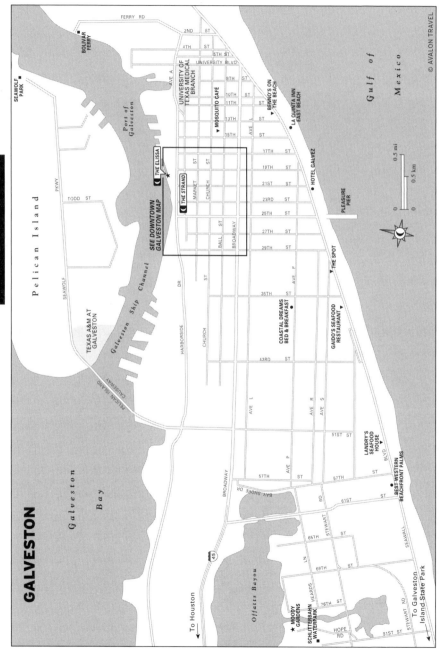

GALVESTON

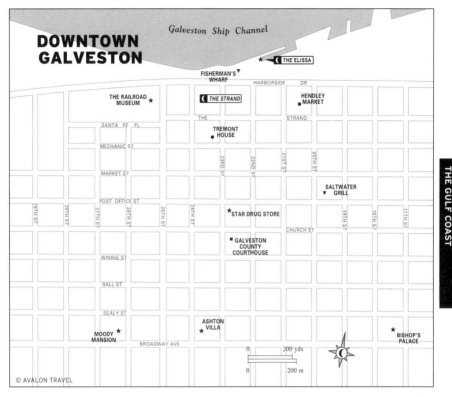

DOWNTOWN GALVESTON

Galveston Ship Channel

THE ELISSA

FISHERMAN'S WHARF

HARBORSIDE DR

THE RAILROAD MUSEUM

THE STRAND

HENDLEY MARKET

SANTA FE PL

THE

STRAND

TREMONT HOUSE

MECHANIC ST

23RD ST

22ND ST

21ST ST

20TH ST

MARKET ST

POST OFFICE ST

SALTWATER GRILL

29TH ST

28TH ST

27TH ST

26TH ST

25TH ST

24TH ST

STAR DRUG STORE

19TH ST

18TH ST

17TH ST

CHURCH ST

GALVESTON COUNTY COURTHOUSE

WINNIE ST

BALL ST

SEALY ST

ASHTON VILLA

MOODY MANSION

BISHOP'S PALACE

BROADWAY AVE

0   200 yds

0   200 m

© AVALON TRAVEL

THE GULF COAST

island's main draw, especially for surf-seeking Houston folks, but its rich historical fabric provides a pleasant slice of Victorian-era life for international visitors.

SIGHTS

Most of Galveston's attractions are heritage related, but they're well worth checking out since they're some of the highest-quality cultural sites in the state. For the past several years, Galveston has been devoting considerable efforts to recovering from 2008's Hurricane Ike, physically (and psychologically). This forward-looking attitude is represented by the new Pleasure Pier and Schlitterbahn Waterpark entertainment complexes on the shoreline. A mile away, the historic commercial buildings along The Strand and the century-old mansions showcase a distinctive and fascinating

time in Texas history that visitors won't find throughout the inland regions.

◖ The Strand

The heart of Galveston's thriving business district in the late 1800s and early 1900s, **The Strand** (Strand and Mechanic St. between 20th and 25th St.) still captures the essence of the city's "Wall Street of the South" era. This 36-block National Historic Landmark District features New Orleans-style hotels, restaurants, art galleries, and boutiques, most of which escaped the devastation of the 1900 hurricane. Today, visitors flock to the antiques and clothing shops, art studios, and seasonal festivals, including the popular Dickens on the Strand and Mardi Gras celebrations. For information about recommended shops, lodging options, and eateries

THE GULF COAST

© ANDY RHODES

Galveston's historic Strand district

throughout The Strand district, consult the corresponding sections in this chapter.

Pleasure Pier

Standing as a testament to Galveston's past and its resolve to move forward, **Pleasure Pier** (2501 Seawall Blvd., 855/789.7437, www.pleasurepier.com, seasonal hours, various ticket options) is a family entertainment complex on the Gulf Coast that opened in 2012. Harkening back to a 1940s facility with the same name (albeit with a slightly slicker customer base), the current Pleasure Pier is hoping the third time's the charm as two previous sites were knocked out by hurricanes (the Flagship Hotel was a victim of 2008's Hurricane Ike).

The Pleasure Pier is an ideal spot to spend an afternoon with the family by reveling in the 15 amusement park rides, midway games, food vendors, and boardwalk-style shopping. Although some locals have complained about the somewhat hefty fees ($20-plus entry, $10 for parking, and another $10 to walk on the

pier), it's a worthy entertainment investment for most visitors. There aren't many other places where you can ride a roller coaster, giant swing, or Ferris wheel over the ocean.

Schlitterbahn Waterpark

Also creating waves of excitement in the realm of new attractions is **Schlitterbahn Waterpark** (2026 Lockheed St., 409/770-9283, www.schlitterbahn.com, $47 adults, $42 children ages 3-11). Although it may initially seem odd to have a massive water-based entertainment facility near the gulf shore, Schlitterbahn is more of an amusement waterpark than a swimming destination.

For example, the gulf can't compete with Schlitterbahn's "uphill water coasters" in a convertible facility that can be opened or closed for indoor or outdoor recreation year-round (the water and air are always in the 80s). Other attractions include traditional twisty water slides, whitewater rapids, a wave pool, playgrounds, hot tubs, a vertical plunge tower, and a surf ride.

the 1877 *Elissa* in Galveston

© ANDY RHODES

THE GULF COAST

an American Treasure by the National Trust for Historic Preservation.

To learn more about *Elissa*'s history and subsequent restoration, visit the adjacent **Texas Seaport Museum.** The portside facility features informative exhibits about maritime culture, a fascinating movie about Galveston's port-based heritage as the "Ellis Island of the West," and a computer database with the names of more than 133,000 immigrants who entered the United States through Galveston.

Ocean Star Offshore Drilling Rig and Museum

When in Texas . . . you know the old saying. To learn about the impact of the oil industry on the Lone Star State and its Gulf Coast, be sure to drop by the **Ocean Star Offshore Drilling Rig and Museum** (1900 Harborside Dr., 409/766-7827, www.oceanstaroec.com, summer hours: 10am-5pm daily, winter hours: 10am-4pm daily, $8 adults, $5 students and seniors). Located just a block from the Strand historical district, this distinctive museum educates visitors about the offshore oil and gas industry by means of a refurbished drilling rig. Visitors can take a self-guided tour through three levels of the retired rig to learn about oil exploration, drilling, and production through informative exhibits and videos.

The Bishop's Palace

Grand. Stately. Enormous. However you choose to describe it, the spectacular 1886 **Bishop's Palace** (1402 Broadway St., 409/762-2475, www.galvestonhistory.org, 11am-6pm daily, guided tours every hour, $10 adults, $7 students) is the centerpiece of Galveston's historical Broadway Street. The American Institute of Architects designated Bishop's Palace as one of the 100 outstanding buildings in the country, and it's easy to see why. This Victorian castle exudes elegance, from its ornate fireplaces (one is lined with pure silver) to its grand stairway to its stained-glass windows and intricately carved furnishings and details. The Bishop's Palace is Galveston's most visited historical attraction

The *Elissa* and Texas Seaport Museum

One of the city's most treasured landmarks is the 1877 ship *Elissa* (Pier 21, 409/763-1877, www.tsm-elissa.org, 10am-5pm daily, $8 adults, $5 students ages 6 and up). This remarkable ship is the second-oldest operational sailing vessel in the world and one of the three oldest merchant boats still afloat. Get a feel for seafaring life by walking across the sturdy wooden decks under massive masts and 19 sails and by exploring the sleeping quarters and mechanical room. While below deck, be sure to take a few minutes to watch the professional documentary about the boat's dramatic shipyard rescue. Incidentally, the *Elissa* was one of the few historical attractions in Galveston that was largely unharmed by Hurricane Ike, losing only a few sails while remaining anchored to the seafloor. A tangible piece of history, the ship has been designated for good reason—its stately design and detailed furnishings transport visitors to another era and offer an escape to the past unmatched in this part of the country.

The Moody Mansion

Nearly as impressive in its opulence is the nearby **Moody Mansion** (2618 Broadway St., 409/762-7668, www.moodymansion. org, 11am-3pm daily, tours held on alternate hours, $8 adults, $5 students). Renowned Galveston entrepreneur and businessman W. L. Moody Jr. purchased the four-story, 32-room, 28,000-square-foot limestone and brick mansion a week after the 1900 hurricane. The stately home features rare hand-carved wood, coffered ceilings, stained glass, and heirlooms from the Moody family, who established one of the country's most heralded financial empires through various entrepreneurial endeavors (cotton, banking, ranching, and insurance). Marvel at the manicured grounds, exquisite furnishings, the expansive ballroom, and the dining room's gold-leaf ceiling.

Moody Gardens

Natural wonders await beneath three enormous glass pyramids at **Moody Gardens** (1 Hope Blvd., 409/744-4673, www.moodygardens.com, 10am-6pm daily, $50 for a one-day pass, $18 for individual pyramid tickets). One of Galveston's most popular and prominent attractions, Moody Gardens offers an elaborate and stunning collection of plants, animals, and educational exhibits inside its colossal 100-foot-tall structures. The all-access day pass carries a hefty price tag, so if you'd rather choose just one area to explore, go with the Rainforest Pyramid. The Aquarium Pyramid has more animals and features, but the Rainforest environment is a unique experience, where you'll find yourself face to face with African jungle animals, tropical birds, and colorful reptiles. Massive plants, cascading waterfalls, and the constant chatter of birds and insects transport you across the planet to these exotic habitats. Be sure to check out the bat cave, with various species of bats hanging upside down, nibbling on fresh fruit.

The Aquarium Pyramid takes you on a journey across the world's oceans, viewed at two levels—surface and underwater. Marvel at penguins as they waddle and dive, and catch an up-close view of sea lions as they glide and play. Sharks, sea turtles, rays, and tropical fish lie below the surface, which you can view in a traditional aquarium tank setting or from the underwater tunnel where you're surrounded by one million gallons of water.

Other notable attractions include the Discovery Pyramid, featuring science and nature exhibits; three IMAX "ridefilm" theaters; kids' activities aboard the *Colonel* paddlewheel boat; seasonal recreation at Palm Beach (swimming lagoons, whirlpools, volleyball, and paddleboats); formal gardens; nature trails; and the esteemed Moody Gardens conference center, hotel, and spa.

Ashton Villa

Also of interest to history enthusiasts is the remarkable 1859 **Ashton Villa** (2328 Broadway St., 409/762-3933, www.galvestonhistory.org, call in advance about visiting the mansion). This stately mansion, built for one of Texas's wealthiest businesspeople, James Moreau Brown, set the standard for the exquisite Galveston homes that followed. Experience the Victorian lifestyle through the home's grand entryway, life-size paintings, and beautifully landscaped grounds. The house contains many pieces of artwork, furniture, and mementos the family acquired during its travels to the Far East. Ashton Villa now houses the city's Heritage Visitors Center, which is open daily, but as of 2012, tours of the mansion were only being held sporadically because of restoration challenges associated with Hurricane Ike.

The Railroad Museum

Anchoring Galveston's historical downtown Strand district is the former Santa Fe Union Station, home to **The Railroad Museum** (2602 Santa Fe Pl., 409/765-5700, www.galvestonrr-museum.com, 10am-5pm daily, $6 adults, $4 students). More than 20,000 railroad items and several dozen vintage passenger, dining, and kitchen cars provide fascinating views of railroad life from the late 19th and early 20th centuries. The main terminal, located at the heart of this impressive art deco building, contains interactive exhibits and a collection of unique plaster sculptures depicting "ghosts of travelers past." Kids will love the miniature model trains and the historical rail cars behind the passenger depot.

BEACHES

Galveston has two main beaches: the mellow family beach and the raucous singles beach. Both serve important purposes, but it's probably best that they're separated.

The family-friendly spot is **Stewart Beach** (6th St. and Seawall Blvd., 409/765-5023, $8 admission per car—cash only, open Mar.-mid-Oct.), where you'll find moms, dads, and kids building sand castles, playing volleyball, and body surfing. Nearby amenities include a children's playground with water slides, umbrella and chair rentals, concession area, souvenir shop, restrooms, and a bathhouse.

Things get a bit crazier at **East Beach** (1923 Boddeker Dr., 409/762-3278, $8 admission per car—cash only). This is where Houston's younger crowd comes to party, a rare surfside treat since East Beach is one of the few places where drinking is legal on the beach. As a result, you'll find more concerts, promotions, and festivals than other public stretches of shoreline. Up to 7,000 cars can pack the beach (parking and drinking while sunbathing is a popular activity), and the bar area is a magnet for partygoers. East Beach also includes restrooms with showers, volleyball courts, chair and umbrella rentals, and a souvenir shop.

RECREATION

Recreational opportunities abound in Galveston. Many of these outdoor-based activities have expanded in recent years, as visitors are increasingly searching for physical challenges and workout opportunities while on the coast. Why would you sit in a hotel and watch TV when you can go kayaking, biking, or surfing?

Galveston Island State Park

One of the most popular places on the island to enjoy the outdoors is **Galveston Island State Park** (14901 FM 3005, 409/737-1222, www.tpwd.state.tx.us, $5 entrance fee ages 12 and up). The popular park encapsulates the spirit of recreation, offering camping, hiking, biking, fishing, swimming, and birding.

The park is an ideal place to spend an afternoon hiking or biking, followed by a dip in the ocean or the simple pleasure of beachcombing. There are four miles of trails to explore, mainly through bayside salt marshes and prairie grassland. Although the beach has no lifeguards, swimmers can take comfort in the provided amenities of restrooms and rinse showers.

Biking

Tired of driving your car around while on vacation? You're not the only one. Bike rentals have become a popular way for visitors to experience Galveston, especially because cyclists don't have to worry about megafreeways and crazy traffic jams.

To rent a bike and learn about Galveston's best cycling areas, head directly to **Island Bicycle Company** (1808 Seawall Blvd., 409/762-2453, www.islandbicyclecompany.com). The shop claims to have the largest selection of rental bikes in the city and even offers hotel pick-up service. The best service is the self-guided tour: For $30, you can take a bike at your own pace and explore points of interest (including lunch at a local restaurant and a ferry ride). The package includes a lock and map.

Paddling

For a slightly more adventurous and innovative way to explore Galveston Island, consider renting a kayak, paddleboard, or canoe.

A good starting point is **Galveston Island State Park.** The park has an established waterway trail system, allowing paddlers to put in and take out their vessels at convenient locations. Paddlers have three different park "trails" to choose from: the 2.6-mile **Dana Cove Trail,** beginning at Lake Como and meandering

HURRICANES: DEADLY TROPICAL CYCLONES

Hurricane season is a tumultuous time for Gulf Coast residents. These devastating tropical cyclones can come ashore anytime between June and November, though most strike in the hot summer months of August and September.

Hurricanes originate when ocean waters reach their highest temperatures, leading to thunderstorms with winds of up to 40 miles per hour (officially a tropical storm). At this point, the National Hurricane Center names the storm, working from a predetermined alphabetical list of names. Tropical storms get their energy from warm humid air over the ocean, and the release of this force is what drives the powerful winds of a hurricane.

Historically the probability of a hurricane hitting Texas hasn't been too severe, but the past decade has been a different story. In September 2005, **Hurricane Rita,** a Category 5 storm with intense 120-mph winds, made landfall near Sabine Pass on the Texas-Louisiana border. It ultimately caused more than $11 billion in damage and is linked to seven deaths. Even more devastating size-wise was **Hurricane Ike,** which slammed into Galveston Island in September 2008, leaving an enormous swath of destruction in its wake. Ike completely leveled several nearby communities, and its 110-mph winds ripped apart hotels, office buildings, and countless homes in Galveston, Houston, and the surrounding area.

In general, however, the statistical possibility of Texas being hit by a hurricane is not too severe (one every six years along any 50-mile segment of the Texas coast). The recent experiences, plus the fresh memory of 2005's devastating Hurricane Katrina in New Orleans, are serious enough to make residents tune in to the weather radar every time the words *tropical depression* surface. More often than not, the storm bypasses the gulf or dissipates by the time it reaches the Texas coast. According to weather researchers, annual probabilities of a hurricane striking a 50-mile segment of the coast range from roughly 30 percent near Port Arthur to nearly 40 percent at Matagorda Bay northeast of Corpus Christi.

That being said, some of the strongest hurricanes to hit the U.S. coast have come ashore in Texas. Unlike the overwhelmingly destructive effects of Hurricane Ike in Galveston, however, the storms that historically ravaged Texas are typically in uninhabited areas. In 1970, meteorologists recorded wind gusts of 180 miles per hour near Aransas Pass, and in 1961, Hurricane Carla brought 175-mph winds to Port Lavaca. By comparison, Katrina's wind speeds were 140 miles per hour at landfall, but its extremely low barometric pressure made it improbably intense.

In the wake of the devastating losses associated with Hurricane Ike, Texas officials have organized emergency plans and evacuation routes for coastal cities. Public awareness campaigns focus on the importance of being informed and prepared. The unpredictable nature of these storms makes evacuation planning a challenge, but an increasing number of Gulf Coast residents are erring on the safe side when an intensifying tropical storm is on the horizon by packing up and moving inland until the tempest subsides.

through shallow seagrass-lined waters; the **Oak Bayou Trail,** a 4.8-mile course beginning near the boardwalk and following along inlets and breakwaters of Galveston Bay; and the **Jenikins Bayou Trail,** a 2.8-mile trail traversing a freshwater pond and small bay inlet. For kayak rental at the park, contact the Friends of Galveston Island State Park (email FoGISP@aol.com or visit http://fogisp.org).

Another worthy outfit for kayak rental and excursion info is **Gulf Coast Kayak Adventures** (979/215-6319, www.gulfcoast-kayakadventures.com). The company offers shuttle service to specified locations, as well as full-day rentals ($65 for a single kayak or $80 for a tandem). Guided kayak tours are also available for $150 (plus $60 per person), ranging from beginner trips exploring birding opportunities to advanced tours offering potential porpoise sightings.

© ANDY RHODES

Galveston Island

Bird-Watching

The Gulf Coast is a bird-watcher's paradise, with ample opportunity for birders to catch glimpses of their favorite flying species during migrations in spring and fall. Galveston Island offers a few extra incentives for birds to make a landing and stay grounded for a while. The natural barrier island habitat provides protection, and more importantly, food-rich bayous and marshes.

Galveston Island State Park is an ideal place to find a perch for prime bird-watching opportunities. Keep an eye (and camera) out for great blue herons, white ibis, great egrets, and white spoonbills, and don't forget to keep your eyes to the skies for hawks, gulls, and terns.

Surfing

"Galveston" and "surfing" don't usually appear in the same sentence . . . or even the same thought. But there are occasional days and locations where surfing exceeds expectations.

Although many people choose to wind-surf with the steady coastal winds, those committed to catching a wave the old-fashioned way can often find decent conditions along the **Seawall** (between 21st and 51st Streets). Waves tend to be most consistent during the spring, and their gentle nature offer a good opportunity for beginners to hone their skills. Be sure to keep an eye out for the beach patrol's red flag warnings on especially gusty days. To keep up with weather conditions, contact the **Galveston Beach Patrol** (409/763-4769, www.galvestonbeachpatrol.com). For information about surf equipment rental, contact one of the city's most popular surf shops, such as **Ohana Surf & Skate** (2814 Avenue R, 409/763-2700, www.ohanasurfandskate.com).

Fishing

Fishing opportunities abound in Galveston, from solo shoreline casting to chartered group tours. Do note, however, that a fishing license is required. To obtain one ($30 for nonresidents, $19 for residents) drop by the **Super Wal-Mart** (6702 Seawall Blvd.) or call the Texas Parks and

Wildlife Office at 800/895-4248 and purchase one by credit card.

Those in search of something simpler should head to **Galveston Island State Park** for bayside fishing. Spotted sea trout, black drum, and flounder can be caught along the shore, and a fish cleaning station is available at the end of the park road near the camping area. For information about licensing and conditions, contact the park's administrative office at 409/737-1222.

One of the most popular fishing spots on the island is the **Galveston Fishing Pier** (90th Street and Seawall Blvd., 409/744-2273). The 300-foot-long T head is an ideal spot to take in the sights of the shoreline while casting a line for redfish, jackfish, and sea trout. To make things even easier, the pier offers equipment rental, bait, chairs, and mobile carts. Admission to the pier is $9 for adults and $5 for children (11 and under). Rod and reel rental is $9. Payment is cash only.

ENTERTAINMENT AND EVENTS
Nightlife

Like most beach towns, Galveston's nightlife scene is a mix of touristy surfside venues (often the most fun and memorable options) and standard beer joints or restaurant-and-bar combos. Unlike other popular travel destinations, however, the bar scene tends to shut down earlier than usual (10pm at many locations), so be sure to call ahead if you're planning a pub-crawl itinerary.

Offering the sometimes rare combination of "touristy" and "genuinely fun" is **Float** (2828 Seawall Blvd., 409/765-7946). The main attraction (during hot summer months) is the outdoor pool, where customers are encouraged to enjoy a cold beverage while . . . floating. The atmosphere is like a supersized backyard pool party, albeit with a full bar offering exotic drinks and views of the Gulf of Mexico. For those who didn't bring a bathing suit (or are visiting during one of the few months of the year when the temperatures are below 80 degrees), indoor seating and standard pub grub are another option, though not as fun.

Another beach-based venue is the **Beach Hut** (731 Seawall Blvd., 409/770-0089). Its claim to fame is being the only bar directly on the beach in Galveston, with a long ramp offering access from the patio to the sandy shoreline. This isn't a late-night hot spot (it closes at 9pm), but the sunset view is magnificent, and its beauty is enhanced by a margarita or cold lager. Live music is on tap most weekends.

Brews Brothers Brew Pub (2404 Strand St., 417/230-6644) attracts those who take their drinking slightly more seriously. You won't find any thirst-quenching commercial light beers here, and that's undeniably refreshing. As its name implies, the brewpub specializes in craft beers (though they currently do not have their own brews on tap). Regardless, the staff is extremely knowledgeable about beer and will gladly describe and recommend any of their countless options from independent craft brewers across the country.

If you're looking for a good spot to grab a meal followed by some drinks, people watching, and a steady ocean breeze, drop by **Yaga's Café and Bar** (2314 Strand St., 409/762-6676, www.yagaspresents.com). Located in the heart of the Strand district adjacent to Saengerfest Park, Yaya's is known for its large outdoor patio and dance parties (live music on weekends and a dance floor).

Performing Arts

Most island visitors searching for nighttime entertainment tend to gravitate toward bars rather than theaters, but Galveston has a few notable venues worth discovering. First and foremost is the **Grand 1894 Opera House** (2020 Post Office St., 409/765-1894, www.thegrand. com). It has truly stood the test of time (and torrential weather), having survived the devastating storms of 1900 and 1915 as well as Hurricanes Carla, Alicia, and Ike. Listed in the National Register of Historic Places, the Grand was also officially proclaimed "The Official Opera House of Texas" by the state legislature in 1993. The building's rich history is immediately apparent upon entering the theater, featuring a grand staircase, wooden walls, and turn-of-the century furnishings. Friendly ushers offer a helpful hand (and stories) for attendees, who regularly pack the house for Texas legends (Lyle Lovett, Jerry Jeff Walker, Robert Earl Keen) and classic artists (Oak Ridge Boys, Kingston Trio).

Another worthy theater option is **Island Etc.** (2317 Mechanic St., 409/771-0165, www.islandetc.org). Billed as Galveston County's only professional repertory theater company, Island Etc. (short for East-End Theater Company) stages up to six productions a year, mostly traditional shows such as *Cat on a Hot Tin Roof, Avenue Q,* and *Harvey.* The venue also screens classic movies, ranging from *The Wizard of Oz* to *Rocky Horror Picture Show* to *Back to the Future.*

Like the Grand Opera House, Island Etc.'s theater building is a strong survivor of several devastating storms. Hurricane Ike destroyed its previous location on Post Office Street just as the company was making plans to relocate to its location in the former Strand Theatre.

Events

By far the biggest annual event in Galveston (and one of the biggest in Texas) is **Mardi Gras** (888/425-4753, www.mardigrasgalveston.com). Held in late winter/early spring (two weeks before the beginning of Lent), this all-out "party of a lifetime" draws more than a quarter of a million people. That's not a misprint.

Held on the island for more than a century (Mardi Gras celebrated its 100th anniversary in 2011), this crazy days-long party features extravagant parades, exhibits, live entertainment, and galas. One of the biggest attractions: the three million beads thrown from floats and balconies . . . just for fun!

Many beachside communities host sand castle competitions, but most of them aren't like Galveston's annual event on East Beach in mid-June, **AIA Sandcastle** (1923 Boddeker St., www.aiasandcastle.com). Instead of just stacking a few pails of sand together, these sand castle architects are actual architects. Hosted by the Houston chapter of the American Institute

of Architects since 1986, Galveston's event is a sight to behold. The imaginative and professionally designed sand structures have to be seen to be believed.

Aside from Mardi Gras, one of Galveston's most venerable annual events is **Dickens on the Strand** (502 20th St., 409/765-7834, www.galvestonhistory.org). Held the first weekend of December, the festival transports participants and visitors to the past for a weekend of 19th-century high society Galveston style. Costumed revelers, carolers, entertainers, and attendees recreate the festive atmosphere of 1800s Galveston, then Texas's largest and richest city.

The city's other major holiday-related event is the **Moody Gardens Festival of Lights** (1 Hope Blvd., 800/582-4673, www.moodygardens.com). Billed as one of the largest holiday celebrations in the region, the Festival of Lights lives up to its name by showcasing more than one million lights on displays and throughout the site's signature pyramid structures. The festival features a rarity in Texas during December: an outdoor ice skating rink and Ice Slide ride.

SHOPPING

Shopping is one of Galveston's main draws, with abundant fashion boutiques and knick-knack shops throughout the historical downtown area. Keep in mind, this is where wealthy Houstonians come to play, so items are often priced for this clientele.

The gas-lit street lamps, ornate architectural detailing, and lofty display windows along the 36-block **Strand district** with its Victorian-era charm even attract those with no interest in shopping. One of the first places many people start their browsing is the eclectic **Hendley Market** (2010 Strand St., 409/762-2610, www.hendleymarket.com). This fascinating emporium contains a little bit of everything, from Mexican imports to vintage jewelry to kitschy knickknacks to antique medical instruments. Kids will love the baskets filled with hand-crafted toys and plastic novelty trinkets.

Not quite as charming yet equally beguiling

with its amazing array of objects is **Big House Antiques** (2212 Mechanic St., 409/762-0559). Shoppers will find many estate-sale pieces here, including furniture, jewelry, decorative items, and books.

For a modest increase on the price and quality scale, step into the **Front Parlor** (2111 Strand St., 409/762-0224, www.thefrontparlor.com), where the sign out front promises "Books, Gifts, and Surprises." Though the store specializes in fancy Lampe Berger lamps imported from Paris, the Front Parlor also features home accessories and women's clothing.

Looking for something shiny but tasteful? You'll find it at **The Jewel Garden** (2326 Strand St., 409/766-7837). This elegant yet relaxed shop offers a range of quality gifts, including silver jewelry, home decor objects, wind chimes, and hand-carved woodwork.

If you forgot your flip-flops or lost your sunglasses on the beach, drop by **Jammin' Sportswear** (2314 Strand St., 409/763-4005). Every beach town needs a few good T-shirt shops, and Jammin' Sportswear is one of the most popular on the island. Pick up towels, caps, sunscreen, or even one of those alligator toys here.

A step up is **Surf Styles** (2119 Strand St., 409/763-0147), where you can get a T-shirt for the beach and some stylish cruise wear for a night on the town. Brands include Stussy, Miss Me Denim, Converse, and Lucky Brand.

A mandatory stop on The Strand is the venerable **Old Strand Emporium** (2112 Strand St., 409/515-0715). The longest-running spot in the district, the Old Strand Emporium offers fresh fudge, ice cream, deli sandwiches, and cold drinks, including beer and wine. Texas foods are the specialty here, so be sure to grab a jar of salsa, a pecan praline, or some tangy barbecue sauce.

ACCOMMODATIONS

Galveston's popularity as a tourist destination means there's no shortage of lodging options. From cheap beachside motels to luxurious resorts, the island has something for everyone.

Strand District

If you'd rather be within walking distance of shopping than seashells, make reservations at the exquisite **Tremont House** (2300 Ships Mechanic Row, 409/763-0300, www.wyndham.com, $179 d). Located in the heart of The Strand historic commercial district, the Tremont is a stunning 1879 Victorian hotel that transports guests to Galveston's heyday as the "Wall Street of the South." In its rooms you'll notice the lofty ceilings and incredibly tall windows. Wrought-iron beds, marble bathrooms, antique furnishings, and a stylish black-and-white color scheme add to the elegant environment. Modern touches include free wireless Internet access and web TV.

Just down the street is the **Harbor House** (28 Pier #21, 409/763-3321, www.harborhousepier21.com, $199 d), which is fancy in a completely different way. It's not historical, but the Harbor House offers the amazing vantage point of the busy harbor and bustling marina. One of the best seafood restaurants in town (Willie G's) is across the street, and the hotel provides free passes to a nearby fitness center. Amenities include wireless Internet access and a free continental breakfast.

Seawall Boulevard

For most visitors, the best way to experience an island vacation is on the shoreline. Though the following selection of hotels aren't technically on the beach (you'll have to cross busy Seawall Boulevard to get your toes in the sand), they're close enough to smell the salty air and see the sailboats and barges.

At the affordable end of the scale is the no-frills yet dependable **Gaido's Seaside Inn** (3700 Seawall Blvd., 409/762-9625, www.gaidosofgalveston.com, $99 d). Gaido's is perhaps best known for its incredible adjacent seafood restaurant, but the hotel has some tasty amenities too, including a free continental breakfast, an outdoor pool with splash shower, and free coffee and juice in the lobby.

Another well-regarded local establishment is the nearby **Commodore on the Beach** (3618 Seawall Blvd., 409/763-2375, www.

commodoreonthebeach.com, $109 d). The Commodore features rooms with balconies facing the beach, a large pool with a cascading fountain, and several complimentary services, including wireless Internet access, continental breakfast, coffee and juice, and late-afternoon cookies.

Some travelers value the comfort and familiarity of chain hotels. Although the corporate options are nearly outnumbered by independent establishments on Seawall, several offer competitive rates and reliable service. Among them is **La Quinta East Beach** (1402 Seawall Blvd., 409/763-1224, www.lq.com, $139 d), featuring an outdoor pool along with a free continental breakfast and Internet access. Though the accommodations aren't luxurious, the comfy beach-town vibe here is appealing, not to mention the ocean view (and smell) directly outside your hotel room door. Another option farther down the island is the more expensive and fancier **Best Western Beachfront Palms Hotel** (5914 Seawall Blvd., 409/740-1261, www.bestwesterngalveston.com, $169 d), offering a free continental breakfast, Internet access, and free cappuccino and hot chocolate. The Best Western also claims to have the only heated pool on the island.

Those willing to drop some extra cash for a truly memorable vacation experience should consider the remarkable **Hotel Galvez** (2024 Seawall Blvd., 409/765-7721, www.wyndham.com, $242 d). Known as the "Queen of the Gulf" when it opened in 1911, the Galvez is stunning in its Victorian elegance. Luxurious amenities include a pool with swim-up bar, marble bathrooms, wireless Internet access, and an impressive spa and workout facility. Not nearly as historical but similarly stylish is the **Hilton Galveston Island Resort** (5400 Seawall Blvd., 409/744-5000, www.galveston-hilton.com, $295 d), featuring large rooms with plush robes, Wi-Fi service, gulf-view rooms with private balconies, a tropically landscaped pool with a swim-up bar, and a fitness center.

Bed-and-Breakfasts

With so many impressive historic structures

in a pedestrian-friendly vacation environment, Galveston is an ideal place to stay in a B&B. One of the more popular options is **Avenue O Bed and Breakfast** (2323 Ave. O, 409/762-2868, www.avenueo.com, rooms start at $99), just a few blocks away from the beach. This 1923 Mediterranean-style home sits on a sizable piece of property surrounded by tropical foliage. Breakfasts are hearty here, and snacks are available throughout the day. Avenue O also provides bikes for island excursions. Just down the street is **Coastal Dreams Bed & Breakfast** (3602 Ave. P, 409/770-0270, www.coastaldreamsbnb.com, rooms start at $139). Built in 1887, this remarkable home boasts 12-foot ceilings, stained-glass windows, and an inviting pool. Breakfasts feature stuffed French toast, thick bacon slices, and omelets, and daytime treats include freshly baked cookies, brownies, and other sweets.

Camping

If you prefer lodging in an RV or tent, you'll enjoy **Galveston Island State Park** (14901 FM 3005, 409/737-1222, www.tpwd.state.tx.us, daily entry fee $5 per person ages 13 and older, camping fees $15-25 per night). Located on the west end of Galveston Island about 10 miles from town, Galveston Island State Park offers 2,000 acres of natural beauty along the Gulf Coast. Even if you aren't planning to spend the night, the park is a great place for swimming, hiking, bird-watching, and mountain biking. Educational tours of the coastline's native plants and animals are available by appointment—contact the park to make arrangements. Expect to encounter and learn about trout, redfish, croaker, and flounder as well as tropical birds, ducks, marsh rabbits, and armadillos.

Park facilities include four miles of hike and bike trails, an interpretive center and nature trail, concrete boat ramp, fish-cleaning shelter, campsites with water and electricity, screened camping shelters, restrooms with showers, outdoor showers, picnic sites, and Wi-Fi access. The park contains 140 campsites with electricity and water hookups, and 10 screened shelters.

Less scenic but more centrally located is the **Bayou Shores RV Resort** (6310 Heards Ln., 409/744-2837). Located just off the causeway, the RV park offers standard hookups as well as a fishing pier and exercise facility.

FOOD

What else are you going to eat in Galveston but seafood? The city is brimming with quality restaurants, and almost all of them survived Hurricane Ike. So savor the local flavor. Fresh seafood is everywhere with several of the best places right on the bay just a few blocks from The Strand district. After you've had your fill of shrimp and oysters, try some of the Southern-style comfort food at one of the island's neighborhood joints.

Strand District

Something about arriving in a seaside town creates an instant yearning for a plate of shrimp or oysters or fish—sometimes all three—while overlooking the water. If you're in the downtown area, satisfy this urge at the low-key yet high-quality **Willie G's** (2100 Harborside, 409/762-3030, www.willieg.com, 11am-9:30pm daily, $9-31). Opt for bayside seating and let your ocean vacation begin. Order some peel-and-eat shrimp to start: squeeze fresh lemon on top and dip them in tangy cocktail sauce. Then proceed to the fresh catch of the day, from grilled flounder to fried trout. Welcome to Galveston!

Next door is the larger and consistently dependable **Fisherman's Wharf** (Pier 22 and Harborside Dr., 409/765-5708, 11am-10pm Sun.-Thurs., 11am-11pm Fri.-Sat., $9-30). Red snapper is the specialty here, but feel free to cast your eyes and teeth on the entire menu—shrimp kisses, oysters on the half shell, calamari, and even the steak and pasta are all tempting and tasty. Be sure to ask for a table with a view of the bay, where you can sit on the deck and watch the shrimp boats slowly glide by.

About a half mile inland you'll find one of the finest (and most expensive) restaurants in town. The fabulous 🅒 **Saltwater Grill** (2017

Post Office St., 409/762-3474, 11am–2pm and 5–10pm Mon.-Fri., 5-10pm Sat., $12-42) feels urban and spare like Houston but tastes fresh and flavorful like a Gulf Coast restaurant should. At Saltwater, *fresh* isn't just an appealing adjective, it's a genuine approach to food preparation. The restaurant utilizes a bizarre but effective steam-kettle device that's linked to a large heater, pipes, and steel buckets that cause water to boil in merely three minutes. The result is rapidly cooked fresh seafood as opposed to reheated or perpetually boiling (and soaking) fare. Enjoy the results on a plate of mussels, clams, or shrimp, and be sure to order the grand gumbo. Another must-taste is the appetizer dish with fried asparagus topped with crabmeat and entrées of grilled yellowfin tuna and seafood linguini. It's worth dropping by the next day for a big bowl of gumbo. Reservations are recommended.

For old-school, affordable, flavorful seafood, head to **Shrimp n' Stuff** (3901 Ave. O, 409/763-2805, www.shrimpnstuff.com, 11:30am-9pm Sun.-Thurs., 11:30am-2am Fri.-Sat.). Skip the "stuff" and head straight for the shrimp—fried, boiled, or grilled. This is a classic local joint, where you order at the counter, get your food in a Styrofoam box, and sit in packed quarters. Don't be surprised if you find yourself here for your next meal, drawn by another round of shrimp (prepared in a different style) and the lively atmosphere.

Despite its location on the Gulf Coast, Galveston doesn't have a strong Cajun flavor. That's not the case at **Little Daddy's Gumbo Bar** (2105 Post Office St., 409/744-8626, 11am-10pm Sun.-Thurs., 11am-11pm Fri.-Sat.). The tasty seafood gumbo, packed with oysters, shrimp, and crab, is worth the trip. For something heartier, feast on the meaty Mumbo Gumbo, a concoction of sausage, prime rib, and chicken. *Bon temps!*

The Strand is filled with confectioners' shops and small eateries that come and go, but several have become mainstays for lunch breaks during prolonged bouts of shopping. Among them is the aptly named **Lunchbox Cafe** (213 23rd St., 409/770-0044, www.

GALVESTON **91**

thelunchboxcafegalveston, 8am-3pm Mon.-Fri., 11 am-3pm Sat.-Sun., $8-19), a family-friendly spot with character that specializes in healthy sandwiches and salads. Sandwiches are a step beyond expectations, with nice touches like fresh organic apple slices on turkey and brie. The Cape Cod salad is also excellent, with a flavorful blend of field greens.

Step back in time at the charming and moderately priced **Star Drug Store** (510 23rd St., 409/766-7719, www.galvestondrug.com, 9am-3pm Sun.-Thurs., 9am-4pm Fri.-Sat., $6-11). The antique neon and porcelain Coca-Cola sign out front sets the tone for this establishment, featuring an almost century-old horseshoe-shaped lunch counter with soda fountain. Not surprisingly, the menu options are typical old-time lunch fare: burgers, Reubens, pimiento cheese sandwiches, chicken salad, dilled pasta salad, and ice-cream floats. The drugstore's signature item is a tasty tomato-basil soup.

Although it's nothing to write home about, **Schutte's Crossroads Cafe** (801 Post Office St., 409/762-2777, hours vary Mon.-Sat.) was a staple of nearby med school students before the university relocated after Hurricane Ike. Regardless, the café's reputation for providing affordable quality breakfasts and lunches remains intact, an often-welcome option for visitors who've shelled out big bucks for meals. Popular (and filling) lunch plates include meat loaf, fried chicken, and turkey wraps, accompanied by sweet potato fries.

Seawall and Vicinity

If you're staying in a hotel on Seawall Boulevard, your inaugural meal should definitely be at **Gaido's Seafood Restaurant** (3800 Seawall Blvd., 409/762-9625, 11am-9pm Sun.-Thurs., 11am-10pm Fri.-Sat., $9-30). This venerable institution has been serving memorable meals since 1911, and its legendary reputation is evident everywhere, from the time-honored trimmings to the traditional menu and attentive service. The shrimp bisque is exquisite and the crab cakes are outstanding.

For an amazing lunch with an outstanding view you gotta hit **The Spot** (3204 Seawall Blvd., 409/621-5237, www.thespotgalveston.com, 11am-10pm Sun.-Thurs., 11am-11pm Fri.-Sat., $8-19). After a morning or afternoon of beachcombing, this is a spot-on place for a shrimp po'boy, fish-and-chips, or even a big ol' burger. What sets this place aside from others is the crunchy breading and homemade bread, with a perfectly crispy texture encasing fresh seafood and top-notch sandwiches. A big bonus: The second-floor deck offers panoramic views of the gulf almost as tasty as the food in front of you.

Although it's a regional chain, **Landry's Seafood House** (5310 Seawall Blvd., 409/744-1010, www.landrysseafoodhouse.com, 11am-10pm Sun.-Thurs., 11am-11pm Fri.-Sat., $6-27) is a respected eatery, even in a Gulf Coast town known for its local legends. Opt for the fresh catch Lafitt or broiled flounder. Landry's also does shrimp well, including a fried option stuffed with seafood.

Specializing in the Cajun variety of seafood is **Benno's on the Beach** (1200 Seawall Blvd., 409/762-4621, www.bennosofgalveston.com, 11am-10pm daily, $8-19). This is a very unassuming place—guests order at the counter beneath dim fluorescent lights and sit on hard plastic booth chairs, but as soon as the food arrives, it's apparent where Benno's focuses its resources. The shrimp dishes are spectacular, bursting with flavor and perfectly seasoned with Cajun spices. You also can't go wrong with Benno's crawfish étouffée, jambalaya, spicy crab, or oysters.

For a true waterside dining experience, be sure to have a meal at **Jimmy's on the Pier** (9001 Seawall Blvd., 409/974-4726, www.galvestonfishingpier.com, 8am-2am daily, $8-27). Located at the base of the popular T-head fishing pier, Jimmy's is a step above other pier-based gulf restaurants, offering a variety of menu items (as opposed to beach grub from a greasy grill). Try to grab a table near the edge of the deck for the best view of surfside activity and a sunset. Jimmy's food ranges from standard burgers and pizza to blackened fish and broiled oysters. Everything on the menu is above average, especially paired with a St. Arnold's lager on tap.

One of the best restaurants in the entire region is just a few minutes from the shore at **◖ Mosquito Café** (628 14th St., 409/763-1010, www.mosquitocafe.com, $7-22, open at 11am Tues.-Fri., 8am Sat.-Sun.). You'll definitely want to have breakfast here at least once, and you may find yourself returning for each meal because the flavor-packed, creatively inspired, healthy food makes such an impression. Grab a hot mug of strong coffee and try to decide among the delectable options such as Mosquito Benedict (a fresh-baked scone covered with portabella mushrooms, sautéed shrimp, sun-dried tomatoes, artichoke hearts, asparagus, and poached eggs topped with serrano hollandaise sauce), cinnamon-tinged French toast, fluffy pancakes, or bagels and lox. Lunch items include hearty bowls of pasta with homemade pesto, olives, and feta cheese, or tasty sandwiches on delicious fresh-baked bread with hickory-smoked bacon, avocado salsa, and goat cheese.

For a simple, low-key breakfast, lunch, or dinner, drop by the nearby neighborhood stalwart, **Sunflower Bakery and Cafe** (512 14th St., 409/763-5500, 8am-7pm Mon.-Fri., 8am-9pm Sat., 8am-3pm Sun., $5-14). You'll find soft, warm fresh-made bakery items (breads, pastries, desserts) and flavor-packed sandwiches (the turkey, bacon, and avocado on honey wheat bread is especially tasty) along with healthy salads and even a few eclectic daily specials. The Sunflower has expanded its options from its humble beginnings as a modest bakery, offering a fresh and full menu complete with crab cakes, burgers, and po'boys. Incidentally, this is the perfect place to order a to-go lunch for the beach—just don't forget to include brownies and their legendary strawberry lemonade.

INFORMATION AND SERVICES

The **Galveston Convention and Visitors Bureau** (523 24th Street, 866/505-4456, www.galvestoncvb.com) offers brochures and maps with friendly staff on hand to answer questions. Contact the **Galveston Historical Foundation** (502 20th Street, 409/765-7834, www.galvestonhistory.org) for information about the island's impressive historical attractions.

GETTING THERE AND AROUND

The island's unique public transportation service, **Galveston Island Trolley** (409/797-3900, www.islandtransit.net, $1.25 adults), was damaged in Hurricane Ike but is back on the rails in a limited capacity. Call ahead to determine if it is offering similar services to its pre-Ike days: transportation from the Seawall to The Strand district and Pier 21. The cars are charming replicas of those used in Galveston from the late 1800s to the 1930s.

Brazosport Area

Brazosport isn't a town name, but a collection of eight Brazoria County communities southwest of Galveston offering an unassuming mix of lightly developed beachfront and petrochemical plants. It's not as bad as it sounds—the beaches are pleasantly uncrowded (most days), and the factories are beyond the view from the shoreline. For the record, the Brazosport communities are Clute, Freeport, Jones Creek, Lake Jackson, Oyster Creek, Quintana Beach, Richwood, and Surfside Beach.

The area is rich in Texas history, with the state's earliest explorers landing on nearby beaches nearly 500 years ago and Stephen F. Austin's first colony settling along the rich bottomlands of the Brazos, Colorado, and San Bernard Rivers in the early 19th century. The venerable Texas term "Old Three Hundred" refers to the 300 settlers who received land grants for Austin's first colony, where each family received up to 4,000 acres of fertile farm and ranch property in the area.

The massive Gulf Intracoastal Waterway carves a path along the coastal lowlands. This commercial boating canal, constructed in the 1940s, is considered the most valuable waterway in the country, transporting as much tonnage annually as the Panama Canal. The protected waterway stretches more than 1,000 miles from Brownsville to Florida.

Visitors to the Brazosport region enjoy the small-town specialty and antiques shops, beach home rentals, and casual ocean-based recreation. Drive, walk, or swim along the 21-mile stretch of beach or watch the seagulls and ocean barges lazily glide by. Other popular recreational activities include fresh- and saltwater fishing, boating, crabbing, and surfing.

SIGHTS

For a destination comprised of a collection of communities, the Brazosport area offers an intriguing mix of cultural attractions. Fortunately, the communities are within about a 20-minute drive of each other, so getting from one place to another takes the same amount of time as it does in a big city, just without the traffic (or stoplights).

Sea Center Texas

A must-see attraction in the Brazosport area is the spectacular **Sea Center Texas** (300 Medical Dr. in Lake Jackson, 979/292-0100, www.tpwd.state.tx.us, 9am-4pm Tues.-Sat., 1pm-4pm Sun., free admission). Sea Center Texas is a multiuse facility combining several aquariums, an education center, and a fish hatchery along with an outdoor wetland exhibit and a kids' fishing pond. The education center's main exhibit is a 50,000-gallon aquarium containing Gulf of Mexico marine animals such as nurse sharks, Atlantic spadefish, red drum, gray snapper, and an enormous moray eel. Other large aquariums house tropical species found in area salt marshes, coastal bays, jetties, artificial reefs, and coral reefs. Kids will love the center's "touch pool," where they can gently handle marine animals including several varieties of crabs, snails, and anemones. Outside, the wetland exhibit is accessible

by a long boardwalk over several marsh areas. Families can bring along a nature checklist and activity book to identify species in the area, including green tree frogs, turtles, and a wide variety of birds. The adjacent hatchery has the capacity to produce 20 million fingerlings each year (mostly spotted sea trout and red drum) for release into Texas coastal waters. Tours are available by reservation only.

The Center for the Arts & Sciences

Regional culture converges at the **The Center for the Arts & Sciences** (400 College Blvd. in Clute, 979/265-7661, www.bcfas.org, 10am-4pm Tues.-Sat., 2pm-5pm Sun., free admission). This all-inclusive facility is home to the Brazosport Art League, the Brazosport Museum of Natural Science, the Center Stages Theater, and Brazosport Planetarium. With so many cultural activities sharing space under one roof, you'll find an amazing array of attractions, from a colossal collection of seashells to an art gallery and studio to a theater staging regional productions. Perhaps most impressive is the natural science museum, containing wildlife, fossils, and an aquarium. Be sure to check out the exhibit featuring the Lightning Whelk (Texas's state shell) and the planetarium, which offers public viewings and previously served as a training facility for astronauts from NASA's nearby Johnson Space Center.

Varner-Hogg Plantation

Visitors strolling beneath outstretched oaks are immediately swept into a bygone world of Southern heritage at **Varner-Hogg Plantation** (1702 N. 13th St. in West Columbia, 979/345-4656, www.visitvarnerhoggplantation.com, closed Mon., $6 adults, $4 students). There's an undeniable charm to the lush grounds and distinguished historical buildings, occupied for most of the 1900s by the larger-than-life Hogg family, including the unfortunately named Miss Ima Hogg.

The site, owned by the Texas Historical Commission, showcases the Hogg family's remarkable 19th-century furnishings acquired

© ANDY RHODES

Varner-Hogg Plantation

from profits associated with the vast oil reserves discovered in the 1920s (at one point bringing in nearly $40,000 daily). Recently, efforts have turned toward the era of Columbus Patton, the plantation's second owner (following site namesake Martin Varner). During insightful tours of the historic plantation home, held seven times daily, guides educate visitors about the legacies of the three families connected to the property: Varner, Patton, and Hogg.

Brazoria National Wildlife Refuge

The sizable **Brazoria National Wildlife Refuge** (24907 FM 2004 in Angleton, 979/964-4011, www.fws.gov) contains protected habitats offering safe harbor for animals, particularly birds. Its prime location on the Gulf Coast draws more than 200 bird species, one of the highest counts in the nation. In winter, more than 100,000 snow geese, Canadian geese, teal, ducks, and sandhill cranes fill the numerous ponds and sloughs. In summer you'll find herons, egrets, white ibis, spoonbills, seaside sparrows, and scissor-tailed flycatchers. Alligators

occupy the refuge year-round on Big Slough and in ponds. Look for their trails through the mud and "gator holes" in dryer months.

San Bernard National Wildlife Refuge

The other major refuge in the Brazosport area is **San Bernard National Wildlife Refuge** (6801 County Rd. 306 in Brazoria, 979/849-6062, www.fws.gov). This 24,000-acre protected area is a haven for snow geese, warblers, herons, egrets, ibis, gulls, and terns. Most of the refuge is closed to the public, but the accessible three-mile car tour and several miles of hiking trails offer access to high-quality wildlife viewing.

BEACHES

The appeal of a low-profile beach can be soothing. The words "Brazosport area beaches" don't always prompt excitement or jealousy. And sometimes, that's exactly what visitors are seeking. Granted, these beaches can get crowded on summer weekends, but they're certainly not major tourist destinations. At Surfside and Bryan, the swimsuits are a couple seasons out of style, the beachcombers' bodies aren't designed for a *Sports Illustrated* cover, and the vibe is easy breezy.

Surfside Beach

If you don't mind a petrochemical plant just a mile away (fortunately not dominating the view), **Surfside Beach** is a delightful getaway for some low-key recreational activity. Though most of the folks here are Houston residents looking for a respite from the Galveston crowds, you'll find other beach lovers here from across the state seeking similar solace. Popular Surfside Beach pastimes include fishing, swimming, sailing, camping, and shell collecting. For information about the village of Surfside Beach, including restaurants, shops, and lodging links, visit www.surfsidebeachtx.org or call 979/233-1531.

Bryan Beach

Just a few miles away near the community of Freeport is **Bryan Beach,** another casual, scenic stretch of surf and sand. Grab a bucket for some sand dollar collecting, a pole for shallow surf fishing, or a towel and sunscreen for sunbathing. Primitive campsites are available nearby. To reach the beach from Freeport, travel two miles southwest of town on FM 1495, then head three miles south on Gulf Beach Road.

RECREATION

Two of the most popular recreational activities in the Brazosport Area are swimming and birding (see previous entries). However, fishing is one of the top draws, and kayaking and canoeing are emerging as viable options.

Fishing

The Brazosport Area offers a multitude of facilities for fishing, either inshore or deep sea. If you choose to keep your feet on the ground, plenty of jetties, piers, and beaches are available where you can cast a line for speckled trout, flounder, redfish, sheepshead, and gaff-topsail catfish. Nearby marinas and beachside shacks

sell tackle and bait. For deep-sea fishing, you can hire a service to provide charter boats to take you out farther for big-time catches including marlin, king mackerel, and sailfish. Two reputable outfits are **Easy Going Charters** (979/233-2947, www.easygulffishing.com), which can accommodate up to six people on its 35-foot-long boat, and **Johnston's Sportfishing** (979/233-8513).

A popular place to spend a weekend of fishing, camping, and lounging is **Quintana Beach County Park** (330 5th St., 979/233-1461 or 800/872-7578, www.brazoria-county.com), located on a picturesque barrier island near Freeport. The park's multilevel fishing pier is a favorite among anglers, and the day-use facilities include shaded pavilions, restrooms, showers, and the historic Coveney House, which houses a museum and natural history display. The camping sites include full hookups, showers, and laundry facilities. From Freeport, take FM 1495 south nearly two miles to County Road 723, then head east three miles to the park entrance.

Paddling

For some low-impact coastal kayaking or canoeing, give yourself a gift and head to **Christmas Bay Paddling Trail** (515 Amigo Ln., Freeport, 979/233-5159, www.tpwd.state.tx.us). The trail is about 19 miles long, with a 4-mile option. Known for its fishing and birding opportunities, the Christmas Bay trail also has extensive oyster reefs and a salt marsh.

Another good area to explore via kayak is the **Brazos River Trail** (www.houstonwilderness.org). Part of a 125-mile system stretching upriver to Houston, the water trail winds through the dense bottomlands, towering trees, and palmetto thickets. Paddlers can experience a wide variety of wildlife species and migrating birds. Launch points in the Brazosport Area are Brazos River County Park in Angleton and Wilderness Park in Lake Jackson.

ACCOMMODATIONS

Here's a nice change of pace: The Brazosport area is overrun with local lodging options,

THE GULF COAST

© ANDY RHODES

Cedar Sands Motel on Surfside Beach

with nary a garish hotel-chain sign in sight. Independently owned hotels are the norm, and many travelers opt to rent a beach house or cabin for the weekend.

Hotels

Those looking for a clean, comfy place to stay within walking distance of the beach should consider the **Cedar Sands Motel** (343 Beach Dr. in Surfside Beach, 979/233-1942, www.cedarsandsmotel.net, $75-150, depending on room size and season). One-bedroom options are available, but you may want to splurge for the kitchenettes, including pots and pans, a queen-size bed, and a pull-out bed. All rooms have refrigerators, microwaves, and free wireless Internet access.

For a step up in quality and price, head to **Ocean Village Hotel** (310 Ocean Village Dr., 979/239-1213, www.oceanvillagehotel.com, rooms start at $149 d). Surfside Beach's newest hotel, the Ocean Village is a nice spot with several amenities not found at other accommodations in the area, namely, direct beach

access and an attached restaurant and bar (Pirate's Alley Café). The hotel offers ocean-view rooms with large private decks, free Wi-Fi, pet-friendly rooms, and extended-stay suites with kitchens.

More casual and representative of many of the sun-bleached, wind-worn, slightly shabby beach hotels is **Surfside Motel** (330 Coral Ct. in Surfside Beach, 979/233-4948, www.surfsidemotel.biz, $65-120). The motel offers kitchenettes with two queen-size beds, one twin bed, and a full kitchen, or two-room suites with one queen-size bed, a pull-out bed, small refrigerator, and microwave. Check with the front desk if you need beach towels, board games, or horseshoes.

Of course, chain hotels provide reliable consistency for some travelers, so if slightly shabby isn't your thing, you'll have to venture four miles off the coast to the nearby community of Clute. The best option is **La Quinta** (1126 Hwy. 332 W., 979/265-7461, www.lq.com, $69 d), featuring free wireless Internet access, a free continental breakfast, and an outdoor pool.

Another fine choice is **Holiday Inn Express** (1117 Hwy. 332 W., 979/266-8746, www.hiexpress.com, $107 d), offering wireless Internet access, a workout facility, and a free continental breakfast.

Beach Home Rentals

Hundreds of rooms are available in cabins and beach homes along the gulf in the Brazosport area. The best way to find something that fits your specific needs (pets, kids, weekends, beach access, etc.) is to contact a rental locating service. Two of the more commendable outlets in the area are **Beach Resort Services** (800/382-9283, www.beachresortservices.com) and **Brannan Resort Rentals, Inc.** (979/233-1812, www.brri.com). For a comprehensive list of companies, visit the following visitor-related sites: www.visitbrazosport.com and www.surfsidetx.org.

Camping

Families and RVers make repeated returns to **Quintana Beach County Park** (979/233-1461,

Pirate's Alley Cafe on Surfside Beach

www.brazoriacountyparks.com, $15-27), featuring 56 paved and level camping sites, full hookups, primitive tent sites, a bathhouse with restrooms, showers, and laundry facilities. Cabins—complete with TVs, microwaves, kitchenettes, and charming wooden detailing—are also available for rent, ranging from $135 to $160, depending on the season.

A popular option for anglers is **Surfside Beach RV Park** (102 Fort Velesco Dr., 979/233-6919, www.surfsidebeachrv.com, $25-30), offering full hookup RV sites, free parking for fishing boats, an on-site laundry, and free wireless Internet access.

FOOD

Let's assume you'll be spending most of your time at the beach. And we can presume you'll also be hungry at some point. The good news is Surfside Beach has several good vacation-style eateries. The best of the bunch is the **Red Snapper Inn** (402 Bluewater Hwy., 979/239-3226, www.redsnapperinn.com, 11am-2pm Mon.-Fri., 5pm-9pm, 11am-9pm Sat.-Sun., $9-23). This quality surf-and-turf restaurant is best known for its seafood items, including the grilled boneless flounder stuffed with crabmeat dressing, the fried soft-shell crabs with rémoulade sauce, bacon-wrapped oysters, and sautéed garlic shrimp. For the turf, most diners opt for the spaghetti and charbroiled Greek-style meatballs or the classic chicken-fried steak.

The newest eatery in Sunset Beach doesn't have the greatest food. But it certainly has the greatest view, and sometimes that's a deciding factor. **Pirate's Alley Cafe** (310 Ocean Ave., 979/239-2233, www.piratesalleytx.com, 11am-9pm Sun.-Thurs., 11am-10pm Fri.-Sat., $5-14) has the best deck on the beach, featuring dozens of tables overlooking the surf and sand. The food isn't quite as stunning, but if you arrive with realistic expectations, you won't be disappointed. For example, instead of anticipating an award-winning gulfside seafood meal, look to enjoy a cold beer and hearty burger on the porch. Rather than a fancy breakfast, opt for a hot coffee and bagel.

Just around the corner, you can't miss **Kitty's**

THE GULF COAST

Purple Cow (323 Ocean Ave., 979/233-9161, www.kittyspurplecow.com, 10am-10pm Mon.-Fri., 7am-10pm Sat.-Sun., $4-9). The food isn't quite as attention grabbing as the restaurant's facade, a distractingly purple building just a block off the beach. Regardless, Kitty's specializes in tasty meaty burgers and even a little seafood (boiled shrimp) from the unfortunately named "app-moo-tizers" menu. Breakfast is also available (after 10am on weekdays), with hearty portions of biscuits and gravy and standard egg dishes.

Locals loiter at the low-key **Jetty Shack** (412 Parkview St., 979/233-5300, hours vary, $5-11), a beachside dive offering a tasty Angus burger, plenty of fried food, grilled cheese, and cold beer.

Any beach town worth its weight in sand dollars has a classic burger joint—in Surfside, that's **Castaway Bar & Grill** (979/233-7270, www.castawaybar.net, hours vary, $5-12), where you can order a big ol' greasy burger and fries to eat in or take out and enjoy with the waves.

INFORMATION AND SERVICES

The **Brazosport Visitors and Convention Council** (main office at 300 Abner Jackson Pkwy. in Lake Jackson, 979/285-2501 or 888/477-2505, www.brazosport.org) provides details on area attractions, accommodations, and restaurants, as well as brochures and maps to help you find your way around

Corpus Christi

Corpus Christi (population 305,215) is the largest city on Texas's Gulf Coast and one of the most popular destinations in the state for seaside recreation, including fishing, sailing, swimming, and windsurfing.

The city has experienced a precipitous history, with drought, conflicts with Native American tribes, and various wars preventing settlements from taking hold until the mid-1800s, when a trading post was established and a small village developed that eventually became known as Corpus Christi, which translates into "the Body of Christ." Just when the town started growing, a yellow fever epidemic decimated the population, and it was subsequently plagued for decades by the lack of a deepwater port.

In 1916 and 1919, torrential storms destroyed portions of the city, erasing grand hotels and palatial homes. As a result, Corpus Christi, dubbed the "Sparkling City by the Bay," can appear historically lackluster, with a deficiency of significant structures reflecting its heritage. Regardless, historical homes and churches still exist in downtown neighborhoods unaffected by hurricanes and wrecking balls.

By the middle of the 20th century, Corpus

(as it's known throughout the state) became a major petroleum and shipping center, with coastal shipments of gasoline, crude petroleum, and natural gas bringing increased corporate activity. Also contributing to the economy were the military bases and the petroleum and petrochemical industry, particularly the six refineries making good use of the approximately 1,500 oil wells in the area.

Despite its fairly large population, Corpus retains the feel of a small city, albeit one with remarkable museums and top-notch seafood restaurants. Corpus Christi's mild year-round temperatures and inviting tropical climate draw visitors from across the country to its cultural and recreational opportunities and the abundant sunshine glistening on this "Sparkling City by the Bay."

SIGHTS
◖ Texas State Aquarium

The magnificent **Texas State Aquarium** (2710 N. Shoreline Blvd., 361/881-1200, www.texas-stateaquarium.org, 9am-5pm daily, $17 adults, $16 seniors, $12 children ages 3-12, parking $5) offers an ideal way to take a quick break from the beach while still being surrounded by

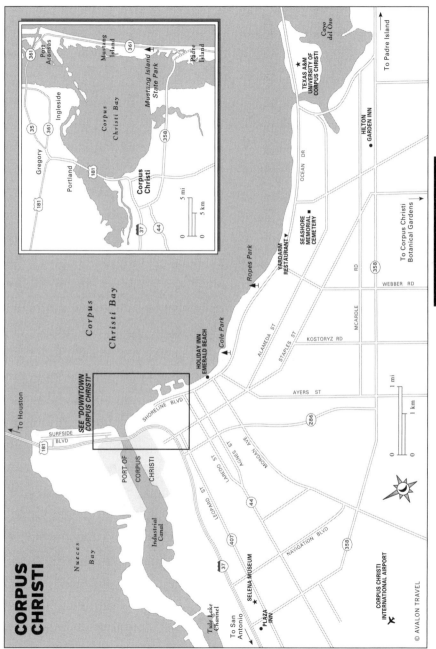

CORPUS CHRISTI

THE GULF COAST

To Houston

Nueces Bay

SURFSIDE BLVD

181

PORT OF CORPUS CHRISTI

Industrial Canal

Tule Lake Channel

To San Antonio

37

SELENA MUSEUM ★

PLAZA INN ●

LEOPARD ST

LAREDO ST

AGNES ST

MORGAN AVE

407

44

NAVIGATION BLVD

358

CORPUS CHRISTI INTERNATIONAL AIRPORT ✈

© AVALON TRAVEL

Corpus Christi Bay

SEE "DOWNTOWN CORPUS CHRISTI"

SHORELINE BLVD

HOLIDAY INN EMERALD BEACH ●

Cole Park

Ropes Park

ALAMEDA ST

STAPLES ST

AYERS ST

286

0   1 mi

0   1 km

YARDARM RESTAURANT ▶

SEASHORE MEMORIAL CEMETERY ■

OCEAN DR

RD

MCARDLE

KOSTORYZ RD

WEBBER RD

358

To Corpus Christi Botanical Gardens

TEXAS A&M UNIVERSITY OF CORPUS CHRISTI ★

Cayo del Oso

To Padre Island

HILTON GARDEN INN ●

Inset map:

361

Port Aransas

Mustang Island

361

Padre Island

Ingleside

Mustang Island State Park

35

361

Gregory

Portland

181

Corpus Christi Bay

358

Corpus Christi

37

44

0   5 mi

0   5 km

THE GULF COAST

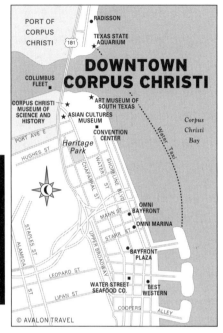

the region's fascinating natural resources. The layout of the aquarium is rather clever, leading visitors into Texas's marine world at sea level with exhibits containing birds, alligators, and stingrays, and proceeding to explore the Gulf of Mexico at sequentially deeper levels. One of the aquarium's main exhibits showcases menacing sharks, a 350-pound grouper, and hundreds of other species as they slither and glide around the barnacle-encrusted poles of a replicated off-shore oil rig. The 350,000-gallon Dolphin Bay habitat uses seawater from Corpus Christi Bay for the Atlantic bottlenose dolphins that cannot live in the wild. A shaded seating area provides respite from the relentless sun for daily interpretive programs, and a lengthy viewing window allows visitors to get nose to nose with the dolphins. Other popular exhibits include Otter Space, featuring the frisky fellas cavorting on slides and in pools, and Living Shores, allowing kids to handle nonthreatening sea creatures. The aquarium expanded to include terrestrial critters, particularly in the Amazon

rain forest exhibit, containing boa constrictors and poison dart frogs, and in the bird theater, featuring "flight performances" by hawks, falcons, and parrots. In 2010, the aquarium introduced Swamp Tales, an exhibit dedicated to conservation efforts in the region, especially with American alligators like Bo, the museum's featured 10-foot 'gator.

◖ USS *Lexington* Museum

You can't miss the massive **USS *Lexington* Museum** (2914 N. Shoreline Blvd., 361/888-4873, www.usslexington.com, open 9am-5pm daily Labor Day-Memorial Day, until 6pm in the summer, $14 adults, $12 seniors and military, $9 children ages 4-12). Looming large in the Corpus Christi Bay, the USS *Lexington* is a decommissioned World War II naval aircraft carrier now serving as a 33,000-ton floating museum to transport visitors back in time with tours of the ship's decks and quarters, educational exhibits, restored aircraft, a high-tech flight simulator, and a collection of historical memorabilia. The music and voices blaring from speakers and interaction with the ship's docents gives an authentic feel for life aboard the nation's longest-serving aircraft carrier. The best way to experience the *Lexington* is via one of the five self-guided tours covering 100,000 square feet on 11 decks. Afterward, take some time atop the flight deck to soak up the view of the bay, the city skyline, and the impressive vintage aircraft.

Corpus Christi Museum of Science and History

To get a better sense of the area's colorful past, drop by the **Corpus Christi Museum of Science and History** (1900 N. Chaparral St., 361/826-4667, www.ccmuseum.com, 10am-5pm Tues.-Sat., noon-5pm Sun., $14.50 adults, $12 seniors, $8 children ages 5-12). The museum features a myriad of educational exhibits emphasizing how the Gulf Coast and the natural and cultural world relate. Particularly fascinating is the *Ships of Christopher Columbus* exhibit, featuring authentic reproductions of the *Niña, Pinta,* and *Santa Maria.* The three

Texas State Aquarium

vessels, located outside the museum and accessible to visitors, were built in Spain to commemorate the 500th anniversary of Christopher Columbus's voyage to the New World. Each ship was made with authentic 15th-century materials such as hand-forged nails and wood from the same forests used for Columbus's ships. The museum's other noteworthy exhibits are also maritime related, including an interactive shipwreck display containing artifacts from three Spanish treasure ships that ran aground on Padre Island in 1554, an exhibit featuring artifacts related to the ill-fated *Belle* shipwreck of French explorer Robert Cavelier, Sieur de La Salle, and the Children's Wharf, a bustling learning area for youngsters. The remainder of the museum contains a comprehensive collection of more than 28,000 objects (shells, Native American crafts, bird and reptile eggs) representing the history and culture of South Texas.

Heritage Park

Just down the street from the science museum is the city's **Heritage Park** (1581 N. Chaparral St., 361/826-3410, www.cctexas.com, 9am-5pm Tues.-Thurs., 9am-2pm Fri., Galván House is free to the public). These 12 restored Victorian-era historic homes were moved to the city's cultural area to protect them from being demolished and to showcase the city's diverse past. The centerpiece is the Cultural Center's Galván House, open for free tours.

Asian Cultures Museum

Also located in the city's cultural district is the **Asian Cultures Museum** (1809 N. Chaparral St., 361/882-2641, www.asianculturesmuseum. org, 10am-4pm Tues.-Sat., $6 adults, $4 students, $3 children 12 and under), offering an interesting array of objects and artwork from across the Pacific. What started as a local resident's personal collection of cultural objects has evolved into a full-fledged museum containing thousands of items representing nearly a dozen Asian countries. Billie Trimble Chandler spent decades as a teacher and art collector in Asia and brought items back to share with Corpus residents and to educate them about

LA SALLE'S LEGACY

French explorer Robert Cavelier, **Sieur de La Salle,** left an enormous legacy in Texas. Though he's well known for his exploration in the Great Lakes region, La Salle's ambitious nature and tremendous hubris ultimately led to his demise after a doomed colonization effort on the Texas Gulf Coast.

In 1684, La Salle embarked on a mission to build forts along the mouth of the Mississippi River to attack and occupy Spanish territory in Mexico. His expedition proved to be a series of failures, beginning when pirates in the West Indies captured one of his ships and continuing with sickness, misdirection, and shipwrecks.

While searching for the mouth of the Mississippi, La Salle missed his target (by a wide margin—nearly 500 miles) and instead landed at present-day Matagorda Bay on the central Gulf Coast of Texas. One of his ships was lost offshore, and another, La Belle, became stranded on a sandbar during a storm.

La Salle made several more attempts to find the Mississippi, but they ultimately proved unsuccessful. Though he eventually established Fort St. Louis near the coast, his subsequent attempt to lead a party in search of reinforcements proved to be the last adventure this famed explorer would take—he was killed by his own men near present-day Navasota, Texas.

La Salle's legacy would be rekindled nearly 300 years later when his wrecked ship La Belle was discovered by marine archaeologists with the Texas Historical Commission. Considered one of the most important shipwrecks ever discovered in North America, the excavation produced an amazing array of finds, including the hull of the ship, three bronze cannons, thousands of glass beads, and even a crew member's skeleton. The artifacts have been carefully cleaned and preserved and are currently displayed at numerous Gulf Coast museums.

faraway lands. Since then, the museum has grown to include clothing, furniture, paintings, dolls, statues, and other art objects from Japan, Korea, China, the Philippines, Taiwan, and other Asian countries. The museum also features international traveling exhibits and offers educational classes for students and the general public.

Selena Museum

Latin-music fans often make a pilgrimage to the **Selena Museum** (5410 Leopard St., 361/289-9013, www.q-productions.com, 10am-4pm Mon.-Fri., $3 admission 12 and up, $1 children). It's not an easy place to find, though. The museum is located downtown just off I-37 in a warehouse-type building with no sign (look for the painted mural of Selena on the outside) and was created by Corpus resident Abraham Quintanilla to honor the memory of his daughter, the famous Tejana singer who was killed by the president of her fan club in 1995. The

museum showcases many of Selena's personal memorabilia, including the outfits and dresses she designed and wore at concerts, her red Porsche, penciled sketches, her prized egg collection, and letters of sympathy from fans across the world.

Art Museum of South Texas

Culture converges at the **Art Museum of South Texas** (1902 N. Shoreline Blvd., 361/825-3500, www.stia.org, 10am-5pm Tues.-Sat., 1pm-5pm Sun., $8 adults, $6 seniors and military, $4 students 12 and older). The three-story building is unmistakable, with bright white concrete walls and 13 rooftop pyramids overlooking the bay. Inside, you'll find several galleries showcasing the museum's 1,300 works of art, primarily paintings and sculpture representing the Americas with a focus on Texas, Mexico, and the Southwest. The museum also contains an interactive kids' playroom, classrooms, studios, a gift shop, and an auditorium.

Corpus Christi Botanical Gardens and Nature Center

Those who want to appreciate the area's natural beauty beyond the beach should visit the **Corpus Christi Botanical Gardens and Nature Center** (8545 S. Staples St., 361/852-2100, www.stxbot.org, 9am-6pm daily, $7 adults, $6 seniors and military, $3 children ages 5-12). Exotic gardens and perfectly landscaped lawns await visitors at this popular attraction, which takes full advantage of its tropical climate to produce vibrant colors and lush landscapes. One of the center's showpieces is the Rose Garden, featuring 300 roses, a large pavilion, and a beautiful lightly lapping fountain. Other noteworthy areas are the hummingbird garden, the orchid garden with 2,500 flowering plants, and the hibiscus garden.

BEACHES

Serious beachcombers and bodysurfers skip the bayside beaches and head straight to the long stretches of sand on the barrier islands 10 miles east of town on the Gulf of Mexico. If you're staying downtown and need a quick beach fix, go to **Corpus Christi Beach** (just north of the USS *Lexington,* 361/880-3480). It's not quite picturesque, and the shoreline sand is pretty coarse, but it's great for a leisurely stroll or swim with a pleasant view of Corpus Christi Bay. You'll see lots of local families playing in the sand or flying kites, and several spots offer rinse-off showers, restrooms, and small cabana huts with picnic tables. Much smaller in size yet within walking distance of downtown hotels is **Magee Beach** (Shoreline Blvd. at Park St., 361/880-3461). This 250-yard stretch of sand on the bay isn't designed for shell collecting, but it's a good place to get your feet wet without worrying about them being pulled away by the undertow you'll encounter on the larger ocean beaches. Showers and restrooms are located on the north end of the beach.

RECREATION
Paddling

Kayakers are increasingly flocking to Corpus Christi for the variety of options and conditions. The two primary options—saltwater kayaking and bay paddling—offer beginners and experienced paddlers a fun way to spend a few hours on the water.

Saltwater kayaking, aka sea kayaking, is typically more difficult since it can involve choppy and unpredictable conditions. Still, it's often more fun because the waves don't tend to reach intimidating or dangerous heights, and the routes can be longer and less restricted.

Bay paddling is ideal for beginning kayakers and offers calmer conditions and shorter trail options. A good starting point is the **Mustang Island State Park Paddling Trail** (www.tpwd.state.tx.us) with several routes ranging from the 5-mile **Shamrock Loop** to the 8.5-mile **North Trail,** which meander through coves and marshes. The park's **Ashum Trail** (nearly 7 miles) traces the Corpus Christi Bay shoreline and includes some quality birding and fishing opportunities.

Several area outfitters offer rental and tour options, including **Capt. Sally's Rockport Outdoors** (204 S. Austin St. in Rockport, 361/205-9624) and **Coastal Bend Kayak** (1125 S. Commercial St. in Portland, 361/557-7003, www.coastalbendkayaking.com).

Fishing

Corpus is a major destination for fishing and has plenty of locations and services to accommodate those interested. You'll find anglers with poles anchored in the sand at several city beaches, including Corpus Christi Beach, where fishers often gather at the **Nueces Bay Pier** at the end of Hull Street. Lines are also cast along the bay on the massive concrete downtown piers (known locally as T heads), at several spots along the seawall, and at lighted breakwater jetties. Another popular spot is **Bob Hall Pier** at Padre Balli Park on North Padre Island. Its prime location and abundance of fish species (tarpon, mackerel, redfish, and even shark) have drawn anglers to this venerable and productive location since the 1950s.

If you'd rather get out to sea for some big-game fishing, contact a charter or rental company to set you up with all the gear, guides,

© ANDY RHODES

Corpus Christi Beach

and good advice you'd ever want. Deep-sea boats are available for those who want to troll for Gulf of Mexico species such as marlin, sailfish, tuna, and kingfish. Reputable companies include **C&T Bay Charters** (4034 Barnes St., 888/227-9172, www.ctbaycharters.com) and Port Aransas-based **Deep Sea Headquarters** (416 W. Cotter Ave., 361/749-5597, www.deepseaheadquarters.com), providing private excursions to anglers of all ages and skill levels.

Windsurfing

Thanks to its constant easy breeze (averaging 15-20 mph), Corpus is a mecca for windsurfers. Although some try their sails on the bay at city locales like **Cole Park** (near the 2000 block of Ocean Dr., restrooms available), most windsurfers head to North Padre Island, particularly **Bird Island Basin** at the Padre Island National Seashore. This half-mile stretch of beach is internationally recognized as one of the top windsurfing sites on the continental United States. If you've never grabbed hold of a sail, this is the best place to learn because a breeze

is always a blowin'. To set yourself up with all the gear, contact **Worldwinds Windsurfing** (11493 S. Padre Island Dr., 361/949-7472, www.worldwinds.net) or **Wind & Wave Water Sports** (10721 S. Padre Island Dr., 361/937-9283, www.windandwave.net).

Hiking and Biking

Recreational opportunities in Corpus are almost exclusively water based. With so many options available in the bay and gulf, the development of organized land-based trails for hiking and biking has not been a priority for government entities or private organizations.

Regardless, a couple of trails are available for those in search of something more inspiring than the hotel treadmill. The city's primary option is known as **Bay Trail,** an 8-mile route hugging the namesake bay. An extremely scenic option, it offers views of downtown buildings, tourist attractions, and bird habitats. To download a copy of the trail map, visit www.ccparkandrec.com.

Another option is the hike-and-bike trail on the campus of **Texas A&M Corpus Christi.**

© ANDY RHODES

Windsurfing is a breeze on the Gulf Coast.

Although students and faculty primarily populate the 3-mile route, it's open to the public, and offers a well-lit paved path for safety. For a map, visit www.tamucc.edu.

Horseback Riding

Have you ever wanted to ride a horse on the beach, with the waves gently crashing at your trusty steed's feet with the ocean breeze whipping through your hair? Then gallop over to **Horses on the Beach** (16562 S. Padre Island Dr., 361/443-4487, www.horsesonthebeachcorpus.com, several rides offered daily, reservations required), located just north of Padre Island National Seashore. Horses are available for first timers, children, and experienced riders, and the stable owners also handle lessons. You're welcome to walk, trot, or ride your horse into the surf.

ENTERTAINMENT AND EVENTS
Bars and Clubs

Although many visitors choose to sip their cocktails on the beach or in the hotel bar, there are options available for the adventurous souls who want to see some live music or perhaps even mingle with the locals.

The best place to soak up the scene without feeling like an outsider is the downtown **Executive Surf Club** (309 N. Water St., 361/884-2364, www.executivesurfclub.com). Located adjacent to the Water Street Seafood Co., the Surf Club's decor reflects its name, with vintage surfboards on the walls and refurbished as tables. The scene is lively yet casual, with live music most nights (mainly Texas rock and blues acts, often with a cover charge), more than 30 beers on tap, and a kitchen serving up tasty grub.

Another visitor-friendly spot is the decidedly more upscale **Republic of Texas Bar & Grill** (900 N. Shoreline Blvd., 361/886-3515, www.omnihotels.com/republic). Sitting atop the 20th floor of the Omni Bayfront hotel, the Republic of Texas bar is dimly lit and heavily wooded in a welcoming way. The views of the bay and city are outstanding, the drinks are expertly made, and the pianist provides a perfect soundtrack. Grab a Scotch, margarita, or a draft beer and soak up the surrounding scenery.

Veering in a local direction is the younger and more boisterous **Dr. Rockit's Blues Bar** (709 N. Chaparral St., 361/884-7634, www.dr-rockitsbluesbar.com). Located along a formerly vibrant stretch of Chaparral Street in the heart of downtown, Dr. Rockit's is still thriving, and it's still all about the blues. Live bands from Corpus and across the state play here nightly, and the place can get pretty rockin' when the bands get rollin'. Check the website for a live music schedule and cover charges.

Just down the street is a laid-back locale, **Bourbon Street Bar and Grill** (313 N. Chaparral St., 361/882-2082), a New Orleans-style establishment with Cajun food and free-flowing drinks. The activity kicks up a notch in Bourbon Street's Voodoo Lounge and next door at **Porky's Saloon.** For something a little more lively and trendy, consider dropping by **Havana Club** (500 N. Water St., 361/882-5552). Havana is the place to go for salsa dancing, live jazz bands, and DJs spinning club music. The club's motto is "Enjoy your life!" so plan accordingly.

Performing Arts

The grand dame of Corpus Christi's performing arts scene is **Corpus Christi Ballet** (1621 N. Mesquite St. 361/882-4588, www.corpuschristiballet.com). Staging several ballets annually, including classics like *The Nutcracker* and children's fare like *Cinderella,* Corpus Christi Ballet is a first-rate classical company that emphasizes the importance of teaching the cultural arts to younger residents and audience members.

One of the newest classical venues in town is the **Performing Arts Center at Texas A&M Corpus Christi** (6300 Ocean Dr., 361/825-5700, www.pac.tamucc.edu). The impressive $18 million facility is known for its excellent sound and quality amenities. The performers here are mainly from the classical realm, with featured names from the past few years including pianist Van Cliburn, Mezzo Soprano Frederica von Stade, and violinists Itzhak Perlman and Joshua Bell.

Perhaps the most venerable performing arts organization in Corpus Christi is the **Harbor Playhouse** (1 Bayfront Park, 361/882-5500, www.harborplayhouse.com). The non-profit community theater traces its history to 1925. Corpus residents have spent nearly a century enjoying the group's staging of classic musicals and plays such as *Annie, The Sound of Music,* and *A Christmas Carol.*

Events

Since Corpus is known primarily for its recreational activities and natural resources, its annual events tend to be more community oriented than splashy statewide destinations. As a result, the local charm on display is worth making an effort to experience.

The city's most venerable annual event is **Buccaneer Days** (www.bucdays.com). Held every April, the (somewhat) pirate-themed event plays up its swashbuckling theme with the mayor being captured by pirates and forced to "walk the plank." Founded in 1938, Buc Days features a rodeo, carnival, and parades.

The other long-standing major event in town is **Bayfest.** The three-day music festival prides itself on being an entirely volunteer-run event, and attracts more than 100,000 people each year for local, regional, and statewide bands.

SHOPPING

Corpus has several malls that don't differ much from others across the country, and many of the vacationers looking for trinkets and T-shirts opt for the souvenir shops in Port Aransas. However, several places in town are worth checking out that offer quality clothing and jewelry, imported goods, and beach gear. Among them is **Pilar Gallery** (3814 S. Alameda, 361/853-7171), a colorful shop with quality women's clothing, tapestries, rugs, and imported jewelry and folk art from Mexico and across the globe. You'll also find an amazing array of imports and curios at **El Zocalo Imports** (601 N. Water St. in the Omni Bayfront hotel, 361/887-8847). Though the primary focus here is Mexican jewelry, shoppers will find an interesting mix of objects, from crosses and candleholders to books and belt buckles.

Every beach city needs a good surf shop, and Corpus has several rad options to choose from. Hodads to heroes will find boards, surf wear, kayaks, skateboards, and surf and skate accessories at **Wind & Wave Water Sports** (10721 S. Padre Island Dr., 361/937-9283, www.windandwave.net) or **Worldwinds Windsurfing** (11493 S. Padre Island Dr., 361/949-7472, www.worldwinds.net).

ACCOMMODATIONS

Corpus has no shortage of lodging options, and most have decent views with easy access to the bay and fairly reasonable rates for a vacation destination. Plenty of budget options are available in the area near the airport and greyhound racetrack, but most leisure travelers feel it's worth dropping the extra cash to stay in a place by the sea. If you're looking for a nice spot away from the city, consider a condo (nightly rates available) on alluring Mustang Island or North Padre Island, about 10-15 miles from downtown directly on the Gulf Coast.

$50-100

You can do the beach on a bargain, if you consider lodging in the $90s a good deal. Not surprisingly, the more affordable hotels tend to be farther down the shoreline, but for many visitors, the key word is *shoreline,* so proximity isn't a concern.

One of the better deals in town is the **Budget Inn & Suites** (801 S. Shoreline Blvd., 888/493-2950, www.budgetinnandsuitescc.com, $69 d), located within walking distance of Cole Park, one of the city's premier windsurfing spots. The hotel's amenities include a free continental breakfast, free wireless Internet service, and an outdoor pool and sundeck.

A bit closer to the action is **Knights Inn** (3615 Timon Blvd., 361/883-4411, www.knightsinn.com, $78 d), sitting just a couple blocks off the bay and offering private balconies, several ocean-view rooms, free wireless Internet access, refrigerators, microwaves, and an outdoor pool.

A reasonable deal in the heart of downtown is the **Bayfront Plaza Hotel** (601 N. Water St., 361/882-8100, www.bayfrontplazahotelcc.com, $89 d). The 10-story atrium lobby and interior corridor is pleasant, unless you're trying to get to sleep while a jazz band is enthusiastically playing in the bar. You can walk to restaurants and nightclubs from here and even stroll down to the T-head piers or tiny Magee Beach. The hotel's amenities include a free breakfast, a large outdoor swimming pool, wireless Internet access, and free covered parking.

The best deal in the $100 range is **Quality Inn & Suites** (3202 Surfside Blvd., 361/883-7456, www.qualityinn.com, $99 d), thanks to its prime location on Corpus Christi Beach in the shadow of the USS *Lexington* and Texas State Aquarium. The hotel also features an outdoor beachside pool and a hot tub, free continental breakfast, and rooms with microwaves and refrigerators.

$100-150

A bit farther up the road in location and price is **Days Inn** (4302 Surfside Blvd., 361/882-3297, www.daysinn.com, $119 d), a block off Corpus Christi Beach. Amenities include rooms with microwaves, fridges, and free Wi-Fi access, along with a complimentary continental breakfast and outdoor pool.

Closer to downtown is the **Plaza Inn** (2021 N. Padre Island Dr., 361/289-8200, www.plazainnhotels.com, $129 d), offering a nice range of complimentary eats, from hot breakfast in the morning to popcorn and soda in the afternoon to beverages and appetizers in the evenings. The Plaza Inn also has an outdoor pool, free Wi-Fi service, and is pet friendly.

Another good option in this price range is the **Holiday Inn Express** (5213 Oakhurst Dr., 361/857-7772, www.hiexpress.com, $118 d), with free Wi-Fi service, a complimentary hot breakfast bar, and a fitness center with an indoor pool and a whirlpool.

A bit farther east is **Hilton Garden Inn** (6717 S. Padre Island Dr., 361/991-8200, www.hiltongardeninn.hilton.com, $119 d), which has a heated outdoor pool with Jacuzzi, complimentary high-speed Internet access, a microwave and minifridge in each room, and 32-inch flat-screen LCD TVs.

Just off the busy South Padre Island Drive is **Hampton Inn** (5209 Blanche Moore Dr., 361/985-8395, www.hamptoninn.com, $119 d), featuring free Internet access, a complimentary breakfast, to-go breakfast bags (on weekdays), an outdoor pool, and a fitness center.

Another downtown option is the **Best Western Marina Grand Hotel** (300 N. Shoreline Blvd., 361/883-5111, www.bestwestern.com, $139 d), offering rooms with private balconies and marina views, wireless Internet access, microwaves, refrigerators, a free continental breakfast, and an outdoor pool and exercise facility.

Farther south along the bayside is **Holiday Inn Emerald Beach** (1102 S. Shoreline Blvd., 800/465-4329, www.ichotelsgroup.com, $143 d). Also located along a nice stretch of beach, the Holiday Inn has an indoor pool and fitness center along with an indoor recreation area (heated pool, playground, Ping-Pong tables, billiard tables, vending machines, etc.).

THE GULF COAST

The hotel offers wireless Internet access and free meals for children.

A bit farther away from the bay is **Staybridge Suites** (5201 Oakhurst Dr., 361/857-7766, www.staybridgecc.com, $149 d). Features include a "sundowner reception" (Tues.-Thurs.) with complimentary light meals along with beer, wine, and soft drinks, as well as a free hot breakfast. Other amenities include a fitness center, whirlpool, outdoor pool, and free Wi-Fi service.

The best choice for those who want to stay directly on the beach is the **C Radisson** (3200 Surfside Blvd., 361/883-9700, www.radisson.com, $149 d). Step out the back doors and onto the sand of Corpus Christi Beach, a pleasant stretch of shoreline on the bay that often plays host to a large number of families, flotsam and jetsam, and the USS *Lexington*. Though the interior corridors are somewhat dark, the rooms are bright and cheery, with private balconies, microwaves, refrigerators, and free Internet access. The hotel features a splendid outdoor pool with swim-up bar service, a full-fledged fitness center, and a decent restaurant, the Blue Bay Grill.

$150-200

For something more intimate and less corporate, consider the new and cozy **V Boutique and Hotel** (701 N. Water St., 361/883-9200, www.vhotelcc.com, $189 d). Located among the bayside businesses, the V features modern decor with a residential feel, including flat-screen TVs, free Internet access, fancy bedding, minibars, and a fitness center.

Looming large along the Corpus Christi Bay are the **C Omni Towers: Marina and Bayfront** (707 and 900 N. Shoreline Blvd., 361/887-1600, www.omnihotels.com, $199 d). Located within a block of each other, the towers are connected by a walkway to form a deluxe complex. They're similar in price and amenities, although the Bayfront Tower offers additional upscale room options. Both towers provide rooms with wireless Internet access, free meals for kids, a fancy fully equipped health club, an indoor/outdoor heated swimming pool, an in-house massage therapist, bike rentals, and free covered parking.

Camping

An ideal spot for RVers looking to set up shop in town is **Puerto Del Sol RV Park** (5100 Timon Blvd., 361/882-5373, $25-35 nightly rates), located at the northern edge of Corpus Christi Beach. Amenities include full hookups, a rec room, laundry facilities, restrooms with hot showers, Internet access, and a book exchange. Farther out of town at the entrance of Padre Island is **Colonia Del Rey** (1717 Waldron Rd., 361/937-2435 or 800/580-2435, $25-35 nightly rates), offering a heated pool, hot tub, recreational facility, laundry room, convenience store, and wireless Internet service. Nearby is the minimal yet affordable **Padre Balli Park** (15820 Park Rd. 22, 361/949-8121, $10-20 nightly rates), encompassing 54 paved campsites with water and electric hookups, 12 hardtop campsites for pitching a tent with water and electric hookups, and primitive camping on the beach. A bathhouse and laundry facility are also available.

FOOD

Seafood is the favored item on the menu for most Corpus Christi diners, and the variety of restaurants in the downtown area offers plenty of options. Since the city has such a large Hispanic population, you'll also find high-quality (and quantity) Tex-Mex restaurants.

Seafood

You'll catch the city's best seafood at **C Water Street Seafood Co.** (309 N. Water St., 361/882-8683, www.waterstreetrestaurants.com, 11am-10pm Sun.-Thurs., 11am-11pm Fri.-Sat., $9-22). In fact, if you're in Corpus for more than a day, it's practically required to eat a meal at this legendary downtown locale at its adjacent sister location, Water Street Oyster Bar. Water Street takes everything tasty in the region—fresh seafood, Mexican influences, Cajun flavors, and good ol' Southern cooking—and combines it on a menu that yields the ultimate Texas Gulf Coast eating experience.

For first timers, the best place to start is the big blackboard, where you'll find fresh catches and daily specials (think blackened snapper, broiled flounder). The regular menu is equally appetizing, featuring consistently in-demand items such as crab cakes served with a spicy rémoulade and mango salsa; seafood jambalaya packed with shrimp, chicken, sausage, and crawfish tails in a creamy tomato sauce; and Southern-fried catfish stuffed with shrimp. For a simple seafood delight, order a double-sized peel-and-eat shrimp plate accompanied by a hoppy pale ale draft.

Slightly more upscale and not quite as family oriented is the next-door **Water Street Oyster Bar** (309 N. Water St., 361/881-9448, www.waterstreetrestaurants.com, 11am-11pm Sun.-Thurs., 11am-midnight Fri.-Sat., $9-25). This is a great spot to have a few cocktails and order some freshly shucked gulf oysters on the half shell. The menu is virtually the same as the Seafood Company's, so the aforementioned recommendations still apply. You'll just be able to enjoy them in a more refined atmosphere. Two additional recommendations: Order your salad with the walnut-based tangy dressing, and try to save room for the hot chocolate brownie with ice cream.

One of the fanciest places in town to delight in a dish of succulent seafood while gazing upon its place of origin is the **Yardarm Restaurant** (4310 Ocean Dr., 361/855-8157, 5:30pm-10pm Tues.-Sat., $10-30). This modestly sized, cozy spot (snug, even) offers tantalizingly fresh seafood, including succulent oysters, flavorful shrimp, and thick, juicy steaks. Due to its limited size and popularity, reservations are recommended.

On the opposite end of the sophistication scale is the consistently tasty but quite casual **Snoopy's Pier** (13313 S. Padre Island Dr., 361/949-8815, www.snoopyspier.com, 10am-10pm daily, $6-19). Located on the bay, Snoopy's is an ideal place to grab a cold beer and a plate full of fried or boiled shrimp. Watch the sun set as you lazily peel shrimp or enjoy the flaky goodness of fresh catches like flounder or mahimahi.

If you're staying on Corpus Christi Beach, you'll find two quality laid-back seafood restaurants within walking distance of your hotel and the beach. **Pier 99** (2822 N. Shoreline Blvd., 361/887-0764, 11am-9pm Sun.-Thurs., 11am-10pm Fri.-Sat., $7-21) is a Corpus Christi stalwart on the beach across from the massive USS *Lexington*. The portions here are nearly as big, particularly the combo plates overflowing with shrimp, crab legs, oysters, crawfish, and catfish. Be sure to order a bowl of the fresh seafood gumbo. Mellow live music keeps the atmosphere spirited most nights, providing a perfect *Margaritaville* moment for your tropical getaway.

Not quite as aesthetically pleasing but reliable in its good food is the misleadingly named **Blackbeard's on the Beach** (3117 E. Surfside Blvd., 361/884-1030, www.blackbeardsrestaurant.net, 11am-9pm Sun.-Thurs., 11am-10pm, Fri.-Sat. $6-19), located across the street from the Radisson and a couple blocks away from the ocean. This is another casual, family-friendly place where you'll find a bar full of bric-a-brac and hearty helpings of fresh seafood and Tex-Mex specialties.

Slightly more trendy is **Dragonfly** (14701 Park Rd. 22 S., 361/949-2224, 11am-2pm Tues.-Fri., 5-9:30pm Tues.-Thurs., 5-10pm Fri.-Sat., $8-23), offering a fresh take on seafood and other standard fare. The salmon has a wonderful curry seasoning and is accompanied by a tasty side of baby bok choy and carrots while the cheesy lasagna somehow manages to be hearty without being overly filling. Other menu highlights include the slightly spicy shrimp skewer and tasty grilled tuna. Parents take note: Dragonfly doesn't officially have a kids menu, but they'll whip up a bowl of creamy mac and cheese upon request.

Steak Houses

By nature, beach towns are populated with casual eateries catering to flip-flopped families and sun-soaked seafarers. Still, vacations are often an opportune time to celebrate the special occasion of being away from home in an exciting unfamiliar locale. A fancy meal is one of the best ways to commemorate a well-deserved break, and in Corpus it doesn't get much fancier than the **Republic of Texas Bar & Grill** (900 N. Shoreline Blvd., 361/886-3515, 5:30-10:30pm Mon.-Sat., 5:30-9pm Sun., $10-42). Located on the 20th floor of the Omni Bayfront hotel, this restaurant serves upscale Texas fare in a refined environment with incredibly stunning views. Meat is the main event here, and the range of options and methods of preparation are as impressive as the surrounding scenery. Can't-miss menu items include Chateau steak with sautéed asparagus and broccoli, pork rib chops in an apple-ginger glaze, Texas crab cake with lobster and cognac sauce, and perfectly prepared venison, buffalo, and redfish.

One of the newer entries to the Corpus upscale food club is **Katz 21 Steak & Spirits** (317 N. Mesquite St., 361/884-1221, www.katz21. com, 5-10pm Mon.-Thurs., 5-11pm Fri., $13-39). A traditional steak house specializing in prime grade A beef, Katz's features quality cuts of beef as well as fresh seafood, veal, and lamb. Unlike many traditional stuffy steak houses, however, Katz's offers a lighter lunch menu with soups, salads, sandwiches, and pastas. Popular menu items include the prime rib served au jus with horseradish sauce, the bone-in rib eye, the rack of lamb, and veal piccata. Reservations are encouraged.

When in Texas, even on the Gulf Coast, some travelers find it necessary to eat at a classic steak house. It's an understandable quest, and in Corpus, it can be successfully achieved at **Niko's Steakhouse** (5409 Saratoga St., 361/992-2333, www.nikossteakhouse.com, 11am-11:30pm daily, $25-35). Prime rib is a favorite among locals, but the rib eye and sirloin steaks are worthy considerations. Although the sides at Niko's appropriately play second fiddle to the main meat events, several options are notable, including the asparagus and Yukon potatoes.

Barbecue
Corpus isn't known as a barbecue mecca, but it has a couple of noteworthy restaurants where out-of-staters can experience the mystique and magnificence of Texas-style 'cue. One of the best options is **Miller's Bar-B-Q** (6601 Weber Rd., 361/806-2244, 11am-9pm Mon.-Sat., $9-18). Miller's is known for its tender brisket and beef ribs, along with pork, chicken, and sausage. The sides here are better than average, so be sure to load up on the sweet potato salad and coleslaw.

Mexican and Tex-Mex
Unlike its seafood restaurants, most of Corpus Christi's Mexican spots are not on the waterfront. Regardless, several are worth the inland drive, particularly **La Playa** (5017 Saratoga Blvd. and 7118 S. Padre Island Dr., 361/986-0089, www.laplaya.cc, 11am-10pm Tues.-Sat., 11am-9pm Sun., $8-19). This is the place to go for a top-notch traditional Tex-Mex meal. Feast on chicken enchiladas in a tangy tomatillo sauce or savor the sizzling beef fajitas. You won't regret ordering the stuffed fried avocados, either. This being a seaside town, you can also order Tex-Mex-style dishes featuring fresh fish and gulf shrimp.

Another commendable spot offering some coastal flair to the Tex-Mex offerings is **La Costenita** (4217 Leopard St., 361/882-5340, hours vary, closed Sun., $8-17). This downtown eatery is small in size but huge on taste, particularly the shrimp dishes and traditional enchilada and taco plates. Try not to fill up too quickly on the amazing chips and perfectly spicy homemade salsa.

Locals flock to **Kiko's** (5514 Everhart Rd., 361/991-1211, 6am-9pm Mon.-Thurs., 6am-10pm Fri.-Sat., $7-17) for the enchiladas. Cheese enchiladas with zesty ranchero sauce are the specialty here, but you can't go wrong with most menu items, including the green chile burrito, guacamole salad, and tortilla soup. Better yet, sample all the goodness the restaurant has to offer with the Kiko's platter, offering a signature cheese enchilada, beef fajita tacos, and a crispy chalupa.

Also drawing Corpus crowds is **Solis Mexican Restaurant** (3122 Baldwin Blvd. and 5409 Leopard St., 361/882-5557, hours vary,

$7-16). This classic taqueria is known for its tasty tacos and enchiladas, all prepared with fresh homemade tortillas. Locals love their stuffed breakfast tacos (served all day) and *liquados* (fruity Mexican drinks).

Standard Tex-Mex is also the main draw at **Café Maya** (2319 Morgan Ave., 361/884-6522, 11am-10pm daily, $7-16), where you'll find massive plates of flavorful favorites, including beef enchiladas, chicken tacos, and cheesy quesadillas. For over-the-top goodness, order the shrimp-stuffed avocado.

Casual

If you've had enough with the fancy stuff, try one of Corpus Christi's most venerable downtown eateries, specializing in comfort food in a casual atmosphere. The 1950s-style **City Diner & Oyster Bar** (622 N. Water St., 361/883-1643, 7am-10pm Sun.-Thurs., 7am-11pm Fri.-Sat., $6-16) is known for just about everything on the menu except its unremarkable oysters. From greasy burgers to zesty peppercorn ranch onion rings to classic chicken-fried steak to snapper smothered in a creamy crab and shrimp sauce, this retro establishment gets home-style regional fare right.

Just a few blocks down the street is another esteemed local hot spot, the tourist-friendly **Executive Surf Club** (309 N. Water St., 361/884-7873, www.executivesurfclub. com, 11am-11pm Sun.-Weds., 11am-midnight Thurs.-Sat. , $7-16). This is an ideal place to grab a big ol' juicy cheeseburger and a Shiner Bock while you contemplate your next beach activity. Standard bar fare is the main draw here, and the Surf Club delivers with fish and chips, fried shrimp, tortilla wraps, and chicken-fried steak, all served on tables fashioned from old surfboards. Stick around after dinner for some local hot blues and rock bands.

Asian

Corpus has a long-standing connection with Asian cultures, reaching back nearly a century to the days when shrimpers and rice farmers arrived in the developing coastal town. Only recently, however, have Thai, Chinese,

and Japanese restaurants come to the general public's awareness. Among the most popular is **Yalee's Asian Bistro** (5649 Saratoga Blvd., 361/993-9333, www.yaleesasianbistro. com, 11am-10pm Sun.-Thurs., 11am-10:30pm Fri.-Sat., $7-18). The counter-service arrangement may lower expectations, but the food at Yalee's is top notch, featuring popular menu items like the spicy Ma Po tofu and flavorful standards like Kung Pao shrimp and General Tso chicken.

Sushi fans should head directly to **Aka Sushi** (415 N. Water St., 361/882-8885, 11:30am-2pm Mon.-Weds. and Fri., 5-10pm Mon.-Tues. and Thurs., 5-10:30pm Fri.-Sat., $7-19). There's something for everyone here, from classic tuna and shrimp rolls to more elaborate options such as a dragon roll and its off-menu variation known as an ecstasy roll. The seaweed salad is a popular dish, and the sake selection is impressive.

Although the Asian population in Corpus is fairly sizable, only a handful of restaurants adequately represent the Thai options. If you're only able to visit one, make sure it's **Thai Spice** (523 N. Water St., 361/883-8884, www.thaispicecc.com, 11am-11pm daily, $9-19). The most popular dishes (and deservedly so) are the coconut curry options, served in actual coconuts. It helps that the flavorful curry is tempered by the sweetness of the coconut and accompanying fresh pineapple. Another notable option is the lemongrass soup, though it can be a bit spicy for some.

Not quite as authentic, **Vietnam** (701 N. Water St., 361/853-2682, www.vietnam-restaurant.com, 11am-10pm Mon.-Sat., $10-23) is a similarly high-quality option just a few blocks away. This is the place to go for amazing soups, including varieties of pho and surprisingly tasty catfish soup. Seafood and veggie dishes are also worth ordering.

Breakfast

For a hearty breakfast or lunch with a colorful cast of local residents, head on over to **Hester's Café and Coffee Bar** (1714 S. Alameda St., 361/885-0558, www.hesterscafe.

com, 7am-3pm Mon.-Sat., $8-20). Known as a reliable spot for comfort food, Hester's offers classics like eggs and hash browns with delectable additions like fresh avocado and thick-cut bacon. Popular lunch options include the stacked Laguna Club sandwich (with melted cheese on top), hearty Victoria Pasta, and fresh salads.

INFORMATION AND SERVICES

The **Corpus Christi Area Convention & Visitors Bureau** (101 N. Shoreline Blvd., 361/881-1800 or 800/766-2322, www.visitcorpuschristitx.org) contains scores of brochures, maps, and helpful information on local attractions and recreation. Similar information is available at the bureau's downtown visitor information center (1823 N. Chaparral St., 800/766-2322).

GETTING THERE AND AROUND

Located five miles west of downtown, the **Corpus Christi International Airport** (1000 International Blvd., 361/289-0171, www.cctexas.com/airport) offers service from several major airlines (Southwest, United, and American Eagle), including service to Monterrey, Mexico. The city's bus system, **Regional Transportation Authority** (1806 S. Alameda St., 361/883-2287, www.ccrta.org), provides citywide service. Check the website for updated fare and route information.

Mustang Island

When people say they're going to Corpus Christi to hit the beach, they're often referring to adjacent Mustang Island. Located on the island's northern tip, about 15 miles north of Mustang Island State Park, is the charming little beach town of Port Aransas. Port A, as it's known locally, has services catering to everyone from beach bums to big spenders.

PADRE ISLAND NATIONAL SEASHORE

Don't let the name of **Padre Island National Seashore** (3829 Park Rd. 22, 361/949-8068, www.nps.gov/pais, $5 entry fee for walkers and bikers, $10 fee for vehicles, passes valid for seven days) fool you. Just south of Mustang Island State Park, this low-key, nature-oriented, protected shoreline is not to be confused with the commercial-minded party atmosphere of South Padre Island, a nearly three-hour drive to the south. Padre Island National Seashore is the longest remaining undeveloped stretch of barrier island in the world and appeals primarily to naturalists who delight in its primitive shoreline and birding and fishing opportunities. Bird-watchers arrive in droves during the fall and spring migration seasons when thousands of birds drop by the island, including sandhill cranes, hawks, and songbirds. The park is also considered the most important nesting beach in the country for the most endangered sea turtle in the world (Kemp's ridley). Park officials incubate sea turtle eggs found along the coast and release the hatchlings into the gulf during the summer. The public is invited to view this fascinating natural event—for release dates and directions to the site, call the Hatchling Hotline at 361/949-7163. Other popular activities at the park include swimming, fishing, windsurfing, and beachcombing. Visit the website for detailed information about camping locations and fees. To reach the park from Corpus, take South Padre Island Drive (Highway 358) to Padre Island, then head south on Park Road 22 for 13 miles to the Malaquite Visitor Center.

MUSTANG ISLAND STATE PARK

Don't miss the beautiful shoreline along **Mustang Island State Park** (17047 State Hwy. 361, 361/749-5246, www.tpwd.state.tx.us, $4 daily ages 13 and older), just north of Padre Island National Seashore. Named for the wild horses that escaped from Spanish explorers and roamed free across this 18-mile-long island, Mustang Island park comprises five miles of pure outstretched beach, perfect for swimming, fishing, sunbathing, hiking, biking, and even low-intensity surfing. Birding is another popular activity along this 4,000-acre island, notable for its distinctive ecosystem based on 20-foot-high sand dunes that protect the bay and mainland and can reduce powerful hurricane-driven waves. To get there from Corpus, take South Padre Island Drive (Highway 358) to Padre Island, then head north on Highway 361 for five miles to the park headquarters.

SAN JOSE ISLAND

If you're seriously into beachcombing—we're talking shell collections, mounted driftwood, maybe even a metal detector—then **San Jose Island** is your paradise. This privately owned property across the bay from Port Aransas is the definition of pristine—it's almost as untouched as it was when the Karankawa native people occupied the place nearly a thousand years ago. In the 1830s, locals found the remains of a pirate camp on the island, and rumor has it pirate Jean Lafitte's Spanish dagger with a silver spike is still somewhere guarding his booty of silver and gold. These days, the island affectionately called "Saint Joe" is safe for visitors, who can access it via a short boat ride and partake of its premier swimming, fishing, sunbathing, and treasure hunting. To arrange transport, drop by Port A's **Fisherman's Wharf** (900 N. Tarpon St., 361/749-5448, www.wharfcat.com, call for seasonal rates).

PORT ARANSAS

The origins of Port Aransas (population 3,480) are traced to an English farmer who used the area as a sheep and cattle grazing station in the mid-1800s. Decades later, New Jersey entrepreneur Elihu Ropes attempted to organize a massive project to dredge a 30-foot shipping channel across Mustang Island to allow access to the deep waters of the gulf. He was ultimately unsuccessful in his quest, but his efforts resulted in the town briefly being named Ropesville in his honor.

By the mid-20th century, Port Aransas had become synonymous with recreation, drawing tens of thousands of anglers, swimmers, boaters, and beachcombers to its magnificent open beaches and charming seaside village atmosphere. The town's population swelled from 824 residents in 1960 to several thousand by the end of the century. As many as 20,000 vacationers descend on Port Aransas during peak periods, packing the island's motels, cottages, beach houses, condos, resorts, seafood restaurants, tackle shops, and boutiques.

Sights

Port A isn't known for its dynamic cultural attractions—at all. It's a small beach community where the biggest and best attraction is . . . the beach. Besides, with big ol' Corpus Christi just a few miles away, it doesn't need any of those pesky multistory buildings and parking lots. In fact, the only real destination in town is beach related: the **Marine Science Institute** (630 E. Cotter Ave., 361/749-6729, www.utmsi.utexas.edu, 8am-5pm Mon.-Fri., free admission). At the risk of learning something on a beach vacation, consider a visit. The oldest marine research station on the Texas Gulf Coast, it is dedicated to sciences relating to plants and animals of the sea (ecology, biochemistry, physiology, and the like). Its visitors center offers educational movies (3pm Mon.-Thurs.) and self-guided tours of marine-related research-project exhibits, stunning photographs, and seven aquariums housing offshore artificial reefs, black mangrove marsh, and Spartina, often over an open seafloor.

Recreation

When it comes to activities in Port Aransas, the key word is "outside." Water is the main reason most people visit the area, and fortunately it has many noteworthy places to explore and enjoy all year.

FISHING

Port Aransas is a fishing mecca. Some claim the area is overfished, but it's clear why so many anglers are angling to get here—easy

JELLYFISH JAM

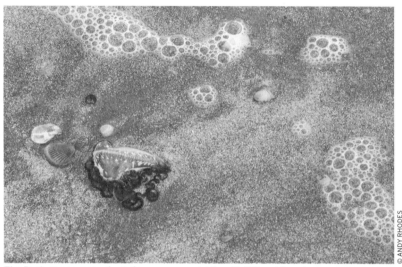

© ANDY RHODES

The Portuguese man-of-war is a common sight on Gulf Coast beaches.

The "jellies" on Texas's Gulf Coast aren't tasty fruit-filled breakfast treats. They're jellyfish, and despite their iridescent and wiggly appearance, they'll cause much more pain than pleasure.

One of the most common creatures washed up on the shore isn't technically a jellyfish, despite its translucent air bubble and blue tentacles. The Portuguese man-of-war (aka the blue bubble, bluebottle, or man-of-war) is actually a colony of organisms, each with its own distinct function. Its name comes from the air bubble's resemblance to the sails of an ancient Portuguese war vessel.

The man-of-war floats on ocean currents and is deposited ashore on Texas beaches during the spring to late summer. These crafty carnivores feed on small fish and other small animals that get caught in their venom-filled tentacles. The other washed-up organisms that visitors may encounter on the shoreline are traditional jellyfish—gelatinous invertebrates with tentacles of varying sizes that hang from the main "body" of the organism (technically referred to as the mollusk).

You won't find an abundance of these bizarre animals on a typical beach stroll, but

it's worth keeping an eye out for them because their stings pack quite a wallop. They're much harder to see in the water, but a good indication of their presence is the appearance of any washed-up organisms on the beach. The man-of-war is especially difficult to see since it's translucent and often blends in with wave foam.

Aside from avoiding areas of the ocean where you see beached jellies, you'll have to make sure you don't step anywhere near the washed-up variety since their stinging cells remain toxic even when the rest of the body has died. Often, the tentacles are nearly invisible, though you'll definitely feel the sharp shot of pain jetting up your leg.

If this happens, scrape the tentacles off with a driver's license or credit card. If a jellyfish stings you, place the affected area under hot water and apply hydrocortisone cream to relieve the itching. For a man-of-war sting, splash the area with saltwater, then apply vinegar or a diluted bleach solution (1 part bleach to 10 parts water) to the sting site without pressing too hard on the skin. The pain should go away within an hour.

access to the bay and deep-sea gulf fishing provide species aplenty throughout the year. Those looking to keep their feet on solid ground or a wooden dock can take advantage of the free fishing from beaches, jetties, or one of the three lighted piers (**Charlie's Harbor Pier, Ancel Brundrett Pier,** and **J.P. Luby Pier**) extending into the Corpus Christi Ship Channel. You'll have to pony up a dollar to use the popular and well-lit **Horace Caldwell Pier,** with its access to the gulf via Magee Beach Park. The pier stands more than 1,200 feet long and stays open 24 hours a day, with bait, tackle, rental equipment, and munchies available at a nearby concession stand.

Many anglers prefer the challenge of the larger deep-sea species, including kingfish, mackerel, tuna, shark, and even mahimahi. Group boats offer bay and deep-sea fishing, and popular fishing tournaments take place throughout the summer. The Deep Sea Roundup, held each July, is the oldest fishing tournament on the Gulf Coast. As a testament to the overwhelming allure of fishing in Port A, the town has several hundred fishing guides. Inquire about group fishing at **Fisherman's Wharf** (900 N. Tarpon St., 361/749-5448, www.wharfcat.com), or to arrange a private rental, contact **Woody's Sports Center** (136 W. Cotter Ave., 361/749-5252, www.woodysonline.com).

SWIMMING
The swimming on the northern tip of the island can't compare to **Mustang Island State Park,** which has the best swimming in the area. But visitors can still access portions of the wide and welcoming beach among the condos and private property just off the island's main road (Highway 361). Swimming and camping are also available just outside Port A at **Magee Beach Park** (321 North on the Beach, 361/749-6117, www.nuecesbeachparks.com). This 167-acre park isn't quite as breathtaking as other portions of Mustang Island or San Jose Island, but it's a good spot to dip your toes in the water and soak up the salty sea air. A park office provides limited

visitor information, and the beach bathhouse contains publicly accessible showers.

Accommodations
INNS
For a truly memorable experience in this quaint seaside village, stay at the charming **◖ Tarpon Inn** (200 E. Cotter Ave., 361/749-5555, www.thetarponinn.com, $89-195 depending on room size and season). An "inn" in every sense of the term, this historic establishment offers a slice of what life was like in the late 1800s. In fact, it's so authentic, you won't even find a TV (or phone!) in your room. Fortunately, Wi-Fi service is available, so if you prefer, you can get online and avoid doing old-fashioned pastimes like book reading, relaxing in a rocking chair, playing croquet and horseshoes, or even talking. The rooms are small, but the lack of stuff in them—vintage beds and furniture notwithstanding—is imminently refreshing. Be sure to check out the old tarpon fish scales on the wall in the lobby, including those autographed by famous actors and politicians. The trolley stops out front every day to take guests to the beach or nearby shops.

Not quite as charming yet just as appealing in its local flavor is **Alister Square Inn** (122 S. Alister St., 361/749-3003, www.portaransastexas.com, $89-189). Though it's a bit rough around the edges, this welcoming accommodation appeals to families and anglers alike with its various lodging options (two-bedroom apartments, kitchenette suites, and standard hotel rooms), each featuring microwaves, refrigerators, and wireless Internet access. Alister Square is within walking distance of the beach, shopping boutiques, and restaurants.

HOTELS
In Port Aransas, visitors have to pay more for the comfort of a familiar chain hotel than a local inn. Among the corporate options are **Best Western Ocean Villa** (400 E. Ave. G, 361/749-3010, www.bestwestern.com, $197 d), located within walking distance of beaches, fishing piers, and local shops. Amenities include rooms with microwaves, refrigerators,

and Internet access, along with a free continental breakfast and an outdoor swimming pool.

Just a couple of blocks closer to the beach, the **Holiday Inn Express** (727 S. 11th St., 361/749-5222, www.ichotelsgroup.com, $228 d) offers a fitness center, a pool and spa area, a free continental breakfast, and rooms with microwaves, refrigerators, and Internet access.

CONDOS

Condos proliferate on Mustang Island's shoreline like barnacles on a shrimp boat—albeit really nice barnacles. Condos make perfect sense in a beach environment: Visitors can traipse back and forth between the surf and their temporary home, sand gathers guiltlessly on all surfaces, and beer and pizza fill the fridge. Perhaps most popular among the dozen or so options is **Beachgate CondoSuites & Motel** (2000 On the Beach Dr., 361/749-5900, www.beachgate.com, $230-310, depending on room size and season). Situated adjacent to the sandy shores of Mustang Island (meaning no boardwalks or long trails through the dunes) Beachgate offers everything from efficiency-size motel rooms to full-size three-bedroom condos, accommodating everyone from the solo angler to the sizable family reunion. Larger options contain fully equipped kitchens, and all units have small refrigerators, microwaves, and coffeemakers. Additional amenities include a fish-cleaning facility, boat parking, and washers and horseshoe sets for fun on the beach.

Another commendable option is the **Sand Castle Condominium** (800 Sandcastle Dr., 361/749-6201, www.sandcastlecondo.com, $185-295), offering 180 units (efficiencies and one, two, and three bedrooms) with complete kitchens and laundry and maid service. The Sand Castle also features a fitness center, large outdoor pool and hot tub, a boardwalk to the beach, and a fish-cleaning facility.

Also drawing hordes of regulars is **La Mirage** (5973 Hwy. 361, 361/749-6030, www.lamirage-portaransas.com, $120-350), with clean and comfortable units in a three-story building surrounding a tropical courtyard. Options include studios; one-, two-, and three-bedroom

condos, each offering fully equipped kitchens; free Internet access; a laundry room; and living and dining areas.

Food
SEAFOOD

One of the best seafood restaurants on the Gulf Coast is the unassuming but spectacular **Shells Pasta & Seafood** (522 E. Ave. G, 361/749-7621, www.eatatshells.com, $10-32, 11:30am-2pm, 5pm-9pm Wed.-Mon.). Housed inside a modest blue building, Shells is a tiny place—plastic chairs at nine tables—with an enormous reputation for quality fresh seafood and pasta dishes. Order from the daily blackboard specials or the regular menu, featuring classic and perfectly prepared seafood dishes such as the signature pan-seared amberjack, grilled shrimp, blue crab cakes, or sumptuous shrimp linguine in a delightfully creamy Alfredo sauce. This is elegant food in a casual shorts-wearing environment. Finding Shells will be a highlight of your trip to Port A.

Not quite as fancy yet well worth a visit is **Lisabella's** (224 E. Cotter Ave., 361/749-4222, $9-27, 5:30pm-10pm Mon.-Sat.). Locals love Lisabella's mermaid soup, a tasty concoction of lobster, shrimp, coconut milk, curry, and avocado. The crab cakes and sautéed grouper are similarly enticing.

If you're looking for an ultracasual spot where you can wear T-shirts and flip-flops while gazing upon old fishermen's nets, mounted marlin, and the ocean itself, head to **Trout Street Bar & Grill** (104 W. Cotter Ave., 361/749-7800, www.tsbag.com, 11:30am-9pm Sun.-Thurs., 11:30am-10pm Fri.- Sat., $9-26). Sit outside on the covered veranda to gaze upon the marina and ship channel activity while feasting on jumbo fried shrimp, grilled amberjack, tuna, or steak. A bonus: Trout Street will cook your fresh-caught fish as long as it's cleaned and ready for the kitchen.

Another venerable seafood spot is the "downtown" **Pelican's Landing Restaurant** (337 N. Alister St., 361/749-6405, www.pelicanslanding.com, 11:30am- 9pm Sun.–Thurs., 11:30am-10pm Fri.-Sat., $8-27). The portions are enormous here, and shrimp is the specialty. Go for the gusto and order one of the Mambo Combos (fried shrimp, steak, crab cakes, beer-battered fries), and savor the flavor on your surfboard table.

ITALIAN

There are two kinds of Italian restaurants in many coastal communities: beach grub and upscale cuisine. Port A has both. For a quick slice of pizza in an ultra laid-back environment, check out the immensely popular **Port A Pizzeria** (407 E. Ave. G., 361/749-5226, www.portapizzeria.com, 10am-2pm, 5pm-9pm daily, $7-16). The biggest draw is the buffet, allowing diners to immediately devour hot slices of cheesy goodness. Some diners even choose to wait a few minutes for the tasty calzone. The big crowds usually ensure a quick turnaround on the pizza varieties.

The fancy Italian option in town is the consistently top-notch **Venetian Hot Plate** (232 Beach Ave., 361/749-7617, www.venetian-hotplate.com, $9-33, 5pm-10pm Tues.-Sat.). Named for the sizzling iron plates some of the meals arrive on, this upscale spot specializes in tender and succulent meats, including filet mignon medallions, veal, and lamb. The wine selection is excellent, and the desserts are spectacular. Reservations are recommended.

Information and Services

Pick up a handy brochure with island visitor info and a map of the trolley route at the **Port Aransas Chamber of Commerce and Tourist Bureau** (403 W. Cotter St., 361/749-5919, www.portaransas.org). The **Island Trolley** (aka "The B" and "The #94 Shuttle") will take you pretty much anywhere you want to go in Port A, from the beach to the wharf to shops and back to your hotel—for only 25 cents. It's particularly handy when you're on beer number four and dinner is calling. For more information about the trolley, contact the city at 361/749-4111.

GETTING THERE

To reach Mustang Island from Corpus Christi, take South Padre Island Drive (Highway 358) across the John F. Kennedy Memorial Causeway. Alternatively, if you have the time and interest, take the **Port Aransas Ferry,** which provides free marine transportation service year-round 24 hours a day. The 15-minute ride connects Port Aransas with the mainland at Aransas Pass, north of Corpus Christi (take 181 across the bay to get there). It's well worth the extra time and effort. Look for dolphins behind the ferry as they tumble over each other in the bay, snatching up fish in the boat's wake. There are six ferries in operation, each carrying up to 20 vehicles per trip. During the busy season, particularly holidays and some summer weekends, you may have to wait up to 30 or 45 minutes for the next ferryboat, but typically the wait is no longer than 5-10 minutes. For more information, call 361/749-2850.

THE GULF COAST

Kingsville

Located about 40 miles southwest of Corpus Christi, Kingsville (population 26,213) is the birthplace of the American ranching industry. It's the main commercial center of the legendary King Ranch, which sprawls across 825,000 acres and boasts 60,000 head of cattle.

The community is named for the famous riverboat baron and rancher Richard King, who used his business profits to purchase the vast piece of property that would become the legendary ranch. Kingsville's roots as a city are traced to the St. Louis, Brownsville and Mexico Railway, which put the town on the map when its tracks were laid in the early 1900s. Most of Kingsville's early business activity, however, was related to the King family, who started a weekly newspaper and built a hotel, an ice plant, and a cotton gin. Kingsville went on to become a busy trade center for ranching families across South Texas.

Kingsville's population grew significantly when Exxon relocated a district office here in the 1960s. A surge in enrollment at the Texas College of Arts and Industries (now Texas A&M Kingsville) brought even more folks to town, numbering nearly 30,000 by the late '70s. Exxon closed its regional office in 1985, and the population has slowly declined since then.

Regardless, Kingsville remains a major draw for birders and naturalists, who delight in the area's million acres of habitat. Visitors from across the state and the country travel to the historical downtown area to learn about the heritage of King Ranch and to shop at the boutiques and antiques stores.

SIGHTS
◖ King Ranch

For many Texas visitors, King Ranch is the embodiment of the Lone Star State's legacy. Longhorn cattle, vast ranchlands, and genuine cowboys evoke a sense of mystique and grandeur that Texas alone can claim.

As improbable as it may seem, America's

King Ranch Saddle Shop

© ANDY RHODES

ranching legacy was revolutionized by a man who arrived as a preteen stowaway on Texas's Gulf Coast. Richard King, who escaped an indenture in New York City in 1835 and stowed away aboard a cargo ship, went on to become a steamboat baron along the Rio Grande before overseeing his ranching empire.

The origins of King Ranch, now an esteemed National Historic Landmark, date to 1853 when Richard King purchased 68,500 acres of property that had been Spanish and Mexican land grants. Between 1869 and 1884, King sent more than 100,000 head of livestock from his ranch to northern markets on now-legendary routes like the Chisholm Trail. Many of these herds were marked with the iconic symbol for the King Ranch, the Running W brand, which first appeared in the 1860s. Though the origins of this distinctive shape aren't known, local legends claim it represents the sweeping horns of a longhorn bull or a slithering diamondback rattlesnake.

One of King Ranch's biggest claims to fame is its development of the Western Hemisphere's first strain of beef cattle: Santa Gertrudis. Based on the name from the property's original land grant, this breed of cattle was developed in the 1920s to produce cows that could withstand the oppressive South Texas conditions—heat, humidity, and biting insects. To accomplish this, breeding experts (including Richard King's grandson) crossed Indian Brahman cattle with British Shorthorns.

King was also one of the first ranchers to move Texas Longhorns from Mexico to markets in the Midwest. The innovations developed at his ranch, from cattle and horse breeding and disease control to improving the blood lines of the quarter horse to well drilling, earned it the proud title "birthplace of American ranching."

Today, King Ranch sprawls across 825,000 acres, an area larger than the state of Rhode Island. The **King Ranch Visitor Center** (2205 Hwy. 141 W., 361/592-8055, www.king-ranch. com, tours at 10am, noon, and 1pm Mon.-Sat., 12:30 and 2pm Sun., $12 adults, $10 seniors, $5 children ages 5-12) offers daily guided tours along an old stagecoach road past majestic Longhorns with the iconic Running W brand on their hindquarters and a 100-year-old carriage house with a mission-style roofline and distinctive arches. Other highlights include the Victorian-era cabin homes of King's working families (known as *Kineños*) and a horse cemetery with graves of famous racing thoroughbreds from the 1950s. Bring plenty of water since it gets plenty hot out on the ranch. Special tours devoted to birding, native wildlife, and agriculture are available in advance by reservation.

To learn more about the fascinating history of the King family and property, move 'em up and head 'em out a couple miles down the road to the **King Ranch Museum** (405 N. 6th St. in Kingsville, 361/595-1881, www.king-ranch. com, 10am-4pm Mon.-Sat., 1pm-5pm Sun., $6 adults, $3 children ages 5-12). Housed in a historic downtown ice plant, the museum contains

stunning 1940s photos of the ranch by award-winning photographer Toni Frissell, fancy saddles and firearms, antique coaches and carriages, and other historical ranch items. One of the most intriguing objects on display is "El Kineño," a custom-designed 1949 Buick Eight hunting vehicle—complete with rifle holders and a shiny Running W hood ornament—made by General Motors especially for R. M. Kleberg Sr., a congressional representative.

Another must-see (and smell) is the restored 1909 Ragland Mercantile Building that now houses the leather-filled **King Ranch Saddle Shop** (201 E. Kleberg Ave., 877/282-5777, www.krsaddleshop.com, 10am-6pm Mon.-Sat.). Originally used to supply gear exclusively to the King Ranch cowboys known as *Los Kineños* (King's people), the store now offers leather goods and clothing to the world (its website does brisk business). The charming downtown shop also contains exhibits and photos on ranch history and information about the governors, presidents, and foreign dignitaries it has outfitted.

1904 Train Depot and Museum

Located a block away from the saddle shop is the restored **1904 Train Depot and Museum** (102 E. Kleberg Ave., 361/592-8515, www. kingsvilletexas.com, 10am-4pm Mon.-Fri., 11am-2pm Sat., free admission), providing a glimpse into Kingsville's bustling past. Photos and artifacts, including an operational telegraph, highlight the historical significance of this hub of regional activity.

Kenedy Ranch Museum of South Texas

Richard King isn't the only famous rancher in these parts. His longtime pal Mifflin Kenedy also accumulated great wealth and property thanks to his successful commercial and ranching endeavors. His legacy is on display at the **Kenedy Ranch Museum of South Texas** (200 E. La Parra Ave., 361/294-5751, www. kenedyranchmuseum.org, 10am-4pm Tues.-Sat., noon-4pm Sun., $3 adults, $2 seniors and children ages 13-18). Located 20 miles south

THE GULF COAST

KING'S PEOPLE

At the heart of the King Ranch are the *Kineños* (King's people), a group of several hundred ranch employees whose families have dedicated their lives to operating the property for generations. From training horses to clearing fields to promoting the King Ranch's original cattle breed, the *Kineños* provide a vital link with the ranch's past and are responsible for maintaining its ongoing legacy.

If you schedule a visit to the ranch or take part in one of the tours, you'll likely get a chance to visit with one of these *Kineños*. Several now serve as visitor guides, even though they occasionally take on some of their traditional ranch-hand duties. By the way, many are men in their 80s.

Some of these men spent their early days "breaking" thoroughbred horses. In the 1940s and '50s, King Ranch trained racing horses and developed many well-known and successful thoroughbreds. The *Kineños* also worked extensively with the ranch's quarter horses, using the handling techniques passed down through generations of *vaqueros* (Mexican cowboys).

Other *Kineños* worked closely with the Santa Gertrudis cattle breed, specifically developed and marketed by the ranch. They helped promote the breed by attending livestock shows across the world and even slept in the barns with the animals and woke up early to clean, feed, water, and brush the cattle in preparation for the shows. *Kineños* also worked with the breed by administering vaccinations, helping in the pastures, and maintaining records.

Some of these stories have been captured for posterity's sake in print. For a fascinating collection of colorful *Kineño* tales, pick up a copy of Alberto "Beto" Maldonado's book *The Master Showmen of King Ranch*.

of Kingsville in the little town of Sarita, the museum showcases Kenedy's illustrious past through exhibits dedicated primarily to family, particularly the Mexican heritage of his wife, Petra Vela de Vidal. Through his successful business ventures, Kenedy accumulated 400,000 acres of Gulf Coast property and was among the first ranchers to hold cattle inside wire fences. Housed in the 1927 Kenedy Ranch headquarters, the museum also details the family's many successful philanthropic programs.

John E. Conner Museum

Regional history and the natural world are the main areas of interest at the **John E. Conner Museum** (905 W. Santa Gertrudis Ave., 361/593-2810, www.tamuk.edu, 9am-5pm Mon.-Fri., 10am-4pm Sat., free admission). Located on the campus of Texas A&M University-Kingsville, this modest museum offers exhibits devoted to the cultural groups that have historically occupied the area, from Native Americans to Spanish to Mexican and pioneer settlers. Native plant and animal species and their environments are also on display, as well as artwork from students and Texas artists.

ACCOMMODATIONS

If you find yourself making an overnight trip to Kingsville, only a few options are available for lodging. On the affordable side is **Best Western Kingsville Inn** (2402 East King Ave., 361/595-5656, www.bestwestern.com, $89 d). Amenities include a complimentary hot breakfast, Wi-Fi access, standard rooms with microwaves and refrigerators, and an outdoor swimming pool and hot tub.

For just a little more money, consider the newer **Holiday Inn Express** (2400 S. Hwy. 77, 361/592-8333, www.hiexpress.com, $108 d), offering a free hot breakfast bar, Wi-Fi access, and a heated outdoor pool.

FOOD
Seafood

Kingsville isn't a highly regarded destination for fine dining, but a few places are worth dropping by if you're visiting King Ranch or even headed down to South Padre. One of the best places to eat in the entire region is about 20 miles south of Kingsville in a tiny town called Riviera. ◼ **King's Inn** (1116 S. County Rd. 2270, 361/297-5265, 11am-10pm Tues.-Sat., $12-25) is billed as one of the best seafood restaurants on Texas's southern Gulf Coast, and for good reason. It doesn't look like much from the outside, and the outdated ambience isn't really charming either, but that matters not as soon as your food arrives. Be sure to order the lightly breaded fried shrimp, loaded with freshly caught flavor and accompanied by the restaurant's famous spicy tartar sauce (the waiter claimed to be sworn to secrecy, though he eventually let it slip that the tartar sauce contained bread crumbs, "lots of eggs," and serrano peppers). This stunning sauce enhances everything from the interesting choice of fish (drum) to the homemade bread to the avocado salad with slices of fresh, juicy tomatoes. It's absolutely worth the 20-minute detour to eat like a king.

Burgers

Just south of the downtown area is an ideal lunch spot, the occasionally rowdy **Big House Burgers** (2209 S. Brahma Blvd., 361/592-0222, www.mybighouseonline.com, 11am-10pm Mon.-Sat., $7-12). The sports bar atmosphere can be a bit overwhelming on weekends (reminding you there's a college in this town) but worth enduring the noise and blaring TVs for the immense and flavorful burgers. Try the quadruple burger if you dare. These juicy treats will fill you up, so split some of the crunchy fries or crispy onion rings with a pal.

Mexican and Tex-Mex

One of the most popular places in town to grab an authentic Tex-Mex meal is **El Tapatio**

Mexican Restaurant (630 W. Santa Gertrudis St., 361/516-1655, 6am-10pm Mon.-Sat., 6am-2pm Sun., $8-15), on the edge of Kingsville A&M campus. Although most of the food is standard Tex-Mex fare, a few items set El Tapatio apart from other spots in town. The *carne guisada*, in particular, is spectacular, with a hearty gravy that brings out the rich flavor of the beef. Like the salsa, it has an extra kick and after-bite that leaves your mouth feeling warm and satisfied.

Another worthy local eatery is **Lydia's Homestyle Cooking** (817 W. King Ave., 361/592-9405, 5am-1:30pm Mon.-Sat., $8-17). Lydia's is known throughout town for its tremendous breakfast taquitos (try the potato, eggs, and sausage) and the *machacado* plate, featuring shredded dry beef scrambled with eggs along with grilled onions, tomato, and serrano peppers. Lydia's lunches are legendary too, including the Barbacoa plate, tamales, and chicken flautas. If necessary, you can also order gringo fare (burgers, sandwiches, etc.).

Another reputable Mexican restaurant is **El Dorado** (704 N. 14th St., 361/516-1459, 6am-10pm Mon.-Sat., 6am-2pm Sun., $6-13). There's nothing too fancy here, but the traditional Tex-Mex fare is consistently decent, including the beef tacos, chicken enchiladas, and burritos.

INFORMATION AND SERVICES

For information about other area attractions, accommodations, and restaurants, visit the **Kingsville Convention and Visitors Bureau** (1501 Hwy. 77, 361/592-8516, www.kingsvilletexas.com, 9am-5pm Mon.-Fri., 10am-2pm Sat.-Sun.).

South Padre Island

South Padre is the ultimate beach vacation in Texas. Its soft smooth sand is far more inviting and picturesque than the grainier, darker versions farther north along the coast. The resort community offers everything seaside travelers seek—beachcombing, fishing, windsurfing, dolphin viewing, biking, snorkeling, and scuba diving. Island time is good for the soul. Everything slows down, priorities shift to beach activities and seafood options, and even tightly wound drivers lay off their car horns. It may take a day or two to assimilate to South Padre mode, but once you're there, you won't want to leave.

The massive 130-mile-long Padre Island is home to the longest sand beach in the United States. Never stretching more than three miles wide, the island was formed by the methodical process of sea erosion and deposition. The northern portion, adjacent to Corpus Christi, has a modest collection of hotels and residences and is mostly recreation oriented. The central portion is the natural protected wonderland of Padre Island National Seashore. And the southern tip is a major resort area lined with hotels and restaurants catering to a thriving tourist industry.

South Padre Island isn't technically a separate island; rather, it's the name of the resort community (population 2,871) at the southern portion of the big island. The town is flanked by the Gulf of Mexico to the east, a narrow ship channel to the north, and the Laguna Madre, the narrow bay leading to the Texas mainland.

Spanish explorers visited the area in the 1500s, but the resort community remained a barren stretch of pristine seashore until the 1950s when a causeway bridge connected Port Isabel to South Padre Island. Although it provided access to the nicest beaches on the Texas coast, the community remained a low-key resort destination until the late 1970s, when insurance companies were required to provide hurricane coverage and the population increased rather dramatically (from 314 to 1,012 residents) thanks to the increased emphasis on tourism. For the past two decades, it's become a major spring break destination for college students, who descend on the small town in the thousands for revelry and recreation each March.

If you're visiting in the winter, you'll be surrounded by Midwestern license plates and polite retirees taking advantage of the restaurants' early-bird specials. In the summer, Texas families flock to the island to play in the gentle waves and devour fried shrimp. Any time of the year is a good time to visit South Padre because the beach is always pleasant and the vibe is always mellow (except during spring break).

The islanders take their enviable natural resources seriously, offering opportunities for visitors to experience the wonders of this region. Make a point of taking a dolphin tour and visiting the sea turtle research center to get a true appreciation of the sea life that doesn't end up on your dinner plate.

Although it takes some effort to get to South Padre, once you're there, maneuvering around the small town is a breeze. After crossing the Queen Isabella Causeway, take a left onto Padre Boulevard to reach the main drag, with hotels, shops, and restaurants. Take a right off the causeway to reach the public beaches and seaside attractions.

SIGHTS
Schlitterbahn Beach Waterpark
Despite the fact real waves are lapping at the shore just 100 feet away, families still flock to the water rides at **Schlitterbahn Beach Waterpark** (33261 State Park Rd. 100, 956/772-7873, www.schlitterbahn.com, 10am-8pm daily Apr.-Sept., $40-48). Without any pesky sand and saltwater to worry about, kids and adults can spend the day gliding and cruising along water trails and rides, including tube chutes, the Boogie Bahn surfing ride, uphill water coasters, the Rio Ventura, and other popular attractions. In 2012, the park

added an indoor year-round area as part of its Beach Resort hotel, allowing travelers to experience the thrill of playing in an 80-degree environment of wavy water even if it's in the 50s outside. Despite having "only" a half-dozen attractions, the indoor area is immensely fun, offering giant twisty water slides, a riveting tube ride in a propulsive river, the Pirate's Cove kid's area with mini slides and engaging activities, and even a traditional carousel. Unlike the original Schlitterbahn in New Braunfels, which is far more spread out with meandering, lazy inner tube rides, the South Padre version is more compact and beach oriented, with a five-story sand castle fun house and a surprisingly good restaurant (the Shrimp Haus). Also, if you find you've had enough of the fake wave action, the resort provides a bonus amenity: easy beach access. Guests can walk down a short boardwalk to the real beach for some enjoyable bodysurfing and beachcombing. Schlitterbahn even provides umbrellas and lounge chairs to let you kick back, relax, and soak up the genuinely relaxing sounds of waves, seagulls, and seaside activity.

Sea Turtle, Inc.

A heartwarming experience awaits at **Sea Turtle, Inc.** (6617 Padre Blvd., 956/761-4511, www.seaturtleinc.com, 10am-4pm Tues.-Sun., donations requested), an unassuming little spot at the end of South Padre's main strip. Inside, you'll find tanks full of various types and sizes of sea turtles, several native to the nearby Gulf Coast. Each turtle is identified in a separate tank, often with a tear-jerking tale about the unfortunate experience (boat propeller, fishing line, animal attack) that brought it to the rehab site. Try to arrive at 10am for the informative presentation offering context about the several dozen friendly and fascinating creatures on-site. Kids can feed the turtles, and everyone has a chance for a photo op. Marvel at these prehistoric animals—some can reach 450 pounds—and toss an extra few dollars in the box for this organization that works tirelessly to protect and promote these endangered sea creatures.

Dolphin Research and Sea Life Nature Center

Kids aren't the only ones who'll learn something at the **Dolphin Research and Sea Life Nature Center** (110 N. Garcia St. in Port Isabel, 956/299-1957, www.spinaturecenter.com, 10am-6pm daily, $3 donation requested). This low-key locale just across the causeway from South Padre has about 20 aquariums filled with sea creatures from the gulf waters. Shrimp, starfish, rays, and eels await at the center, which offers a children's program at 11am and 2pm (call ahead to ensure it's available) that allows youngsters to handle and feed some of the nonthreatening species in the touch tanks. Knowledgeable staffers educate visitors about environmentally responsible ways to enjoy their time on the island.

◖ Port Isabel Lighthouse

It's well worth the 74-step climb up the tight spiral staircase to experience the breathtaking views from the **Port Isabel Lighthouse** (421 E. Queen Isabella Blvd. in Port Isabel, 800/527-6102, www.tpwd.state.tx.us, summer hours: 10am-6pm Sun.-Thurs., 11am-8pm Fri.-Sat., winter: 9am-5pm daily, $3 adults, $2 students). From the bug-size cars passing over the gorgeous Laguna Madre Bay on the San Isabella Causeway to the remarkable view of adjacent historic downtown Port Isbell, the vantage point from this historical lighthouse is truly a sight to behold. Constructed in 1852 at the request of sea captains frustrated by visibility issues along the low-lying Texas coast, the lighthouse was a prominent and necessary fixture in the region until the early 1900s, when newer, more efficient, and more powerful towers were constructed. Sixteen similar lighthouses graced the Texas coast at one time, but the Port Isabel structure is the only facility remaining open to the public.

Pan American Coastal Studies Laboratory

Not quite as family-oriented as other area attractions, the **Pan American Coastal Studies Laboratory** (100 Marine Lab Dr.,

THE GULF COAST

SAVE THE SEA TURTLES

© ANDY RHODES

an injured sea turtle at South Padre Island's Sea Turtle Inc. rescue center

Padre Island National Seashore is undertaking extensive efforts to protect an endearing creature that nests along its shoreline. The most endangered species of sea turtle, the Kemp's ridley was nearly lost forever in the 1960s, due to massive exploitation of eggs and meat at its primary nesting beach in Mexico. Once the home to nearly 40,000 turtles, the 16-mile stretch of sand at nearby Playa de Rancho Nuevo, in Tamaulipas, Mexico, now sees fewer than 5,000 turtles nesting there each year.

To help save the turtle, the U.S. and Mexican governments have worked together to reestablish a nesting beach at Padre Island, utilizing the theory that turtles will return to the beach where they were born to lay their own eggs. Over 10 years (1978-1988), scientists collected more than 22,000 eggs at Rancho Nuevo and transported them in Padre Island sand to a lab at the national seashore for incubation. The hatchlings were released on the beach, where they then crawled to the surf, with the hopes they'd be naturally imprinted with the location in their memories for future reference.

Biologists have attempted to gauge the turtles' successful rate of return by marking their shells and fins with identification tags and even GPS devices. Each year more turtles revisit their birthplace. Nearly 60 percent of the species' eggs are now found on Padre Island, making it the most important Kemp's ridley nesting beach in the United States. Park officials still incubate turtle eggs and release the little guys into the gulf each summer. The public is invited to view this fascinating natural event; for release dates and directions to the site, call the Hatchling Hotline at 361/949-7163.

Visitors who see a live or dead turtle on the beach are encouraged to immediately contact a park ranger or the seashore's turtle biologist at 361/949-8173. Messing with these endangered turtles in any way is considered a felony, with fines ranging up to $20,000. Many Kemp's ridleys have been identified and protected as a result of visitors' efforts. Perhaps your next stroll on the beach will yield something far more valuable than an intact sand dollar.

© ANDY RHODES

Port Isabel Lighthouse

956/761-2644, www.utpa.edu/csl, 1:30pm-4:30pm Sun.-Fri., free admission) is designed more with researchers in mind than kiddos. Regardless, you'll learn things here about the plant and animal life in the Laguna Madre and Gulf of Mexico through interactive displays (shark jaws, turtle shells) and limited aquariums.

BEACHES

The beach is everywhere at South Padre, so you won't have any trouble finding a place to park and tote your gear to the soft white sand (don't forget to bring plenty of sunscreen and bottled water). Look for public beach access points every few blocks along Gulf Boulevard.

For a few more amenities (pavilions, picnic tables, and playgrounds in addition to the restrooms and showers) go to one of the county beach parks on the southern or northern ends of the island. The most popular of the two is the southern option—**Isla Blanca Park** (33174 State Park Rd. 100, 956/761-5494, www.co.cameron.tx.us/parks, 7am-11pm daily, entry

$4 per vehicle). Referred to as the "crown jewel of the system," it features a mile-plus of pristine white sand and bright blue gulf water for swimming, surfing, and fishing. Parking is easily available, and beachcombers can step right out of a surface lot and onto the beach, where they'll encounter pick-up volleyball games, surfers, Frisbee-catching dogs, and friendly folks strolling along the low-key surf. Nearly 600 RV slots are also available.

At the northern end is **Andy Bowie Park** (7300 Padre Blvd, 956/761-3704, www.co.cameron.tx.us/parks, 7am-11pm daily, entry $4 per vehicle). More "rural" in nature, Andy Bowie offers access to a beachfront road that eventually opens up to 20 miles of scenic driving that certainly qualifies as off the beaten path. Horseback riding is popular here, as is wade fishing and windsurfing on the bay side.

RECREATION
Water Sports
Your one-stop shop for all things recreational in South Padre is **South Padre Island Water Sports/Air Padre** (SPIWS, 5709 Padre Blvd., 956/299-9463, www.spiws.com). The company's credo says it all: "beautiful South Padre Island is best seen from the water." Who knew there were so many ways to experience this view? Each of the following provide a compelling option:

Kayaks are probably the most popular way for visitors to get a steady vantage point of island scenery while getting a nice workout. SPIWS offers a surprising number of kayaks for rent, including single, tandem, fishing, surfing, and even glass-bottom varieties. Prices range from $25-95.

Kiteboarding is another fun way to get a (major) workout at South Padre, though you may spend more time looking at the sky than the shoreline sights. Kiteboarding is a fairly new sport developed by thrill seekers who grew bored with simple waves or sails as a primary source of surfboard acceleration. The island's steady winds and shallow surrounding waters are optimal for this activity. Since most visitors are new to the sport, SPIWS strongly suggests

THE GULF COAST

THE GULF COAST

© ANDY RHODES

Gulf Coast surfing

scheduling an initial lesson (starting at $99) before venturing out on their rental equipment.

Windsurfing represents a step down in intensity from kiteboarding, though it's still an active pursuit requiring plenty of stamina. Fortunately, the island's steady 18-mph winds make things a bit easier for consistent movement. Combined with Laguna Madre Bay's relatively calm waters and shallow sandy floor, windsurfing offers a fun and easy way to zip around the shoreline.

Traditional **surfing** remains an appealing option for many island visitors, and you'll see board-toting guys and gals on most stretches of the beach. The waves aren't major, but they're ideal for honing new (or improving existing) skills. One of the best ways to get your feet wet is through an SPIWS group lesson, offered daily. And you'll find all the equipment you'll ever need for rent or purchase, from soft-stop surfboards to traditional longboards to leashes.

Stand-up paddleboarding is certainly the "easiest" way to experience South Padre via

watersport, and it represents a viable option for visitors seeking a low-key way to see the sights while maintaining an exercise routine. The wide boards help with stability and balance, and the canoe-style paddles provide plenty of propulsion power. SPIWS offers lessons for newbies and rental equipment.

Snorkeling and Scuba Diving

With its clear water and fine sand, the South Padre Island area is a haven for scuba divers and snorkelers. The fish aren't as varied and colorful as you'll find in more exotic locales, but the marine life is certainly intriguing, and you never know what you might find among the reefs and rigs.

Those interested in snorkeling and shallow shore dives can explore the underwater action at the **Mansfield Jetties,** the beach at **Dolphin Cove** (look for sand dollars here), and the adjacent Barracuda Bay. Scuba divers will enjoy the artificial reef (a wreck dive known as "the tug") located seven miles southeast of the **Brazos Santiago Pass Jetties.** Farther out and most compelling to experienced divers are the oil rigs, where fish of all sizes are plentiful.

South Padre has several full-service dive shops offering equipment for rent and sale, organized excursions to prime spots, instruction, and service. One of the most reputable companies is **Southern Wave** (201 W. Pike St., 956/772-7245, www.sailspi.com). Another noteworthy option is **American Diving** (One Padre Blvd., 956/761-2030, www.divesouthpadre.com).

Fishing

Like most coastal communities, fishing is a huge draw in South Padre. Everywhere you look, you'll see men and the occasional woman with a fishing pole standing on a beach, jetty, or pier. If they aren't standing on shore, they're in a chartered boat. Shoreline anglers tend to snag redfish, speckled trout, and flounder while deep-sea adventurers seek tarpon, marlin, kingfish, mackerel, and wahoo.

Many anglers use the services of the venerable **Jim's Pier** (209 W. Whiting St., 956/761-2865), which bills itself as the original South Padre Island fishing-guide company. Jim's provides boat slips, fueling docks, a launching ramp, and fish-cleaning facilities. The company also offers two bay fishing trips daily on its renowned 40-person-capacity party boat. To find out more about fishing locations and services, consult the **Port Isabel/South Padre Island Guides Association** at www.fishspi.com, offering a lengthy list of endorsed professional fishing guides.

Dolphin Viewing

Even though you don't technically get in the water to take on this activity, it's ocean based and certainly worth experiencing. The Laguna Madre Bay is home to a myriad of bottlenose dolphins, and there's nothing like the thrill of seeing them up close in their natural environment. The best way to get an intimate experience is through an independent tour company like **Fins to Feathers** (tours operate from Port Isabel's Sea Life Center, 956/299-0629, www.fin2feather.com; tours run 7am-sunset daily,

$25 per person). Enjoy a personalized experience from a small boat, allowing up-close views and interaction with the knowledgeable guide, a colorful character accompanied by a dolphin-finding dog. Anticipate the surge of excitement you'll feel when that first dorsal fin ascends from the water and the sun glistens off the smooth gray surface of these magnificent and elegant creatures.

Hiking

South Padre is not known as a hiking destination. That being said, it has plenty of shoreline to explore by foot, just not in the traditional way of strapping on boots and following trails. To experience the island as a biped, head to **Andy Bowie Park** (7300 Padre Blvd., 956/761-3704, www.co.cameron.tx.us/parks, 7am-11pm daily). The park offers access to a beachfront road trail (watch out for rogue vehicles) that eventually opens up to extremely isolated areas.

Biking

Like hiking, South Padre isn't the first place that comes to mind when most cyclists are looking for an adventurous trail to tackle. Most bikes on the island are either loud motorcycles or the basket-toting variety operated by Winter Texans. However, cyclists will certainly enjoy the novel challenge of pedaling a Fat Sand Bike on the beach, a surprisingly quick and easy way to navigate in the soft sand. Rentals are available at **South Padre Island Water Sports/Air Padre** (5709 Padre Blvd., 956/299-9463, www.spiws.com) from half days to a week ($40-250).

ENTERTAINMENT AND EVENTS
Bars and Clubs

After a day of playing in the ocean, the perfect place to relax and enjoy a cold glass of quality suds is **Padre Island Brewing Company** (3400 Padre Blvd., 956/761-9585, www.pibrewingcompany.com, $6-17). Not surprisingly, beer is the main theme here, with home-brew supplies such as kettles, burlap sacks, and vintage bottles serving as surrounding scenery. It provides a refreshing change of pace from the

THE GULF COAST

THE GULF COAST

© ANDY RHODES

a dolphin sighted on the Fins to Feathers tour

ubiquitous corporate light-beer signs in most beach establishments. Fortunately, the hand-crafted beer is commendable, particularly the Padre Pale Ale and Spotted Trout Stout. There's food too, including seafood (natch) and tradi-tional bar fare like burgers, nachos, ribs, and sandwiches. Look for a seat on the second-floor outdoor deck.

For the ultimate sampling of island leisure activity, belly up to ◖ **Louie's Backyard** (2305 Laguna Dr., 956/761-6406, www. lbyspi.com, $9-26). During Spring Break, Louie's is party central, with multiple decks of dance floors and swirling light shows. The bartenders work quickly and ably, and the drinks are potent and tasty. Speaking of tasty—before hitting the bar, consider going to the sumptuous buffet. Choose from boiled shrimp, crab legs, fish, and scallops along with ribs, pasta, and salad. The full menu has even better options, including a buttery and flaky red snapper fillet and crispy, fla-vorful fried shrimp. Top off your experience with a stunning view of the sunset over the

bay while sipping Louie's signature cocktail, mixed with multiple liquors and aptly named the Whammy.

South Padre regulars have been celebrating the return of a favorite bar in a new location. **Parrot Eyes** (5801 Padre Blvd., 956/761-9457, www.parroteyesspi.com) has a definite Jimmy Buffet feel, with its laid-back vibe and beach-lovin' patrons, who also enjoy indulging in a cocktail or four. Grab a drink and try to snag a spot on the small deck overlooking the bay. If you're feeling adventurous (during Spring Break or any time at all), order the Parrot-Head Paralyzer, a crazy concoction of multiple liquors and fruit juices that helps you hang on (to the bar).

Those seeking the Spring Break vibe will find it at **Coconuts Bar and Grill** (2301 Laguna Dr., 956/761-4218, www.coconutsspi.com). Coconuts has good food but is known mainly for its festive activities during the day—water-sport rental and recreation—and night—oc-casionally raucous bar scene with friendly and generously pouring waitstaff.

THE GULF COAST

© ANDY RHODES

Padre Island Brewing Company

Events

The community of South Padre knows how to show its visitors and residents a good time, as evidenced by several fun annual outdoor events. One of the first to draw big crowds each year is early February's **SPI Kitefest** (956/761-1248, www. bskites.com). Held at the Sand Flats north of the South Padre Island Convention Centre, Kitefest features hundreds of colorful kites punctuating the crisp blue sky. The steady ocean breeze helps keep even beginners' kites aloft, but experts are also on hand to showcase new equipment, demonstrate kite-flying skills, and distribute prizes.

Of course, the community's (and even one of the state's) biggest beach event of the year is **Spring Break,** when tens of thousands of college students and similarly minded partiers descend on South Padre en masse to . . . party. Although revelers arrive throughout the entire month of March, the heaviest dose of craziness occurs during Texas Week, typically the second or third week of March. To find out more about joining (or avoiding) the chaos, visit http://springbreak.sopadre.com.

Much more mellow is the island's annual **Texas State Surfing Championship,** usually held in late April or early May (dates are based on surf swell). This invitational competition for all ages is held in Isla Blanca Park, located on the extreme southern tip of the island and considered the area's crown jewel. For updates and more information about the event, visit www. surftgsa.org.

ACCOMMODATIONS
Hotels

Lodging rates in a beach town are akin to those in a ski village—they can be mile-high in the busy season and downright affordable the rest of the year. The following South Padre accommodations include prices for a weekend stay in midsummer (the busy getaway season in Texas, despite the fact that it's 93 degrees and humid).

Among the affordable options is **South Beach Inn** (120 E. Jupiter Ln., 956/761-2471, www.southbeachtexas.com, $49-119 depending on room size and season), an independently owned 12-unit establishment nestled among

SPRING BREAK AT SOUTH PADRE

This low-key, unassuming beach community turns into a high-octane, raucous party town for several weeks each March. Nearly 100,000 students from across the country descend on South Padre Island from approximately March 10 through March 20, prompting locals to skedaddle from their quiet seaside homes quicker than a college kid can chug a beer.

Rivaling Florida's Daytona Beach as the nation's ultimate spring break destination, South Padre has become party central for college students primarily from Texas and the Midwest. Though the town doesn't quite have the infrastructure to handle the hordes—eight-hour waits on the causeway are common on peak arrival days—it ultimately benefits from the millions of dollars spent on lodging, food, and DWI tickets (be forewarned: take the Wave shuttle if you've had a few drinks).

Speaking of drinking, one of South Padre's biggest spring break assets is its on-the-beach consumption policy: Unlike most American seashores, it's completely legal to consume here if you're 21 or older. The undercover TABC (Texas Alcoholic Beverage Commission) agents are out in full force looking for MIPs (minors in possession), so make sure you're of legal age or at least extremely discreet. In other drinking-related news, visitors may want to consider renting a hotel with kitchenette or, even better, a condo for easy access to a fridge, ice, and countertops. For a comprehensive list of condo options, visit www.service24.com.

Spring breakers often take advantage of the various package deals offered by travel agencies. Most involve flights and lodging, but several feature mini excursions around the area for those seeking a brief respite after four or five days of constant drinking and sunbathing. One of the most popular activities is a professionally operated surfing lesson, complete with board, wet suit, and individual instruction. Those in search of a change of scenery while downing drinks can sign up for a party-yacht cruise originating at Coconuts Bar and Grill.

the palms just a block from the beach. One of the oldest hotel buildings on the island (1961), South Beach offers mostly efficiency-style kitchenettes with full-size stoves, refrigerators, microwaves, and toasters. Pets are welcome, and Wi-Fi service is available.

The next step on the price ladder gets you a bit closer to the action with some added amenities. One of the more popular and reliable options is the **Ramada Limited** (4109 Padre Blvd., 956/761-4097, www.ramadasouthpadreisland.com, $119 d), offering a free hot breakfast, an outdoor pool and hot tub, and rooms with microwaves, fridges, and free wireless Internet access. Also worth noting: pets are welcome at the Ramada. Closer to the Queen Isabella Causeway is the casual yet consistent **Super 8** (4205 Padre Blvd., 956/761-6300, www.super8padre.com, $123 d), with a heated outdoor pool, free continental breakfast, free Wi-Fi access, and mini microwaves and refrigerators.

The **Travelodge** (6200 Padre Blvd., 956/761-4744, www.southpadretravelodge.com, $140 d) has a large outdoor pool and hot tub, a private walkway to the beach, free wireless Internet access, a deluxe continental breakfast, and microwaves and refrigerators in each room. Another good option is **Beachside Inn** (4500 Padre Blvd., 956/761-4919, www.padrebeachside.com, $184 d), featuring clean, simple rooms within walking distance of the beach, an outdoor pool with hot tub, and kitchenettes with microwaves and refrigerators. For a clean and reliable chain hotel, consider **Holiday Inn Express** (6502 Padre Blvd., 956/761-8844, www.hiexpress.com, $199 d). What sets it apart from the other corporate choices is the massive aquarium in the lobby with dozens of colorful fish darting about. Otherwise, the amenities here are pretty standard, including an outdoor pool, a fitness center, beach access, Wi-Fi access, and rooms with microwaves and refrigerators.

Resorts

The newest place to stay and play on the island is **Schlitterbahn Beach Resort** (33261 State Park Road 100, 956/772-7873, www.schlitterbahn.com, starting at $209 d). Opened in 2012, the resort is an ideal family getaway at any time of the year because it includes an indoor water park. The brand-new accommodations are clean and comfortable, with quality bed linens, fancy flat-screen TVs, and an interesting heavy-timber theme, reportedly hewn from remnants of a devastating Central Texas forest fire. Be sure to set aside some time in the evening to experience the pleasure of ordering a nightcap cocktail at the resort's swim-up bar in the heated pool.

The recently renovated (former Best Western) is now **La Copa Inn Beach Resort** (350 Padre Blvd., 956/761-6000, www.lacoparesort.com, $199 d). Upgrades to the former chain include free Internet service, a free deluxe continental breakfast, and nightly happy hour with beer, wine, and snacks.

For a step up, consider another hotel-to-resort renovation: the **Pearl South Padre** (310 Padre Blvd., 956/761-6551, www.pearlsouthpadre.com, $279 d). Occupying 15 tropical beachside acres, this former Sheraton hotel is a comfortable yet fancy spot with ample amenities and several types of accommodations. Choose from standard guest rooms, kitchenettes, suites, or even fully equipped two- and three-bedroom condominiums, all with private balconies. Other amenities include an enormous 6,000-square-foot swimming pool complete with waterfall and swim-up bar, a separate oversize Jacuzzi, volleyball nets, an exercise and weight room, and seasonal parasailing.

Just down the street is the upscale (and pricey) **Peninsula Island Resort & Spa** (340 Padre Blvd., 956/761-2514, www.peninsulaislandresort.com, $329 d), featuring one-, two-, and three-bedroom units with kitchenettes, a swim-up pool bar, large edgeless pool, hot tub, rooms with fancy Brazilian furniture, a gym,

THE GULF COAST

© ANDY RHODES

Schlitterbahn Beach Resort

and an on-site convenience store. Seasonal spa services are available.

Among the most well-known and luxurious choices on the island is the **Isla Grand** (500 Padre Blvd., 800/292-7704, www.isla-grand.com, $279 d), boasting perhaps the best beachfront location in town with excellent services. Rooms include free Internet access, microwaves, and refrigerators. Consider upgrading to a condo suite—the spacious rooms, living area with a couch and second TV, fully equipped kitchen, and separate bathrooms (a godsend for those with kids) provide a perfect home away from home. The hotel's grounds, though, is what keeps guests coming back for repeated recreational relaxation. Enjoy the direct beach access, two outdoor swimming pools with a cascading waterfall, three whirlpools, four lighted tennis courts, shuffleboard courts, and plenty of lounge chairs.

Camping

Beachfront property is too valuable to allow for many camping options in the commercial area of South Padre. In fact, there are really only a couple main options for serious RV-style campers.

The **South Padre Island KOA** (1 Padre Blvd., 800/562-9724, www.southpadrekoa.com, $30-60 nightly) is geared toward RVs and mobile homes, but it also has a few cabins and lodges available. Site amenities include an outdoor pool, a fitness center, recreation room, and free wireless Internet service. Bonus: The adjacent Pier 19 restaurant is one of the best places on the island to enjoy a quality seafood meal.

Another busy option for RVers is **Isla Blanca Park** (33174 State Park Rd. 100, 956/761-5494, www.co.cameron.tx.us/parks). Referred to as the "crown jewel of the system," the park offers nearly 600 RV slots. Other features include a mile-plus of pure white sand and glistening blue gulf water for swimming, surfing, and fishing.

Those looking for a more rustic, natural experience have the option of pitching a tent (or parking an RV) on the vast unpopulated stretch of sand north of all the major

recreational activity. Local officials caution campers to drive on the wet sand to avoid getting stuck in the soft tractionless powder farther away from the surf. Also, be sure to bring your garbage back with you (there aren't any trash cans in these remote areas) and take the No Trespassing signs seriously.

FOOD
Seafood

One of the first places many beach-town visitors go is a seaside seafood restaurant. Even before you check in to your hotel room you may want to drop by a low-key local eatery like **Palm Street Pier Bar & Grill** (204 W. Palm St., 956/772-7256, www.palmstreetpier.com, 11am-midnight daily, $7-18), known for its tantalizing seafood and sunsets. Overlooking the scenic Laguna Madre Bay, Palm Street Pier specializes in tasty shrimp dishes. The fried shrimp is especially wonderful, and the coconut and stuffed varieties are nearly as tasty. Don't miss the cheap margaritas and summertime Friday-night fireworks over the bay. Another bonus is the "you hook it, we'll cook it" policy, allowing diners to bring in their own fresh catch and have it expertly prepared—blackened, grilled, or fried with two sides—for $6. Worth noting: Palm Street operates on island time, so don't expect your food to arrive quickly.

Also drawing regular return customers is the venerable and well-regarded **Blackbeard's** (103 E. Saturn Ln., 956/761-2962, www.blackbeardsspi.com, 11am-10pm daily, $7-20), a swashbuckling-themed spot with surprisingly refined food. Fresh gulf catches are the main draw here, including flounder and tilapia, but the landlubber options are equally commendable, including charbroiled steaks and grilled chicken. Incidentally, the burgers here are the best on the island.

A local favorite in a new location is **Daddy's Cajun Kitchen & Seafood Market** (1801 Padre Blvd., 956/761-1975, www.daddysrestaurant.com, 11am-10pm daily, $9-20). Housed in the two-story building previously occupied by Garcia's, Daddy's offers a slightly different take on traditional South Texas Gulf Coast seafood, with Creole and Cajun specialties. Choose from popular standards like jambalaya, gumbo, and crawfish étouffée, or opt for one of the in-house lunch specials such as a crispy panko-breaded shrimp or almond-crusted fish fillet topped with crab and cheese sauce.

South Padre also has a couple of highly recommended seafood restaurants that are more upscale in nature. In a casual town like this, however, that simply means the quality and prices are higher—you can still wear shorts and sandals. One of the most popular is the remarkable **C Sea Ranch Restaurant** (1 Padre Blvd., 956/761-1314, www.searanchrestaurant.com, 4:30-9pm Sun.-Thurs., 4:30-10pm Fri.-Sat., $9-40), the kind of place where you can't go wrong with anything on the menu, be it "from the sea" or "from the grill." The options change regularly, but the mantra of the Sea Ranch remains constant: serving quality "local wild-caught" seafood directly from the gulf. Signature dishes include boiled king crab legs, gulf shrimp and bay oysters, and an amazing ahi tuna served rare with soy sauce and wasabi. Topping it all off is an exceptional view of the sea. Reservations are suggested.

Another popular seafood spot is **Pier 19** (1 Padre Blvd, 956/761-7437, www.pier19.us, hours vary, $8-39). Don't let the KOA Kampground sign scare you away—simply drive past a few hundred campers until the road ends at this fine local establishment. Located literally on the water, this seafood and steak restaurant gets marks for its consistent, high-quality food. Highlights on the menu include shrimp (the peel-and-eat plates are perfectly prepared, as are the sautéed and fried options), blackened rockfish, and local flounder, pompano, and amberjack. The baja tacos (with grilled shrimp) are especially tasty, bursting with the complimentary flavors of savory shrimp, spicy jalapeño, and sweet mango. An added bonus: On some weekends, the staff "treats" diners to a pirate-themed show; if you're unable to witness this performance, keep your eye out instead for dolphins, which are known to make occasional appearances in the water below.

Burgers

If you've somehow exhausted your craving for seafood, your next best bet is standard beach fare—burgers, pizzas, fried stuff, and in South Padre, Tex-Mex. One of the best places in town to combine all these things with a cold glass of quality suds is **Padre Island Brewing Company** (3400 Padre Blvd., 956/761-9585, www.pibrewingcompany.com, 11:30am-11:30pm Mon.-Thurs., 11:30am-midnight Fri.-Sat., 11:30am-10:30pm Sun., $6-17). Not surprisingly, beer is the main theme here, with home-brew supplies such as kettles, burlap sacks, and vintage bottles serving as surrounding scenery. It provides a refreshing change of pace from the ubiquitous corporate light-beer signs in most beach establishments. Fortunately, the handcrafted beer is commendable, particularly the Padre Island Pale Ale and Spotted Trout Stout. There's food too, including traditional bar fare like burgers, nachos, ribs, and sandwiches. To experience a combination of the island's most tantalizing taste bud sensations, order a pale ale with a gulf-stuffed flounder, a flavorful fillet packed with crab and topped with a creamy shrimp sauce. To enhance the experience even further, ask for a seat on the second-floor outdoor deck.

For a tasty burger and cold beer, head to **Tom & Jerry's Beach Bar & Grill** (3212 Padre Blvd., 956/761-8999, 11am-11pm daily, $6-18). The seafood dishes here are commendable, but the beach grub is the main draw, from the burgers to the chicken plates to the chicken-fried steak and club sandwich. After your meal, head to the raised bar, where friendly staffers will gladly pour you a cold draft beer or expertly mix a frozen concoction.

Mexican and Tex-Mex

If you're in the mood for some traditional Tex-Mex, head to the extremely popular and immensely satisfying **Jesse's Cantina & Restaurant** (2700 Padre Blvd., 956/761-4500, hours vary, $7-15). Jesse's is famous for its potent margaritas and top-notch traditional dishes like tacos, enchiladas, carnitas, and

Pier 19

quesadillas. Naturally, they serve fried shrimp here too, and it's some of the best on the island.

INFORMATION AND SERVICES

The incredibly friendly and helpful people at the **South Padre Island Convention & Visitors Bureau** (600 Padre Blvd., 800/767-2373, www. sopadre.com, 8am-5pm Mon.-Fri., 9am-5pm Sat-Sun.) will provide you with brochures, maps, and information about area attractions. You can also check with them about activities and events related to fishing, boating, and other ocean-based recreation.

GETTING THERE AND AROUND

The Brownsville South Padre Island International Airport (700 S. Minnesota Ave., 956/542-4373, www.flybrownsville.com) is the closest airport to South Padre. At 27 miles

away, it's not too far, especially if you need to get to the beach in a hurry and don't feel like making the nearly nine-hour drive from Dallas or approximately five-hour trek from Houston and Austin. The airport offers several American Eagle and United Airlines flights daily to and from Houston. Rental car services are available at the airport.

Once on the island, feel free to ditch the car in favor of the city's reliable and often necessary **Wave transportation system** (866/761-1025, visit www.townspi.com for schedule and stops). If you plan to have a beer or six during spring break, you'll be glad these small buses are there to cart your body safely home. Although the Wave typically operates 7am-9pm among local businesses and services, it's also available for late-night stops during spring break to shuttle impaired revelers. Incidentally, the belligerent scene on the ride back from the bar at 3am is one of the most insane experiences imaginable.

EAST TEXAS GETAWAYS

For many Houston residents and visitors, a "getaway" is defined as a day trip to Galveston (50 miles southeast of town) or an overnight camping excursion to Sam Houston National Forest (70 miles north). Those journeys take about as long as an average weekday commute in the sprawling ciy. Consider devoting a morning's drive to a true getaway further up the coast in Beaumont or deeper into the East Texas Piney Woods. Both offer a true diversion from big-city life via slower-paced scenic roadways and charming encounters with genuine local characters.

Instead of spending big bucks on a trendy new restaurant or chartered fishing expedition, take a load off your wallet (and wardrobe) with a casual trip to a historical Main Street community like Marshall or a modest-sized city like Lufkin. These and other East Texas towns offer surprisingly high-quality food options and attractions at a fraction of Houston costs.

A weekend in East Texas will help urbanites and tourists recharge and reacquaint themselves with bygone days. Texas history plays a major role in the region's cultural destinations, and the occasional pocket of dropped cell phone service proves that Facebook updates and work messages aren't always a priority.

Take a hike in the Big Thicket National Preserve. Eat a perfectly fried catfish fillet. Gaze at the spot where an oil gusher forever changed the fate of the Lone Star State. And soak up a different pace and time during your East Texas getaway.

© ANDY RHODES

EAST TEXAS

HIGHLIGHTS

LOOK FOR ◖ TO FIND RECOMMENDED SIGHTS, ACTIVITIES, DINING, AND LODGING.

◖ **Spindletop-Gladys City Boomtown Museum:** The 1901 oil gush heard 'round the country erupted at this site, where a museum now chronicles Beaumont's boomtown days (page 138).

◖ **Bird-Watching at Big Thicket National Preserve:** This swath of East Texas Piney Woods contains a host of species from the Gulf Coast, Central Plains, and Southeastern forests coexisting with critters from the deserts, bayous, woods, and swamps (page 146).

◖ **Aldridge Sawmill:** Enormous and stark concrete walls are all that remain of the century-old lumber operation, offering an eerie juxtaposition to the surrounding dense forest that emerged in its place (page 151).

◖ **Texas State Railroad:** Experience the old-time feel of riding the rails on this rickety but enchanting locomotive, which chugs, clanks, and charms its way through the East Texas Piney Woods (page 160).

◖ **Caddo Lake:** Way up in the northeast corner of the state, Caddo Lake, the only natural lake in Texas, is worth a visit for its scenic backdrop of wispy Spanish moss and outstretched cypress trees, best viewed while hiking, swimming, fishing, or boating (page 172).

PLANNING YOUR TIME

Since the region is so large, it may be easier to think of East Texas as offering a series of distinctive getaways, depending on what strikes your fancy on a particular weekend. For Texans, the opportunity to spend a few days surrounded by the sights, sounds, and smells of a dense pine forest is worth prioritizing. Even travelers from pinier parts of the country can appreciate the region's national forests (Big Thicket, Sam Houston, Davy Crockett, Angelina, and Sabine), ripe with Texas-worthy elements such as massive reservoirs, barbecue restaurants, and a sawmill ghost town.

Although a tent is the optimal way to spend a night or two in a forest campground, plenty of other lodging options are available, including rustic cabins and hotels. And if you're angling to catch some bass or catfish, you'll find plenty of places to rent boats and equipment. For a more low-key recreational experience, consider bringing a bike or pair of hiking boots to explore the forest trails.

For those more interested in discovering local cuisine, culture, and shopping, a weekend is also the perfect amount of time to soak up one of East Texas's charming communities. Beaumont is the closest getaway (about 80 miles east of Houston) and delivers an impressive array of Cajun restaurants, heritage attractions, and entertainment options.

A bit further away from Houston (but completely worth the drive) are Lufkin and Nacogdoches, about two-and-a-half hours

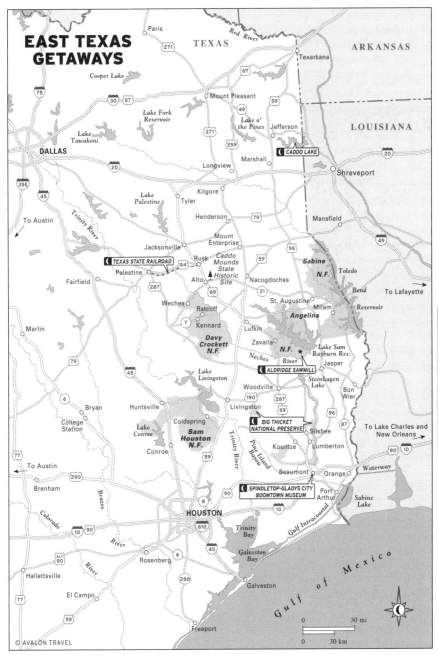

EAST TEXAS GETAWAYS

TEXAS

ARKANSAS

LOUISIANA

Paris
Red River
Texarkana
Cooper Lake
Mount Pleasant
Lake Fork Reservoir
Lake o' the Pines
Jefferson
CADDO LAKE
Lake Tawakoni
DALLAS
Longview
Marshall
Shreveport
To Austin
Trinity River
Lake Palestine
Tyler
Kilgore
Henderson
Mansfield
Jacksonville
Mount Enterprise
Caddo Mounds State Historic Site
Sabine N.F.
Fairfield
TEXAS STATE RAILROAD
Rusk
Palestine
Alto
Nacogdoches
Toledo Bend Reservoir
To Lafayette
Weches
Ratcliff
Kennard
St. Augustine
Milam
Angelina
Marlin
Davy Crockett N.F.
Lufkin
Zavalla
N.F.
Lake Sam Rayburn Res.
Jasper
Neches River
ALDRIDGE SAWMILL
Steinhagen Lake
Bon Wier
Lake Livingston
Woodville
Bryan
Huntsville
Livingston
College Station
Coldspring
Lake Conroe
Sam Houston N.F.
BIG THICKET NATIONAL PRESERVE
Silsbee
To Lake Charles and New Orleans
Conroe
Kountze
Lumberton
To Austin
Brenham
Trinity River
Pine Island Bayou
Beaumont
Orange
Waterway
Brazos
SPINDLETOP-GLADYS CITY BOOMTOWN MUSEUM
Port Arthur
Sabine Lake
Colorado River
HOUSTON
Hallettsville
Rosenberg
Trinity Bay
Gulf Intracoastal
El Campo
Galveston Bay
Galveston
Gulf of Mexico
Freeport

EAST TEXAS

0   30 mi
0   30 km

© AVALON TRAVEL

north. Consider devoting two or three days to exploring this area, just to soak up all the uniquely East Texas elements like the state railroad, forestry museum, and Caddo mounds.

Finally, those with a little extra time will be rewarded for their nearly four-hour drive to northeastern Texas (home of the historically Deep South communities of Marshall and Jefferson). This region offers a true step back in time to the antebellum south, with plantation museums, majestic lakes, down-home restaurants, and genuinely friendly townsfolk.

Beaumont and Vicinity

Beaumont (population 118,296) isn't your average Texas midsize city. More connected to the eastern United States than other Southern communities, it has a working-class union element (due to the propensity of oil workers), and it has a denser historical downtown than its wide-open West Texas brethren. Its proximity to New Orleans and the Gulf Coast along with its two nearby sister cities of Port Arthur and Orange have earned the area the nickname "the Cajun Triangle."

The city's (and state's and country's) fate was forever changed on the morning of January 10, 1901, when the Lucas Gusher erupted from the Spindletop oilfield. Tens of thousands of people flocked to Beaumont to capitalize on the oil boom and in the process built an impressive collection of churches, civic buildings, and residences. The impact on Beaumont resulted in a true American melting pot, with Italian and Jewish influences combined with Cajun and African American inspirations. The city's architectural treasures remain an integral part of downtown's distinctive historical charm.

Although the corporate oil scene would eventually move to nearby Houston (about 80 miles to the southwest), Beaumont's petroleum-related legacy remains its true identity. In 1901, the first year of the boom, three major companies formed—the Gulf Oil Corporation, Humble (later Exxon), and the Texas Company (later Texaco). One year later, more than 500 Texas corporations were doing business in Beaumont.

However, the boom soon went bust as Spindletop quickly fell victim to an overabundance of wells. Two decades later, new advancements in the oil industry allowed riggers to dig wells deeper, resulting in another Spindletop boom. In 1927, the oilfield yielded its all-time annual high of 21 million barrels.

The Beaumont area never experienced another major surge, but the city had landed on the map, with corporations and families from across the country relocating to the region. During World War II the city prospered as a shipbuilding center, and the petrochemical industry continued to sustain the economy for decades to come.

Meanwhile, the nearby coastal communities of Port Arthur and Orange benefited from Beaumont's corporate and cultural activity. Although the oil money never made the Golden Triangle as prosperous as its name implies, the region benefited by opening several art museums, forging a soulful music identity, and capitalizing on its Cajun culture with fabulous food establishments.

SIGHTS
C Spindletop-Gladys City
Boomtown Museum

To get a true sense of the craziness that befell Beaumont upon the discovery of the Spindletop oilfield, visit the intriguing **Spindletop-Gladys City Boomtown Museum** (5550 University Dr., 409/880-1750, www.spindletop.org, 10am-5pm Tues.-Sat., 1pm-5pm Sun., $5 adults, $3 seniors, $2 children ages 6-12). Located near the site of the famous Lucas gusher, the museum offers a self-guided tour of 15 clapboard building replicas from the oil-boom era, including a general store, saloon, post office, stable, and blacksmith shop. The buildings and associated photos and interpretive panels tell the story of the

BOOM! GOES THE TOWN

In the early 1900s, East Texas was a land of opportunity, with prospectors speculating about the location of the next big oil field. More often than not, their efforts were unsuccessful. But when they guessed correctly and tapped into a fertile patch of petroleum, the fortunes of everyone associated with the discovery exploded like the gusher of oil that burst into the East Texas sky.

The wildcatters working at the base of Beaumont's Lucas gusher certainly couldn't have predicted the global impact they'd helped create on January 10, 1901. Once word spread about the gusher's subterranean Spindletop oil field, tens of thousands of people flocked to Beaumont to make their fortunes.

Everyone wanted a piece of the action, from engineers and riggers to real estate companies and saloon owners. Virtually overnight, the oil discovery transformed Beaumont from a small village of several hundred rice farmers and cattle raisers to a big ol' boomtown of petroleum barons, field workers, and the people who provided services to them.

A lesser-known East Texas boomtown was Kilgore, about 30 miles east of Tyler. Kilgore's glory years began in 1930, when the first oil gusher arrived; within weeks, the town's population surged from 500 people to more than 10,000. Before well-spacing regulations were adopted, Kilgore boasted a small section of downtown that became known as the "World's Richest Acre," where 24 oil wells once stood.

At the height of Kilgore's boom, residents woke up to find their yards filled with strangers covered with boxes, sacks, and newspapers. People installed iron doors on their homes for protection from the influx of newcomers, and they stopped hanging their clothes out to dry since they'd be stolen right off the line.

Not surprisingly, the oil boom also brought professional undesirables in the form of con men, criminals, and prostitutes to these small East Texas towns. The Texas Rangers were assigned to clean up the area, and they often had to resort to unorthodox means—like the time they "remodeled" an old church into a makeshift prison with padlocked prisoners lining the interior walls—to address the newfound population of ne'er-do-wells.

These stories, along with photos and artifacts, are often on display at local history museums in East Texas. For a full-fledged step back in time to the region's oil boomtown glory years, visit Kilgore's comprehensive and compelling **East Texas Oil Museum** (at the intersection of Hwy. 259 and Ross St., 903/983-8295, www.easttexasoilmuseum. com, 9am-4pm Tues.-Sat., 2pm-5pm Sun., free admission).

EAST TEXAS

massive and unprecedented boomtown saga, when Beaumont transformed from a village of several hundred to a city of nearly 30,000 in a matter of weeks. The museum also features wooden oil derricks of the era, including a life-size *water*-spewing gusher that keeps families entertained and refreshed during the hot summer months.

McFaddin-Ward House

One of the city's top tourist destinations is the remarkable 1906 **McFaddin-Ward House** (1906 Calder Ave., 409/832-2134, www.mcfaddin-ward.org, 10am-3pm Tues.-Sat., 1pm-3pm Sun., closed at lunch, $3 guided tours,

$2 group tours, reservations recommended). This impressive neoclassical beaux arts-style mansion features beautiful decorative exterior detailing and opulent interior furnishings reflecting the lifestyle of William McFaddin, a member of one of Texas's oldest and wealthiest families. McFaddin was a Texas Army veteran who created a cattle and oil empire from the land he received for his military service. The guided tours of his family's fabulous home and adjacent carriage house provide anecdotal and architectural background information along with up-close views of furniture, artwork, and mementos showcasing this prominent Texas family.

EAST TEXAS

Texas Energy Museum

Somewhat surprisingly, Beaumont boasts nearly 20 museums. Among the best is the downtown **Texas Energy Museum** (600 Main St., 409/833-5100, www.texasenergymuseum. org, 9am-5pm Tues.-Sat., 1pm-5pm Sun., $2 adults, $1 seniors and children ages 6-12). This spacious two-story facility features a fascinating collection of exhibits dedicated to, appropriately enough, oil-based energy sources. Interactive displays highlight the history of oil as a versatile resource and provide vital information about the global significance of this local commodity. Though the name is somewhat misleading—there aren't any power plants or light bulbs here—the museum succeeds in educating visitors about the remarkable history and relevance of the petrochemical industry.

Fire Museum of Texas

The nearby **Fire Museum of Texas** (400 Walnut St., 409/880-3927, www.firemuseumoftexas.org, 8am-4:30pm Mon.-Fri., free admission) is another unexpected gem. The small museum, housed in the 1927 Beaumont Fire Department Headquarters Station, is practically dwarfed by the massive black-and-white spotted "world's largest fire hydrant" in front of the building. Now considered the not-quite-as-impressive third largest in the world, this 24-foot-tall hydrant was donated to the museum by Disney Studios in conjunction with the release of the animated movie *101 Dalmatians*. Inside, the facility showcases the importance of firefighters in Texas and across the country through vintage fire engines and equipment, educational exhibits, and the Texas Firefighter Memorial.

Babe Didrickson Zaharias Museum

Babe who? You'll be telling everyone about her after experiencing the captivating **Babe Didrickson Zaharias Museum** (1750 I-10 E., 409/833-4622, www.babedidriksonzaharias.org, 9am-5pm daily, free admission). Port Arthur native Zaharias was a pioneer in women's sports who was voted the world's greatest woman athlete of the first half of the 20th century in a poll conducted by the Associated Press. Nicknamed "Babe" after swatting five home runs in one baseball game, Zaharias was an accomplished Olympic athlete, tennis player, basketball player, diver, bowler, and most notably, golfer. She won every major professional golf championship at least once and is credited with single-handedly popularizing women's golf. The museum features trophies, golf clubs, photos, newspaper clippings, Olympic medals, and films representing her fascinating and enormously successful athletic career.

ACCOMMODATIONS

For a modest-sized city, Beaumont is surprisingly lacking in downtown hotels within walking distance of its many museums and cultural attractions. Regardless, one of the better deals in town is **La Quinta Midtown** (220 I-10 N., 409/838-9991, www.lq.com, $45 d), located about five minutes from the city center on busy I-10. La Quinta offers a free continental breakfast, free Internet access, and an outdoor pool.

A popular and reliable option is **Sleep Inn & Suites** (2030 N. 11th St., 409/892-6700, www.choicehotels.com, $79 d), featuring free wireless Internet access, a free deluxe continental breakfast, fitness center, and an outdoor pool. Another consistently solid choice is **Homewood Suites by Hilton** (3745 I-10 S., 409/842-9990, www.homewoodsuites3.hilton.com, $79 d), located four miles from downtown. The suites feature separate living and sleeping areas, fully equipped kitchens with full-size fridges, and Wi-Fi. Accommodations include a full breakfast each morning, evening dinner and drinks (Mon.-Thurs.), and even a complimentary grocery-shopping service. For those traveling with four-legged companions, it's worth noting that Homewood Suites is a dog-friendly hotel.

The best bang for the buck is **◖ Holiday Inn Beaumont-Plaza** (3950 I-10 S., 409/842-5995 or 800/465-4329, www.holidayinn.com, $82 d). An enormous three-story cascading waterfall greets guests as they enter the spacious garden atrium, and the renovated rooms provide clean and comfortable accommodations. The Plaza location (not to be confused with Holiday Inn Midtown) features free Wi-Fi service, an indoor pool and whirlpool, a full fitness center, and free meals for kids 12 and under.

Representing the upper tier of Beaumont's lodging options is the regional chain **MCM Elegante** (2355 I-10 S., 409/842-3600, www.mcmelegantebeaumont.com, $99 d). The hotel features a tropical outdoor pool, a fancy fitness center, free Wi-Fi access, refrigerators, and microwaves.

FOOD

Despite being only one city block, the historical **Crockett Street District** is a fun little stretch of downtown that gives Beaumont an extra dash of flavor. The area was once the center of illicit activity, with bordellos and bars keeping roughnecks and port visitors plenty entertained. These days, most of the establishments are respectable bars and restaurants. Although the recent economic downturn has affected some of the vibrancy here, locals are optimistic that the current surge in the area's oil-related activity will get things, er, booming again soon.

Classic American

Two of Beaumont's most popular restaurants are within walking distance from each other on Dowlen Road. For a lively dinner-and-drinks atmosphere, go to **Madison's on Dowlen** (4020 Dowlen Rd., 409/924-9777, www.madisonsoftexas.com, 11am-2am daily, $9-22). Classic American fare is the best option here, with reliable (and huge) burgers, chicken, and fried food. For an added burst of flavor, try the bacon-wrapped shrimp with jalapeño. Things pick up at Madison's after dark, when bands often take the stage and the bar gets busy.

Just down the street, **Goodfellas** (3350 Dowlen Rd., 409/861-2500, 11am-11pm daily, $8-20) trends toward Italian but is known as one of the city's best steakhouses. The 16-ounce bone-in rib eye is a local favorite, and the pasta dishes are consistently well prepared. This is fine dining in classic Beaumont style: quality food with decent service in a relaxed atmosphere.

Much more inspiring than its name implies is **The Grill** (6680 Calder Ave. 409/866-0039, www.theaspgrill.com, 3-10pm Tues.-Sat., 10am-2pm Sun., $9-32). For fine dining with modern Beaumont style, The Grill delivers quality food with attentive service in a refined atmosphere. Recommended menu items include the parmesan-crusted Chilean sea bass, grilled rack of lamb, and au poivre tournedos (beef tenderloin with a tasty cognac mushroom sauce). Be sure to save room for the amazing *tres leches* cake, topped with a velvety goat's milk caramel.

Cajun and Seafood

Beaumont is one of the best places in Texas to get authentic Cajun food, and the city's proximity to the Gulf means the seafood is always fresh and flavorful.

The Crockett Street District's consistent culinary destination is **Zydeco Louisiana Diner** (270 Crockett St, 409/835-4455, open for lunch 11am-2pm Mon.-Fri., www.zydecolouisianadiner.com, $8-16). A popular import from Houston, Zydeco specializes in southern Louisiana home-style cooking, with regional favorites like po'boys (go for the shrimp or crawfish), gumbo, and étouffée. If you're fortunate enough to be in town on a Friday, be sure to order the daily special of stuffed pork chops with jambalaya, a slightly indulgent plate of Southern goodness, with perfectly seasoned meat accompanied by just the right amount of spicy rice.

A favorite among locals is the no-frills **Sartin's West** (1990 I-10 S., 409/861-3474, 11am-9pm Mon.-Thurs., 11am-10pm Fri.-Sat., 11am-3pm Sun., $9-22). Beaumonters can't get enough of their fantastic barbecued crabs, and for good reason: These tasty morsels are succulent and slightly spicy, an ideal representation of Beaumont's distinctive cuisine. Other popular menu items include the broiled seafood platter and any variety of shrimp (fried, grilled, or peel-and-eat).

Another spot where locals line up is the consistently delectable **Vautrot's Cajun Cuisine**

EAST TEXAS

(13350 Hwy. 105, 409/753-2015, www.vautrots.com, 11am-2pm and 5-9pm Tues.-Fri., 11am-9pm Sat., $7-18). Start with the tasty crawfish étouffée or jam-packed gumbo, or go crazy and proceed directly to the ridiculously large and immensely flavorful Uncle Emrick's Seafood Sampler, a spread of gumbo and étouffée along with fried crawfish, fried catfish, fried shrimp, fried oysters, onion rings or French fries, and . . . a salad.

Floyd's Cajun Seafood (2290 I-10 S., 409/842-0686, www.floydsseafood.com, $8-19) is a small regional chain that's huge on authentic flavor. You'll find all the reliable standards here, from crawfish and shrimp to oysters and catfish.

INFORMATION AND SERVICES

To get a handle on the layout of the city and where things are in relation to your hotel, contact the friendly folks at the **Beaumont Convention & Visitors Bureau** (505 Willow St., 409/880-3749 or 800/392-4401, www.beaumontcvb.com). Maps, brochures, and staff members are available at the CVB's information centers. The main office, 505 Willow Street, is open 8am-5pm Monday-Friday. The other visitors center is at the **Babe Zaharias Museum** (1750 I-10, 409/833-4622, open 9am-5pm daily).

GETTING THERE

With Houston being such a megalopolis, it's not surprising that the 75-minute drive on I-10 to Beaumont is considered somewhat of a suburban commute. Although the cities have completely different identities, the "quick" jaunt between them (by Texas standards) makes it an easy day trip.

If you're traveling to the region by air, your closest options are in Houston. The **George Bush Intercontinental Airport** (2800 N. Terminal Rd., 281/230-3100, www.fly2houston.com) is located just north of town, and the city's old airport **William P. Hobby Airport** (8183 Airport Blvd., 713/640-3000, www.fly2houston.com) is now the major hub for Southwest Airlines.

Once you're in Beaumont, you can get most places in about 15 minutes. If you don't have a car, several cab companies are available, including **Beaumont Taxi** (409/893-1318) and **Yellow Cab Beaumont** (409/860-3335 6594). If you're feeling adventurous, you may even consider tackling the **Beaumont Municipal Transit System** buses (409/835-7895, www.beaumonttransit.com).

PORT ARTHUR

It's worth making the short drive (20 miles) from Beaumont to Port Arthur (population 53,818), even if only to spend an afternoon at a museum or sample some seafood. With three major oil refineries in operation, Port Arthur's economy remains primarily petro-centered. Named for Arthur Stillwell, a Kansas City businessman who brought the railroad to town, this low-key community has been tied to the shipping industry since a navigable canal was dredged in the early 1900s.

Aside from oil and ocean commerce, Port Arthur is known for churning out music stars (Janis Joplin, the Big Bopper, Johnny Winter, and Tex Ritter are area natives) as well as its Cajun food, fishing, and legendary Mardi Gras celebration, drawing tens of thousands of people each February for the festive atmosphere.

Sights

Get a grasp on the Golden Triangle's illustrious history at the **Museum of the Gulf Coast** (700 Proctor St., 409/982-7000, www.museumofthegulfcoast.org, 9am-5pm Mon.-Sat., 1pm-5pm Sun., $4 adults, $3 seniors, $2 students ages 6-18). Located in a large downtown two-story former bank building, the museum covers a lot of ground. From prehistoric items to Texas Revolution artifacts to modern mementos, the Museum of the Gulf Coast offers a comprehensive representation of cultural events in the region. Be sure to check out the replica of Janis Joplin's painted psychedelic Porsche in the museum's music exhibit, where visitors can play songs on a jukebox (for free) and browse among the displays dedicated to the surprising number of musicians from the area, including Joplin,

George Jones, the Big Bopper, Tex Ritter, and members of ZZ Top. Nearby, a similarly large (head-scratchingly so) number of sports legends and celebrities are featured in the pop culture exhibit, including Jimmy Johnson, Bum and Wade Phillips, and perhaps most confounding, two *Police Academy* stars (G. W. Bailey and Charles "Bubba" Smith).

The **Sabine Pass Battleground** (6100 Dick Dowling Rd., 512/463-7948, www.visitsabine-passbattleground.com), 12 miles south of town, is worth visiting even if you aren't a history buff. Owned and operated by the Texas Historical Commission, this 58-acre site tells the story of a fierce Civil War battle where severely outnumbered Confederate troops prevailed over a formidable Union fleet. Interpretive panels in a large concrete kiosk, several historical markers, and a big bronze statue help portray the conflict. Visitors also have access to walking trails and camping facilities overlooking the Sabine Ship Channel.

For a unique experience, drop by the **Buu Mon Buddhist Temple** (2701 Procter St., 409/982-9319, www.buumon.org). Established as the first Buddhist center in Beaumont (its namesake), the temple is now located in a former Baptist and Vietnamese Catholic church. Where there was once a steeple, a stupa now exists. Instead of a crucifix, a seven-foot-tall gilt bronze Buddha now rests on the altar. The temple's annual spring garden tour attracts hundreds of Texans in search of pleasing colors and smells in the lotus garden. Monks are always on hand to enthusiastically guide visitors through the temple and the garden and even offer a cup of freshly brewed green tea.

Food
Port Arthur is known across Texas for its excellent seafood and Cajun restaurants. One of the best spots in town is the bland-looking yet consistently tasty **Bruce's Seafood Deli** (6801 9th Ave., 409/727-3184, 10am-9pm Mon.-Sat., $8-18). You can't go wrong with the basics here—shrimp, crawfish, and catfish. Although just about everything is deep fried, it's incredibly flavorful and fresh. The uninspiring decor

(it appears to have been a former fast-food or pizza chain restaurant) allows you to focus on the main event: fine seafood. Another favorite Bayou-style eatery is **Larry's French Market and Cajun Cafeteria** (3701 Atlantic Hwy. in nearby Groves, 409/962-3381, www.larrys-frenchmarket.com, 11am-2pm Mon.-Weds., 11am-9pm Thurs., 11am-10pm Fri., 5-10pm Sat., $7-19), offering an ideal all-inclusive combo (the Captain's Platter), featuring fresh and flavorful shrimp, catfish, oysters, barbecue crabs, fried crawfish, seafood gumbo, and Cajun fries. Alternate menu options include the "boiled water critters" (crawfish and crab) served with corn, potatoes, and a dipping sauce, as well as fried critters (alligator, frog legs).

Locals tend to loiter at the traditionally minded and classically decorated (aka dated) **The Schooner** (1507 S. Hwy. 69, 409/722-2323, 10am-9pm Mon.-Sat., $8-23). Seafood is the main catch here, ranging from fresh fillets to fried platters. Popular menu items include stuffed crab and oysters.

ORANGE
One of Texas's easternmost and oldest cities is Orange (population 18,595), a border town (with Louisiana) named for orange groves along the Sabine River. It never experienced the same gushing levels of successful oil activity as Beaumont and Port Arthur, but it was an important industrial port during the two world wars, boasting its highest population of 60,000 in the mid-1940s.

Decades earlier, Orange was infamous for its red-light district and outlaw reputation. Its respectability increased when shipbuilding kept the local economy afloat during wartime. Although many residents fled to larger cities in subsequent decades, Orange continues to draw hordes of anglers and outdoors enthusiasts for its abundant hunting, birding, and fresh- and saltwater fishing.

Sights
You're already in the bayou, so why not *really* get into the bayou? **Adventures 2000 Plus Swamp and River Tours** (409/883-0856,

www.swampandrivertours.com, several tours offered daily, call for reservations, $25 adults, $20 seniors and students, $15 children 11 and under) educates locals and visitors about the fascinating biodiversity of the region, so don't look for any high-powered, speedy water vessels here. Instead, the boats are designed for comfort and relative quiet, allowing a better chance of seeing wild alligators, eagles, rare birds, and various swamp plants and creatures. (Note: The company is in search of new ownership. Check beforehand regarding a potential change in name and hours of operation.)

On the opposite end of the cultural scale is the highbrow **Stark Museum of Art** (712 Green Ave., 409/886-2787, www.starkmuseum.org, 9am-5pm Tues.-Sat., free admission). Named for Orange native Henry J. Lutcher Stark, a successful lumber baron and entrepreneur, the museum showcases the family's extensive collection of art related to the American West. Paintings, prints, and sculpture depict the breathtaking landscapes and natural features of the West, along with bronze Remington sculptures, Native American pottery and baskets, Steuben crystal, and other artistic media.

To learn more about the intriguing life of the Stark family, visit the remarkable **W. H. Stark House** (610 W. Main St., 409/883-0871, www.whstarkhouse.org, 10am-3pm Tues.-Sat., $5 adults, $2 seniors and children ages 10-17). The magnificent 1894 Queen Anne mansion contains 15 rooms of opulent furnishings, artwork, carpet, and silver and porcelain settings. The family's financial success afforded them the rare luxury (in this part of Texas) of purchasing expensive housewares and artwork, including fancy cut glass, imported bronzes, and Asian antiques. The Stark House is listed on the National Register of Historic Places and is designated a Recorded Texas Historic Landmark by the Texas Historical Commission.

Food

Like the other apexes of the Golden Triangle, Orange is known for its top-notch Cajun food. Although the options here are slightly more limited, they're still quality locales. One of the most popular options in town is **Crazy Jose's** (110 Strickland Dr., 409/883-6106, 11am-10pm Sun.-Thurs., 11am-11pm Fri.-Sat., $7-16). As the name implies, Crazy Jose's is an eclectic mix of Mexican, Cajun, and seafood items, providing a welcome mix of tantalizing flavors, from the superb chiles rellenos to the spicy seafood gumbo to the flaky catfish fillets.

If you're more in the mood for turf than surf, belly up to the consistently reliable **J.B.'s BBQ Restaurant** (5750 Old Hwy. 90, 409/886-9823, 10am-9pm Tues.-Sat., $7-16). J.B.'s doesn't offer table service (customers place and pick up their orders at the counter), and that's good news—it means less time to wait on the fabulous food. You can't go wrong with any of the classics here. Ribs, brisket, sausage, and chicken are all perfectly smoked and smothered in a sweet and spicy sauce.

Another popular local hangout is **Spanky's Restaurant** (1703 N. 16th St., 409/886-2949, www.spankysgrill.com, 10:30am-10pm daily, $6-17). You'll find everything you'd ever want or need here, including steaks, seafood, burgers, and sandwiches. Noteworthy menu items include the mega one-pound "Flookburger" and the deep-fried peppers stuffed with crabmeat and cheese.

Big Thicket National Preserve

The Big Thicket National Preserve's name is somewhat misleading. Sure, it has areas of dense forest seemingly impenetrable to human or beast. But for the most part, this National Park Service property is merely woodsy, with pines, oaks, and swamplands dominating the landscape. It's what occupies this flora that makes the Big Thicket a national treasure.

Species from the Gulf Coast, Central Plains, and Southeastern forests coexist with critters from the deserts, bayous, woods, and swamps. Birds from all regions of the country that should never be sharing air space pass through the area on migratory routes. There are 85 tree species, nearly 186 kinds of birds, and 50 reptile species, including a small, rarely seen population of alligators. In short, the tremendous variety of habitats coupled with the thicket's geographic location result in a unique destination for nature lovers and wildlife enthusiasts.

SIGHTS

A good place to start is the Big Thicket's **visitors center** (409/951-6725, 9am-5pm daily), located seven miles north of Kountze at the intersection of U.S. Highway 69 and FM 420. The center provides brochures and maps, and includes a discovery room with interactive and educational exhibits related to the history and scope of the Big Thicket. Speaking of scope, it can take awhile to get a full grasp of the Big Thicket's layout since it consists of nine separate "land units" (basically separate park areas) over an expanse of East Texas. To get your bearings, be sure to view the visitor center's 30-minute orientation film and talk to an NPS nature guide about taking a short excursion to several of the ecosystems found in the preserve.

Lake Tombigbee

Lake Tombigbee is located in one of only three Indian reservations in Texas, the Alabama-Coushatta. In previous decades, the tribe was much more active with its tourist activities, offering a museum, guided hikes, and cultural events. Although these resources are no longer available, visitors are encouraged to spend time at the reservation's Lake Tombigbee campground.

Lake Tombigbee offers primitive camping sites, full-capacity RV stations, restrooms with bathhouses, swimming areas, and hiking and nature trails. Fishing is also popular on the lake, though visitors are encouraged to bring their own equipment because rental operations are scarce in the area.

Call 936/563-1221 or 800/926-9038 for camping information and to obtain a map of the facilities. For additional information about the tribe, call 936/563-1100 or visit their informative website at www.alabama-coushatta.com.

RECREATION
Hiking

Those planning to stick around the Big Thicket for a while can take advantage of many recreational opportunities, including hiking, with eight trails offering more than 45 miles of mild terrain through the muggy forest. The ideal time to plan a hike in Big Thicket is in the late fall, early winter, or spring because the summer is brutally hot. The trails truly offer something for everyone, ranging from wheelchair-accessible 0.5-mile loops to an 18-mile cross-forest trek. Of the eight trails, the following offer the best slices of Big Thicket life:

Located in the southeast corner of the preserve's Big Sandy Creek Unit, the 1.5-mile **Beaver Slide Trail** encircles several ponds formed by old beaver dams. The towering shaggy-barked cypress trees are another main attraction.

The **Kirby Nature Trail System** offers a lot of flexibility with distance and environments. A printed guide at the trailhead is a handy item to have in your back pocket, providing basic maps and information about the ecosystems and trails, ranging from a 0.5-mile loop through a cypress slough to a 2.4-mile hike traversing the southern edge of the Turkey Creek Unit.

ALABAMA-COUSHATTA INDIAN RESERVATION

One of only three Indian reservations in Texas, the Alabama-Coushatta Reservation represents the distinctive heritage of this small yet proud group. At one time the tribe offered tours, a museum, and cultural events for tourists; unfortunately, much of this is no longer operating, apart from occasional events. Regardless, visitors are encouraged to spend time at the reservation's campground or fishing on Lake Tombigbee.

Located on 4,600 acres of dense woodland close to the center of the Big Thicket National Preserve, the Alabama-Coushatta Reservation was established in 1854 by Sam Houston as a reward to the tribes for their courage in remaining neutral during the Texas War for Independence from Mexico. Both groups had been living in the Big Thicket area since circa 1800, when they migrated westward to hunt and build homes out of the abundant East Texas timber.

White settlers displaced countless tribe members, prompting many Coushattas to relocate near Kinder, Louisiana, where a major-ity still resides today. Malnutrition and disease took their toll on the Alabama-Coushatta, resulting in a disturbingly low population of 200 members in the late 1800s.

By the 1920s, the state and federal government recognized the people's poor living conditions and appropriated funds to purchase additional land, construct frame houses to replace meager log cabins, dig wells to help eliminate long water treks to natural springs, and provide medical and educational resources.

Despite the closing of the tribe's cultural facilities, the reservation still operates the popular Lake Tombigbee Campground, offering primitive sites, full-capacity RV stations, restrooms with bathhouses, swimming areas, and hiking and nature trails.

Call 936/563-1221 or 800/926-9038 for camping information and to obtain a map of the facilities. For additional information about the tribe, call 936/563-1100 or visit their well-organized and regularly updated website: www.alabama-coushatta.com.

For a distinctive trek through diverse ecosystems, take the 1-mile **Pitcher Plant Trail** through a mixed pine forest to a wetland savannah to a mixed hardwood-pine forest. Be sure to keep an eye out for the sundews and pitcher plants as you stroll along the wooden boardwalk.

To get a comprehensive feel for the preserve's Turkey Creek unit and its namesake creek, consider hiking the lengthy **Turkey Creek Trail** (15 miles long). Environmental highlights include baygalls, floodplains, sandhill pine uplands, and mixed forests.

Biking

Because of the Big Thicket's remote location, cyclists should bring their own bikes to the preserve (instead of hoping for a nearby rental location). A bike will allow you to experience even more of the park's incredible biodiversity than a mere hike would.

The biggest complaint most cyclists have about the park is its limited access. Bikes are only allowed on the Big **Sandy Creek Horse/Bike Trail** in the southern portion of the Big Sandy Creek Unit. Fortunately, it's the Big Thicket's longest trail, offering 18 miles of beautiful natural scenery. Highlights include a diverse hardwood forest of sweet gum, basket oak, and hornbeam; dense and fragrant upland pine forests; and a mixed area with loblolly pines and beech-magnolia trees. Be sure to check beforehand about trail access (it's occasionally closed during hunting season) and keep an eye and ear out for horses.

Bird-Watching

One of the most popular activities at Big Thicket is bird-watching, and several popular trails, including the Big Thicket Loop and Sundew Trail, offer ideal opportunities for serious and amateur birders with nearly 185 species in the park either year-round or along one of the two major migratory flyways. Bird migrations peak between March and May, and some of the most sought-after species in the park include the red cockaded woodpecker and the Bachman's sparrow. In the spring, bird and wildflower enthusiasts flock to the Sundew Trail in the park's Hickory Creek Savannah Unit to catch sight of a rare brown leaded nuthatch or an eye-catching pitcher plant.

Paddling

The Big Thicket has traditionally been known for its hiking and fishing, but it's gaining a reputation for its quality paddling opportunities. Canoeists and kayakers are especially fond of the Village Creek area, where they can spend an afternoon or entire day exploring the lush waterway and camping opportunities. Another popular area is the **Lower Neches River Corridor,** a larger body of water with East Texas-style bayous and swamps leading all the way south to the Gulf of Mexico. Equipment rentals and shuttles are also available—check with the visitors center for a list of currently operating companies.

Backcountry Camping

The Big Thicket is more of a hard-core camper's destination than a traditional park. There are no developed sites with water and electricity; rather, campers are required to procure a permit for a primitive site. For some, this is an ideal situation since it offers a true natural getaway without the distractions of a classic campground.

Campers must have a valid Backcountry Use Permit, available for free at the visitors center or headquarters offices. Naturalist activities are available with reservations or on selected weekends. Call 409/951-6725 or visit www.nps.gov/

bith to learn about the park and its activities or to find out more about making reservations.

ACCOMMODATIONS AND FOOD

Since the Big Thicket is divided among nine separate park units across a large geographic area, there isn't one specific town where most visitors go for food or lodging. Typically restaurants, hotels, or campgrounds are selected based on proximity to a traveler's recreational activity. The preserve's sections range 80 miles west-to-east from Livingston to Kirbyville (with dozens of small communities in between) and 70 miles north-to-south from Jasper to Beaumont. Nearby communities with more than just a hotel or two include Woodville and Kountze. Since **Beaumont** is less than an hour from most of the Big Thicket's nine park areas, consider budgeting some time to drive to this comparatively big city for a tasty and reliable Cajun meal or a clean hotel.

INFORMATION AND SERVICES

The best place to find out everything you need to know about the Big Thicket (trail maps, boating conditions, nearby restaurants, etc.) is the visitors center. It's located seven miles north of Kountze at the intersection of U.S. Highway 69 and FM 420 (409/951-6725, 9am-5pm daily). Visit www.nps.gov/bith to learn more about the park or to find out more about making reservations.

Those interested in visiting the Alabama-Coushatta reservation for fishing or camping should call 936/563-1221 or 800/926-9038. For information about the tribe, call 936/563-1100 or visit www.alabama-coushatta.com.

Piney Woods National Forests

The Piney Woods are the natural heart of East Texas. Comprised of several national forests and not much else, most of this vast area remains as it has for centuries, when Native American tribes and pioneers hunted wild game in the dense woods by day and slept under the canopy of pine boughs by night.

The moniker "Piney Woods," a Texas colloquialism, is an endearing term describing this forested region, an image many visitors don't associate with the stereotypical desert landscape of the Lone Star State. Regardless, these aren't dense, lush groves of evergreens—they're mainly shortleaf and loblolly pines, sprinkled liberally with hardwoods such as oak, elm, ash, and maple. The combination is especially appealing in autumn, when in another unexpected Texas scene, occasional bursts of changing colors offer a scenic outdoor escape.

Nearly 750,000 acres of East Texas pine forests remain standing because the federal government became involved. The trees were mostly clear-cut during the zealous timber harvesting of the early 1900s, but the U.S. Forest Service eventually became involved as an "administrator" of the vast woodlands, allowing them to be responsibly maintained through professional oversight of harvesting and replenishing.

The four national forests of East Texas are ideal destinations for a natural weekend getaway. Campers will want to pack more than hiking boots and mountain bikes—these woods are filled with rivers and lakes ideal for canoeing and fishing, drawing tens of thousands of recreation seekers to these natural playgrounds. Texans accustomed to their state's hot summers and unpredictable winters will frequent the forests throughout the year while out-of-staters prefer to enjoy them during the temperate months of spring and late fall.

These wooded areas provided shelter and sustenance for the region's earliest inhabitants, the Native American tribes that were largely displaced by westward frontier expansion. The

legacy of the native Caddo people is evident in the rich history of Piney Woods communities like Nacogdoches, and the Alabama-Coushatta tribe remains a vital cultural presence on its reservation in the Big Thicket National Preserve.

The forests also had a significant impact on East Texas's economy when the lumber industry became a major contributor to the state's agricultural output in the late 19th and early 20th centuries. Though much of the area was initially overharvested, the industry eventually recovered and remains an essential economical element today. Several of the forests, Angelina in particular, feature logging-related trails and historical exhibits. A highlight is the abandoned and ghostly Aldridge Sawmill in Angelina National Forest.

SAM HOUSTON NATIONAL FOREST

Located approximately 40 miles north of Texas's largest city, Sam Houston National Forest contains 162,984 acres of short- and long-leafed pine, hardwood forests, and abundant recreational opportunities appealing to visitors, big-city dwellers, and small-town folk. Camping is the main draw here, complemented by daytime activities on Double Lake and Lake Conroe and the 140-mile-long Lone Star Hiking Trail.

Recreation

The **Lone Star Hiking Trail** contains approximately 140 miles of walkways open to foot travel only. The trail traverses the entire Sam Houston National Forest through woodlands, swamps, and meadows via five loops to accommodate various starting points and parking for day hikers or overnight backpackers. Trail maps and brochures are available at the park headquarters in New Waverly.

Cyclists will enjoy the eight-mile trail on the east side of the forest custom built by mountain bikers. Though most of the East Texas forests are devoid of significant slopes, this hilly trek

LOGGING TIME WITH THE COMPANY

From the 1880s until the 1920s, East Texas's Piney Woods became a lot less piney—and a lot less woodsy. During these four decades, the "lumber bonanza" resulted in 18 million acres' worth of timber being cut.

Lumber production started out with small owner-operated sawmills and eventually evolved into sophisticated operations that dominated the East Texas economy in the early 1900s. These corporations built their own railroads into the forests and connected their isolated sawmills with major cities and shipping points for their wood products.

One of the more fascinating aspects of this era was the establishment of lumber "company towns." The men who worked in the sawmills and on the cutting crews were encouraged to remain with a company for the long haul, and one of the main incentives was the promise of caring for their wives and children.

The companies would choose a location on a rail line and construct a makeshift town, complete with all the basic necessities, including homes, schools, churches, stores, and hospitals. The workers were often paid with credits they could use for food, merchandise, and services in the company town facilities.

Sometimes, the towns would pick up and move along with the ever-changing frontier of virgin forest. Homes located in rail cars allowed for easy mobility, leaving behind a ghost town of clapboard buildings and dirt roads.

By the 1920s, the depletion of the East Texas timber resources combined with the effect of the Great Depression caused the decline of the lumber bonanza. Some of the companies went into bankruptcy while several of the larger timber corporations moved to the fertile forests of the Pacific Northwest.

offers terrain-filled passages winding through the pine forests.

The 22,000-acre Lake Conroe is one of the biggest draws to the Sam Houston forest, particularly for its swimming, boating, fishing, and sailing. The lake is stocked with bass and bluegill, and boats are available for rent at various marinas along the lakeshore.

Camping

Sam Houston National Forest contains three developed campgrounds. **Cagle Recreation Area** is a campground with 48 camping units offering electric, water, and sewer connections; hot showers; lakeshore hiking, biking, and equestrian trails; fishing; and swimming. **Double Lake Recreation Area,** constructed in 1937 by the Civilian Conservation Corps, surrounds a 24-acre lake and includes family camping units (a tent pad, parking area, picnic table; some with water, sewer, and electrical hookups), a swimming area and beach, and a concession stand with bathhouse. **Stubblefield Recreation Area** has 28 camping units, hot showers, and access to fishing and hiking. Double Lake facilities are available by reservations, but Cagle and Stubblefield are available on a first-come, first-served basis only.

Food

When in East Texas, it's best to stick with the foods the locals know best: barbecue and Southern. Although it may be tempting to snack on a taco or find a fine Italian meal, save those cravings for the cities.

When it comes to barbecue, one of the most popular spots in the Sam Houston Forest area is on the northeastern edge of the property line in the small town of Coldspring. **Lone Star BBQ** (300 FM 2025, 936/653-2586, hours vary, $9-16). This down-home, charmingly cluttered local establishment specializes in the classics, like sliced brisket and pork ribs. The menu offers more variety than most barbecue joints, with shrimp and catfish (most East Texas restaurants find a way to get catfish on the menu).

Just up the road from Coldspring in the slightly larger town of Livingston is **Courthouse**

Whistlestop Cafe (318 N. Washington Ave., 936/327-3222, www.courthousewhistlestop. com, 9am-2pm Mon.-Thurs., 9am-3pm Fri.-Sun., $7-15). Located across from the stately Polk County Courthouse in the historical downtown district, the Whistlestop is an ideal place to grab a hearty breakfast before venturing out on a hiking trail or paddling trip. Start with a strong mug of coffee and pair with a meaty omelet or stack of buttermilk pancakes. If you're looking for lunch, opt for a big ol' deli sandwich (the Reuben is a local favorite) or bowl of chili.

Information and Services
For more information about recreational opportunities at the forest, including all-important maps, contact the **Sam Houston National Forest headquarters** (394 FM 1375, 936/344-6205 or 888/361-6908, www.fs.fed. us/r8/texas, 8am-4:30pm Mon.-Fri.), located two miles west of I-45 and New Waverly. For **campground reservation information,** call 877/444-6777 or go to www.recreation.gov.

Getting There
Since the national forests are located in rural areas of East Texas, the only way to access them is by car. Assuming many visitors are traveling to the Sam Houston forest from Houston, take I-45 north out of town for about 40 miles, all the way to the small town of New Waverly. The forest's visitors center is just a couple miles west of the interstate at New Waverly. Drivers can also take State Highway 59 northeast out of Houston. When you reach Cleveland or Shepherd look for signs directing you to county roads heading westward into the forest.

DAVY CROCKETT NATIONAL FOREST
For hiking enthusiasts, the Davy Crockett National Forest is a welcome wild frontier. With more than 160,000 acres of scenic woodlands just west of Lufkin, the Davy Crockett forest has some of the region's best opportunities for hiking and horseback riding.

Recreation
The most popular hiking trail in the forest is the **Four C National Recreation Trail,** named after the Central Coal and Coke Company that logged the forest's stately trees from 1902 to 1920. The 20-mile trail traverses moderate terrain amid lofty pines, swampy bogs, and hardwood forests. Horses and hikers share the woodsy, mossy, and boggy 50-mile **Piney Creek Horse Trail.**

Visitors are also drawn to the **Ratcliff Lake Recreation Area,** built in 1936 by the Civilian Conservation Corps around a 45-acre lake that was once a log pond and source of water for the Central Coal and Coke Company Sawmill. The area offers camping, a swimming beach and bathhouse, an interpretive trail, showers, boating, and fishing.

While you're hiking be on the lookout for the forest's abundant wildlife, including deer, turkey, dove, quail, and various waterfowl. The endangered red-cockaded woodpecker also lives in a managed habitat within the forest.

Camping
Some of the forest's most scenic camping sites are along the Four C trail at the **Walnut Creek campsite** (five tent pads, a shelter, and a pit toilet) and at another small campsite, farther north on the trail, with two tent pads. Another option is the **Ratcliff Lake Recreation Area.** Campers comfortable with primitive sites should head to the nearby **Neches Bluff Overlook** at the north end of the trail, where they can enjoy a panoramic view of pine-hardwood forests in the Neches River bottomlands.

Information and Services
To obtain a trail map of the forest or to learn more about camping and boat accessibility, contact the **Davy Crockett National Forest headquarters** (Route 1, Box 55 FS, 936/655-2299), near Kennard. To find out more about the forest and its seasonal activities, visit www. fs.fed.us/r8/texas. The ranger district office is located near Ratcliff on Highway 7, about a quarter mile west of FM 227.

Getting There

Assuming you'll be arriving by car from Houston, take I-45 north to State Hwy. 19 in the town of Crockett. Take a right on State Hwy. 7 for a few miles, where you'll find the main visitor center in Ratcliff. You can also take U.S. Hwy. 59 northeast out of Houston. When you reach Lufkin, take a left on State Hwy. 103, which turns into State Hwy. 7 and leads to the visitors center.

ANGELINA NATIONAL FOREST

Located just east of Lufkin, the 153,179 acres of Angelina National Forest stand as one of the most popular East Texas forests for fishing and boating excursions. Angelina completely encapsulates most of the massive Lake Sam Rayburn, a 114,500-acre lake on the Angelina River formed when the Sam Rayburn Dam was constructed in the early 1960s.

The forest itself is like most of its East Texas brethren, with gently rolling landscapes covered mostly with shortleaf and loblolly pine, hardwoods, and a swath of longleaf pine in the southern portion. When it was acquired by the federal government in 1935, Angelina was in pretty bad shape—most of the property had been forested and left without adequate protection. The Texas Forest Service's fire prevention efforts resulted in much of the land "seeding in" naturally, a practice that continues to this day.

◖ Aldridge Sawmill

Though Angelina is focused primarily on water-based activities, the most memorable experience in the forest is a surreal (and spooky) abandoned sawmill. All that's left of the old **Aldridge Sawmill** are huge concrete structures serving as reminders of the region's timber-industry heritage.

Nearly 100 years ago, thousands of people thrived in a busy logging community called Aldridge before abandoning the site practically overnight. Now located in a remote and dense

EAST TEXAS

© ANDY RHODES

Aldridge Sawmill

area of the Angelina forest, the dead-quiet ruins offer a completely contrary scene to its previous buzz of equipment and activity.

Once bustling with hundreds of homes and several saloons, hotels, and churches, Aldridge workers logged East Texas's largest longleaf pines—some more than 30 inches in diameter. When the tree supply was depleted by 1920, however, the residents and their families packed up and moved on to the next swath of dense woodland, leaving behind several large-scale mill facilities.

The enormous and stark concrete walls of these buildings are all that remain, offering an eerie juxtaposition to the surrounding natural beauty of the enchanting second-growth forest that emerged in its place. Similarly intriguing are the remnants from local teenagers—graffiti, beer bottles, and flip-flops—who frequent the ghost town to do what they do best (a Forest Service guide simply noted, "A lot of innocence has been lost here").

Although forest officials discourage publicizing Aldridge's location to deter even more teenagers from discovering and destroying it, legitimate visitors can get a map and directions (look for the Sawmill Hiking Trail) from the visitors center.

Recreation

Lake Sam Rayburn is a popular destination for anglers, who return regularly for the lake's abundant largemouth bass, crappie, and catfish. Recreational boating is also a major activity, with water-skiers, sailboats, and personal watercraft dotting the water's surface.

Even if you don't have a boat, it's worth driving across Lake Sam Rayburn on the lengthy Hwy. 147 bridges. On the east side of the bridge, there's an access road to Jackson Hill park, where you can explore the lakeside and catch a picturesque sunset.

The Angelina forest is also a popular place for visitors to view the hundreds of wildlife species, including deer, wild turkey, woodcock, quail, and the year-round resident population of wood ducks. During the winter, bald eagles occupy the area surrounding the reservoir, and

the forest is also home to the endangered red-cockaded woodpecker, a small black-and-white bird that visitors often make (largely unsuccessful) quests to locate.

Camping and Lodging

The park's two main recreation areas, Caney Creek and Sandy Creek, offer camping, boating, and fishing on or near the shores of Sam Rayburn Reservoir. Camping and fishing are also popular at Bouton Lake Recreation Area and Boykin Springs Recreation Area, including historical structures built by the Civilian Conservation Corps and offering camping, swimming, fishing, and canoeing.

Another option worth considering is a cabin rental. A local real estate company offers a lone 1940s-era historical **log cabin** (936/240-1700, www.vrbo.com, $80 nightly for two people) near the south shore of Lake Sam Rayburn. Surprisingly available at many times of the year, the rustic two-bedroom home is sparse yet perfectly suited for a low-key weekend getaway. Nestled in a pine grove, the cabin offers modern conveniences (central air/heat, a full kitchen and bathroom, satellite TV, even Wi-Fi) with the charms of a woodsy home (large front porch, bunk beds, comfy furniture, and a charcoal grill).

Food

Much like the Davy Crockett forest, nearby eating options are minimal. To get a decent meal, make the 15-mile drive to Lufkin for quality regional cuisine. However, if you're in the Zavalla area and are willing to keep your expectations fairly low, there's **Carlene's Place** (594 E. Main St., 936/897-2900, 6am-9pm Sun.-Thurs., 6am-10pm Fri.-Sat., $6-10). Carlene's "features" a buffet (mostly fried food and a salad bar) along with standard American fare like burgers, chicken-fried steaks, and sandwiches.

Information and Services

To learn more about the Angelina forest's campsite availability and fees, lake access points, and trail maps, contact the **Angelina**

National Forest headquarters (111 Walnut Ridge Rd. in Zavalla, 936/897-1068, www.fs.fed.us/r8/texas, 8am-4:30pm Mon.-Fri.).

Getting There

Take State Hwy. 59 northeast out of Houston. When you get to Lufkin, take a right on State Hwy. 103. To reach the visitors center, head southeast from Lufkin on U.S. Hwy. 69 to Zavalla.

SABINE NATIONAL FOREST

Totaling 160,656 acres, Sabine National Forest is the easternmost of Texas's four national forests and is dominated by the massive Toledo Bend Reservoir along the Louisiana border.

Considered the second-largest lake in Texas and the fifth-largest artificially made reservoir in the United States, Toledo Bend offers extensive recreational opportunities, from boating and fishing to swimming and lakeshore camping.

Recreation

Outdoor recreation opportunities in the Sabine National Forest include fishing, hunting, camping, hiking, horseback riding, and mountain biking. One of the most popular destinations in the forest is the 12,369-acre **Indian Mounds Wilderness Area,** designated by the U.S. Congress as a site "to allow the Earth's natural processes to shape and influence the area." Unfortunately, it was misnamed since the mounds are actually just normal hills; fortunately, these natural formations shelter beautiful flora, including American beech, southern magnolia, yellow lady's slipper orchids, and broad beech ferns.

Hikers should hoof it to the 28-mile **Trail Between the Lakes,** extending from the Toledo Bend Reservoir's Lakeview Recreation Area to Highway 96 near Sam Rayburn Reservoir. Contact park headquarters for a map showing the many miles of roads throughout the forest that are open to mountain bikers and horseback riders.

Fishing is another recreational activity that draws people to Sabine National Forest. The reservoir is ideal for catching striped bass, and the forest's rivers and creeks teem with crappie, bass, and bluegill.

Birding is also popular with forest visitors, who flock to the area during the spring and fall to catch a glimpse of migratory waterfowl and other species of neotropical migratory birds such as songbirds, hawks, and shorebirds. Like in the other East Texas forests, the red-cockaded woodpecker, an endangered species, receives special habitat management.

Camping

To get a true sense of the rural forest camping experience, get a spot at **Indian Mounds Wilderness Area.** Less primitive is the **Ragtown Recreation Area,** offering opportunities for hiking, fishing, and bird watching atop a bluff that faces the lake. Camping with electrical hookups is available only at **Red Hills Lake** and **Boles Field.**

Food

Since the forest runs along the state line with Louisiana, this is a good opportunity to make a run for the border to experience an authentic meal in another state. One of the best options is about 15 miles east of the state line in Leesville, Louisiana, at a homey spot called **Mustard Seed** (1152 Entrance Rd., 337/537-1933, hours vary, $8-19). Go for the local specialties here, specifically the crispy and tender fried catfish and savory gumbo (chicken or sausage). Be sure to order or share some side dishes too because you don't always get a chance to eat Louisiana-style collard greens or brown gravy.

If you'd prefer to stay in the Lone Star State, stick with the food that Texans do best: barbecue. One of the only recommended options near the Sabine forest is **Hemphill BBQ** (3285 South Bayou Rd., 409/787-1814, 11am-3pm Mon., 11am-8pm Tues.-Thurs., 11am-9pm Fri.-Sat., $8-18) in the small town of Hemphill. Because this is East Texas, the specialties tend to shift away from beef and toward pork, so order the baby back ribs or a pulled pork sandwich. The sides tend to be sweeter in this part of the state, which works well for Hemphill's cole slaw and potato salad. Locals come here

EAST TEXAS

for the homemade desserts alone, so try to save room for a pie or pastry.

Information and Services

For a comprehensive list of Toledo Bend reservoir-related services—fishing guides to private resorts to boat launch sites—visit www.toledo-bend.com. To learn more about Sabine forest's campsite availability and fees, lake access points, and trail maps, contact the **Sabine**

National Forest headquarters (201 South Palm in Hemphill, 409/787-3870). To learn more about the park's recreational opportunities and seasonal news, visit www.fs.fed.us/r8/texas.

Getting There

Take State Hwy. 59 northeast out of Houston. When you reach Lufkin, take a right on State Hwy. 103. To reach the park's visitors center, head south on State Hwy. 87 in Milam for three miles.

Lufkin

Lufkin (population 35,062) is worth visiting for its unique role as a major logging town in Texas's history. Founded in 1882 as a stop on the Houston, East and West Texas Railway, the town was named for Abraham P. Lufkin, a Galveston cotton merchant and close friend of the railroad company president.

The construction of railroad lines in the early 1880s allowed access to the forests' interiors, and the lumber industry and regional economy began to flourish. In fact, between 1890 and 1900, the forest industry contributed more to Texas's economy than any other industry, including the traditional stronghold markets of cattle and cotton.

As a result, lumber "company towns" flourished in the Lufkin area. The corporations provided jobs for men and prioritized family life by building and advocating schools, churches, and medical facilities. Often, the workers were paid in coupons and credits redeemable for merchandise and services in the company town facilities. Although some sawmill workers were later drawn to the oil fields for higher wages, many men chose to stay with their families in the lumber company towns because they were good places to raise a family in a community environment.

The lumber industry continues to play a significant role in Lufkin's economy. Each year, the region produces more than a million board feet of saw timber and has significant manufacturing of pulpwood from the nearby pine and hardwood forests.

Visitors, especially antiques shoppers and history buffs, are drawn to downtown Lufkin's quaint mix of restaurants and retail shops. A walking tour showcases several remarkable historic buildings, including the 1925 Pines Theater and the location of the first Brookshire Brothers grocery store. Along the way, look for the five colorful murals by artist Lance Hunter depicting historical businesses and stories from the area.

SIGHTS
Texas Forestry Museum

An essential stop in Lufkin is the **Texas Forestry Museum** (1905 Atkinson Dr., 936/632-9535, www.treetexas.com, 10am-5pm Mon.-Sat., free admission). The museum showcases both the history and contemporary growth of the region's lumber industry in two main areas—the forest history wing and the resource and management wing.

Highlights include a compelling exhibit about life in a lumber company town, complete with model buildings and a large collection of artifacts from early logging camps. Historical equipment, a fire lookout tower cab, paper mill room, and an educational exhibit detailing the natural succession of a forest are other noteworthy attractions at the Texas Forestry Museum. A children's area is well intentioned and fairly educational, though the early '90s signage and videos are becoming dangerously dated. Visitors can learn more about the region's natural resources on the scenic Urban Wildscape Trail located behind the main building.

© ANDY RHODES

Lufkin's Ellen Trout Zoo

Museum of East Texas

Despite its all-encompassing name, the **Museum of East Texas** (503 N. 2nd St., 936/639-4434, www.metlufkin.org, 10am-5pm Tues.-Fri., 1pm-5pm Sat.-Sun., free admission) isn't as grand as it sounds. Built in 1976, the museum primarily features exhibits showcasing the talents of regional artists. Though it features occasional traveling shows and science or children's exhibits, the museum devotes much of its attention to the work of locals, which is certainly commendable yet somewhat limited in scope. The museum also hosts occasional lectures, performances, classes, kids' art camps, and publications dedicated to the character and heritage of East Texas.

Ellen Trout Zoo

File this one under expectations exceeded. Far larger than it has to be is the impressive **Ellen Trout Zoo** (402 Zoo Circle, 936/633-0399, www.cityoflufkin.com/zoo, 9am-5pm daily, $5 adults, $2.50 children ages 4-11).

Home to more than 700 animals from all over the planet, the zoo contains a surprising variety of jungle beasts, tropical birds, and swamp creatures in a well-organized and spacious setting. Be sure to set aside three or four hours to get a full appreciation for the animals you typically see in big-city zoos, including monkeys, a giraffe, rhinos, and hippos. Also keep an eye out for alligators, seals, and birds around every corner.

Another highlight for families is the miniature train, which circles the zoo, then makes an unexpected detour across Ellen Trout lake (look for the elusive gators), and then makes a small loop through the nearby forest.

The History Center

Located just 11 miles outside Lufkin in the small town of Diboll is a fascinating attraction known simply as **The History Center** (102 N. Temple St., 936/829-3543, www.thehistorycenteronline.com, 8am-5pm Mon.-Fri., 9am-1pm Sat., free admission). Appropriately situated in Diboll, the oldest continually operated forest company site in Texas, the 12,000-square-foot History Center is technically a public archives facility dedicated to East Texas history. But that makes it sound rather boring, which it's not.

The vaguely named History Center did not get a specified moniker because organizers did not want it to be classified as simply a museum or a library. Although it contains many reference materials, it's more than a research center. Likewise, it features artifacts, but it is not really a museum. It's best described as a public history and archive center that collects, preserves, and explores the heritage of East Texas.

Visitors are immediately drawn to the facility by its exquisite woodwork, consisting of cypress walls preserved from the 1950s along with floors of locally harvested yellow pine. Exhibit panels feature remarkable century-old photos showcasing Diboll's dynamic past as a lumber company town, and an impressive collection of archives, including 70,000 photos, decades' worth of community newspapers, lumber company log books. For children (and sometimes even their parents), the History Center's

© ANDY RHODES

the steam train at Diboll's History Center

EAST TEXAS

highlight is parked behind the building: an authentic 1920 Baldwin 68-ton steam locomotive, which visitors can explore by climbing in, on, and around. The best part? Experience the immense satisfaction of pulling on a rope and hearing the authentic throaty sound of the engine's steam whistle.

RECREATION

Lufkin is close to four national forests, so if you're interested in boating, hiking, camping, or biking, that's where you should spend your time. However, if you're in town for a limited stay and looking for somewhere to jog or walk your dog, the city manages 16 municipal parks through **Lufkin Parks and Recreation** (936/633-0250, www.lufkinparks.com). Check the website for information on hours of operation and access to swimming pools, jogging trails, playgrounds, picnic areas, and the like.

ACCOMMODATIONS

Lufkin's lodging options are somewhat limited, but several chains offer reliable

accommodations and amenities. Those looking for an affordable rate in a commendable hotel should consider **La Quinta** (2119 S. 1st St., 936/634-3351, www.lq.com, $95 d). Features include an outdoor pool, free continental breakfast, and free Internet access. A step up on the price and quality ladder is **Best Western Crown Colony Inn & Suites** (3211 S. 1st St., 936/634-3481, www.bestwesterntexas. com, $113 d), offering spacious rooms with microwaves and refrigerators, free Internet access, a deluxe continental breakfast, outdoor pool, and fitness room. Similar in price and scope is **Hampton Inn & Suites** (4400 S. 1st St., 936/699-2500, www.hamptoninn. com, $129 d), featuring a free hot breakfast, to-go breakfast bags (on weekdays), and free Internet access.

A suggested alternative to the chain hotels is the welcoming **Wisteria Hideaway** (3458 Ted Trout Dr., 936/875-2914, rooms start at $95). Located in a 1939 colonial-style home, this B&B provides genuinely charming Southern hospitality without being too fancy—or frilly.

ROSENWALD SCHOOLS

Rosenwald schools represent a brief yet far-reaching cultural phenomena that impacted the lives of thousands of underserved East Texans. These rural facilities were built throughout East Texas and the entire South in the early 1900s to benefit the African American population thanks to Julius Rosenwald, a Chicago philanthropist and former president of Sears, Roebuck and Co.

Rosenwald felt compelled to address the educational needs of African Americans in the rural South, who had previously attended makeshift schools in churches, shacks, and cabins. Rosenwald intended his facilities to serve as models of modern schoolhouse construction.

The Rosenwald program provided facilities (built from standardized architectural plans) that attracted qualified teachers and became community educational centers. These schools served as models for rural African Americans to develop quality facilities and a better-educated population. To be comparable with the education in Anglo communities, Rosenwald required his schools to have certified college-educated teachers and a calendar year of at least five months. State and national funding paid for educational supplies, lesson plans, and more importantly, additional high school levels. With the establishment of African American colleges throughout the state, black students were able to complete 12 years of public school and go on to receive a college education, ultimately allowing them the freedom of working for themselves.

The last Texas Rosenwald building was constructed in 1931. School district consolidation and desegregation rendered most of the facilities obsolete by the late 1950s, but by that time, 527 Rosenwald schools had been built in Texas. With the abandonment and neglect of these largely rural buildings, only 30 of them remain standing. Fortunately, these existing structures are being documented and protected, and preservationists throughout East Texas are working to restore and adapt these significant buildings.

Rooms are tastefully decorated, and the breakfasts are outstanding, starting with the freshly made buttermilk biscuits and continuing with fluffy and flavorful egg casseroles and sausage or bacon. Enjoy the feast in the dining room or the privacy of your own quarters.

FOOD
Barbecue

If you only eat one meal in Lufkin, head directly to the unassuming, 1950s-era strip mall housing **Lufkin Bar-B-Q** (203 S. Chestnut St., 936/634-4744, 10am-9pm daily, $8-17). Before you get to the meat, consider yourself forewarned: the lightly fried rolls served before the meal are so astoundingly tasty, you'll be tempted to make a meal out of their doughy deliciousness. If possible, maintain some self-control (limiting yourself to three or four rolls) and save space for the main event: succulent barbecue. The hearty and perfectly smoked brisket and spicy sausage are the way to go, or try a chipped beef sandwich if you're not in the mood for quantity. The sides aren't too memorable, so . . . go ahead and have another roll!

To experience a classic East Texas barbecue joint, drop by **Bryan's Smokehouse Bar-B-Q** (609 S. Timberland Dr., 936/632-2255, 10am-10pm Mon.-Thurs., 10am-11pm Fri.-Sat., 10am-3pm Sun., $9-18). This small, rustic smokehouse has everything a barbecue place should—smoke-stained photos of local and regional musicians, hearty portions of succulent meat, and a sticky, tangy sauce. Brisket and pork ribs are the favorites here, and you can't go wrong with the better-than-average sides, particularly the savory beans and sweet potato salad. If you're feeling adventurous, give the fried cabbage a try.

Mexican

Lufkin is known more for its barbecue than Mexican food, but several places in town draw sizable lunch crowds. One worth visiting is the

© ANDY RHODES

Lufkin Bar-B-Q

consistently reliable **Cafe Del Rio** (1901 S. 1st St., 936/639-4471, 11am-9:30pm Mon.-Thurs., 11am-10:30pm Fri.-Sun., $7-15). From the crispy chips and spicy salsa to the loaded nachos and sizzling fajitas, Cafe Del Rio doesn't disappoint. Also recommended is **Casa Ole** (2109 S. 1st St., 936/632-2653, 11am-10pm Sun.-Thurs., 11am-midnight Fri.-Sat., $6-14), offering tasty tacos and hearty enchiladas. Another local hot spot is **El Taurino Mexican Grill** (3774 Hwy. 69 N., 936/699-3344, www.eltaurinomexican-restaurant.com, 11am-9:30pm Mon.-Thurs., 11am-10pm Fri.-Sun., $5-14), featuring classic Mexican combo dishes with enchiladas, tacos, chiles rellenos, and burritos.

Lunch

As its name implies, **Mar Teres Tea Room** (3157 Ted Trout Dr., 936/875-6200, 11am-2pm Tues.-Fri., reservations recommended, $9-21) is a classic luncheon spot filled with antiques and a fair share of pink decor. However, this tightly packed home is known throughout town as the ultimate destination for quality cuisine in Lufkin. Husbands and boyfriends take note: it's worth spending an hour outside your comfort zone to experience the powerful flavors packed into the food at Mar Teres. The almond tea is the talk of the town, and entrees like chicken spaghetti, chicken salad, and French onion soup are outstanding. Not surprisingly, the desserts here are top notch, especially the lemon cake, coconut pie, and old-fashioned chocolate cake.

Casual

For good ol' fashioned Southern comfort food, it doesn't get much better than **Mom's Diner** (900 W. Frank Ave., 936/637-6410,10am-8pm daily, $6-14, cash only). As its name implies, this semi-rustic spot specializes in comfort food, including one of the best chicken-fried steaks in the area, as well as juicy burgers, fried chicken, and outstanding peppered cream gravy. Take note: Mom doesn't accept credit cards, just cash.

For old-time greasy and tasty burgers, head to **Ray's Drive In Cafe** (420 N. Timberland

Dr., 936/634-3262, 10am-10pm daily, $5-9). Locals love the classic 1950s feel and fare of this original drive-in restaurant, from the mouthwatering bacon cheeseburger with onion rings to the mushroom burger, chili dog, and chocolate milk shake. The surrounding sound of classic oldies music completes this nostalgic scene.

INFORMATION AND SERVICES

To get the scoop on additional lodging and dining options or to pick up a handy map or brochure, stop by the **Lufkin Convention & Visitors Bureau** (1615 S. Chestnut St., 936/633-0349 or 800/409-5659, www.visit-lufkin.com, 8:30am-5pm Mon.-Fri.).

Nacogdoches and Vicinity

Nacogdoches (population 32,996) claims to be Texas's oldest town, and though some historians debate this, there's no denying the wealth and breadth of its East Texas heritage and culture.

Named for the Caddo tribe (the Nacogdoche) that lived in the area, Nacogdoches was an active Native American settlement until 1716 when Spain established a mission at the site. In 1779, Nacogdoches received official designation from Spain as a pueblo (village), prompting locals to deem it Texas's first official "town."

Soon after, Nacogdoches became a hotbed of trading activity, much of it illicit, primarily among the French and Americans, with much of the action centered around the Old Stone Fort. The frequent activity coupled with the town's prime location on several major trade routes made Nacogdoches prominent in early military and political arenas.

By the mid-1800s, Nacogdoches lost its distinction in these areas because of its lack of modern transportation, which at that time meant steamboats and railroads. Growth remained relatively stagnant until the 1920s, when Stephen F. Austin State Teachers College (now Stephen F. Austin State University) opened its doors, bringing fresh faces, jobs, and cultural activities to town. With a current enrollment of nearly 12,000 students, the university remains the lifeblood of Nacogdoches.

SIGHTS
Old Stone Fort Museum
The **Old Stone Fort Museum** (1936 North St., 936/468-2408, www.sfasu.edu/stonefort, 9am-5pm Tues.-Sat., 1pm-5pm Sun., free

admission), located on the Stephen F. Austin State University campus, is a 1936 replica of the home of Don Antonio Gil Y'Barbo, considered the founder of present-day Nacogdoches. The original facility, dating to the 1700s, was considered the oldest standing stone structure in Texas before it was torn down amid much protest in 1902. Now officially historic itself, this replica remains an important Nacogdoches landmark, featuring a permanent exhibit on the fascinating history of the building that served as a trading post, church, jail, private home, and saloon but never an official fort. The Old Stone Fort Museum also contains artifacts related to the early history of East Texas, with a special focus on the Spanish and Mexican periods (1690-1836).

Sterne-Hoya House
One of the oldest homes in East Texas is the 1830 **Sterne-Hoya House** (211 S. Lanana St., 936/560-5426, www.ci.nacogdoches.tx.us/departments/shmuseum.php, 10am-4pm Tues.-Sat., free admission and tours). Built by Adolphus Sterne, a prominent leader of the Texas Revolution, the modest yet stately home is still standing on its original site, a rare claim for many structures of this era, which were either moved or demolished. Prominent figures of the time, including Davy Crockett, Sam Houston, and Cherokee Chief Bowles, visited the Sterne home in the mid-1800s. Tour guides explain the significance of the period antiques and the prominent families who occupied the home, which is now listed on the National Register of Historic Places.

EAST TEXAS

© ANDY RHODES

the Sterne-Hoya House in Nacogdoches

◖ Texas State Railroad State Historical Park

The rich throaty sound of a steam train whistle beckons visitors to the **Texas State Railroad** (Park Rd. 76 off Hwy. 84 W., 888/987-2461, www.texasstaterr.com). The nearest depot is located in Rusk, approximately 30 miles northwest of Nacogdoches, where passengers get all aboard on a historical journey through the East Texas Piney Woods. Trains have rolled on these 25 miles of rustic yet sturdy tracks between Rusk and Palestine since 1881, when the state prison system began constructing the railway to transport iron ore and timber.

The 90-minute trek between the two towns is a thoroughly enjoyable and relaxing journey into the past, with gently rolling train cars clickety-clacking over bridges and through the dense green forest. Sit back and let time slowly slip by while the steam locomotive's whistle bellows and the genial conductor checks your ticket. Before you know it, you'll be at the Victorian-style depot at the end of the line, where you'll find historical exhibits, gift shops, and food service.

Round-trip excursions depart each weekend year-round from both the Rusk and Palestine depots at 11am and return to their point of origin by 3:30pm Be forewarned: Tickets for the train are pretty pricey, but the experience is one-of-a-kind. Adult fares run $56, and child (ages 3-11) fares are $38. A 90-minute layover is scheduled at the opposite train depot, where a variety of lunch options await. Snacks, beverages, and restrooms are available on the train.

Caddo Mounds State Historic Site

Just south of Rusk near the small town of Alto is the compelling **Caddo Mounds State Historic Site** (1649 State Hwy. 21 W., 936/858-3218, www.visitcaddomounds.com, 8:30am-4:30pm Tues.-Sun., $4 adults, $3 students). Caddo-speaking farmers built these ceremonial burial mounds more than 1,200 years ago, and historians now realize that they are the southwestern-most structures of the legendary Mound Builders of the eastern North American woodlands. Three of these earthen mounds, used for burials, temples, and religious ceremonies, still

© ANDY RHODES

Caddo Mounds

rise from the East Texas forests. Visitors can walk among the gently sloping structures, explore the interpretive center's exhibits and displays, and view a reconstructed Caddo house built with Stone Age tools.

RECREATION
Hiking
Looking for a quiet retreat to the surrounding woodlands? Then hoof it to the **Stephen F. Austin Experimental Forest** (eight miles southwest of Nacogdoches at 6598 FM 2782, 936/564-8924, www.srs.fs.usda.gov). Not quite as compelling at its name implies, the forest is dubbed "experimental" for its crazy variety of tree species planted in the 1940s. A century ago, the area was logged and abandoned for use as cotton fields, but the U.S. government's purchase of more than 600,000 acres of East Texas property—eventually becoming the region's national forests—allowed for the reforestation of hardwoods and pines that would eventually populate the area. The Experimental Forest contains three miles of trails with interpretive

signs. Visitors and locals regularly traverse the wooded trails to catch a glimpse of the more than 150 species of birds and 80 kinds of butterflies throughout this peaceful site.

Biking
If you're in town with a bike and are looking for a scenic and pleasant place to ride for an hour or so, head directly to the campus of **Stephen F. Austin State University** (1936 North St., 936/468-3200, www.sfasu.edu). Soak up the tree-lined streets and classic collegiate structures while keeping an eye out for thousands of meandering (while texting) students.

More adventurous souls in search of a lengthy ride can meet up with cyclists knowledgeable about the area at the **Nacogdoches Bicycle Club** (www.bikenacogdoches.org). The group meets several times a month, almost always on Saturday mornings for a 30-mile ride on the rolling rural roadways outside of town. Membership is not required, and visitors are welcome to drop in. As of late 2012, the group was meeting on Saturday mornings near the SFASU campus at **Java Jack's** (1122 North St., 936/560-3975, www.javajacks.com).

ACCOMMODATIONS
Like Lufkin, Nacogdoches's lodging options are primarily chains, with most located near the Stephen F. Austin campus. The best budget choice is **Best Western Inn of Nacogdoches** (3428 South St., 936/560-4900, www.bestwestern.com, $75 d), offering rooms with free Internet access along with microwaves and refrigerators, a free continental breakfast, and an outdoor pool. One of Nacogdoches's few locally run establishments is the pleasant downtown six-story **Hotel Fredonia** (200 N. Fredonia St., 936/564-1234, www.hotelfredonia.com, $89 d), which opened in 1955. Recently restored, the Fredonia features Wi-Fi access, a large outdoor pool, and a fitness center.

Moving into the slightly-more-expensive range is the clean and comfortable **Hampton Inn & Suites** (3625 South St., 936/560-9901, www.hamptoninn.com, $119 d), which provides free Internet access, a complimentary hot

Hotel Fredonia

breakfast buffet, an outdoor pool, and a fitness center. A popular option with business travelers is the nearby **Holiday Inn Express Hotel & Suites** (3807 South St., 936/564-0100, www. hiexpress.com, $139 d), with amenities such as free wireless Internet service, a fancy fitness center, and an outdoor pool.

FOOD
Barbecue

Don't let the shiny new decor fool you at the **Barbecue House** (704 N. Stallings Dr., 936/569-9004, 11am-9pm daily, $8-16, cash only). Just because the building is new, it doesn't mean the food is fancy. This is classic East Texas-style barbecue done right: sweet tomato-based sauce smothering delicious brisket, savory sausage, and meaty pork ribs. Instead of pinto beans and coleslaw, opt for the red beans and rice. Houston-based **Harlon's Bar B Que** (603 Old Tyler Rd., 936/564-4850,

11am-8:30pm Mon.-Thurs., 11am-9pm Fri.-Sat., $7-14) isn't quite as tantalizing, but it'll satisfy your craving. The brisket and chicken are popular here, as are the weekend late-night gatherings, where blues music, karaoke, and dancing are often on the menu.

Mexican

Nacogdoches isn't really known for its quality Mexican restaurants, but it has a couple options in town if you need a fajita fix. **San Miguel Mexican Restaurant** (2524 South St., 936/569-2082, hours vary, $6-15) offers all the classics: chicken enchiladas with green sauce, tacos, burritos, and even fried ice cream. Another option is **Restaurant El Ranchero** (123 King St., 936/569-2256, hours vary, $7-14), featuring some of the hottest and heartiest salsa in town, along with traditional favorites such as quesadillas, fajitas, and flautas. Call in advance to see if they're offering their "two free margaritas" special.

Lunch

If you're in the downtown area at lunch, drop by the wonderful **Shelley's Bakery Cafe** (112 N. Church St., 936/564-4100, www. shelleysbakerycafe.com, 10am-3pm Tues.-Sat., $5-14). The salads are a big draw here, as are the hearty sandwiches. Billing itself as a European-style bistro, Shelley's is one of those tucked-away little places that's ideal for grabbing a midmorning coffee and pastry while perusing the local paper. Another popular lunch spot is the campus-area **Stacy's Deli** (3205 N. University Dr., 936/564-3588, closed Sun., $4-8). Students and professors line up at this shopping-center deli for tasty BLTs, Reubens, and meatball subs accompanied by salty chips and a large iced tea. Stacy's spicy pickles are legendary among SFASU students. Locals also love the regional chain **Clear Springs Cafe** (211 Old Tyler Rd., 936/569-0489, www.clearspringsrestaurant.com, 11am-9pm Mon.-Fri., 11am-10pm Sat.-Sun., $6-19). Seafood is the main draw here, including popular dishes such as the pan-seared tilapia, salmon or crawfish salad, and catfish étouffée.

INFORMATION AND SERVICES

While strolling historical downtown Nacogdoches, drop by the town's two main tourism offices. The **Nacogdoches Convention & Visitors Bureau** (200 E. Main St., 888/653-3788, www.visitnacogdoches.org, 9am-5pm Mon.-Fri., 10am-4pm Sat., 1pm-4pm Sun.) has information on the city's history and local sites of interest. Just around the corner is the office headquarters of the **Texas Forest Trail Region** (202 E. Pilar St., 936/560-3699, www. texasforesttrail.com, 8:30am-5pm Mon.-Fri.). Operated by the Texas Historical Commission, the Forest Trail Region oversees heritage travel destinations and cultural activities in Nacogdoches and the entire East Texas Piney Woods region. Drop by to pick up brochures and maps and talk to the friendly and knowledgeable staff.

Tyler

Slow-moving Tyler will never be confused with fast-paced Austin, but this large town, or small city, (population 98,564) certainly has a distinctive feel—Southern. From stately plantations to hospitable residents to deep-fried cooking, Tyler has a strong cultural connection to the Deep South.

The city's biggest draw is its roses. Once responsible for more than half of the country's rose bush supply, Tyler now provides 20 percent of the roses in the United States. The Tyler Municipal Rose Garden contains more than 35,000 rosebushes representing nearly 500 varieties. The gardens attract bees, butterflies, and more than 100,000 people annually from across the world. Many visitors come especially for the Texas Rose Festival, a tradition held each October since 1933, featuring events such as the queen's coronation, the rose parade, the queen's tea, and the rose show.

Tyler changed dramatically in 1930, when the discovery of a nearby East Texas oil field turned this small agricultural and railroad city into a major destination for workers and corporations. The town received an added boost in the 1940s when Camp Fannin was established nearby, with a troop capacity of 19,000 at the height of World War II.

In the following decades, Tyler's economic base shifted from agriculture to industry. Most were petroleum related, but other manufacturing plants soon followed, including metal and fabricating companies, railroad and machine shops, furniture and woodwork manufacturers, aluminum foundries, and air-conditioning and refrigeration plants.

In the 1970s and '80s, Tyler was best known as the hometown of football legend Earl Campbell, who earned the Heisman Trophy at the University of Texas and went on to become a Hall of Fame running back in the National Football League. Campbell's nickname, "The Tyler Rose," forever linked him with his hometown.

SIGHTS
Tyler Municipal Rose Garden and Museum

The region's most popular tourist attraction is the **Tyler Municipal Rose Garden and Museum** (420 Rose Park Dr., 903/597-3130, www.texasrosefestival.com, 9am-4:30pm Mon.-Fri., 10am-4:30pm Sat., 1:30pm-4:30pm Sun., $3.50 adults, $2 children ages 3-11). The museum is well worth visiting, with numerous displays showcasing the elaborately jeweled, hand-sewn gowns worn by rose queens dating back to 1935. Be sure to check out the scrapbook pages from each rose queen, including memorabilia, personal recollections, and photos (including one with a queen and her freshly killed deer). Visitors can also view videos about the history of Tyler's rose industry and rose festival and experience an interactive "attic" exhibit with a bizarre collection of antiques and collectibles from Tyler's past.

The municipal garden is the primary draw, however, with its sea of colorful roses—more

© ANDY RHODES

Tyler Municipal Rose Garden

than 35,000 bushes representing the nearly 500 distinct varieties. Although the blooming period is from May through November, early May is the peak of the flowers' natural growing cycle. This is when the garden's 14 acres burst with the bright sight and sweet scent of fresh roses.

Plantation Museums

Tyler's heritage is on full display at Tyler's three plantation museums, where the Old South comes to life through antique furniture, artifacts, and photos. This lifestyle, typically associated with the Deep South, wasn't prevalent in most of Texas, so it's worth dropping by one of these sites just to get a feel for the ornate homes and luxurious grounds. If you're lucky, the docents and tour guides may even be dressed in period costume.

The Goodman Museum (624 N. Broadway Ave., 903/531-1286, www.cityoftyler.org, 10am-4pm Tues.-Sat., free admission) was the home of Dr. W. J. Goodman, a local doctor and Civil War surgeon for 72 years (1866-1938).

Originally built in 1859, the house is Tyler's first property to be listed on the National Register of Historic Places. The museum features original furnishings, including hand-carved tables and chairs, a grandfather clock from the colonial era, surgical tools and medical cases, and fine silver and china. It's open for walk-in tours.

Just as impressive is the 1854 **Dewberry Plantation** (14007 FM 346 W., 903/825-9000, www.dewberryplantation.com, open by appointment, tours are $8 adults and seniors, $5 children ages 6-18). The plantation site served as a campground for the officers of the Army of the Republic of Texas prior to their final battle with the Cherokee. The home, billed as the only original two-story pre-Civil War house still standing in Smith County, was built for War of 1812 hero Colonel John Dewberry, who moved to the Tyler area in 1835.

Also noteworthy is the grand 1878 **McClendon House** (806 W. Houston St., 903/592-3533, www.mcclendonhouse.net, 10am-4pm Fri.-Sat., tours $7). Once a hub for

Tyler's eloquent Victorian society, the home was eventually purchased by the McClendon family, whose youngest daughter, Sarah, became a noted Washington DC journalist with a presidential-coverage career spanning from Franklin Roosevelt to George W. Bush. The home is now primarily used as a wedding and events site but is open to the public for tours.

Caldwell Zoo

Big cities don't necessarily have the best zoos. One of the best-run and highly acclaimed zoos in the state is Tyler's **Caldwell Zoo** (2203 W. Martin Luther King Jr. Blvd., 903/593-0121, www.caldwellzoo.org, 9am-5pm daily Mar. 1-Labor Day, 9am-5pm daily in the off-season, $9.50 adults ages 13-54, $8.25 seniors, $6 children ages 3-12). What started in 1938 as a backyard menagerie of squirrels and parrots for schoolchildren has evolved into an 85-acre zoo containing more than 2,000 animals representing species from East Africa, North America, and South America. Animals on display in naturalistic habitats include monkeys, rhinos, elephants, giraffes, cheetahs, and mountain lions.

Tyler Museum of Art

For a dose of traditional culture, visit the respectable **Tyler Museum of Art** (located on the east side of the Tyler Junior College campus at 1300 South Mahon Ave., 903/595-1001, www.tylermuseum.org, 10am-5pm Tues.-Sat., 1pm-5pm Sun., $7 adults, $5 seniors and students). The museum primarily showcases local and regional artists with an emphasis on contemporary works; however, occasional traveling exhibits feature centuries-old European paintings, Japanese artwork, and Native American pottery and ceramics. It contains three galleries on the main level, a smaller gallery for special exhibits upstairs, and a children's gallery.

Discovery Science Place

If you're in Tyler with the family in tow, this is the place to go. The **Discovery Science Place** (308 N. Broadway, 903/533-8011, www.discoveryscienceplace.org, 9am-5pm Mon.-Sat., 1pm-5pm Sun., $8 adults, $6 children and seniors) offers three large exhibit halls with fun interactive features like the earthquake shake, cavern crawl, dinosaur exhibit, and bat cave.

ENTERTAINMENT AND EVENTS

For a city of nearly 100,000, Tyler has a surprising number of entertainment options. Perhaps that's due to the increasing number of retirees who have been steadily moving from large metroplex areas to Tyler for its proximity and slower-paced lifestyle (and traffic). Regardless, the number and quality of people involved with the local arts scene has certainly improved over the past decade, resulting in a top-notch ballet, symphony, and cultural offerings.

Ballet Tyler

One of the organizations drawing a lot of local attention is **Ballet Tyler** (4703 D.C. Dr., Ste. 105, 903/596-0224, www.ballettyler.org). The 2009 convergence of two programs, the School of Ballet Tyler and Tyler Junior College dance program, has helped raise the group's profile. Dancers range in age from 11 to 20, and the company stages several performances throughout the year. Visit its website for performance schedules and prices.

East Texas Symphony Orchestra

One of Tyler's enduring cultural entities is the **East Texas Symphony Orchestra** (522 S. Broadway Ave., Ste. 101, 903/526-3876, www.etso.org). Newly named to encompass a larger region (as opposed to just Tyler), the orchestra has also bumped up its mission to bring classical music to a larger segment of the community. The organization offers a wide range of concerts, from contemporary to Renaissance.

Cowan Center

For big-name touring acts, Tyler residents and visitors head to the University of Texas-Tyler's **Cowan Center** (3900 University Blvd., 903/566-7424, www.cowancenter.org). This is the stage for international and touring stars from all aspects of entertainment, including comedy, jazz, and Broadway shows. Past performers and performances include Bill Cosby, David Copperfield, Lyle Lovett, *Cats*, *Stomp*, and Larry Hagman.

Gallery Main Street

The "cornerstone of Tyler's Arts District" is **Gallery Main Street** (110 W. Erwin St., 903/593-6905, www.heartoftyler.com). The gallery, affiliated with Tyler's Main Street program, features a rotating schedule of juried exhibits for local art lovers. It's open Monday through Saturday and free of charge.

SHOPPING
East Texas Fresh Farmer's Market

Tyler isn't really known as a major shopping destination; however, locals are increasingly spending time and money at **East Texas Fresh Farmer's Market** (5725 Old Bullard Rd.). Held each Saturday, the market features regional vendors offering fresh produce, flowers, and wares. It's a good way to soak up a slice of the local scene and support the local farming community in the process.

ACCOMMODATIONS

Chain hotels are pretty much the only choice in Tyler; fortunately, the available options are safe, reliable, and relatively affordable. On the lower end of the price spectrum is **La Quinta** (1601 W. Southwest Loop 323, 903/561-2223, www.lq.com, $75 d), featuring free Internet access, a free continental breakfast, and an outdoor pool.

Perhaps the best deal in town is the **Comfort Suites at South Broadway Mall** (303 E. Rieck Rd., 903/534-0999, www.choicehotels.com, $99 d), offering rooms with free Internet access, microwaves, and refrigerators plus hotel amenities such as an exercise room, free continental breakfast, manager's reception (free happy hour drinks), and an indoor heated pool and whirlpool. The only drawback is its location: far away from the downtown activity.

On Broadway (about 10 minutes from downtown) is the recommended **Country Inn & Suites** (6702 S. Broadway Ave., 903/561-0863,

www.countryinns.com, $90 d). There's plenty of space to spread out here, with a mini kitchen (refrigerator, microwave) and rooms offering free Wi-Fi. The free breakfast includes meats, eggs, bagels, and cereals. Nearby is the city's largest hotel—the comfortable **Holiday Inn Select** (5701 S. Broadway Ave., 903/561-5800 or 800/465-4329, www.holidayinn.com, $99 d). The Holiday Inn features free Wi-Fi service, an outdoor pool, a full fitness center, and free meals for kids 12 and under.

FOOD

Tyler's quality restaurant options are better than you'd expect, particularly for a smallish city in a largely rural area of the state. Perhaps it's the steady arrival of Dallas retirees demanding fine-dining establishments, but the end result is good news for everyone, from travelers to locals to newcomers.

Contemporary and Fusion

A stalwart on the scene is 🄲 **Rick's on the Square** (104 W. Erwin St., 903/531-2415, www.rix.com, 11am-midnight Mon.-Fri., 4pm-1 am Sat., $10-32), a swanky lunch and dinner joint and rowdy blues bar by night. Located in the heart of downtown in an old saloon and theater, Rick's is the kind of place that gets everything right—tempting appetizers (shrimp and oysters), gigantic juicy burgers with chunks of fried potatoes on the side, and exquisite entrées ranging from chicken dumplings to tortilla-crusted mahimahi to the indulgent yet highly recommended crawfish-stuffed filet mignon. A similar menu can be found at the popular **Potpourri House** (3200 Troup Hwy., 903/592-4171, www.potpourrihouse.com, 11am-9pm Mon.-Sat., $9-29). This welcoming spot is combined with a retail establishment offering candles, antiques, jewelry, more candles, and probably even some potpourri. The restaurant's offerings range from club sandwiches to baked fish and chicken to prime rib.

Barbecue

A local legend and a must for barbecue fans is **Stanley's Famous Pit Bar-B-Q** (525 S. Beckham Ave., 903/593-0311, www.

stanleysfamous.com, 7-10 am Mon.-Fri., 11am-9pm Mon.-Sat., $7-19). The smoked ribs here have been placed atop "best of" barbecue lists all across Texas, and for good reason—their tender, succulent taste will have you thinking about them for days. Try the smoked turkey and sausage, or sample a sliced brisket sandwich. Better yet, tackle the Brother-in-Law sandwich, teeming with sausage, chopped beef, and cheese.

Mexican

Tyler is pretty far away from the border, but that doesn't prevent it from having a few worthy Mexican restaurants. Among the most popular are the homegrown regional chains of Mercado's and Posado's.

If you're downtown, drop by **Posado's** (2500 E. 5th St., 903/597-2573,11am-10pm daily, $7-15). The mission-style decor adds to the authentic Mexican taste, including interior-style dishes such as marinated quail fajitas and shrimp or fish platters. You can't go wrong with the classics here either, including chicken enchiladas and spicy beef tacos. A big bonus: The chips and salsa and dessert (ice cream or sopapillas) are free.

Locals also love **Taqueria El Lugar** (1716 E. Gentry Pkwy., 903/597-4717, 10am-9pm Mon.-Sat., $8-16). As the name implies, tacos are the specialty here, and they're listed on the menu by number (up to 16). Order anything with the amazing guacamole and tasty beef (the cabbage isn't quite as recommendable), and be sure to ask for it on a corn tortilla.

Coffee

As its name implies, the **Downtown Coffee Lounge** (200 W. Erwin St., 903/266-9192, hours vary, $4-9) is an ideal place to grab a coffee while downtown. It certainly helps that the coffee is exceptional, and the downtown is inviting. Although there are other spots in Tyler to experience a more authentic and hearty East Texas-style lunch, the Downtown Coffee Lounge offers decent food (salads, chicken wraps, soups) if you're in the area at lunchtime. The real draw, however, is the coffee—a double latte provides a perfect mid-morning pick-me-up or works well as an accompaniment for a stroll around the adjacent courthouse square.

INFORMATION AND SERVICES

The **Tyler Convention & Visitors Bureau** (315 N. Broadway Ave., 903/592-1661 or 800/235-5712, www.visittyler.com) is located just a few blocks north of the downtown square on the first floor of the historic Blackstone building. The friendly staffers will provide brochures, maps, and general information to help you get around the Rose Capital.

GETTING THERE

If, for some reason, you really need to get to Tyler in a hurry, you can actually take a commercial flight to **Tyler Pounds Regional Airport** (700 Skyway Blvd., 903/531-9825, www.cityoftyler.org). United and American airlines fly regional jets to Tyler several times a day. From Houston, flights cost around $275 round-trip and sometimes a bit more. Most people opt for the modest automobile, however, which takes about three and a half hours from Houston (about the same amount of time it would take to fly, considering the security lines, runway taxi time, and so on).

EAST TEXAS

Marshall

Although some people might think a nearly four-hour drive (from Houston to Marshall) is a bit of a stretch for a getaway, it's not that uncommon. In Texas, three or four hours is "just down the road," so a long weekend in Marshall (population 23,523) is certainly a consideration for Houston residents and visitors. Besides, the drive is part of the appeal, with most of it meandering through the picturesque Piney Woods. Once there, visitors find Marshall's laid-back Southern charm to be a welcome respite from the coastal plains and urban environs of Southeastern Texas.

Perhaps even more intriguing is the town's burgeoning cultural scene. Believe it or not, the heart of rock n' roll may have started beating in Marshall. This compelling community is at the center of a musically fertile region that spawned such legendary artists as Scott Joplin, Lead Belly, and Don Henley.

Marshall's new slogan is "The Birthplace of Boogie Woogie," and the city is grooving to its musical moniker. This barrelhouse style of piano playing likely originated in logging camps along the tracks of the Texas and Pacific Railway, headquartered in Marshall during the late 1800s. Now, thanks to some professional research and eager townsfolk, the city is celebrating this slice of its cultural heritage with weekly piano gigs, festivals, and associated artistic endeavors. It's certainly not a typical East Texas town.

SIGHTS
Texas & Pacific Railway Museum

To get a sense of the city during its railway heyday, visit the **Texas & Pacific Railway Museum and Depot** (800 N. Washington St., 903/938-9495, 10am-4pm Tues.-Sat., $2 admission). Housed in a striking crimson building that still serves as an active Amtrak station, the museum contains an impressive collection of railroad-related photos, memorabilia, and hands-on displays including a pull whistle and operable model train. The 1912 depot depicts an authentic slice of life in late-1800s Marshall, when the railroad company employed nearly a third of the town.

Starr Family Home

Part of the Marshall community for more than a century, the **Starr Family Home** (407 W. Travis St., 903/935-3044, www.visitstarrfamilyhome.com, open 10am-4pm Tues.-Sun., $4 adults, $3 students ages 6-18) is a remarkable example of 19th-century Texas. Visitors to the home can see hand-carved furnishings, family portraits, and delicate glassware collections. The site's collection is composed of original pieces from the Starr family, which played an important role in the state's history from the formative years of the Republic of Texas. The Starr Family Home has become a community cornerstone, hosting events ranging from weddings to family reunions to an annual croquet tournament and holiday candlelight dinner.

Harrison County Courthouse

Serving as the visual centerpiece of downtown is the stately **Harrison County Courthouse** (200 W. Houston St., 903/935-8402, 9am-5pm Mon.-Fri.). Recently restored to its original grandeur, the 1901 neoclassical-style building features remarkable architectural elements, including eagle statues along the roofline and a beautifully renovated cupola. The ornate courtroom offers a step back in time with its handcrafted detailing and curvilinear balcony. Inside, the **Harrison County Museum** provides an overview of the many factors that shaped the city, including the railroad, boogie-woogie music, and Wiley College, the first African American college west of the Mississippi River certified by the Freedman's Aid Society.

Michelson Museum of Art

A few blocks away is the modest yet impressive **Michelson Museum of Art** (216 North Bolivar St., 903/935-9480, www.michelsonmuseum.org, open 10am-4pm Tues.-Fri., 1pm-4pm Sat., free admission). This modest downtown museum showcases a colorful compilation of more than 1,000 paintings and sketches by Russian-American artist Leo Michelson (1887-1978). The museum has expanded its collection to include early 20th-century American prints and international objets d' art such as Chinese opera puppets and African masks.

SHOPPING
Marshall Pottery

The city's best-known shopping destination is **Marshall Pottery** (4901 Elysian Fields Rd., 903/927-5400, www.marshallpottery.com, 9am-5pm Mon.-Sat.). Billed as the largest manufacturer of red clay pots in the United States, this enormous store draws pottery people from across the South in search of handcrafted and customized stoneware to better their homes and gardens.

© ANDY RHODES

Marshall's Texas & Pacific Railway Museum

Weisman Center

Located in a century-old mercantile store just a couple blocks from the historic downtown courthouse is the popular **Weisman Center** (211 North Washington Ave., 903/934-8836, www.theweisman.com, open 10am-5:30pm Mon.-Sat.). The two-story classic shop is home to an eclectic mix of antiques, artwork, and locally made crafts. A portion of this former department store hosts Central Perks, offering coffee, salad, and sandwiches accompanied by panoramic views of Marshall's downtown historical district.

ACCOMMODATIONS

With a major freeway (I-20) traversing the southern edge of Marshall, hotel options are plentiful, though fairly expensive. A consistently reliable option is **Holiday Inn Express** (500 E. I-20, 903/934-9700, www.hiexpress.com, $94 d), offering free Wi-Fi service, a pool, full fitness center, and free meals for kids 12 and under. More memorable is **Fairfield Inn & Suites** (105 W. I-20, 903/938-7666,

www.fairfieldmarshall.com, $99 d), featuring Marshall's only indoor swimming pool. Other amenities include a hot tub, complimentary hot breakfast, free Internet service, and microwaves, refrigerators, and bonus DVD players in each room.

Slightly closer to town is **Hampton Inn** (5100 SE End Blvd., 903/927-0079, www.hamptoninn3.hilton.com, $104 d), offering free Internet access, a complimentary hot breakfast (including a to-go breakfast bag Mon.-Fri.). The Hampton also provides unexpectedly high-quality bed linens, coffee at any time of the day, a fitness center, and outdoor pool.

FOOD

Considering its remote location and modest population, expectations for quality food options in Marshall should be realistic (that is, not high). Fortunately, there are a few places to get a decent meal. The best place to soak up the local scenery while enjoying good food is on the downtown square at **OS2 Restaurant and Pub** (105 E. Houston St., 903/938-7700,

EAST TEXAS

© ANDY RHODES

the OS2 Restaurant and Pub in downtown Marshall

www.os2marshall.com, 5-9pm Mon.-Thurs., 5-10pm Fri.-Sat., $10-29). Located inside a quaint historic building in the shadow of the stately courthouse, the OS2 is primarily known for its steaks. The tenderloin medallions and salmon fillet are worthy, and the sides (mainly buttery vegetables) offer a nice accompaniment. Be sure to stick around for a drink at the attached pub, and if you're lucky, you may be able to shake a leg with Marshall's finest local dancers as part of the town's boogie-woogie live music program.

Just down the street, **Central Perks** (211-A N. Washington St., 903/934-9902, www.centralperks.us, 8am-5:30pm Mon.-Weds. and Fri., 8am-8pm Thurs., 8am-5pm Sat., $4-14) is the place to go for lunch. Located on the ground floor of the historic Weisman Center mercantile building, Central Perks is an ideal spot to enjoy a sandwich, soup, or salad while gazing out the window at Marshall's version of downtown "hustle and bustle." Even if you're not here at mealtime, it's worth getting a coffee or tea to go.

Although Tex-Mex in Texas is typically best when it's closer to the Mexican border, Marshall offers a decent option at **Jalapeño Tree** (1000 E. End Blvd., 903/927-2777,11am-10pm daily, $7-15). A small regional chain, Jalapeño Tree provides all the standard Tex-Mex fare for those needing a fix. The restaurant is best known for its fajitas (go with beef instead of chicken), but you can't go wrong with traditional menu items here either, particularly the enchiladas and tacos. The margaritas are better than average, and if you still have room after your meal, the soft-serve ice cream is free of charge.

Jefferson

If you've decided to invest a few hours into making the northeastern Texas getaway trip, you should set aside a few hours to explore Jefferson (population 1,869). This quaint Deep Southern community is nestled among the forests, offering a pleasant escape to the Piney Woods' past. In its glory days of the mid-19th century, Jefferson was a burgeoning boomtown containing a kaleidoscope of cultures, from entrepreneurial East Coast shop merchants to newly freed slaves to westward-moving pioneers. For more than a decade, Jefferson welcomed a steady flow of steamboats bringing worldly influences and people.

In 1870, Jefferson had a population of 4,180 and was the sixth-largest city in Texas. Between 1867 and 1870, steamboats became a tremendous factor in the town's commercial trade, which grew from $3 million to $8 million. By 1870, only the port of Galveston exceeded Jefferson in volume.

In 1873, things changed dramatically for Jefferson. The destruction of the Red River raft, a natural dam on the river, lowered the water level of the surrounding lakes and streams, making navigation to Jefferson via steamboat nearly impossible. Also that year, the Texas and Pacific Railway, which bypassed Jefferson, was completed. Without steamboat or railroad access, people started leaving Jefferson in droves.

In the mid-1900s, locals began looking at Jefferson's distinctive past as a way to preserve and promote the town's heritage, particularly its remarkable 100-plus state and nationally recognized historic structures. Known as the Bed and Breakfast Capital of Texas, tourism is now Jefferson's most important economic base.

SIGHTS
Historic Buildings

With so much Southern heritage in such a small town, it's necessary to visit some of the sites that make Jefferson so historically significant. One of its crown jewels is the amazing

House of the Seasons (409 S. Alley St., 903/665-8000, www.houseoftheseasons.com, tours available at 11am Mon.-Sat., $7.50 per person). Built in 1872 by Colonel Benjamin Epperson, a prominent businessman and friend of Sam Houston, this magnificent home contains architectural elements representing styles ranging from Greek Revival to Italianate to Victorian. The house gets its name from the glass encasement on top of the house, featuring colored glass representing each season of the year.

A visit to Jefferson is incomplete without a stop at the fascinating **Jefferson General Store** (113 E. Austin St., 903/665-8481, www.jeffersongeneralstore.com, 9am-6pm Sun.-Thurs., 9am-10pm Fri.-Sat.). Walking through the creaky front screen doors offers a true step back in time, with vintage trinkets and current-day souvenirs mingling in an 1870s mercantile setting. Touches of bygone days are everywhere, from the signature five-cent cup of coffee to the homemade pecan pralines to the soda fountain. Jams, salsas, T-shirts, and candy round out this unique experience.

Also well worth a visit is **The Grove** (405 Moseley St., 903/665-8018, www.thegrove-jefferson.com, call for tour information, $6 admission). Referred to as "the most haunted house in Jefferson," The Grove is a private residence built in 1861 that was listed on the National Register of Historic Places. An hour-long tour offers a fascinating glimpse into the home, along with stories about the supernatural experiences of the owners, including a lady in a white dress who always takes the same path through the house when she appears. Its paranormal activity is so legendary, *This Old House* placed it on its list of Top 12 Haunted Homes, and it graces the cover of *A Texas Guide to Haunted Restaurants, Taverns, and Inns.*

Just outside of town, approximately one mile west, is the stately **Freeman Plantation** (Hwy. 49 W., 903/665-2320), built on nearly 1,000

EAST TEXAS

acres in 1850 by Williamson M. Freeman. Guided tours educate visitors about the Victorian antiques and the family who occupied the home during the antebellum period.

The Atalanta Railroad Car

The Atalanta (210 W. Austin St., 903/665-2513, open daily) was a private rail car used by railroad tycoon Jay Gould. It's rather odd that this elaborately designed and elegantly furnished car ended up in Jefferson since the city rejected Gould's plans to bring a railroad through the town. Upon being spurned, he hightailed it out of there, predicting Jefferson's demise (he was partly right as the town never regained its steamboat-era splendor of the 1860s). The Atalanta features nearly a dozen rooms containing opulent interior materials such as mahogany, crystal light fixtures, and silver bathroom accessories. Located downtown across from the Excelsior Hotel, it remains a major attraction in Jefferson's heritage tourism industry.

Scarlett O'Hardy's Gone With the Wind Museum

If you're still pining for historical ties to the Old South, drop by the campy and somewhat strange **Scarlett O'Hardy's Gone With the Wind Museum** (408 Taylor St., 903/665-1939, www.scarlettohardy.com, 10am-5pm Thurs.-Sat., $3 adults, $1 children 12 and under). The jam-packed museum contains everything imaginable related to the classic film, including posters, photos, costume reproductions, dolls, and seats from the Atlanta theater where the movie premiered in 1939. Perhaps most interesting is the collection of autographs from the movie's stars, most notably Clark Gable and Vivien Leigh, Leslie Howard, Hattie McDaniel, and Butterfly McQueen.

Lake o' the Pines

The nearby **Lake o' the Pines** is just as charming as its name implies. This popular destination is particularly known for its fishing, with bass, catfish, and crappie as the main biters. Recreational boating is another common activity, especially waterskiing, sailing, or relaxing on pontoon boats, party boats, and "floating cabins," all available at several lakeside marinas. Campers also flock to Lake o' the Pines, pitching tents and parking RVs at one of the four U.S. Army Corps of Engineer parks or privately owned campgrounds. Other options include guesthouses, cabins, or motels. For more information about lake services, contact the local chamber of commerce at www.lakeothepines.com or 903/755-2597.

Caddo Lake

For the area's premier recreational destination, head just downriver from Jefferson to **Caddo Lake,** the only natural lake in Texas (all the others were created by dams). Stringy Spanish moss and outstretched cypress trees surround this mysteriously beautiful and sometimes marshy lake. The native Caddo people claimed a giant flood formed the lake, but scientists believe massive logjams blocked the Red River, causing it to back up into the Cypress Bayou watershed, which formed the lake. Popular lake activities include camping, hiking, swimming, fishing, and boating. Among the many attractions at Caddo Lake is **Caddo Lake State Park** (take State Hwy. 43 to FM 2198, 903/679-3351, www.tpwd.state.tx.us) operated by the Texas Parks and Wildlife Department. The park offers access to diverse fishing, canoe rentals, and quaint cabins, built by the Civilian Conservation Corps in the 1930s.

ACCOMMODATIONS
Bed-and-Breakfasts

Jefferson is the Bed and Breakfast Capital of Texas, so if you were ever going to stay in a B&B, this is the place to do it. The nearly 40 B&Bs far outnumber the measly hotel options, and the town is a Victorian-era playground, so you may as well go all the way.

Among the popular choices is the **Claiborne House Bed & Breakfast** (312 S. Alley, 903/665-8800, www.claibornehousebnb.com, $109-179), a stately Greek Revival home built in 1872. The Claiborne House offers six rooms—four in the main house and two in the carriage house, each named after romantic poets (Yeats, Wilde, Dickinson, etc.). All rooms have a framed poem, book of the poet's work, wireless Internet access, private baths, and color TVs. A full Southern gourmet breakfast is served at 9am, and a day spa features massages, body wraps, hot rock treatments, and salt scrubs.

Guests make regular returns to the remarkable **McKay House Bed & Breakfast Inn** (306 E. Delta St., 903/665-7322, www.mckayhouse.com, $139-149). The McKay house is famous for its attention to detail (Victorian nightgowns, sleep shirts, and period hats await on guests' beds) and its Gentleman's Breakfast (French toast, bacon, shirred eggs with ham, pineapple zucchini muffins, strawberry cheese blintzes). Seven rooms feature period furnishings, private baths, and Wi-Fi access, and the B&B provides lemonade, fireside coffee, a Packard pump organ, and a lush garden.

The **Old Mulberry Inn Bed & Breakfast** (209 Jefferson St., 903/665-1945, www.jeffersontexasinn.com, $85-169) is recommended by *Southern Living* magazine and even the *New York Times,* for good reason. This antebellum home has five guest rooms and two cottages with private baths featuring footed tubs, family heirlooms, cable TV, and free wireless Internet access. The three-course gourmet breakfasts include delectable items from artichoke quiche and Rocky Mountain grits to baked pears with cranberries and mulberry-almond coffee cake.

Hotels

For those who insist on staying in a normal plush-free hotel in the B&B Capital of Texas, there's really only one option in town: the independently owned **Inn of Jefferson** (400 S. Walcott St., 903/665-3983, www.innofjefferson.com, $89 d). There's nothing fancy about this place but it's certainly pleasant, with a free full hot breakfast, an outdoor pool, and free 24-hour beverage service. A word of caution: The loud whistles from the trains across the highway can be quite distracting—especially at three in the morning.

The historic **Excelsior House** hotel (211 W. Austin St., 903/665-2513, www.theexcelsiorhouse.com, $119 d) is technically a hotel but feels like a B&B (not a surprise in this town). Rich in history and ghosts, it has hosted guests since the 1850s. Fans of paranormal activity claim this is one of the most haunted locations in town. During Jefferson's prosperous days, famous people such as Ulysses S. Grant, Rutherford B. Hayes, and Oscar Wilde stayed here, and its 150-plus years of operation make it one of the oldest establishments of its kind still in business in Texas.

FOOD

Because of the town's modest size, most restaurants in Jefferson are within walking distance of the historical downtown shopping and lodging attractions. One of the stalwarts is the tremendous **Joseph's Riverport Barbecue** (201 N. Polk St., 903/665-2341, 11am-6pm Tues.-Sat., 11am-2pm Sun., $9-17). It serves traditional East Texas-style 'cue, with sweet, spicy sauce covering savory smoked meats, including pork ribs, brisket, and chicken. The turkey and chopped beef sandwiches are amazing, and the sides (potato salad, coleslaw, beans) are far better than average. Drop by on a Friday night for a catfish feast.

Another popular local eatery is **The Hamburger Store** (203 N. Market St., 903/665-3251, 10:30am-8pm Mon.-Sun., $6-15). It should be called the Pie Store, though, because it's best known for its incredible homemade pies. Call in a custom order (it takes about four hours) or pick up an individual slice while strolling through downtown. Of course you can also try to save room for pie after devouring one of the restaurant's enormous juicy burgers. Go full throttle and order a jalapeño chili cheddar burger followed by a piece of chocolate pie. A word of warning: The service here is extremely slow, so arrive early and take some time to work up an appetite.

EAST TEXAS

For a fancier dining experience, make reservations at the top-notch **Stillwater Inn** (203 E. Broadway St., 903/665-8415, www.stillwaterinn.com, 5:30pm-9pm Mon.-Sat., $9-29). Located in an 1890s Victorian house, this busy upscale restaurant is famous for its grilled seafood and steak, veal specials, and roasted rack of lamb.

INFORMATION AND SERVICES

To find out more about the dozens of available B&Bs or other area attractions, pick up a map or brochure from the kind folks at the **Marion County Chamber of Commerce** (101 N. Polk St., 903/665-2672, www.jeffersontexas.com).

BACKGROUND

The Land

As its name implies, the Coastal Plains of Texas include the flatlands that run along the Gulf of Mexico and further inland, part of a larger physical region that starts by the Atlantic Ocean and extends to beyond the Rio Grande. As you drive to the coast from points north and west, the transition is apparent when rolling hills become vast panoramas with little topography.

The official geographic boundary of the Coastal Plains reaches beyond the obvious horizontal stretches near the coast all the way up to San Antonio, Austin, and eastward. A fault line in this area marks the boundary between plains and rocky terrain and is often used to separate Texas into "lowland" and "upland" regions.

In East Texas, the Coastal Plains are largely wooded and once were dense with pine forests before the trees were clear-cut in the early 1900s. Several national forests retain the thick wooded areas representing the western edge of the pine forests that extend across the southern United States.

GEOGRAPHY

The two main geographic areas in this region of the state are the Coastal Plains and Piney Woods. The plains extend westward along the coast from the Louisiana border, reaching

inland up to 60 miles. Between the Sabine River (which marks the border between Texas and Louisiana) and Galveston Bay, the demarcation between the Coastal Plains and the Piney Woods is very noticeable, transitioning from towering trees to grassy scrublands.

The Piney Woods area extends about 100 miles into Texas from the east. Geographically, it's rather diverse, with soil ranging from sandy to rocky to mineral rich (iron deposits are mined near Lufkin). Even more significant are the oil fields in the ground beneath several notable sites in East Texas, including the East Texas Oil Field (Smith, Gregg, and Rusk counties) and most famously, Spindletop near Beaumont.

The Coastal Plains

This area has the lowest elevation in Texas—less than 1,000 feet above sea level—and contains several bands of physical features and soil types formed by the weathering of underlying rock layers. As its name implies, the Gulf Coastal Plains include Texas's entire coastline and the mouths of most of the state's major rivers.

The Pine Belt comprises the eastern portion of this region along the Louisiana border. Pine trees, hay fields, and cattle pastures dominate the area, which is home to several national forests and the state's lumber industry.

West of the Pine Belt lie the Post Oak and Blackland Belts. These regions are known for their fertile soil and rolling prairies, and cotton remains the major crop. These prime agricultural conditions fueled Texas's growth, and the region retains some of the state's most densely populated areas.

Texas's southern tip is mostly comprised of the Rio Grande Plain, which includes the Lower Rio Grande Valley, known throughout the state simply as "the Valley." The Rio Grande Plain extends southward into Mexico for several hundred miles. Cattle production is also significant in the southern Rio Grande Plain, and a prime example is the famous King Ranch, located southwest of Corpus Christi. The Valley, meanwhile, thrives agriculturally,

the coastal plains

thanks to the rich delta soils and absence of freezing weather. It's best known for citrus production, most notably the Ruby Red grapefruits in the Brownsville area.

The region's Coastal Prairies stretch across the Gulf of Mexico coastline, reaching as far as 60 miles inland. The eastern portion of this region is thick with vegetation and supports crops ranging from rice to cotton. The southern portion contains grasslands, citrus fruits, and vegetables.

CLIMATE

Most of Texas has two main seasons—a hot summer that lasts from approximately May through October and a winter that starts in November and usually lasts until March. Things are slightly different along the Gulf Coast, however, as winter is not really a factor.

Houston can get cold, and it has had a few extremely rare instances of snow in the past few years. But it mostly gets cloudy during the traditional winter months, and even then, 70-degree days are not uncommon. Further south along the Gulf Coast, the experience of colder weather is even more rare. That's why so many Northerners flock to the region from November through March, comprising a sizable segment of the population known as Winter Texans.

A weather map in winter tells the story of Texas's variable climate in a visually stunning way—the entire spectrum of colors is represented across the state. The rainbow of Texas's diverse climate is a revealing diagram, from the lower Gulf Coast's balmy 90°F reds to icy 20°F blues in the Panhandle.

The **average rainfall** in the Houston area and East Texas typically exceeds 56 inches annually while parts of West Texas typically receive less than 8 inches each year. One final note of interest: Brownsville, at the southern tip of Texas's Gulf Coast, has no measurable snowfall on record.

Scientists typically divide Texas into three meteorological areas—modified marine (aka subtropics), continental, and mountain. The destinations in this book are mainly located in the subtropics region, which is primarily affected by tropical airflow from the Gulf of Mexico. As a result, Houston and the Gulf Coast are well known for having a humid climate noted for its warm summers.

Dangerous Weather

Even the weather is extreme in this region of Texas. Menacing hurricanes, tornadoes, and floods can strike at any time, wreaking their havoc swiftly before clear skies and calm conditions return. Fortunately, many residents of Houston and along the Gulf Coast have learned from previous storms, putting evacuation plans and safety procedures in place. Though most of these events are seasonal, Texas's nature can be unpredictable, so visitors should be prepared for potential flash floods.

Historically, **hurricanes** have hit Texas's Gulf Coast about once every decade, usually in September or October. Most Gulf Coast communities have evacuation plans in place, along with reinforced buildings and homes to brace against the torrential winds. Many seaside structures are also raised on piers to help prevent damage from the crashing waves during a tropical storm.

In the past decade, however, the hurricane activity in the gulf has been much higher. In addition to the devastation brought by Hurricanes Katrina and Rita, Hurricane Ike slammed into Galveston Island on September 13, 2008, leaving an enormous swath of destruction in its wake. Ike completely leveled several nearby communities, and its 110-mph winds ripped apart hotels, office buildings, and countless homes in Galveston, Houston, and the surrounding area. Of the nearly 7,000 documented historic buildings in Galveston, upward of 1,500 were seriously damaged.

Things were quite different a century ago. Galveston experienced the most destructive storm in U.S. history (before Hurricanes Katrina, Rita, and Ike) in 1900, when a hurricane left at least 6,000 dead and leveled most of the city. A storm of equal intensity hit Galveston in 1915, but the city was prepared with its new seawall. The death toll was a comparatively low 275.

Floods have also taken their toll on the region. **Thunderstorms** are a major event—they typically come barreling in from the west, spewing lightning and firing occasional hailstones everywhere in their path. Appearing as massive, intimidating red blobs on the radar screen, they furiously dump heavy sheets of rain in Houston and the Gulf Coast region, leaving saturated ranches and overflowing rivers and streams in their wake.

ENVIRONMENTAL ISSUES

The oil mecca of Houston probably isn't the first place that comes to mind when talk turns to environmental responsibility, but the state has its fair share of activists and defenders. And despite the influence of the petroleum industry in the region, one of the chief environmental concerns is air pollution, particularly from vehicle emissions.

Since cities like Houston sprawl into outlying wide-open spaces, cars are the preferred method of transportation. The state's steady increase in population has become problematic for environmentalists. Air pollution concerns

in Texas's cosmopolitan areas have prompted ozone alerts, and Houston has been jockeying with Los Angeles for the coveted title of "smoggiest city."

Other troublesome issues for the region's environmental activists are water pollution and unsafe waste disposal. The **Texas Commission on Environmental Quality,** a state agency dedicated to protecting Texas's natural resources, oversees a multitude of monitoring efforts and public awareness campaigns designed to maintain control over potentially dangerous environmental hazards. The agency's air monitoring endeavors, water conservation districts, and efforts to keep tabs on industrial waste are commendable but don't always reach citizens at the local level.

That's where grassroots organizations like the **Texas Campaign for the Environment** come into play. The group's mission is to inform and mobilize area residents to maintain their quality of life and health. Their primary focus is improving trash and recycling policies to limit air, water, and soil pollution. It's reassuring to know that even in more conventional cities and industries, efforts are being made with future Texans' well-being in mind.

Flora and Fauna

The plant and animal kingdoms in the Coastal Plains are a source of fascination. Thousands of plant varieties and hundreds of animal species call the region home, and their compelling assortment is as diverse as the landscape.

Like most places, the vegetation and wildlife in Houston and the Gulf Coast are tied to the geography and climate. Most of the region's mammals (aside from livestock) live in warmer, forested areas, and many exceptional birds and insects pass through on migratory routes. Hundreds of miles of coastline yields hundreds of varieties of marine animals and associated plants.

TREES AND SHRUBS

Like most vegetation, the abundance and assortment of trees and shrubs in this part of Texas is tied to the quality and quantity of soil and water. Compared to the arid conditions on the opposite side of the state, East Texas seems downright lush. Here, tree species include **mesquite, live oak,** and **pecan,** as well as colorfully named shrubs such as **blackbrush, whitebrush,** and **greenbrier.** Meanwhile, the forests consist mainly of **pine trees,** with a healthy mix of oak, elm, and hickory. Interspersed among the pines are **hardwood timbers,** usually in valleys of rivers and creeks. This area is the source of practically all of Texas's commercial timber production.

GRASSES

The region's grasses, though plentiful, aren't exactly intriguing. Although a fair number of native grasses have been lost to overgrazing, the dozens of remaining varieties in the area endure in spite of Texas's variable weather and topography. Tolerant species such as **sideoats grama** (the official state grass), **Texas grama, buffalo grass,** and **Indian grass** still provide meals for livestock while their hardiness also helps contain soil erosion.

The eastern half of the Coastal Plains are covered with thick grass, but the western half typically has short grass, which appeals to the thousands of grazing cattle in the area, many in the famous King Ranch (southwest of Corpus Christi). The ranch is also home to a good amount of prickly pear cactus, with its spiny paddles and occasional source of nourishment for (somewhat desperate) cattle and goats.

WILDFLOWERS

Wildflowers in the eastern portions of Texas are akin to fall foliage in New England. For most of March and April, nature puts on a brilliant display of iridescent blues, dazzling reds, and blinding yellows across fields and along highways in the region. One of the prime viewing areas is just west of Houston (in the Brenham area), where landscapes are painted with **bluebonnets, Indian paintbrush, Mexican poppies,** and **black-eyed Susan.**

These wildflowers have been around for more than 130 million years, and the different species are greatly affected by the differences in the state's soils (for instance, azaleas thrive in acidic East Texas soil but struggle in the chalky earth further west). This biodiversity results in a plethora of springtime wildflowers—nearly 400 varieties in all—and a majority are native species. The scenery is especially prime in East Texas, home to **blooming azaleas, yellow jasmine, dogwoods,** and **wisteria.**

MAMMALS

Mention "mammals" in the Houston and Gulf Coast region, and you may get a few empty stares. But actually quite a few mammals live in this vast expanse of Texas, from the standard variety to the unexpected.

The most interesting mammal by far is the **bottlenose dolphin.** These curious creatures are common along the Gulf Coast, and many small businesses in the area offer dolphin tours, allowing you to venture out onto the water with an experienced guide who knows where the dolphins tend to spend their time. You can see them for free if you happen to be taking the ferry from Port Aransas to the mainland since the dolphins follow the boat to munch on the fish that are dispersed in its wake.

Slightly less exciting mammals in the region include **river otters,** which aren't quite as plentiful but can be a source of entertainment if you're canoeing or hiking along one of the rivers outside of Houston. Of the four-legged variety mammals, the occasional **coyote** may enter the woods outside suburban homes and even a few **javelina** in the southern sections of the coastline, mostly in search of prickly pear cactus on ranchlands.

BIRDS

Eastern Texas is a destination and crossing point for myriad bird species during migratory seasons. It's also home to hundreds of native varieties. More kinds of birds (approximately 600) are in Texas than any other state—primarily because of its south-central location. Feathered pals from the eastern and western part of the country occupy this region's air space, and international travelers cross the Mexican border, drawing avid bird-watchers to the state from across the United States.

Texas birds can be grouped into five major categories: permanent residents (**mockingbirds, roadrunners, screech owls**), winter residents (**common loons** and **terns, red-bellied woodpeckers**), summer residents (**purple martins, yellow-breasted chats, orchard orioles**), migrants (**snow geese, scarlet tanagers, various sandpipers**), and accidentals (**greater flamingos, red-footed boobies, yellow-billed loons**).

Spring is the prime time for bird-watching. Serious and amateur birders from across the country visit the Gulf Coast and Rio Grande Valley to catch a glimpse of migrating and native bird species. **Pelicans, spoonbills, egrets,** and **herons** are fairly easy to spot. Those looking for a unique birding experience can join a boat tour to spy whooping cranes. Boasting a seven-foot wingspan, the massive white birds were nearly extinct before efforts were made to revive the species. Now more than 100 spend their winters in the Aransas National Wildlife Refuge on the Gulf Coast.

MARINE LIFE

An amazing variety of marine animals live in the Gulf of Mexico, home to thousands of fish and shellfish that depend on the coast's diverse habitats for food and shelter. These environs are typically categorized by five distinct water areas—salt marshes, coastal bays, jetties, nearshore waters, and the Gulf of Mexico.

Fish and shrimp enter salt marshes looking for food or for a place to lay their eggs. They're joined by several species of **crabs (fiddler, hermit,** and **stone), snails, mussels,** and

worms. Coastal bays and beaches are home to two types of **jellyfish,** the **Portuguese man-of-war** (stay away from these purplish baggy creatures with the poisonous blue tentacles) and the relatively harmless **cabbage head jellyfish,** which looks like its namesake and are occasionally used by dolphins as toy balls.

The beach area also supports **oysters, spotted sea trout,** and several species of **catfish.** Jetties, which are used to prevent ship channels from piling up with sand and silt, consist of large stones that provide shelter and food for a wide range of sea life, including **sea anemones, urchins, crabs, grouper,** and **sea trout.** Artificial reefs (stone rubble, old ships, oil rigs) make nearshore waters habitable for mussels, shrimp, crabs, and a host of other animals, including the fish that feed on them (**tarpon, kingfish,** and others).

The Gulf of Mexico is home to some of Texas's heaviest hitters. **Great barracuda** and **hammerhead, lemon,** and **bull sharks** devour smaller varieties like bluefish, striped bass, and tuna. When the currents and temperatures are

© LANCE CLEM/123RF

white pelicans

just right, tropical species such as **parrot fish, angelfish,** and **spiny lobsters** also visit the Gulf waters.

REPTILES

Snakes slither across much of eastern and southern Texas's surface, and the range of reptiles is rather impressive. Texas is home to 16 varieties of poisonous snakes (including 11 types of **rattlesnakes**), which can be extremely hazardous to hikers and campers. Other dangerous snakes include **cottonmouth, copperhead,** and **Texas coral snakes.**

Snake bites from these varieties require a few basic first-aid techniques if medical care is not immediately available. The American Red Cross suggests washing the bite with soap and water and keeping the bitten area immobilized and lower than the heart. Equally as important is avoiding common remedy misconceptions: Do not apply hot or cold packs, do not attempt to suck the poison out, and do not drink any alcohol or use any medication.

Texas is also home to hundreds of nonvenomous snake species, some of which mimic their poisonous counterparts. The **Texas bull snake** realistically imitates a rattlesnake, all the way down to the rattling sound, and a **milk snake** and **coral snake** look disturbingly alike, with the same colors but in different orders. A time-honored Texas adage helps differentiate the two: Red and yellow, kill a fellow (the coral snake has red next to yellow stripes); red and black, friend of Jack (the milk snake has red next to black stripes).

Not to be overlooked are Texas's other distinctive reptiles. Noteworthy species in the Gulf Coast region include alligators (fairly common in the bayous and swamps of southeastern Texas) and **sea turtles,** among the oldest creatures on earth now facing an uncertain future due to environmental threats.

INSECTS

Nearly 100,000 different kinds of pesky insects buzz around Americans' heads and ankles, and a third of those bugs have been found in Texas. The Lone Star State proudly claims to have more different kinds of insects than any other state.

Texas also has more butterfly species than any other state. Its 400 varieties number more than half the butterfly species in the United States and Canada. The recognizable **monarch butterflies** make the annual migratory flight along the Gulf Coast region en route to their wintering grounds in Mexico. Their southward flight in late summer and fall can be quite a spectacle, as monarchs fill the air and gather on trees by the thousands.

East Texas's insects are just as numerous but not nearly as charming. Most of these winged and antennaed creatures are ecologically beneficial, but the two insects that creep immediately to most people's minds are the bothersome **mosquito** and the squirm-inducing **cockroach.**

AMPHIBIANS

Like most living things in this region, amphibians are well represented on account of the tremendous diversity in climate and temperature. Frogs, toads, and salamanders are abundant in the relatively wet habitats of the eastern third of the state. Camping near lakes and streams in this area offers visitors an audio sampler of the various croaks and calls of the region's native frog and toad species.

One species worthy of special note (mainly for its subject-appropriate name) is the **Gulf Coast Toad.** Ranging from two to four inches in size, this local amphibian can be found in open grasslands, wooded areas, residential backyards, and of course, along the shoreline of the Gulf Coast.

History

No place has a sense of place like Texas, and that sentiment is indelibly tied to the state's fascinating past. Texans in Houston and the Gulf Coast region are proud of their history, and for good reason. The state was once its own country, and many modern-day residents would likely welcome a return to the idea of isolationism. Above all, there's something reverential about the pride Texans take in their heritage, whether for the (East Texas) Native American contribution of the word *tejas* (meaning friends), the state's nearly 400-year-old Spanish mission buildings, the aforementioned Republic of Texas, the role Texas played in the Civil War, or its ranching and oil heritage.

Being proud of what a state represents is somewhat distinctive to Texas. Not to take away from any other state's history, but a term like "Rhode Island pride" or the concept of a proud Idaho heritage just don't resonate the way "Texas Pride" does. It is a badge of honor, and the state's rough-and-tumble past makes it a deserved title.

Everyone knows about The Alamo, but those who set out to discover Texas's dynamic heritage will encounter fascinating stories, like the 4,000-year-old Native American pictographs in a rock shelter, the discovery of the 1686 Gulf Coast shipwreck of French explorer La Salle, the influence of Mexican *vaqueros* on Texas's cowboys, and life in an oil boomtown in the 1930s. And that's just scraping the surface.

PREHISTORY

Depending on the source, Texas's prehistoric past can be traced as far back as 13,000 years. That's 11,000 BC. That's a lot of years. Most archaeologists and historians divide the state's prehistoric era into three periods: Paleo-Indian, Archaic, and Late Prehistoric.

The Paleo-Indian period is significant for its indicators of the earliest known inhabitants of the state (circa 9200 BC). Archaeologists have discovered numerous distinctive Clovis fluted points (a type of arrowhead) from this era, which were sometimes used for hunting mammoths.

The longest span of Texas's prehistory falls under the Archaic period (circa 6000 BC-AD 700). It's noted for the changes in projectile points and tools and the introduction of grinding implements for food preparation. A significant weapon used during the Archaic period was a spear-throwing device known as an atlatl.

The bow and arrow was introduced during Texas's Late Prehistoric period (AD 700 to recorded times). Pottery was present during this period among the hunters and gatherers in Central, South, and coastal Texas. Bison hunting was also very important to people living in most regions of the state's present-day boundaries.

NATIVE AMERICANS

Historians have identified hundreds of Native American groups in Texas. The validity of these names is problematic, though, because explorers used different languages (mainly Spanish, French, and English) to record what they heard to be the names of the newly "discovered" tribes they encountered.

Regardless, most historians agree that European diseases decimated Texas's native people. Anthropologist John C. Ewers identified at least 30 major epidemics (mostly smallpox and cholera) that wiped out as much as 95 percent of the state's Native Americans between 1528 and 1890. Until then, the four major tribes playing roles in Texas history were the Apache, Caddo, Comanche, and Kiowa.

The **Apache** arrived in the area that would become Texas circa AD 1200. They were a nomadic tribe subsisting almost completely on buffalo, dressing in buffalo skins, and living in tents made of tanned and greased hides. The Apache were a powerful tribe that raided most groups they encountered. Eventually, their aggressive behavior turned their neighbors into enemies, and the Apache ultimately fled before the Comanche entered the region.

The **Caddo** were a collection of about 30 distinct groups who shared a similar language, political structure, and religious beliefs. One such Caddo group was the Tejas Indians, from whom Texas got its name. Based in the current-day East Texas Piney Woods, the Caddo were mainly agricultural and lived in permanent villages (as opposed to being nomadic). They weren't especially warlike, except for minor territorial conflicts they had with smaller nearby tribes over hunting grounds.

The **Comanche** were known to be exceptional at horseback riding and played a prominent role in Texas frontier history in the 1700s and 1800s. Because of their trading skills, the Comanche controlled much of the region's commerce by bartering horses, buffalo products, and even captives for weapons and food. They lived in portable tepees constructed of tanned buffalo hide stretched over as many as 18 large poles.

The **Kiowa** acquired horses, slaves, and guns from the Spanish and eventually evolved into a nomadic, warring lifestyle until they became one of the most feared tribes in the region that became Texas. By the late 1700s, the Kiowa made a lasting peace with the Comanche and continued to live in the area until peacefully joining the Comanche with the Southern Cheyenne and Arapaho.

EUROPEAN EXPLORATION AND SETTLEMENT

The arrival (via shipwreck) of Spanish explorer **Álvar Núñez Cabeza de Vaca** in 1528 was one of Texas's first contacts with the Old World. His subsequent trek across the land that would become the Lone Star State offered Europeans some of the first clues about this newfound foreign region.

By 1685, the French were in on the action, dispatching explorer **Robert Cavelier, Sieur de La Salle,** to find the mouth of the Mississippi River. He missed it by a long shot, ultimately wrecking his ship *La Belle* in a bay between present-day Houston and Corpus Christi. More than 200 years later, the Texas Historical Commission discovered the contents

and remains of *La Belle,* which offered a rare glimpse at a 17th-century New World colony—glass trade beads, dinnerware, gunflints, and even a human skeleton.

By the early 1700s, the Spanish solidified their presence in the region with four new mission buildings (The Alamo being one of them) used primarily to "civilize" the area's Native American tribes by converting them to Christianity. It didn't work as well as they'd hoped. By the early 19th century, European diseases had decimated most of the state's Native Americans, and many tribes had mixed in with other cultural groups, rendering the missions' objective obsolete.

Around this same time, the first wave of Germans arrived in Texas. Word spread quickly about Texas's bountiful land and ideal climate (perhaps they visited in springtime), prompting thousands of Germans to take root along rivers and streams in the state's fertile prairies and scenic hills.

THE REPUBLIC OF TEXAS AND STATEHOOD

An 1835 skirmish between colonists and Mexicans over ownership of a cannon is generally considered the opening battle of the Texas Revolution; subsequently, a provisional government was established in 1836 when delegates adopted the **Texas Declaration of Independence** on March 2 (which remains a state holiday). Texas's most famous battle occurred a week later with the 13-day siege of **The Alamo.** Mexican troops led by **General Antonio López de Santa Anna** eventually killed the remaining Texas defenders.

Later that month, about 350 Texan prisoners were executed by order of Santa Anna at Goliad. With these defeats in mind, the Texans, led by **Sam Houston,** defeated Santa Anna's Mexican army on April 21 with rallying cries of "Remember the Alamo!" and "Remember Goliad!" Houston reported 630 Mexican troops killed, with only 9 Texan lives lost. The revolution's end became official in May 1836 when both sides signed the Treaty of Velasco.

A year later, the United States, France, and England officially recognized the new Republic of Texas, and plots of land were soon sold in the republic's new capital, named for **Stephen F. Austin,** the state's preeminent colonist. In 1845, after the U.S. Congress passed an annexing resolution, which was accepted by the republic's Texas Constitutional Convention and overwhelmingly supported by Texas voters, Texas became a U.S. state. From 1846 to 1848, Texas and Mexico engaged in a boundary battle known as the **Mexican-American War,** which ultimately established the current international boundary.

THE CIVIL WAR AND RECONSTRUCTION

Texas struggled with complexities during the Civil War. Some people supported the Union, including Governor Sam Houston, who refused to take an oath of allegiance to the Confederacy. It eventually cost him his office. For the most part, Texans identified with the rest of the southern United States, and in early 1861 it became official when Texas seceded from the Union and became the seventh state accepted by the provisional Confederate States of America government.

After four years of border skirmishes, Gulf Coast naval battles, and prisoner of war camps, Texas troops marked the true end of the Civil War with a battle near Brownsville, more than a month after the war officially ended (because of the time involved for news to reach Texas back then). In June, it was announced that slavery had been abolished, an event still commemorated today during **Juneteenth festivals** in African American communities statewide.

Much of Texas's history during the late 1800s is centered around the arrival of railroads, which put towns on and off the map depending on the train routes. Cattle drives were an important part of Texas's commerce and identity before railroads took over the responsibility of moving cattle northward. Texas's development was made possible by the railroad. Their construction continued to sustain the local economy for decades because so many areas of the state still needed railroad service, including the lower Rio Grande Valley, the South Plains, the Panhandle, and West Texas.

THE 20TH CENTURY AND BEYOND

Texas's 20th century kicked off with a boom— a 100-foot oil gusher blew in at Spindletop near Beaumont in 1901, boosting Texas into the petroleum age. Oil wells would be discovered for several decades, turning small communities into boomtowns with tens of thousands of wildcatters and roughnecks arriving overnight to work on the rigs.

The Wild West arrived in West Texas when the **Mexican Revolution** (1911-20) spilled across the border; as a result, supply raids and refugee harboring became common occurrences. The notorious Mexican general **Pancho Villa** was involved with some of these skirmishes.

By the 1950s and '60s, Texas was gaining a reputation for its intellectual resources, resulting in the Dallas-based development of the integrated circuit (used in semiconductors and electronics) and the opening of the Manned Spacecraft Center at **NASA** (National Aeronautics and Space Administration) in Houston.

In one of the darker moments of Texas and U.S. history, **President John F. Kennedy** was assassinated in Dallas. It marked the end of the country's optimism during Kennedy's presidency and ushered in a new president—Lyndon B. Johnson, former vice president and a Texan. Johnson would go on to play a major role in advancing the country's civil rights movement. The final two decades of the 20th century were notable for two additional Texans being elected to the U.S. presidency: George H. W. Bush and his son George W. Bush.

Economy and Government

Cotton, cattle, and crude (oil)—Texas's venerable "Three Cs" are staples of the Houston-area economy, and they dominated the state's agricultural and economic development until the mid-20th century. To this day, these land-based resources continue to support much of the state's wealth. Other factors contributing to the regional economy are various industries not exclusive to the area, such as retailing, wholesaling, banking, insurance, and construction.

Many national corporate headquarters have relocated to Texas, and petroleum companies continue to search for new sources of energy to provide fuel. In addition, Houston is home to many federal air installations and NASA's prestigious Lyndon B. Johnson Space Center. Tourism has also become a major business, and Houston has become a leader in the areas of medicine and surgery.

AGRICULTURE

Cattle and cotton remain staples of the region's agricultural economy. The wide open spaces allowed both commodities to grow freely when settlers arrived in the mid-1800s, and the remaining abundance of available land continues to make it the most important cattle-raising state in the country.

Cotton became a prominent crop in eastern and southern Texas because of the immigration of settlers from the Deep South, who continued their plantation system of agriculture when they arrived in the region. Cotton production grew steadily after 1900, and the crop became a major economic factor when suitable varieties were developed for the Texas climate.

MANUFACTURING AND INDUSTRY

The region's manufacturing roots lie with its agricultural processing—cotton gins, cotton-seed mills, meatpacking plants, flour mills, oil field equipment, and canning plants. These days, the largest employment sector is categorized as the "trade, transportation, and utilities industry," which includes jobs in retail, wholesale, and finance.

Jobs in the petroleum, construction, and service industries are also typically steady across the region, reflected in the statewide ranking of top exported products: chemicals, petrochemicals, and transportation equipment. The state's remarkable number of exports is attributed to its proximity to Mexico, which receives nearly half of its products.

PETROLEUM

Oil changed everything for Texas. It transformed the state from a backwoods frontier to an industrial giant. In January 1901, a gusher blew in at Spindletop near Beaumont, and the Texas oil boom erupted into the nation's conscience. Thirty years later, an even more significant event occurred—the discovery of the enormous East Texas Oil Field north of Houston.

Oil became the basis for the region's mammoth petrochemical industry and provided the funding to develop the state's educational and highway systems. On the flip side, a massive drop in oil prices in the early 1980s resulted in a decline in Houston's (and, in turn, the entire state's) economy. Regardless, oil and natural gas remain the state's most valuable minerals, contributing nearly 20 percent of the country's oil production and 30 percent of its gas production in recent years.

GOVERNMENT

Texas was annexed to the United States as the 28th state on December 29, 1845. From Reconstruction (the late 1800s) through the early 1960s, the Democratic Party dominated Texas politics. Keep in mind, the Democrats of those days differed considerably from the current political party. For almost a century, Texas Democrats consisted mainly of Anglo conservatives, who prevailed in almost all statewide elections.

A Texas-worthy phrase was used during this era to describe the especially dedicated party members: "Yellow Dog Democrats" were the state's die-hard partisan loyalists who would vote for a yellow dog if it ran on the Democratic ticket. The phrase is now used to describe any Democratic loyalist, although the recent stronghold of Republicans in Texas is rendering the term nearly obsolete.

Texas's bicameral legislature is comprised of 31 Senate members who serve for four years and the House of Representatives, with 150 members elected for two-year terms. The legislature meets for its regular session in the spring of odd-numbered years, but the governor may convene a special session for the legislators to address particular issues. The governor of Texas is elected to a four-year term in November of even-numbered, non-presidential election years.

People

The people of Houston and the Gulf Coast equally reflect and defy all stereotypes associated with their dynamic nature. For every good ol' boy set in his ways, there's a progressive genius building a web-based empire. For every brash oil executive making millions, there's a humble educator affecting lives. Intense football coaches coexist peacefully with environmental activists.

Like anywhere else, people in this region have their differences, but one thing transcends obstacles that is unique to this state—the common bond of being Texan. Not that it solves all problems, but most Texans look kindly upon their brethren and genuinely display the spirit of Southern hospitality. It's infectious too. "Y'all come back" and "Well, bless your heart" become true expressions of kindness rather than silly stereotypes.

Transplants from the northern and eastern United States may initially be taken aback by random strangers in the grocery store commenting on their purchases, but they'll later find themselves doing the same thing. Offers of assistance are genuine rather than obligatory, and people make direct eye contact when they mutter a polite "Howdy."

These residents could be categorized in many ways—by age, ethnicity, religion, income level, and so on—but labels don't capture the soul of the region's residents, who aptly represent the character of the word *friend* in the origins of the word *Texas*.

POPULATION

The most recent census figures (2010) revealed that Houston has grown at an incredibly impressive rate. With a metro-area population of 6.3 million, the city has experienced an astounding 65 percent population growth in merely two decades. Projections call for another half-million residents to join the fray by 2016, drawn in large part by the city's low unemployment rate, relatively low cost of living, and job growth (particularly in the oil industry).

Houston's intensive growth rate is mirrored in Texas's rate, which has exceeded the nation's in every decade since Texas became a state (1845). The state's population has more than doubled in the past 25 years, from roughly 11.2 million to more than 25 million. Estimates based on recent growth rates suggest the state is growing by nearly 500,000 people annually.

ETHNICITY

Unlike more rural parts of the Lone Star State, Houston is remarkably diverse. The "melting pot" cliché certainly applies here, with city streets, restaurants, and public gatherings reflecting a cultural blend befitting of New York City or London. Based on the most recent census figures documenting Houston's ethnicity (2000), the city's approximate racial population breakdown is 49 percent White (including Hispanic or Latino, with 37 percent identifying as Hispanic), 25 percent African American, and 5 percent Asian.

These numbers are generally reflected in the state's ethnic diversity. Currently about 49 percent of the population is of northern European ancestry, roughly 36 percent are Hispanic, and approximately 11 percent are African American. The remaining 4 percent are listed under "other racial/ethnic groups," though most are of Asian descent.

The healthy pace of Texas's increased population is largely due to international immigration, which represented nearly 77 percent of the state's population growth in recent years. The Texas State Data Center projects that by 2020, Hispanics will represent the majority of the state's population. Of note is the rapid growth of foreign-born residents in Texas's major metro areas (112 percent) compared to border metro cities (51 percent).

Perhaps most significant are major population increases in the southern area of the Gulf Coast, particularly the Lower Rio Grande Valley, with growth rates continually nearing 40 percent and birth rates significantly higher than the rest of the state. As a result, Texas has the country's second-highest Hispanic population, behind California.

According to reports from the 2010 census, Hispanics accounted for two-thirds of Texas's growth over the past decade and now represent about 37 percent of the state's total population (an increase from 32 percent in 2000). Also of interest is the considerably younger age of the state's Hispanic population (25.5 years for the median age versus 38 for Anglos).

RELIGION

When it comes to religion, the city of Houston and the Gulf Coast region are notably different. In the metro area, religion isn't a major factor in many people's lives, with studies showing that approximately 48 percent of residents claim not to be affiliated with a religious group. However, unlike the predominant Christian identity of the rural areas of eastern and southern Texas,

Houston has far more diversity in its religious makeup, including Muslim, Hindu, Buddhist, Jewish, and people of other faiths as well.

Outside of Houston, the two primary religious groups are Baptist (approximately 22 percent) and Catholic (roughly 21 percent). Although it mirrors national trends showing slightly declining congregation numbers, residents in the rural areas remain committed churchgoers.

LANGUAGE

English speakers in Houston and the Gulf Coast region account for the majority of the population, with Spanish running a distant second, yet still notable (26 percent). People speak Vietnamese in pockets of Houston, but for the most part, it's Spanish and English (and a few interesting varieties of the two).

A fair number of Hispanics along the Gulf Coast speak an unofficial language known as **Tex-Mex,** which combines Spanish and English words without any rigid guidelines determining when to use each. It's a distinctive regional practice, resulting from an impulsive tendency to toss in an English or Spanish word when the translation isn't immediately on the tip of the tongue, and it's most evident on Tejano radio stations in Corpus Christi and the Lower Rio Grande Valley, where rapid-fire DJs pepper their announcements in Spanish with random yet instantly recognizable English words.

Learning to speak Texan is an entirely different endeavor. Although it sounds like a Southern accent on the surface, there are distinct dialects in different parts of the state. In East Texas, vowels are more drawn out, and the slower cadence includes inflections of the Deep South. Meanwhile, people on the far western side of the state speak with more of a tight twang. Pronunciation of the word *Texas* is a prime example—in East Texas, it often sounds like "TAY-UX-us," and in West Texas it's pronounced "TIX-is."

HOW TO SPEAK TEXAN

Texas boasts several accents within its own border, from the slowly stretched-out East Texas drawl, to border-hopping Spanglish known as Tex-Mex, to the tight twang of the Panhandle and West Texas.

Even though Texans like to brag about their accomplishments, they can't take credit for the Southern accent that prevails below the Mason-Dixon Line. However, residents of Houston and the Gulf Coast region can claim some of the spice that makes the Southern dialect unique. For the most part, the following examples are found in rural areas of the state, though you'll occasionally hear a "yessir" or "fixin' to" in a downtown urban environment.

Let's start with the obvious: "Howdy, y'all." It's the quintessential Texas and Southern phrase, usually invoked with a mocking twang by Yankees (a name used down here to jokingly refer to anyone north and east of Oklahoma). The truth is Texans actually say these words often, but usually not together. "Howdy" is typically muttered as a polite greeting as opposed to a garish welcome, and its use as a friendly salutation is one of many cultural traditions taught at Texas A&M University. As for "y'all," it just makes sense—why refer to a group of people (women and children, in particular) as "you guys"? The common Texas phrase "all y'all" takes things to a whole new level, however.

Texans also use "sir" and "ma'am" regularly, just not in a formal or subservient way. It's common to hear men respond to each other with a simple "yessir" or "nosir," and it's just plain polite to express appreciation to someone—a police officer, fellow pedestrian, or store clerk—with a simple "thank you, ma'am." Up North, these terms take on military or old maid connotations, but in Texas, people are just being cordial.

Like other Southerners, Texans of all ages refer to their parents as "mother" and "daddy." It's somewhat strange to hear a grown man talk about his "daddy's" influence, but it's charming, nevertheless.

Another Texas phrase that gets the Yankees giggling is "fixin' to." It's a handy term that's quintessentially Southern, indicating someone is getting ready to do something without fully committing to carrying out the task ("I'm fixin' to pay those bills soon"). Incidentally, the "fixin'" also refers to food in Texas, garnishes and side dishes in particular. If you order a burger or barbecue plate with all the fixin's, you'll get onions, pickles, peppers, and any number of sides or sauces piled on the plate.

Speaking of food, occasional confusion arises when Texans refer to "dinner" and "supper." These are interchangeable in other parts of the country, but around here, "dinner" can mean lunch, but "supper" almost always refers to the evening meal.

Other examples of Lone Star speak are evident in the pronunciation of words. You can tell a Texan by the way they emphasize the first syllable in words like *umbrella* (UM-brella), *insurance* (IN-surance), and *display* (DIS-play.). Others are more subtle, like the tendency to flatten out the vowel sounds in words like *mail* (mell), *wheel* (well), and the double whammy *windshield* (wenshell).

Finally, you'll occasionally hear Texans using traditional rural sayings like "over yonder" (over there), "pitch a hissy fit" (a dramatic reaction), and even "gaddum" and its derivative "dadgum." Fortunately, Texans are such a friendly bunch, they won't pitch a hissy fit if you sound like a dadgum Yankee.

Arts and Culture

One of the specialty license plates available to Texans features a bold image of the state flag with the phrase "State of the Arts" at the bottom. This motto might not be the first attribute people associate with Texas (California and New York immediately jump to mind), but it's certainly appropriate for Houston and the Gulf Coast.

World-renowned writers, artists, musicians, and actors call the region home, and their influences and styles are as far reaching as the coastline. Premier exhibits and tours always include Houston on their schedule, and the dynamic magnetism of the region serves as an inspiration for a diverse mixture of creative endeavors.

MUSIC

Texas has perhaps the most compelling music legacy in the country, and Houston and the Gulf Coast region have played a large role. In fact, Houston is an especially significant ambassador of Texas music since its enormous size and influence broadcast many of these artists to a wider audience across the country and the world.

The region's documented musical history begins with Texas's initial wave of settlers in the late 1800s. A fascinating mix of cultures, including German, African American, Czechoslovakian, Mexican, and Anglo, resulted in an equally intriguing blend of musical styles. The best known types of music in the U.S. South—blues and country—evolved into new and intriguing genres when accompanied by a Texas twist. Appalachian "fiddle music" migrated westward with pioneers and merged with distinctly Texan influences such as yodeling, accordions, and 12-string guitar, resulting in unique styles like Western swing, conjunto, and rockabilly.

One of Texas's most influential musicians was **Blind Lemon Jefferson,** who introduced his signature country blues in the 1920s with his raw, potent track "Black Snake Moan." Borrowing the flamenco-influenced guitar work he heard from Mexican migrant workers, Jefferson's fast fingers and ear for melody inspired fellow Texas blues legends and regional natives **Huddy "Lead Belly" Ledbetter and Lightnin' Hopkins.** Their work paved the way for generations of Texas blues heroes, including **Albert Collins, Freddy King, Clarence "Gatemouth" Brown,** and **Buddy Guy.**

A wholly distinct sound from this region of Texas is **conjunto music** (aka **Tejano, Tex-Mex, norteño**), which combines accordion and 12-string guitar to produce lively dance melodies with South Texas soul. The style originated with Texas and Mexican working-class musicians who adopted the accordion and the polka from 19th-century German settlers. Conjunto music was popular along the Rio Grande and throughout Latin America for decades before artists began reaching larger audiences in the late 1960s. The genre's best known artist is **Leonardo "Flaco" Jiménez,** who has performed with renowned acts, such as the Rolling Stones, Bob Dylan, Willie Nelson, Buck Owens, and Carlos Santana.

Although country music has its true origins in Anglo-based folk balladry, Texans took the style and made it their own. Several of country music's offshoots are Texas products, including **Western swing, honky-tonk,** and **outlaw country.** Overall, the Texas contributors to country music, including many regional natives, reads like a track listing from the style's greatest hits: Gene Autry, Buck Owens, George Jones, Kenny Rogers, Larry Gatlin, Barbara Mandrell, Townes Van Zandt, Kris Kristofferson, George Strait, Mark Chesnutt, Lyle Lovett, and Pat Green (and that's just volume one).

During the past 20 years, Texans continued to make their marks on a myriad of musical styles. Corpus Christi's **Selena Quintanilla-Perez** (1971-1995), known simply as Selena, led a surge in the Latino music scene's popularity in the early 1990s with her dancy pop tunes that drew thousands of converts to her spirited

TEXAS IN SONG

Texas is immortalized in song perhaps more than any other state. Several sources list nearly 100 tunes with *Texas* (or *Lone Star*, or Texas cities) in the title, a far cry from the number of songs heralding Idaho's contribution to the cultural landscape.

With all the options to choose from, it's unfortunate that the official state song, **"Texas, Our Texas,"** is unrecognizable to most people, including many Texans. Adopted by the legislature after being selected in a statewide competition, the song features inspirational (and poorly written) lyrics with simple rhymes like "all hail the mighty state" with "so wonderful, so great."

Our country's national anthem is rather difficult to sing on account of its extremely wide tonal range and occasionally confusing lyrics, so Texas's official state song should be something recognizable and easy on the vocal chords. Some Texans have even proposed adopting an updated official tune to rouse the troops at athletic competitions and school or government events.

There are plenty to choose from, including iconic classics such as **"Deep in the Heart of Texas,"** made famous by Gene Autry (and Pee Wee Herman); **"The Yellow Rose of Texas,"** as performed by Bob Wills; Ernest Tubb's version of **"Waltz Across Texas";** or even the fiddle-filled old-school dance craze **"Cotton Eyed Joe."** Collegiately patriotic Texans will insist that their school fight songs are the most iconic Texas tunes, particularly **"The Eyes of Texas"** (University of Texas) and the **"Aggie War Hymn"** (Texas A&M University).

The 1970s were a golden time for Texas-themed songs, particularly in the country music scene. Though the following options haven't attained "official song" consideration status, they're known well enough in pop culture as ambassadors of Texas mystique. Highlights include Willie Nelson's adaptation of **"San Antonio Rose,"** Marty Robbins's **"(out in the West Texas town of) El Paso," "Streets of Laredo"** by Buck Owens, **"Luckenbach, Texas (Back to the Basics of Love)"** by Waylon Jennings, Glen Campbell's **"Galveston,"** ZZ Top's **"La Grange,"** and a couple of George Strait classics, **"Amarillo by Morning"** and **"All My Exes Live in Texas."** Unfortunately, there's also Alabama's hit **"If You're Gonna Play in Texas (You Gotta Have a Fiddle in the Band)."**

The Texas-themed songs haven't been quite as prolific lately, but the state's music scene remains vital. Perhaps in the near future we'll see a remixed version of a Texas classic or a new Lone Star legend penned by one of Austin's indie rock sensations. Stay tuned.

---

shows. Other significant Texas contributions to contemporary music in the early 21st century were Houston acts **Destiny's Child** (rhythm and blues) and **Paul Wall** (rap).

FILM

With mild winters and more than thousands of square miles of diverse landscape to work with, Texas's Gulf Coast region is an extremely versatile place to shoot movies, TV shows, music videos, commercials, and other film projects.

The **Texas Film Commission,** a division of the governor's office, lends filmmakers a hand by providing free information on locations, crews, talent, state and local contacts, weather, laws, sales tax exemptions, housing, and other film-related issues. The assistance certainly pays off, with the state receiving more than $2 billion in film-related expenditures during the past decade. Filmmakers look kindly upon the region because of its experienced crew members, equipment vendors, and support services. On most features shot here, 75 percent of the crew is hired locally, and the production company is 100 percent exempt from state and local sales taxes on most of the services and items they rent or purchase.

Significant film projects shot in Houston

include *Logan's Run* (1976), *Urban Cowboy* (1979), *Terms of Endearment* (1983), *Blood Simple* (1984), *Reality Bites* (1994), *Rushmore* (1997), *Fast Food Nation* (2006), and Terence Malick's *Tree of Life* (2011).

THE ARTS

The visual arts scene in Houston and the Gulf Coast region is particularly captivating, due in large part to available funding from the area's land and oil barons. World-class artwork is regularly exhibited throughout the region in big cities and small towns, where art philanthropists give generously to construct ornate museums and draw exceptional exhibits.

For the most part, the region's fine arts opportunities are located in its metropolitan areas (Houston and Corpus Christi). Houston boasts nearly 20 major museums and galleries. The city's Museum of Fine Arts houses approximately 31,000 works of American, European, Latin American, Native American, and Asian art spanning 4,000 years. Its concentration is on Renaissance and impressionism, but its treasures lie hidden around every corner, like the primitive Native American pieces.

Another worthy Houston museum is the Contemporary Art Museum, which rotates exhibits every six weeks, offering visitors a fresh experience year-round. The Menil Collection also features rotating displays along with its permanent 10,000-piece collection, which includes a stunning mix of styles, from African and Byzantine to surrealist and contemporary.

ESSENTIALS

Getting There

Houston and the Gulf Coast are far removed from the transportation hubs on the East and West Coasts, but they're easily accessible by plane and relatively accessible by car, train, bus, and boat. The only problems travelers have traditionally encountered when entering the southern portion of the region (in Brownsville at the Mexican border) are no longer an issue because travel across the Rio Grande is discouraged on account of the recent unrest and violence associated with drug cartels.

AIR

Houston is so big, it has two airports. The rest of the cities along the Gulf Coast aren't that big, but several have small regional airports to save travelers the long drives across the seemingly endless coastal plains.

The major air hub in the region is **George Bush Intercontinental Airport** (2800 N. Terminal Rd., 281/230-3100, www.fly2houston.com), located just north of Houston. This is one of United Airlines' major hubs, and since it offers nonstop service to and from more than 170 cities around the world, it's typically hustling and bustling at all hours of the day and night. The city's old airfield, **William P. Hobby Airport** (7800 Airport Blvd., 713/640-3000, www.fly2houston.com) is now the center of activity for Southwest Airlines and hosts flights

© BRANDON SEIDEL/123RF

from several other major carriers. Located 10 miles southeast of downtown, Hobby is more accessible than Bush, but it's showing its age. That's often forgiven by travelers who prefer the facilitated accessibility and cheaper cab fares (nearly $20 less than the trek from Bush to downtown Houston).

SuperShuttle (281/230-7275, www.supershuttle.com) offers shuttle service to and from area hotels and Bush Intercontinental and Hobby Airports. Look for the company's ticket counters in the lower-level baggage claim areas of Bush and Hobby. Many downtown-area hotels offer free shuttle service to and from Bush Intercontinental Airport, but check first to make sure they're running.

Another option is a cab. Ground transportation employees outside each terminal of Bush Intercontinental Airport and near the lower-level baggage claim area (Curbzone 1) of Hobby Airport will half-heartedly hail travelers a taxi. All destinations within Houston's city limits to and from Bush Intercontinental are charged a flat zone rate or the meter rate, whichever is less. For more information on zone rates, check out the Ground Transportation section at www.fly2houston.com. To arrange for cab pick-up service from within the city, contact one of the following local companies: **Liberty Cab Company** (281/540-8294), **Square Deal Cab Co.** (713/444-4444), **Lonestar Cab** (713/794-0000), or **United Cab Co.** (713/699-0000).

Many travelers prefer to rent a car, and the powers that be at Bush Intercontinental have attempted to make things easier by establishing the **Consolidated Rental Car Facility** (281/230-3000, www.iahrac.com). All the major rental car companies are accessible from this shared location about five minutes away from the terminals. The rental companies share a shuttle system, designated by the white and maroon buses marked "Rental Car Shuttle" located outside the terminal.

To reach the mid-Gulf Coast area, book a flight to **Corpus Christi International Airport** (1000 International Blvd., 361/289-0171, www.cctexas.com/airport), offering service

from American Eagle, United, and Southwest Airlines. A variety of rental car companies are available at the airport.

The **Brownsville South Padre Island International Airport** (700 S. Minnesota Ave., 956/542-4373, www.flybrownsville.com) is the closest airport to South Padre. At 27 miles away, it's not too far, especially if you need to get to the beach in a hurry and don't feel like making the five-hour trek from Houston. The airport offers several American Eagle and United Airlines flights daily to and from Houston. Rental car services are available at the airport.

CAR
Two major U.S. interstates, **I-10** and **I-45,** lead to Houston, making it easily accessible from the north, west, and east. The roads tend to be in good shape because they don't have to contend with icy conditions, but like most places, construction is a perpetual issue in Houston and Corpus Christi. Increased truck traffic from Mexico has taken its toll on some of the freeways, and rural roads between smaller cities can get a bit rough, but that doesn't deter locals from going 90 mph. The **Texas Department of Transportation** (www.txdot.gov) oversees all aspects of vehicular travel.

Since the majority of the coastline is undeveloped, no major freeways link major cities south of Houston. **State Highway 35** is the closest option, a primarily rural road stretching between Houston and Corpus Christi passing through dozens of small towns along the way. The lengthy Padre Island National Seashore is only accessible by a park road near Corpus Christi; otherwise, the trek to South Padre beaches is more than 20 miles inland via **U.S. Highway 77** through Kingsville, Harlingen, and Brownsville.

BUS AND TRAIN
Houston is large enough to make accessibility by bus and train a viable option (thanks to the frequency in arrivals and departures). Those interested in traveling by bus can contact **Houston Greyhound** (2121 Main St.,

713/759-6565 or 800/231-2222, www.grey-hound.com). Passenger trains arrive in town via **Amtrak's Sunset Limited** line, which runs cross-country between Orlando and Los Angeles. Look for arrivals and departures at the **Houston Amtrak station** (902 Washington Ave., 713/224-1577 or 800/872-7245, www.amtrak.com).

Getting Around

CAR

Houston and the Gulf Coast's major interstates are well maintained, and drivers are largely courteous but have a bit of a lead foot. At times, I-10 east and west of Houston can resemble a racetrack, with cars and semitrucks regularly buzzing along at a 90-mph clip. That being said, some drivers are notorious for hanging in the passing lane at 55 mph, forcing cars to line up behind them and pass on the right when there's a break. Incidentally, freeway ramps can be highly unpredictable—some are only a few hundred yards short while others seem to stretch for miles. Once you're off the interstate or heading into rural areas, be sure to keep an eye out for police because some small towns in the Gulf Coast region rely on speeding-ticket fines to help fund their municipal budgets.

Toll Roads

Unlike other states with well-established turnpike and tollway systems, much of Texas is relatively new to the fees-for-freeways concept. Stretches of Houston highways, including I-10 and I-45, have adjacent tollway options in especially busy areas of town. Currently, about 120 miles of roadway in the metro area require a toll payment.

The city's main toll road is a lengthy 70-mile outer loop known as the Sam Houston Tollway. Like most tollways, it offers a convenient option if you're in a hurry or you don't mind the pay-to-play approach, in this case anywhere between $1 and $5.

For the most part, the tollways are welcome (unless they're placed or proposed on a previously public road) because they ease congestion on busy nearby interstates. Still, they rub some people the wrong way and can be underused because of the perceived expense. The Harris County Tollroad Authority's (HCTA) system is fairly convenient and understandable, although it's primarily designed with locals in mind since it has virtually no stations for payment by cash or credit, instead relying on the **EZ TAG** electronic payment tag system.

If you're renting a vehicle, be sure to ask the rental company if they have a toll tag or if you can purchase a prepaid tag. Otherwise, you may be unpleasantly surprised to later find you've been charged a $50 "convenience" fee for the company to handle the arrangements. If you don't have a tag, be sure to look for the highway signs letting you know if there's an option for paying an actual person at a toll gate; otherwise, you may want to take a more convenient route on a true *free*way.

For more information about Houston's toll roads, contact the **HCTA** (713/587-7800, www.hctra.org) for toll road maps and information about the organization. To learn more about obtaining an EZ TAG, consult the website, call 281/875-3279, or drop by the **West Area EZ TAG Store** (2707 W. Sam Houston Pkwy N.). For roadside assistance on Houston's toll roads, call 713/222-7328.

BIKE

Things are getting better for cyclists in Houston, but it remains challenging to share the road with so many cars in a metropolis so focused on vehicles.

Before planning to spend most of your time attempting to navigate the city on two wheels, it's advisable to contact a local cycling advocacy organization to inquire about accessibility and issues in the areas you'll be visiting. Two of the most reputable groups are **Bike Houston** (713/364-6074, www.bikehouston.org) and **Pedal Houston** (www.pedalhouston.com).

The metro area contains more than 300 miles of interconnected "bikeways": bike lanes, bike routes, hike and bike trails (including rails to trails and other urban multiuse paths). The city also offers more than 80 miles of hike and bike and nature trails within its park system. For information about the location of these lanes and trails, as well as updated news about construction affecting them, visit http://bikeways.publicworks.houstontx.gov.

BUS

To traverse eastern and southern Texas by bus, consider contacting **Trailways** (319/753-2864, www.trailways.com). The company operates eight regional routes in Texas, offering passengers the option of making personalized trips using independently operated bus companies. This is an ideal option for travelers who wish to explore cities or smaller towns at their own pace without having to rely on a major bus tour operation with existing (and less-than-adventurous) itineraries.

Corpus Christi's metropolitan bus system, **Regional Transportation Authority** (1806 S. Alameda St., 361/883-2287, www.ccrta.org), provides citywide service. Check the website for updated fare and route information.

PUBLIC TRANSPORTATION

Houston has a decent public transportation system, but it can be confusing for out-of-towners who haven't yet developed a strong sense of direction. Regardless, a little homework can be helpful in strategizing plans via the Metro, aka the **Metropolitan Transit Authority of Harris County** (713/635-4000, www.ridemetro.org), which offers local and commuter bus service. Tickets are available in vending machines located at each station. Metro's red line services 16 stations near downtown's busiest commercial and recreational sites.

In Galveston, a unique public transportation service, the **Galveston Island Trolley** (409/797-3900, www.islandtransit.net) was damaged in Hurricane Ike, but plans are to have it back on the rails soon. Call ahead to determine if it is offering similar services to its pre-Ike days: transportation from the Seawall to The Strand district and Pier 21. The cars are charming replicas of those used in Galveston from the late 1800s to the 1930s.

In South Padre, feel free to ditch your car in favor of the city's free, reliable, and often necessary **Wave transportation system** (866/761-1025, visit www.townspi.com for schedule and stops). If you plan to have a beer or six during spring break, you'll be glad these small buses are there to cart your impaired body safely home. Although the Wave typically operates 7am-7pm to and from local businesses and services, it's also available during spring break to shuttle late-night revelers.

Sports and Recreation

PROFESSIONAL SPORTS

Houston-area residents spend a lot of time enjoying outdoor activities, despite the intolerably hot summers. For sports, football is the undisputed king, but baseball, basketball, and golf are also popular as they can be played year-round.

The region's mild climate also allows nonprofessional (recreational) sporting activities to continue throughout the year. Campers, hikers, and mountain bikers flock to state and local parks year-round—especially in winter for the warm tropical climate of the Gulf Coast and Rio Grande Valley.

Once home to the storied Houston Oilers football franchise (before they bolted for Tennessee and became the Titans), the city is now home to the NFL's **Houston Texans.** As an expansion team, the Texans were slow to gain their footing in the NFL, but over the past several years have built a formidable franchise that continues to draw substantial crowds to Reliant Stadium, regardless of the team's spot in the standings. For the past several seasons, the Texans have outperformed the state's traditional football powerhouse, the Dallas Cowboys. It's a major point of pride for Houston residents, who are always looking for an opportunity to put points on the scoreboard against their rival city to the north.

Not nearly as pride inducing are the **Houston Astros,** the city's cellar-dwelling Major League Baseball franchise. In 1965, the Astros became the primary occupants of the then-futuristic Astrodome, referred to as the Eighth Wonder of the World. Indeed, it was a sight to behold and an especially welcome respite from Houston's horrendous humidity. The Astros assembled some worthy teams in the 1980s, most notably with hometown hero Nolan Ryan, and two decades later they attained similar success with another local legend Roger Clemens at the helm and a powerhouse offense featuring the "Killer Bs"—Craig Biggio, Jeff Bagwell, and Lance Berkman. By this time, the Astros had fled the Eighth Wonder for the comfy confines of the downtown Minute Maid Park (501 Crawford St.), a classic urban ball field with a modern retractable roof. Locals hope the team's recent move from MLB's National League to the American League will bring a shot of energy and excitement to the franchise.

Basketball isn't as big a draw in Texas as other sports, but the **Houston Rockets** have always had a considerable following. Their successful 1990s teams, featuring top-notch talent such as Clyde "The Glide" Drexler and Hakeem "The Dream" Olajuwon, were the talk of the NBA during their glory years, when they won the NBA title in 1993 and 1994. The Rockets hold court at the downtown Toyota Center.

RECREATIONAL ACTIVITIES

Rivaling Hermann Park for crown jewel of Houston's public green space is **Memorial Park.** What sets Memorial Park apart is its recreational facilities, primarily the hike and bike trails. Located on 1,400 acres formerly dedicated to World War I-era Camp Logan, Memorial Park is now a magnet for all varieties of athletes and exercisers.

The three-mile Seymour **Lieberman**

Exercise Trail is popular with residents who have a daily workout routine and utilize the exercise stations and restrooms along the route. More dedicated runners use the nearby asphalt timing track to work on speed and develop skills while the Memorial Park Picnic Loop offers a smooth surface for in-line skaters, traditional roller skate enthusiasts, and hikers. Dogs are welcome and even encouraged at the park—canine drinking fountains are conveniently located at ground level along the jogging trails. Just remember to keep your pooch on a leash and to bring a doggie bag.

Mountain bikers race to the park for the miles of challenging terrain along the **Buffalo Bayou.** The southwest section of the park contains color-coded trails with maps at the trailheads, and Infantry Woods provides an advanced trail for those with superior skills. The park's other recreational opportunities include a full-service tennis center, swimming pool, golf course, fitness center, baseball diamonds, a croquet field, and sand volleyball courts.

Just east of Memorial Park is the pleasantly modest-sized **Buffalo Bayou Park,** an urban greenbelt with the namesake waterway as its centerpiece. With the towering Houston skyline as a backdrop, the park draws bikers, joggers, art lovers, and walkers from across the city who relish its riverside trails and bustling activity. In addition to the smooth, wide trail system, the 124-acre park contains exercise stations, a recreation center, disc golf course, children's playground, and popular dog-recreation area. Public art abounds along the jogging trail, from stainless-steel objects representing tree roots on an overpass to the large stone blocks, now turned sculpture, that remain from the city's demolished civic auditorium. Visit the park's website, www.buffalobayou.org, to download PDFs of trail maps.

ECOTOURISM

One of the most popular ecotourism destinations in the country is emerging along the Gulf Coast in South Texas, particularly the Lower Rio Grande Valley near South Padre Island. The Valley's immense biodiversity and

© ANDY RHODES

The World Birding Center is an example of ecotourism on the Gulf Coast.

ecological complexity make it a natural crossing point for migratory birds, which traverse the region each fall and spring en route to and from their winter homes in the tropics.

Much like the birds that arrive in the Valley from the East Coast and Midwest, the birders who track and document their feathered friends flock from across the country in search of their favorite and rare species. The McAllen area is home to several acclaimed birding sites catering to the thousands of ecotourists who arrive annually, including the **World Birding Center's Quinta Mazatlan,** the highly regarded **Ana National Wildlife Refuge,** and the **Bentsen-Rio Grande Valley State Park.** These parks retain the region's natural state by maintaining the distinctive woodlands, which draw species popular with the birding crowd, such as the chachalacas, green jays, and broad-winged hawks.

Websites worth exploring to find potential ecofriendly travel options in Houston and the Gulf Coast region include www.ecotourism.org and www.ecotravel.com.

PARKS

Most big cities have a showcase central park offering an inviting natural oasis among the harsh urban environs. Houston's version is Hermann Park. Located in the heart of the Museum District just southwest of downtown, **Hermann Park** is a 400-acre magnet for joggers, dog walkers, bikers, and families in search of some rare green space in a city known for its rampant development. Trails and trees are abundant here, as are the amenities and services, including a theater, golf course, and garden center. The park is filled with statues, too; look for monuments to Sam Houston, Mahatma Gandhi, and namesake George Hermann.

Farther outside of town but worth the 30-minute drive is **Armand Bayou Nature Center.** Located near NASA on the west side of Galveston Bay, the nature center offers residents and visitors a chance to learn about native plant and animal species, hike on the discovery trails, or see the live animal displays featuring the likes of bison, hawks, and spiders. The main area of the park contains a boardwalk traversing the marshes and forests and providing a glimpse of the beautiful bayou region of East Texas. The best way to experience this natural wonder is by boat—consider taking a tour on the Bayou Ranger pontoon boat or signing up for a guided canoe tour.

Camping

Like many other places, funding for parks is scarce in this region of Texas, but the **Texas Parks and Wildlife Department** (TPWD) manages to run a decent operation with limited resources. For years, Texans complained mightily about the hassles of making campground reservations via phone. Several years ago, TPWD finally implemented an online reservation system (http://texas.reserveworld.com), which has added convenience.

If you're considering pitching a tent while visiting Houston, the best camping is about 30 miles southwest of the city at **Brazos Bend State Park** (21901 FM 762). To make reservations, contact the park at 979/553-5102 or via the Texas Parks and Wildlife Department's website at www.tpwd.state.tx.us. Entry fees are $4 daily per person 13 and older.

Covering roughly 5,000 acres, this popular state park offers hiking, biking, equestrian trails, and fishing on six easily accessible lakes. However, visitors are cautioned about alligators, which are numerous in some areas of the park.

Facilities at Brazos Bend State Park include restrooms with showers, campsites with water and electricity, screened shelters, primitive equestrian campsites, and a dining hall. Many visitors make Brazos Bend a weekend destination because of its abundant activities, including free interpretive programs and hikes. A nature center with informative displays contains a "hands-on" alligator discovery area, a model of the park, a freshwater aquarium, live native snake species, and the George Observatory (open 3pm-10pm Sat.).

Closer to town is the unremarkable yet convenient **Alexander Deussen County Park** (12303 Sonnier St.). For reservation information, call 713/440-1587 for information. Named after a respected Houston geologist, Deussen Park offers basic camping services, including site pads, fire pits, picnic areas, and restrooms. Pets are allowed, but they must be kept on a leash.

FISHING

Like other outdoor activities in the Houston and Gulf Coast region, fishing is a popular recreational endeavor because of the mild year-round temperatures. The areas of East Texas just north of Houston (especially near the four national forests) are well known in angler circles for their freshwater reservoirs and streams packed with largemouth bass, smallmouth bass, crappie, panfish (bluegill, sunfish), and catfish. The Gulf Coast, meanwhile, is an angler's paradise for tarpon, amberjack, red drum, and spotted sea trout.

The **Brazosport** area offers a multitude of facilities for fishing, either inshore or deep sea. If you choose to keep your feet on the ground, plenty of jetties, piers, and beaches are available where you can cast a line for speckled trout, flounder, redfish, sheepshead, and gaff-topsail catfish. Nearby marinas and beachside shacks sell tackle and bait. For deep-sea fishing, you can hire a service to provide charter boats to take you out farther for big-time catches including snapper, marlin, king mackerel, and sailfish.

A popular place to spend a weekend of fishing, camping, and lounging is **Quintana Beach County Park**, located on a picturesque barrier island near Freeport. The park's multilevel fishing pier is a favorite among anglers, and the day-use facilities include shaded pavilions, restrooms, showers, and the historical Coveney House, which houses a museum and natural history display. The camping sites include full hookups, showers, and laundry facilities. From Freeport, take FM 1495 south nearly two miles to County Road 723, then head east three miles to the park entrance.

Since Texas is so big and fishing is so popular, it has nearly 1,700 locations to obtain a **fishing license** (a requirement). Anglers can

fishing on South Padre Island

purchase a license at most bait and tackle shops, as well as local sporting goods stores, grocery stores, and even some department stores. Recreational licenses are available on a daily basis (fees vary by location) or with an **annual permit** ($30 freshwater, $35 saltwater, $40 "all-water"). These licenses can also be purchased in advance by phone (800/895-4248 8am-5pm Mon.-Fri.) or via TPWD's website at www.tpwd.state.tx.us. In addition, the site offers information about fishing reports, tides, and advisories, along with a handy service that identifies the nearest local license vendor by city.

HUNTING

Hunting is huge in eastern and southern Texas, and the area's sheer size provides countless opportunities to grab a gun and wait patiently for your critter of choice. **Deer hunting** is one of the biggest draws, and deer season has a major cultural and economic impact on much of the state. Pick up a community newspaper during the winter, and you'll find plenty of photos of

hunters, ranging in age from 8 to 88, in the back of their pickup trucks proudly displaying the rack of the buck they just killed.

In general, this part of Texas offers something for every kind of hunter, from waterfowl along the Gulf Coast to quail and pheasant in South Texas to feral hogs in East Texas. The best place to find all the information you'll ever need about hunting in Texas—seasons, permits, regulations, restrictions, hunting lodges, and hunting leases—is the Texas Parks and Wildlife Department's website: www.tpwd. state.tx.us.

Like fishing licenses, Texas's **hunting licenses** are required and can be obtained across the state. Hunters can purchase a license at a local gun shop, sporting goods store, grocery store, or department store. Resident licenses are available for $25 (fees for out-of-staters are slightly higher) and allow hunting of "any legal bird or animal (terrestrial vertebrates)." The licenses can also be purchased in advance by phone (800/895-4248 8am-5pm Mon.-Fri.) or via TPWD's website. Like the fishing licenses, the website offers a service that identifies local vendors based on the closest city.

Although most locals are well versed in the procedures associated with field dressing and transporting a deer after it's been killed, visitors may need a crash course on the state's requirements. To find out everything you need to know about appropriate tags, processing (four quarters and two backstraps), and keeping the deer in "edible condition," visit www.tpwd. state.tx.us.

Food

Food lovers love Houston, with its more than 8,000 restaurants (that's not a misprint). Turn on the Food Network, and you'll probably soon be watching a feature about a Houston-area restaurant serving up Texas-style barbecue, one of the many varieties of Mexican food, or recipes for the perfect Lone Star chili. Here's a quick overview of the region's culinary icons.

BARBECUE

The prime representation of Texas cuisine—barbecue is all about the meat, from beef (brisket and ribs) and pork (sausage, ribs, and chops) to turkey, chicken, mutton, goat, and anything else you can put in a barbecue smoker. The tradition originated in the Caribbean as a method to cook meat over a pit on a framework of sticks known as a *barbacot,* and it eventually made its way across the southern United States, where it picked up various cultural influences on the way. Even in Texas several different methods for barbecuing meat are used, and the debate rages on about who does it the right way. Fortunately, everyone wins since all styles of Texas barbecue are exceptionally pleasing to the palate.

In general, the East Texas approach is aligned with African American traditions of the South: The sauce is tomato based and somewhat sweet, and the sides (potato salad and coleslaw, in particular) are mayo based and extremely sweet. Moving further west, the 'cue originating in traditional German and Czech communities is considered the ideal representative of the Lone Star State. Based on traditions from European meat markets, the sausage and beef are smoked and served on waxed paper along with side items inspired by the former grocery store-butcher shops where they originated—bread slices, beans, tomatoes, cheese, and jalapeños.

TEX-MEX

For most people, Mexican food means tacos, burritos, and nachos. In this region of Texas, especially moving further south toward the border, Mexican food can mean a variety of things—cuisine from the interior of Mexico with savory sauces and various meats, Southwestern-style Mexican food with green chilies and blue corn, or border-inspired Tex-Mex with gooey cheese, seasoned beef, and tortillas.

Though interior Mexican food is certainly worth sampling if you can find an authentic restaurant, Tex-Mex prevails in this region of Texas, and finding a good representation of this regional comfort food in most cities across the state is not hard to do. In fact, mom-and-pop Tex-Mex restaurants are much like Italian eateries on the East Coast and in the Midwest—the best food is often in the most unassuming spot, like a strip mall or small house on a side street.

The main ingredients in Tex-Mex are ground beef, chicken, cheese, pinto beans, and tortillas. These items are combined differently for tasty variations, including a crispy or soft beef taco; a beef, cheese, or chicken enchilada; a bean chalupa; cheese quesadilla; or beef and chicken fajitas. Salsa, guacamole, lettuce, and tomato are typically added as flavorful accompaniments.

SOUTHERN

Texas doesn't hold exclusive rights to this category, but Southern food is considered

peel-and-eat shrimp

somewhat exotic to more than half the country, and like just about everything else, the Gulf Coast region of Texas puts its own distinct spin on this style of down-home country cuisine.

It's unfair to generalize Southern cooking as being mostly fried, even though a good portion of it is encased in crispy goodness (just not always of the deep-fried variety). One of the best examples of Southern cookin' done right in Texas is chicken-fried steak, a thin cut of cube steak that's tenderized, breaded in egg batter or a seasoned flour mixture, pan fried in lard or vegetable oil, and served smothered in peppered cream gravy. The name likely refers to the similar process used in frying chicken. Other fried favorites include pork chops, catfish, okra, and chicken.

Another Southern cooking tendency is to include meat in veggie dishes (vegetarians should consider themselves warned). Beans, greens, and black-eyed peas are often spruced up with ham hock or bacon, and lard or bacon grease can add an extra dimension of flavor to just about any vegetable or bread

recipe. Incidentally, if you order tea in a Texas restaurant, you'll get iced tea (occasionally sweetened), and you should never skip an opportunity to order a fruit cobbler or pecan pie for dessert.

SEAFOOD

Although the holy trinity of Texas food—barbecue, Tex-Mex, and Southern—is available in all areas of the state, Houston and the Gulf Coast region are the only places where seafood is a viable fresh option. In fact, for many travelers, a visit to the Gulf Coast is incomplete without including shrimp in every meal. One of the best ways to kick off a visit to the coast is by going directly to a seaside restaurant and ordering a plate of peel-and-eat shrimp accompanied by a hoppy local brew. To continue your mealtime quest, consider ordering shrimp in breakfast tacos, in a lunchtime enchilada dish, and in the traditional fried form for dinner.

It's possible that you'll be seeking other varieties of fresh-caught seafood while visiting the area. Feel free to ask a waiter about potential specials that may not be listed on the menu. In some cases, especially in traditional fishing communities like Port Aransas, the restaurants are happy to cook your own fresh-caught fillet, a handy option if you're staying in a hotel or somewhere without easy access to a cooking source. Call ahead to find out the procedures in place for each location.

Tips for Travelers

For the most part, traveling in Houston and the Gulf Coast region is similar to traveling in the rest of the United States, with the main exception being issues associated with crossing the Mexican border (which is avoided by most people these days). Otherwise, it's smooth sailing across state lines, with visitor information centers located on the Texas side of several major freeways as one enters this region of the state.

INTERNATIONAL TRAVELERS

Since Texas shares a lengthy border with another country, international travel has traditionally been commonplace in the Lone Star State. Not anymore. With the recent rise in violence associated with the warring drug cartels in Mexico's border regions and trafficking routes, visitors are advised against traveling to Mexico.

Overseas travel is a different story—recent numbers compiled by state government show Texas ranks seventh as a destination point among mainland U.S. states for overseas travelers, with New York, California, and Florida taking the top spots. Many of these visitors arrive in Houston because it is a major airport hub.

Before international travelers arrive, they're encouraged to address several issues that will make their experience more pleasant and convenient. Suggested action items include the following: consulting their insurance companies to ensure their medical policy applies in the United States; making sure they have a signed, up-to-date passport and/or visa; leaving copies of their itinerary and contact information with friends or family for emergencies; and taking precautions to avoid being a target of crime (don't carry excessive amounts of money, don't leave luggage unattended, and so forth).

TRAVELERS WITH DISABILITIES

Travelers with disabilities shouldn't have much trouble getting around in this part of Texas; in fact, the only places that may not be wheelchair accessible are some outdated hotels and restaurants. Otherwise, parks, museums, and city attractions are compliant with the Americans with Disabilities Act, providing ramps, elevators, and accessible facilities for public-use areas.

Texas law requires cities to appoint one member to a transit board representing the interest of the "transportation disadvantaged," a group that can include people with disabilities. As a result, most cities have addressed accessibility issues in airports and public transportation services. For detailed information, contact the municipal offices in the city you're visiting or the **Texas Department of Transportation's Public Transportation Division** (512/416-2810, www.dot.state.tx.us).

Other handy resources for travelers with disabilities en route to Houston and the Gulf Coast are **Disabled Online** (www.disabledonline.com), offering a page of links with travel tips; the **Handicapped Travel Club** (www.handicappedtravelclub.com), providing information about campgrounds with accessibility; and the **Society for Accessible Travel and Hospitality** (www.sath.org), whose website has a resources page with handy travel tips for anyone with physical limitations.

SENIOR TRAVELERS

For seniors, it's always a good idea to mention in advance if you're a member of AARP or if you qualify for a senior discount (typically for ages 65 and older, but occasionally available for the 60 and older crowd). Most museums in this region offer a few dollars off admission fees for seniors, and many public transportation systems also provide discounts.

If you haven't done so already, inquire about travel options through **Elderhostel** (877/426-8056, www.elderhostel.org), an organization that provides several programs in the Houston area with seniors in mind. Excursions lasting 4-12 days are available, ranging from birding trails to heritage-based tours to art, nature, and fishing trips.

GAY AND LESBIAN TRAVELERS

Texas's rural communities (and even some of its smaller cities) aren't quite as open-minded as its metropolitan areas. Houston has a sizable gay community, with bars, restaurants, and services catering exclusively to gay clientele. To learn more about resources related to gay and lesbian travel in this region of Texas, including accommodations, restaurants, and nightclubs, visit the following travel-related websites: www.gaytravel.com, and www.gayjourney.com. For additional information, contact the **Lesbian/Gay Rights Lobby of Texas** (512/474-5475, www.lgrl.org).

Health and Safety

This region of Texas isn't any more dangerous or safer than other parts of the state (or country), but several environment-related issues (weather, animals) set it apart. Travelers with medical issues are encouraged to bring extra supplies of medications and copies of prescriptions—local visitors bureaus can recommend the best pharmacy or medical center, if needed.

CRIME

Although it's still often considered a Wild West state, Texas is similar to the rest of the nation regarding crime statistics and trends. According to a recent report by the Texas Department of Public Safety, criminal activity in Texas was separated into the following categories: violent crimes (against people, such as robberies, assaults, etc.), which represented 11 percent of the reported offenses, and property crimes (burglary, car theft), representing the remaining 89 percent. The report also revealed that violent crime decreased by 1.5 percent from the previous year while property crime increased 2.6 percent. As always, if you're a victim of a crime in Texas or witness any criminal activity, immediately call 911.

THE ELEMENTS

Eastern and Southern Texas's weather is as volatile as its landscape. Summers regularly reach triple digits, and winters are marked by near-freezing temperatures (and the occasional snowfall). The biggest threat to travelers in winter is **ice**—bridges and overpasses become slick and are usually closed when a rare ice storm barrels through the state. Since Texans in this region are unaccustomed to dealing with such slippery conditions, they often disregard the danger and plow across a patch of ice in their big fancy trucks. The results are predictably disastrous.

Heat is by far the most serious threat to travelers. From the sticky humidity of marshy East Texas to the intense sun further south, the summer months (May-September in Texas) can be brutal. Hikers, bikers, and campers are encouraged to pack and carry plenty of water to remain hydrated.

WILDLIFE, INSECTS, AND PLANTS

This region of Texas has some bizarre fauna and flora, which can occasionally pose a danger to travelers, particularly those who venture to the state's parks and natural areas. Of primary concern are **snakes,** which nestle among rocks and waterways throughout eastern and southern Texas (though rattlesnakes are largely found only in western portions of the state).

Venomous **snake bites** from these varieties require a few basic first-aid techniques if medical care is not immediately available. The American Red Cross suggests washing the bite with soap and water, and keeping the bitten area immobilized and lower than the heart. Equally as important are avoiding remedy misconceptions: Do not apply hot or cold packs, do not attempt to suck the poison out, and do not drink any alcohol or use any medication.

The most dangerous plant in Texas is **cactus.** There are many varieties in the national forests and along the coastal plains, and even though some appear harmless, they may contain barely visible needles that get embedded in your skin and cause major irritation. With cactus, the best approach is to look but don't touch.

Information and Services

The best way to find out about activities and services in the city you're visiting is through the local convention and visitors bureau, or in smaller communities, the chamber of commerce. Each destination in this book includes contact information for visitor services, and even the most rural areas have discovered the value of promoting themselves online thanks to the wonders of the Internet.

MONEY
It's always a good idea to have cash on hand for tips, bottles of water, and parking or tollway fees, but you can get by in most cities across this region with a credit or debit card. Some smaller towns still don't accept them (old-fashioned restaurants and "convenience" stores, in particular), but they're typically modern enough to have ATM machines. Also available, yet not quite as accessible, are wire transfers and travelers checks. Call ahead for the bank's hours of operation because some institutions close at odd hours.

MAPS AND TOURIST INFO
Convention and visitors bureaus are the best resource for planning a trip to Houston and the Gulf Coast. Call ahead to have maps and brochures sent before your trip, or check the town's website for electronic versions of walking tours and street maps available for download. It's also a good idea to check these websites or call in advance to find out if the city you're visiting is hosting its annual pecan days or biker festival at the same time. Depending on your outlook, this can enhance or hinder your excursion.

RESOURCES

Suggested Reading

GENERAL INFORMATION

Alvarez, Elizabeth Cruce, and Robert Plocheck. *Texas Almanac 2012-2013*. Denton, TX: Texas State Historical Association, 2012. Published annually, this handy book includes virtually everything you'd ever need to know about Texas—current and historical information about politics, agriculture, transportation, geography, and culture, along with maps of each county (all 254 of 'em).

Texas Monthly. With an upper-crust subscriber base, this monthly features some of the best writers in the state offering insightful commentary and substantive feature articles about the state's politics, culture, history, and Texas-ness. It's available at most bookstores, coffee shops, and grocery stores.

State Travel Guide. Each year, the Texas Department of Transportation publishes this magazine-size guide with maps and comprehensive listings of the significant attractions in nearly every town, including all the local history museums in Texas's tiny communities.

LITERATURE, FICTION, HISTORY

McCarthy, Cormac. *All the Pretty Horses*. New York: Knopf, 1992. Tracing a young man's journey to the regions of the unknown (though it technically takes place along the Texas-Mexico border), this novel depicts a classic quest with plenty of good, evil, and Texas mystique.

Bissinger, H. G. *Friday Night Lights*. Reading, MA: Addison-Wesley, 1990. This book will tell you more about Texas than you could ever experience in a visit to the state. Not just about football, it details the passionate emotions involved with family, religion, and race in Odessa through the eyes of journalist Buzz Bissinger.

Harrigan, Stephen. *The Gates of the Alamo*. New York: Knopf, 2000. This is gripping historical fiction and a compelling read, with detailed history about the actual people and events associated with the battle of The Alamo.

McMurtry, Larry. *Lonesome Dove*. New York: Simon and Schuster, 1985. Beautifully written by Pulitzer Prize-winning novelist Larry McMurtry, this period piece (late 1800s) chronicles two former Texas Rangers on a cattle drive and leaves readers with a yearning for the compelling characters and the Texas of the past.

Fehrenbach, T. R. *Lone Star*. New York: Da Capo Press, 2000. Considered the definitive book on Texas history, this enormous tome, written by a highly respected historian, covers Texas's lengthy and colorful heritage in fascinating and accurate detail.

Dobie, J. Frank. *Tales of Old-Time Texas*. Boston: Little, Brown, 1955. Known as the Southwest's master storyteller, J. Frank Dobie depicts folk life in Texas unlike any other author, with 28 inspiring stories of characters (Jim Bowie) and culture (the legend of the Texas bluebonnet).

MUSIC AND FOOD

Porterfield, Bill. *The Greatest Honky Tonks of Texas.* Dallas, TX: Taylor, 1983. You'll likely have to do some searching to dig up a copy of this book, but it's worth it for the engaging text about the colorful culture of the state's iconic honky-tonks and historic dance halls.

Walsh, Robb. *Legends of Texas Barbecue.* San Francisco: Chronicle Books, 2002. This book is as fun to read as it is to use—learn about the fascinating history of the many different styles of Texas barbecue while trying out some of the state's best recipes and cooking methods.

Govenar, Alan. *Meeting the Blues: The Rise of the Texas Sound.* Dallas, TX: Taylor, 1995. This thoroughly researched book provides fascinating insight into the development of the Texas blues through historical narrative, interviews, and photos.

Walsh, Robb. *The Tex-Mex Cookbook.* New York: Broadway Books, 2004. Well-researched and comprehensive in approach, this informative book includes cultural information about classic and unknown Tex-Mex dishes and plenty of authentic recipes.

Marshall, Wes. *The Wine Roads of Texas: An Essential Guide to Texas Wines and Wineries.* San Antonio, TX: Maverick, 2002. Covering more than 400 Texas wines and the top wineries in Texas, this book offers a comprehensive sampling of wines from Big Bend to the bayous.

OUTDOORS

Tekiela, Stan. *Birds of Texas Field Guide.* Cambridge, MN: Adventure Publications, 2004. Designed for amateur birders, this handy guide is color coded (corresponding to the birds' feathers) with helpful photos, maps, and descriptions.

Tennant, Alan. *A Field Guide to Texas Snakes.* Houston, TX: Gulf Publishing, 2002. This thorough guidebook provides essential information about understanding and appreciating Texas's venomous and nonvenomous snakes through identification keys and color photos.

Wauer, Roland. *Naturalist's Big Bend.* College Station, TX: Texas A&M University Press, 2002. If you ever wanted to know about the major and minor details of Big Bend's mammals, reptiles, insects, birds, trees, shrubs, cacti, and other living things, this is the place to find it.

Internet Resources

GENERAL TRAVEL INFORMATION

Office of the Governor, Economic Development and Tourism
www.traveltex.com
This indispensable site provides background and contact information for virtually every tourist attraction, major and minor, in the state.

Texas Department of Transportation
www.dot.state.tx.us
Visit this site for information about road conditions and travel resources (maps, travel info center locations, and so forth).

Texas Monthly
www.texasmonthly.com
The site of this award-winning magazine offers samples of feature articles and recommendations for quality dining and lodging options throughout the state.

HISTORIC PRESERVATION

Texas Historical Commission
www.thc.state.tx.us
The official state agency for historic preservation, the THC provides helpful guidelines about its preservation programs and essential travel information about popular historic properties across the state.

Texas State Historical Association,
The Handbook of Texas Online
www.tshaonline.org/handbook/online
The is the online version of *The New Handbook of Texas,* which has long been considered the definitive source for accurate information about Texas's historical events, sites, and figures.

OUTDOORS

Texas Parks and Wildlife Department
www.tpwd.state.tx.us
You can get lost (in a good way) exploring this site, with its comprehensive listings of state parks and detailed information about outdoors activities.

National Parks in Texas
www.nps.gov
Texas's national parks are astounding, and this site provides enough information to put these intriguing locales on your must-visit list.

Texas Campgrounds
www.texascampgrounds.com
Use this site to help find a commendable RV park or campground anywhere in the state.

Texas Outside
www.texasoutside.com
This site contains helpful information and links for outdoor activities in Texas, including hiking, biking, camping, fishing, hunting, and golfing.

Index

A

Adventures 2000 Plus Swamp and River Tours: 143

African American history: Buffalo Soldiers Museum 32; Civil War and Reconstruction 184; Rosenwald schools 157

agriculture: 185

AIA Sandcastle: 87

aircraft carriers: 100

air travel: 192

Alabama-Coushatta Reservation: 146

Alamo, siege of the: 183

Aldridge Sawmill: 18, 20, 136, 151

Alexander Deussen County Park: 198

Alice's Tall Texan: 13, 46

Alley Theatre building: 41

Americana: 34

amusement parks: Kemah Boardwalk 37; Pleasure Pier 80; Schlitterbahn Beach Waterpark (South Padre Island) 122; Schlitterbahn Waterpark (Galveston) 80

Ana National Wildlife Refuge: 197

Ancel Brundrett Pier: 115

Andy Bowie Park: 125

Angelina National Forest: 9, 17, 20, 151

Anvil Bar & Refuge: 11, 43

Apache people: 182

aquariums: Downtown Aquarium 28; Kemah Boardwalk 37; Moody Gardens 82; Sea Center Texas 93; Texas State Aquarium 98

Arboretum of Houston: 12, 35

archaeological sites: 160

architecture/historic homes: Ashton Villa 82; Asia Society Texas Center 32; Bayou Bend Collection 34; Bishop's Palace 81; Harrison County Courthouse 168; Heritage Park 101; Jefferson 171; McFaddin-Ward House 139; mid-century 41; Moody Mansion 82; Plantation Museums 164; sandcastle 87; Skyspace building 35; Starr Family Home 168; Varner-Hogg Plantation 93

Armadillo Palace: 13, 47

Armand Bayou Nature Center: 39, 197

arts, the: 189-191

Ashton Villa: 82

Asian Cultures Museum: 101

Asian Pacific Heritage Festival: 49

Asia Society Texas Center: 32

Astrodome: 41

Atalanta Railroad Car: 172

Austin, Stephen F.: 184

B

Babe Didrickson Zaharias Museum: 140

backpacking: 147, 148, 153

ballet: 48-49, 106, 165

Ballet Tyler: 165

barbecue: general discussion 200; Cajun 8; Corpus Christi 110; Houston 8; Jefferson 173; Lufkin 157; Nacogdoches 162; Orange 144; Tyler 166

Battleship *Texas*: 18, 38

Bayfest: 106

Bayou Bend Collection: 34

Bayou City Cajun Fest: 49

bayou tours: 143

Bay Trail: 104

beachcombing: 113

beaches: Brazosport 94-95; Corpus Christi 103; Galveston Island 83; Gulf Coast 9; Mustang Island State Park 113; Padre Island National Seashore 112; Port Aransas 113; South Padre Island 15, 122, 125

beach home rentals: 97

Beaumont: 138-144, 147

bed-and-breakfasts: 89, 172

Bentsen- Rio Grande Valley State Park: 197

Big Easy Social and Pleasure Club: 12, 44

Big Texas Dance Hall and Saloon: 13, 47

Big Thicket National Preserve: 136, 145-147

biking: Big Thicket National Preserve 146; Corpus Christi 104; Galveston Island State Park 83; Houston 40; Mustang Island State Park 113; Nacogdoches 161; South Padre Island 127; as transportation 194

birds: 179

bird-watching: general discussion 197; Adventures 2000 Plus Swamp and River Tours 143; Angelina National Forest 152; Big Thicket National Preserve 136, 145, 146-147; Brazoria National Wildlife Refuge 94; Corpus Christi Bay Trail 104; Galveston Island State Park 83, 85; King Ranch 119; Mustang Island State Park 113; Padre Island National Seashore 112; Sabine National Forest 153; San Bernard National Wildlife Refuge 94; Stephen F. Austin Experimental Forest 161

Birthplace of Boogie Woogie: 168

Bishop's Palace: 15, 18, 81
Blue Bell Creameries: 71
Blue Fish: 16, 64
blues music: 46-47
boardwalks: 37
boogie woogie: 168
Brain Night at the Museum: 49
Brazoria National Wildlife Refuge: 94
Brazos Bend State Park: 198
Brazosport area: 92-98, 198
Breakfast Klub: 16, 59
Brenham: 71
Brenham Heritage Museum: 71
Brennan's: 16, 59
Brownsville South Padre Island International
    Airport: 76
Bryan Beach: 95
Buccaneer Days: 106
Buddhist temples: 143
Buffalo Bayou: 39, 196
Buffalo Bayou Park: 196
Buffalo Soldiers Museum: 18, 19, 32
bus travel: 193, 195
butterflies: 161
Buu Mon Buddhist Temple: 143

C
Cabeza de Vaca: 183
Caddo Lake: 136, 172
Caddo Lake State Park: 172
Caddo Mounds State Historic Site: 160
Caddo people: 183
Cajun Triangle: 138
Caldwell Zoo: 165
CAM: 30
camping: general discussion 198; Big Thicket
    National Preserve 147; Caddo Lake 172;
    Corpus Christi 108; Galveston Island: 89;
    Houston 57; Lake Tombigbee 145; Piney
    Woods 149, 150, 152, 153; South Padre Island
    132
car travel: 193
Casa Ramirez: 12, 52
Center for the Arts & Sciences: 93
Central School Arts and Humanities Center: 71
Chanukah Fest: 50
Charlie's Harbor Pier: 115
children's activities: Caldwell Zoo 165; Children's
    Museum 31; Discovery Science Place 165;
    Dolphin Research and Sea Life Nature
    Center 123; Downtown Aquarium 28; Ellen
    Trout Zoo 155; Health Museum 31; Houston
    Arboretum and Nature Center 35; Houston

Zoo 31; itinerary for 17-20; Kemah Boardwalk
    37; Museum of Natural Science 29; NASA
    Space Center Kid's Space 36; Schlitterbahn
    Waterpark 80; Schlitterbahn Beach
    Waterpark 122; Sea Center Texas 93; Stewart
    Beach 83; Texas State Aquarium 100
Children's Museum: 17, 31
Chinatown: 27, 53
Christian religion: 187
Christmas events: 87
Churrascos: 16, 61
cinema: 190
Civil War: 143, 184
climate: 177
Coastal Plains: 176
Columbus, Christopher: 100
Comanche people: 183
communications: 70
concert venues, Houston: 48
Contemporary Arts Museum of Houston: 11,
    22, 30
Corpus Christi: 9, 15, 98-112; accommodations
    106-108; beaches 103; children's activities
    19; entertainment/events 105-106; food
    108-112; historical sights 18; maps 99, 100;
    shopping 106; sights 98-103
Corpus Christi Beach: 103
Corpus Christi Botanical Gardens and Nature
    Center: 103
Corpus Christi International Airport: 76
Corpus Christi Museum of Science and History:
    18, 100
country and Western music: 47
Cowan Center: 165
cowboy culture: 13, 119, 120
crime: 203
culture: 189-191
Culture converges at the Art Museum of: 102
cyclones, tropical: 84

D
Davy Crockett National Forest: 150
Day of the Dead Festival: 50
Dean's Credit Clothing: 11, 42
deer hunting: 199
Dewberry Plantation: 164
dialect, regional: 187
Diboll: 9, 155
Dickens on the Strand: 87
disabilities, travelers with: 202
Discovery Science Place: 165
Dolphin Research and Sea Life Nature Center: 123
dolphin tours: 122, 127

Double Lake: 148
Downtown Aquarium: 19, 28
downtown Houston: accommodations 54;
    food 16, 58-60; nightlife 42; orientation 26;
    shopping 50-51; sights 28-29
Downtown Tunnels: 28
driving: 193, 194

E

East Beach: 83
East Texas: 135-174; Beaumont 138-144;
    Big Thicket National Preserve 145-147;
    highlights 136; itinerary 15; Jefferson 171-
    174; Lufkin 154-159; maps 137; Marshall 167-
    170; Piney Woods 148-154; planning tips 9,
    136; Tyler 163-167
East Texas Oil Museum: 139
East Texas Symphony Orchestra: 165
economy: 185
ecotourism: 196
Elissa: 14, 18, 74, 81
Ellen Trout Zoo: 155
Ellison's Greenhouses: 71
El Real Tex-Mex Cafe: 11, 16, 61
emergencies, medical: 69
environmental issues: 178
ethnicities: 186-187
European exploration: 183

F

fall foliage: 148
family vacation itinerary: 17-20
film: 190
Firehouse Saloon: 12, 13, 47
Fire Museum of Texas: 140
Fisherman's Wharf: 113
fishing: general discussion 198; Angelina
    National Forest 151; Brazosport 95; Caddo
    Lake 172; Corpus Christi 103; Galveston
    Island State Park 83, 85; Lake Conroe 149;
    Lake o' the Pines 172; Lake Sam Rayburn
    152; Mustang Island State Park 113; Padre
    Island National Seashore 112; Port Aransas
    113, 115; San Jose Island 113; South Padre
    Island 127; Toledo Bend Reservoir 153
flora: 178-179
folk art: 36
food: 16, 200-202
Four C National Recreation Trail: 150
Freeman Plantation: 171

G

Gaido's Seafood: 19, 91
Galleria: 27
Gallery Main Street: 166
Galveston Fishing Pier: 86
Galveston Island: 9, 14, 76-92; accommodations
    88-89; beaches 83; children's activities 19;
    entertainment 86-87; food 90-92; historical
    sights 18; maps 77-79; recreation 83-86;
    shopping 87; sights 79-83; transportation 92
Galveston Island State Park: 19, 83
gambling: 71
gardens: Buu Mon Buddhist Temple 143;
    Corpus Christi Botanical Gardens and
    Nature Center 103; Houston Arboretum
    and Nature Center 35; Moody Gardens 82;
    Plantation Museums 164; Tyler Municipal
    Rose Garden and Museum 163
Gardere Martin Luther King Jr. Oratory
    Competition: 49
Gatlin's Barbecue: 12, 13, 16, 64
gay travelers: 203
gear: 10
geography: 175-177
George Bush International Airport: 192
George Ranch Historical Park: 18, 38
ghost stories: 171
Ghost Walks: 50
golf: 40
Gone With the Wind: 172
Goode Co. Barbeque: 11, 13, 61
Goodman Museum: 164
government: 185
grasses: 179
Greater Houston: food 66-68; shopping 53;
    sights 27, 36-38
Grove, the: 171
Gulf Coast: 73-134; Brazosport area 92-98;
    Corpus Christi 98-112; Galveston Island 76-92;
    highlights 74; itinerary 14-17; Kingsville 118-
    121; maps 76; Mustang Island 112-117; planning
    tips 9, 75; South Padre Island 122-134

H

Harrison County Courthouse: 168
Harrison County Museum: 168
haunted sights: 171
health: 203
Health Museum: 17, 31
heatstroke: 203
The Heights: food 64-65; nightlife 45;
    orientation 27; shopping 52

Heritage Park: 101
Hermann Park: 39, 197
Hermann Park Golf Course: 41
hiking: Big Thicket National Preserve 145; Caddo Lake 172; Corpus Christi 104; Davy Crockett National Forest 150; Galveston Island State Park 83; Houston 40; Lone Star Hiking Trail 148; Mustang Island State Park 113; Sabine National Forest 153; San Bernard National Wildlife Refuge 94; South Padre Island 127; Stephen F. Austin Experimental Forest 161
history: general discussion 182-184; Sabine Pass Battleground 143; San Jacinto Battleground 38; Sieur de La Salle 102; tour of sights 18; see also specific place
The History Center: 155
Hogg, Ima: 34, 93
Holocaust Museum Houston: 32
home rentals: 97
Horace Caldwell Pier: 115
horseback riding: Corpus Christi 105; Davy Crockett National Forest 150; Sabine National Forest 153
House of the Seasons: 171
Houston: 21-72; accommodations 54-57; children's activities 17; city layout 23; cowboy culture: 13; food 16, 58-68; getaways from 71; highlights 22; historical sights 18, 22; information/services 69-71; itinerary 11-12; maps 24-26; medical center 32; music 46-48; nightlife 42-46; performing arts 48-49; planning tips 8, 23; recreation 39-42; shopping 50-53; sights 28-38; tours 69; transportation 72
Houston, Sam: 183
Houston Arboretum & Nature Center: 35, 40
Houston Astros: 41, 196
Houston Ballet: 48-49
Houston Center for Photography: 32
Houston Grand Opera: 48
Houston International Jazz Festival: 50
Houston Mod: 41
Houston Museum of Fine Arts: 11, 22, 30
Houston Rockets: 42, 196
Houston Symphony: 49
Houston Texans: 41, 195-196
Houston Zoo: 19, 31
Humble Oil Building: 41
hummingbird gardens: 103
hunting: 199
Hurricane Ike: 84

Hurricane Rita: 84
hurricanes: 84, 177

I
ice: 203
ice cream: 71
Imperial Calcasieu Museum: 71
Indian Mounds Wilderness Area: 153
information/services: 204
insects: 181, 203
international travelers: 202
Isla Blanca Park: 125
itineraries: 11-20

J
jazz: 47-48
Jefferson: 171-174
Jefferson General Store: 171
jellyfish: 114
John E. Conner Museum: 120
Johnson Space Center: 36, 37
Joplin, Janis: 142
J.P. Luby Pier: 115
Juneteenth: 49

K
kayaking/canoeing: Big Thicket National Preserve 147; Brazosport 95; Corpus Christi 103; Galveston Island 83; South Padre Island: 125
Kemah Boardwalk: 8, 12, 19, 22, 27, 37
Kenedy Ranch Museum of South Texas: 119
Kilgore: 139
Kineños (King's people): 120
King, Richard: 118
King Ranch: 15, 18, 20, 74, 118, 120
King Ranch Museum: 119
King Ranch Saddle Shop: 119
King Ranch Visitor Center: 119
Kingsville: 118-121
Kiowa people: 183
Kirby Outlet Malls: 27
kiteboarding: 125
kite-flying: 103, 129

L
La Belle: 102
Lake Charles, Louisiana: 71
Lake Conroe: 148
Lake o' the Pines: 172
Lake Sam Rayburn: 151

Lake Tombigbee: 145
language: 187
La Salle: 102, 183
L'Auberge du Lac Hotel & Casino: 71
leaf peeping: 148
leather goods: 119
lesbian travelers: 203
LGBT community: 27, 203
lighthouses: 123
light shows: 35
Lone Star Hiking Trail: 148
Louisiana: 71, 127
Lufkin: 9, 17, 154-159
Lufkin Parks and Recreation: 156
luggage storage: 70
lumber industry: 18, 149, 151, 154

M
Magee Beach: 103, 115
Mam's House of Snoballs: 16, 65
man-of-war jellyfish: 114
manufacturing: 185
maps: 204
Mardi Gras: 87
marine life: 180
marine science: 93, 113, 123
Marine Science Institute: 113
Marshall: 9, 167-170
Marshall Pottery: 168
McClendon House: 164
McFaddin-Ward House: 139
media: 70
medical emergencies: 69
Memorial Park: 39, 40, 196
Memorial Park Picnic Loop: 40
Menil Collection: 12, 34
Mexican-American War: 184
Mexican Army: 38, 183
Michelson Museum of Art: 168
midtown Houston: 26, 43
Mission Control: 37
Molina's: 12, 66
money: 70, 204
Montrose-Kirby: food 60-63; nightlife 43;
    orientation 27; sights 34-35
Moody Gardens: 14, 19, 82
Moody Gardens Festival of Lights: 87
Moody Mansion: 15, 18, 82
Mosquito Café: 14, 92
mountain biking: Buffalo Bayou 40; Lone Star
    Hiking Trail 148; Sabine National Forest 153
movies: 190

Museum District: children's activities 17;
    orientation 26; planning tips 8, 11; sights
    29-33
Museum of East Texas: 155
Museum of Natural Science: 11, 17, 22, 29
Museum of the Gulf Coast: 142-143
music: general discussion 189; Marshall 168;
    Museum of the Gulf Coast 142-143; Selena
    Museum 102
Mustang Island: 9, 15, 20, 112-117
Mustang Island State Park: 112-113, 115
Mustang Island State Park Paddling Trail: 103

NO
Nacogdoches: 159-163
NASA Space Center: 8, 12, 19, 22, 27, 36, 37
Native American history: 182
Native American reservations: 145, 146
Native American sights: 160
naval sights: 100
Nazi history: 32
1904 Train Depot and Museum: 119
Ocean Star Offshore Drilling Rig and Museum: 81
oil/gas industry: general discussion 185;
    Beaumont 138, 139; Houston 29; Ocean
    Star Offshore Drilling Rig and Museum 81;
    Port Arthur 142-143; Spindletop-Gladys
    City Boomtown Museum 138; Texas Energy
    Museum 140
Old Stone Fort Museum: 159
Orange: 143
Orange Show: 12, 22, 36
orchids: 103, 153
Origami Festival at Tansu: 50
Oxheart: 16, 58

P
packing: 10
paddling: see kayaking/canoeing
Padre Island National Seashore: 74, 112
Pan American Coastal Studies Laboratory: 123
parks: 39-40, 197
PBR: 13, 43
performing arts: 86-87, 106
petroleum: see oil/gas industry
photography: 32
Pier 19: 15, 133
Piney Creek Horse Trail: 150
Piney Woods: 9, 17, 20, 148-154
planetariums: 93
plane travel: 192
planning tips: 8-10

Plantation Museums: 164
plants: 178-179, 203
Pleasure Pier: 14, 19, 80
population: 186
Port Aransas: 113
Port Arthur: 142-143
Port Isabel Lighthouse: 15, 74, 123
Portuguese man-of-war: 114
pottery: 168
precipitation: 177
prehistory: 182
public transportation: 195

QR

Quintana Beach County Park: 95, 198
Radisson: 15, 20, 108
Railroad Museum: 82
railroads: Atalanta Railroad Car 172; 1904 Train
    Depot and Museum 119; Railroad Museum
    82; Texas & Pacific Railway Museum 168;
    Texas State Railroad State Historical Park
    160; as transportation 193
rainfall: 177
ranching: George Ranch Historical Park 38;
    Kenedy Ranch Museum of South Texas 119;
    King Ranch 118, 120
Ratcliff Lake Recreation Area: 150
R.A. Vines Trail: 40
Reconstruction: 184
recreation: 10
religion: 187
reptiles: 181
Republic of Texas: 183
Rice Student Center: 35
Rice University: 27, 35
Rice University Art Gallery: 35
Rice Village: 27, 44, 51
Rienzi: 12, 35
rose gardens: 163
Rosenwald, Julius: 157
Rosenwald schools: 157
Rothko Chapel: 34

S

Sabine National Forest: 153
Sabine Pass Battleground: 143
safety: 114, 203
sailing: 81, 149
Saltwater Grill: 15, 90
Sam Houston National Forest: 148
Sammy's Wild Game Grill: 13, 16, 64
San Bernard National Wildlife Refuge: 94

San Jacinto Battleground: 8, 12, 18, 22, 27, 37
San Jose Island: 113
Sandcastle competition: 87
Santa Gertrudis cattle: 119
Scarlett O'Hardy's Gone With the Wind
    Museum: 172
Schlitterbahn Beach Waterpark: Galveston 19,
    80; South Padre Island 15, 122
science museums: 29, 93, 100, 165
scuba diving: 126
sculpture: Houston Museum of Fine Arts 30;
    Menil Collection 34; Orange Show 36
Sea Center Texas: 93
seafood: 201
Sea Ranch: 15, 133
seasons, best for travel: 10
Sea Turtle, Inc.: 15, 123
Seawall: 85, 88, 91
Selena Museum: 102
senior travelers: 202
Seymour Lieberman Exercise Trail: 40, 196
shell collecting: 95, 103, 113
Ships of Christopher Columbus: 100
shrubs: 178
Sieur de La Salle: 102, 183
Skyspace building: 35
snorkeling: 126
songs about Texas: 190
Southern food: 200
South Padre Island: 9, 15, 122-134
space exploration: 36, 37
Spanish explorers: 183
SPI Kitefest: 129
Spindletop-Gladys City Boomtown Museum:
    136, 138
sports: 41, 195-196
spring: 10
Spring Break: 129, 130
stand-up paddleboarding: 126
Stark Museum of Art: 144
Starr Family Home: 168
statehood: 183
Stephen F. Austin Experimental Forest: 161
Stephen F. Austin State University: 159, 161
Sterne-Hoya House: 159
Stewart Beach: 83
storms: 84, 177
Strand district: 14, 18, 74, 79, 88, 90
summer: 10, 203
surfing: Galveston Island 85; Mustang Island
    State Park 113; South Padre Island 126
Surfside Beach: 95

T

temperatures: 10, 177, 203
Texas & Pacific Railway Museum: 168
Texas Campaign for the Environment: 178
Texas Commission on Environmental Quality: 178
Texas Declaration of Independence: 183
Texas Energy Museum: 140
Texas Forestry Museum: 18, 154
Texas Forestry Museum and the History
    Center: 20
Texas General Land Office: 75
Texas Home and Garden Show: 49
Texas Medical Center: 32
Texas Parks and Wildlife Department: 198
Texas Seaport Museum: 81
Texas State Aquarium: 15, 20, 74, 98
Texas State Railroad: 9, 17, 18, 20, 136
Texas State Railroad State Historical Park: 160
Texas State Surfing Championship: 129
Tex-Mex food: general discussion 8, 200;
    Corpus Christi 110; Houston 61, 62, 66, 67;
    Jefferson 170; Kingsville 121; South Padre
    Island 133
Tex-Mex language: 187, 188
theater, Houston: 49
theft: 203
III Forks: 11, 16, 58
thunderstorms: 178
Toledo Bend Reservoir: 153
toll roads: 194
TopWater Grill: 12, 19, 67
tourist information: 204
tours: dolphin 122, 127; Houston 69; Orange
    bayou 143
train travel: 193
transportation: 192-195
Treebeard's: 11, 59
trees: 178
Tremont House: 15, 88
Tunnels, Downtown Houston: 28
turtles: 123, 124
20th century history: 184
Tyler: 9, 163-167
Tyler Municipal Rose Garden and Museum: 163
Tyler Museum of Art: 165

UV

Uchi: 12, 16, 63
Underbelly: 12, 16, 60
uptown Houston: accommodations 56; food
    65-66; nightlife 46; orientation 27; shopping
    52; sights 35-36
Urban Cowboy: 42
USS *Lexington:* 15, 18, 74, 100
Varner-Hogg Plantation: 93
vegetarian food: 68
vegetation: 178-179
Vietnamese community: 44
visual arts: 191

WXYZ

walking/jogging paths: 40, 196
water parks: 80, 122
water recreation: 10
Water Street Seafood Co.: 15, 20, 108
Water Wall: 35
weather: 10, 84, 177
Weisman Center: 169
West University: accommodations 56; nightlife
    44; orientation 27; shopping 51
wheelchair access: 202
W. H. Stark House: 144
wildflowers: 179
wildlife: general discussion 181; Adventures
    2000 Plus Swamp and River Tours 143;
    Angelina National Forest 152; Big Thicket
    National Preserve 145; Brazoria National
    Wildlife Refuge 94; dolphin tours 122; King
    Ranch 119; marine 126, 180; safety 203;
    San Bernard National Wildlife Refuge 94;
    Sea Turtle, Inc. 123; South Padre Island 15;
    turtles 123, 124
windsurfing: 104, 125, 126
winter: 10, 203
World Birding Center's Quinta Mazatlan: 197
Wortham Park Golf Course: 41
zoos: Caldwell Zoo 165; Ellen Trout Zoo 155;
    Houston 31; Moody Gardens 82

List of Maps

Front color section
The Texas Gulf Coast: 2
Houston: 3

Discover Houston & the Texas Gulf Coast
chapter divisions map: 8

Houston
Houston: 24-25
Downtown Houston: 26

The Gulf Coast
The Gulf Coast: 76-77
Galveston: 78
Downtown Galveston: 79
Corpus Christi: 99
Downtown Corpus Christi: 100

East Texas Getaways
East Texas Getaways: 137